The Hamlet of Edwin Booth

THE HAMLET OF EDWIN BOOTH

CHARLES H. SHATTUCK

UNIVERSITY OF ILLINOIS PRESS

Urbana Chicago London

Frontispiece: Edwin Booth as Hamlet, 1870. Photograph by Napoleon Sarony. Courtesy of the Walter Hampden Memorial Library at The Players.

 Manufactured in the United States of America. Library of Congress Catalog Card No. 71-76832.

252 00019 6

PREFACE AND ACKNOWLEDGMENTS

When the curtain rises on a play, we care nothing for the private lives of the actors, but only for their art. No curtains rise on actors of the past, however, and when we wish to learn what their art was, and turn to the books written about them, too often we find little more than their biographies—indispensable, fascinating, meaningful in indirect ways—but hardly telling us what we most want to know: what did the actor do upon the stage and what did it mean to his beholders?

In this study of Booth's Hamlet I have attempted to reverse the emphasis. This is not a life of Edwin Booth, but the life of a single role as Booth played it. Booth was born in 1833 and died in 1893; he played Hamlet for thirty-eight years, from 1853 to 1891. Beyond these statistics I promise no orderly biography, assuming that the reader knows the main facts of Booth's life already. I shall draw upon biography only for those events and circumstances which clarify his work with the play.

Of all the famous Shakespearean performances of the past, Booth's Hamlet is the most fully documented, but the documents have lain unused in special collections, untouched except by passing specialists, their contents little known. Principal among them are the half a dozen major promptbooks which Booth used during the last quarter-century of his career and one or two promptbook-like records of his performance compiled by professional observers;

Booth's own annotations of the play in his *Hamlet* Notebooks; Charles Witham's watercolors of the 1870 scene designs; and above all the massive description of Booth's 1870 performance put together by Charles Clarke. In Part II (Chapter V) of this study I shall describe these and other primary documents in appropriate detail. Newspapers and magazines of the time devoted many hundreds of columns to reportage and criticism of Booth's Hamlet. Of this contemporary journalism I confess at once that I have been able to recover no more than the cap of the iceberg, and have incorporated but a fragment of that fragment. The impact of Booth's playing in Chicago, Philadelphia, New Orleans, Detroit, and a hundred other cities and towns in America, in the provinces of England, and in the German cities, remains largely to be assessed.

In Parts I and III of this study I have endeavored to trace the whole development of Booth's Hamlet: in the first chapter to observe his occasional and uncertain clutchings at the role while he struggled to find his acting style and establish himself as a star; in the second chapter to sort out from the hitherto unexplored letters of Adam Badeau and Mollie Devlin certain personal and intellectual forces which influenced his shaping of the role; in the third chapter to trace the emergence of Hamlet as Booth's acknowledged masterwork; in the fourth chapter to examine his definitive production of the play at his own theatre in 1870. Chapter VII (Part III) traces the fortunes of his Hamlet as it aged, matured, and finally declined during the last two decades of his career. Whenever down through the years Booth's critics, friendly or hostile, defined his Hamlet with especial acuteness, I have given them generous room to speak.

For readers who wish no more than an overview of Booth's Hamlet, Parts I and III will be sufficient. Only those who wish to realize Booth's Hamlet in the utmost possible immediacy should grapple with Part II, which I have called a "reconstruction." The bulk of Part II is Charles Clarke's description of Booth's performance, his extremely minute recording of Booth's stage movement and gesture, emotional expression, and vocal play. It is not holiday reading. Every line or phrase—at times every word—that Booth uttered upon the stage carries its burdens of commentary, and the effects of any one passage can be got at only by painstaking and repeated mulling.

Out of Clarke's record I might have compiled an "original" description of Booth's Hamlet, appropriating only so much of the evidence as suited the criterion of "readability" and discarding the rest. The result would have been dishonest. Clarke saw and heard Booth's Hamlet, and the evidence he set down is more important than would be a filtering of it through me or any single evaluator. Although, as I have explained in Chapter V (The Documents), I have subjected Clarke's often random pilings of fact to severe editing in order to present them more systematically and intelligibly, I have omitted nothing. The evidence as Clarke saved it for us is given complete.

For the reader who wishes only to take samplings of Booth's performance, the Hamlet-Ophelia scene (Act III, 1) or the scene in the Queen's Closet (Act III, 5) may be the most rewarding to begin with. From my own experience with the material I would suggest too that it is best to take in at first reading only the visual images which Clarke gives us; next the emotional effects; the vocal patterns last of all. The difficulties in describing vocal patterns by means of written words are nearly insuperable, and Clarke's notations of Booth's "sound track," though persistent, are inevitably imprecise. Beyond such obvious effects as strong pause, extremes of pitch or tempo, whispering, and the like, Clarke cannot make us "hear" Booth. He cannot re-create the living voice. He does at best make us "see" Booth, however, and the reader who will faithfully apply his own histrionic sensibility to Clarke's data may well find Booth's Hamlet as alive in his imagination as any Hamlet he looked on last year in the flesh.

About fifteen years ago the late Dr. William Van Lennep, Curator of the Harvard Theatre Collection, began to gather materials for a book about Booth's Hamlet, but between his curatorial duties, failing health, and his work on *The London Stage* he was unable to carry the project very far. Through the kindness of his literary executor, George Winchester Stone, and of Mrs. Van Lennep I have had the benefit of his gatherings, which include, along with many suggestive notes, an impeccable transcription of the Charles Clarke manuscript.

The Folger Shakespeare Library, which owns the Clarke manuscript, has permitted me to reproduce its contents. The Players of New York City have given me access to the Booth promptbooks, notebooks, and correspondence in their possession; to the late Pat Carroll of that institution I was indebted from the first for advice and encouragement, and to Louis Rachow of the Walter Hampden

Memorial Library at The Players I am indebted for technical assistance far beyond his line of duty. Paul Myers, Curator of the Theatre Collection of the New York Public Library at Lincoln Center, has recently won the gratitude of all lovers of Booth by his last-minute rescue of several boxes of Boothiana (including the letters of Mary Devlin) from careless destruction; to him and his staff I am grateful for many cordial attentions. Sam Pearce of the Museum of the City of New York, Dorothy Mason of the Folger, Alma DeJordy of the University of Illinois Library, George Nash of the Gabrielle Enthoven Collection, Dr. Willy Unger of the German National Library, and many other librarians in this country and abroad have been generous with assistance.

The Library of the University of Southern California (through the kindness of Lloyd A. Arvidson) and the Hamlin Garland estate (through the kindness of Constance Garland Doyle) have permitted me to quote from Garland's essay-lecture on Booth's Hamlet. Alexander P. Clarke of the Princeton University Library has permitted quotation from the Badeau-Wilson correspondence, and John Y. Simon, Director of the Ulysses S. Grant Association, has generously loaned me his transcription of that correspondence. John Cranford Adams, who owns the James Taylor souvenir promptbook of Booth's late Hamlet, kindly made it available to me for several months of study. Gerald Honaker of Catawba College has given me his as yet unpublished findings of the stage dimensions of Booth's Theatre. Robert Cohen of the University of California at Irvine was the first to call my attention to the Bensen Sherwood stage plans, without which my understanding of stage practice at Booth's Theatre would have been disastrously inadequate. Hennig Cohen of the University of Pennsylvania put me on the trail of Booth's relations with Sandford Gifford and other artists of the time. Pat Ryan of the State University of New York College of Education at Brockport gave me the benefit of his study of the Winter Garden *Hamlet.* Daniel Watermeier of Moorhead University has contributed from his work with the Booth-Winter correspondence countless facts and recognitions which have brought light into dark corners. I am indebted to my colleague Wesley Swanson for advice on an early draft of portions of my manuscript.

Without the resources and services of the Harvard Theatre Collection this study would have foundered long ago. Just at the point when the confusion of available evidence had become most discouraging, Miss Helen Willard, Curator of the Harvard Theatre Collection, discovered, acquired, and put at my disposal the great souvenir promptbook of Booth's 1870 production, which with its explicit stage directions and its watercolors of the scene designs at once solved all that had seemed unsolvable. Miss Willard's later acquisition of the 1866 (Winter Garden) promptbook was another remarkable, and from my point of view most timely, *coup* of curatorship. My obligations to her for workaday assistance are uncountable.

William H. Bond of the Houghton Library has granted permission to reproduce the watercolors from the 1870 promptbook; and I am grateful to Howard Mumford Jones as editor of the *Harvard Library Bulletin* for giving generous space to a preliminary essay on the 1870 promptbook soon after its discovery.

Mrs. Elizabeth Dulany, Associate Editor at the University of Illinois Press, has edited the difficult manuscript and seen it into print with that minute care which is characteristic of her own work and that of the Press staff generally.

To my wife, who has been endlessly patient about this work, and who has provided better criticism of the following pages than I have been able to put to use, I owe most.

I am indebted to the University of Illinois Center for Advanced Study for an appointment as Associate Member in 1966, during which term the research for this study was largely completed. The cost of manuscript preparation was sustained by the University of Illinois Research Board. Funds for travel and for photo-duplication of materials were granted me from the Penrose Fund of the American Philosophical Society.

CHARLES H. SHATTUCK
Urbana, Illinois
November 1, 1968

CONTENTS

Introduction xiii

PART I. BOOTH'S HAMLET, 1853-70

Chapter I. The Apprentice Years 3

Chapter II. An Actor's Education 18

Chapter III. The Emergence of Hamlet 37

Chapter IV. *Hamlet* at Booth's Theatre, 1870 67

PART II. BOOTH'S HAMLET RECONSTRUCTED

Chapter V. The Documents 101

Chapter VI. The Performance

Act I 115

Act II 160

Act III 182

Act IV 240

Act V 250

PART III. THE FINAL YEARS

Chapter VII. *Hamlet* in Repertory, 1870-91 285

Index 311

INTRODUCTION

To our mind, the delineation of Hamlet by Booth comes nearer to the proper idea of Hamlet than that of any other actor of the present generation. It is idle to talk now of Kean and Kemble, just as it will be idle for the old playgoers of 1970 to bring up, in the aggressive manner in which all old playgoers *do* bring up the celebrities of byegone days, the Hamlet of Edwin Booth, with which to crush the rising candidate for histrionic laurels. We of today live in the era of Booth; and Booth, to a majority of us, is Hamlet. The Hamlets of the past are to us really no more than the unimagined Hamlets of the future. There were glorious skies, and bright sunlight, and crimson clouds in the days when the Pyramids were young, and there will be the same in the coming years, when our youth will seem as long past as the youth of Sesostris or Rameses; but to us the sunlight of one day of the present is worth them all.

—The New York *Evening Post*, March 16, 1870

Edwin Booth's Hamlet is the most famous impersonation in the history of the American theatre. In the history of staged Shakespeare it is one of those verbal absolutes, like Mrs. Siddons' Lady Macbeth or Edmund Kean's Othello—a metaphor of perfection which we accept and quote without questioning its meaning.

It was, in fact, more than one Hamlet. Booth studied the role so intensively, played it so long, and became so intimately identified with it, that over the years it took various coloration and emphasis from the courses of his own living. The version of it which comes through to us most clearly defined, and perhaps most satisfying, is that which Booth achieved in 1870. Booth was then in his middle thirties and at the peak of his creative energies—almost miraculously so, one might think, for in recent years he had suffered such buffetings of fortune as would have destroyed a lesser man. In 1863 his beloved young wife had died; in 1865 his brother had assassinated President Lincoln; in 1867 his entire theatrical property was destroyed in the Winter Garden fire. He came through these disasters sobered but strong, with a deepened awareness of the meaning of tragedy. He built a splendid new theatre, called Booth's Theatre, and determined there to climax his already long career as Hamlet with a production and performance which would be definitive. It emerged as the tragedy of a good and brilliant man destroyed by circumstance—"a man of first-class intellect and second-class will," as Charles Clarke, our most discriminating witness, put it. This Hamlet, though outwardly the last word in composure and gentlemanliness, burned inwardly with fierce excitement. In every lesser emergency he penetrated at once to the truth behind surfaces, marshaled his strategies in passionate meditation, and sprang to decisive action. Yet whenever he faced his one major obligation, to kill the King, he faltered and drew back. In the catastrophe, when the killing was done, Clarke saw in his face and action the sorriest bewilderment—no glint of triumph, but doubt, dismay, the beginnings of remorse. Thus, according to Clarke's reading of it, the tragic pattern was firmly conceived, worked out in passion, and sustained to the final curtain.

Fifteen years later the pattern had somewhat softened. This Hamlet, though still impressive, was less active, less agonized, more meditative and stoical, less "tragic," and more obviously a subject for moral admiration. Booth himself, then in his early fifties, had turned prematurely gray, wearying though never breaking as his burden of personal misfortunes continued to mount—the loss of Booth's Theatre and with it the fading of his best professional hopes, financial harassment, the failure of his second marriage, and his wife's collapse into lunacy and death. His Hamlet grew old and steadfast with him: its fires glowed more often than they blazed. When the young Hamlin Garland saw it in 1884 it appeared to him as "the good man enduring," or "the passive suffering center"—a Hamlet who from the beginning was aware of the end of the story, who anticipated his own doom and steadied himself toward it with dignity and a wholly admirable fortitude.

In either of these phases, and until the actor's failing health quite enfeebled it, Booth's Hamlet commanded worship. "Worship" is hardly too strong a word to describe the responses of Booth's following. Although the latter decades of the century in America—the Brown Decades, as Lewis Mumford has called them—may have been a vulgar and immoral time, when the grossest materialism spread like a fungus throughout public life, when every robber baron who died was memorialized in an effigy of bronze or marble, when hypocritic claims to public virtue veiled but thinly the grossest corruption, yet millions of ordinary citizens lived decent lives according to the old-fashioned codes of honesty and kindliness. And Booth, too, however vividly he shone on the public scene, was an innocent; wrapped in Art and the Ideal, he was insulated from corruption. He would have made the Theatre a school and temple as well as a playhouse, and he strove with priestly devotion to make his Hamlet an idol of virtue. For many thousands of playgoers it was a lesson and a rite.

Long before his career ended, his Hamlet had become a legend, for some almost a cult. Thirty years after he died, during the furor over John Barrymore's Hamlet, a group of aging Booth devotees called upon Barrymore in his dressing room to beg him to stop his run of the play on the ninety-ninth night. Their "great master" had played it for one hundred nights, and his record must not be broken. Barrymore pretended he had never heard of Booth's "Hundred Nights." When it was explained to him he told his visitors to stop living in the past, and declared then and there that he would play Hamlet one hundred nights plus one. He did so. But legends are tougher than statistics, impervious to common sense or irreverent gestures. Barrymore's Hamlet became a legend too, but it did not destroy Booth's.

The Booth legend is now too remote to threaten the living theatre as it threatened Barrymore in the 1920's, so that we can now accept it affectionately, along with the lives and works of other saints of the stage. Yet we should disabuse ourselves of certain cultist superstitions which have clustered around it. Booth's Hamlet was not, of course, "the very Hamlet of Shakespeare's imagining" as in the last century a thousand voices proclaimed it to be. The wonder of Shakespeare's Hamlet is its infinite variety, which no one actor in one time can possibly realize. Booth himself called it "the epitome of mankind, not an individual; a sort of magic mirror in which all men and women see the reflex of themselves."[1] Whether Booth had in mind, like his gentle eulogist whose sentences I have taken for epigraph, all men and women from the days of the pyramids into the far future does not appear; but certainly to most of his contemporary admirers his impersonation of Hamlet—mannerly, meditative, darkly romantic, wise, kindly, fierce for good only, pure—answered perfectly to their storybook conception of the prince-figure, their own preferred reflection. What Shakespeare had written did not matter. Booth's audience, bardolators all, typically knew little about Shakespeare beyond what was given them from the stage; and the stage, governed strictly by their own moral and esthetic prejudices, gave them only what they wanted to hear and see. Booth's Hamlet, clad in his personal beauty, flattered the popular ideal. When his admirers called it "Shakespeare's very Hamlet" they were congratulating themselves.

Booth did not honor the text of the play quite as we would expect of a serious producer in our own time. He gave out to the press that "Mr. Booth's artistic and conscientious regard has not permitted him to abbreviate any of its length or beauty," but that is not to be taken literally. Of the 3,930 lines he cut some 1,180. His acting version of 2,750 lines was only about 220 lines longer than the commonly used acting version printed in the *Modern Standard Drama.* Although he claimed privately to have studied the text in a dozen or more modern editions, and although he was careful to collate every reading with that of the 1623 Folio, the popular notion that he "restored the text" is misleading. The fact is that he bowdlerized it and concentrated it around the name-character as relentlessly as any previous actor-manager had done.

The text did not ask to be "restored" in the usual sense, for *Hamlet* had never been rewritten, as *Richard III* or *King Lear* or *The Tempest* had been, by the seventeenth- and eighteenth-century "improvers." Booth only tinkered with the acting version which he had received from tradition. Exactly as his predecessors had done, he omitted the entire "outside story" of the Norwegian wars, and thereby the coming on of Fortinbras, and thereby the great soliloquy of "How all occasions do inform against me." He deprived Laertes

[1] See Booth's "A Few Words About Edmund Kean," in *Actors and Actresses of Great Britain and the United States*, ed. Brander Matthews and Laurence Hutton (New York, 1886), III, 4.

and Polonius of about 40 lines of their advice to Ophelia. He omitted the "dram of eale" speech. In the second act he dropped Reynaldo, much of the amusing small talk between Hamlet and his old school friends, all the topical discussion of the plight of the players, and much of the "rugged Pyrrhus" stuff. He cut most of Hamlet's dialogue with Ophelia during the Play scene and much of the *Mousetrap* dialogue. He cut about 70 lines from the scene between Hamlet and his mother. In the fourth act he economized far beyond his predecessors, omitting scenes 1, 2, 4, and 6 entirely and reducing the whole act by nearly 300 lines. In the fifth act he dropped 50 lines from the Osric scene and the entrance of "a Lord."

His restorations include many small and mostly not very significant scraps. The inclusion of Polonius' advice to Laertes (25 lines) can hardly be counted as a Booth restoration, for although it is not printed in the *Modern Standard Drama* version, most producers from at least Macready's time had included it. He restored the King's Prayer scene and Hamlet's "Now might I do it pat" soliloquy (64 lines). He restored to the fifth act Hamlet's narrative of his sea-adventures (74 lines).

I have based these notes upon his promptbook of 1870, by which time he had made all the restorations he would ever make; thereafter he seems gradually to have discarded most of them, great and small. The 2,750-line version proved to be too long. At Booth's pace of acting it went on for four hours. As he once told William Winter (perhaps exaggerating, for he was trying to convince Winter not to restore too much of the text of another play), "People gaped, slept and left before the final act—in squads." [2] Thus by 1878 when Winter brought out *Hamlet* in the Prompt-Book edition, the narrative of Hamlet's sea-adventures had disappeared and "Now might I do it pat" was indicated as "sometimes omitted." One of the more telling small restorations had been the battery of comical names which Hamlet fires at the Ghost in the cellarage; but audiences disliked to hear the good son addressing his father's spirit disrespectfully, so in 1878 most of the name-calling was suppressed.

But the 1878 version was still too taxing. "My long & varied experience," Booth wrote Winter, "has taught me that the closer and quicker tragedy can be acted the better is the audience pleased." From Booth's later promptbooks we learn that he shortened the open-

[2] Booth to William Winter, June 4, 1878. The Folger Shakespeare Library, Y.c. 215 (282).

ing scene by reducing the Ghost's two entrances to one; that he sometimes omitted the first 40 lines of "Now I am alone"; that he shortened the *Mousetrap* still further and dropped another 30 or 40 lines from the Laertes-King conspiracy of the fourth act. In Boston in 1889 an "Admirer of Mr. Booth" complained bitterly to the *Home Journal* (February 16) of the way the play had been chopped down at a recent Saturday matinee. The opening scene was not performed at all. Hamlet did not give his Advice to the Players. The Prayer scene was hopelessly mangled. The scene in which the King sends Hamlet to England was omitted. Many lines were cut from the soliloquies, which "we have heard so beautifully given in years gone by." The event here complained of was perhaps exceptional, but one fears that in those later years many a worshipful audience, at least at Saturday matinees, got less than its money's worth of the "length or beauty" of the play.

For Booth's uses the play had to be cleansed of its burden of "filth"—lines which many a common reader of those days would have argued had not been written by the "divine Shakespeare" anyway. "Remember," Booth once told a fellow actor, "that Hamlet is not merely a Prince, but a most delicate and exquisitely refined creature—an absolute gentleman." [3] In his *Hamlet* Notebook he added that Hamlet is "feminine, but not effeminate, in feeling." From the lips of such a character the occasional rough talk of Shakespeare's Hamlet would not do.

Producers in our own time perhaps make too much of the sex elements in the play. Somehow they convert the Queen's Closet into the Queen's Bedroom, and loose their Hamlets there to ruffle their mothers over the mattress as if Hamlet meant in his own person to "let the royal bed of Denmark be a couch for luxury and damnèd incest." In Booth's time the fault lay the other way. As Booth staged it the Queen's Closet was a lady's sitting room or study, with chairs for herself and one or two guests and with a library table dressed with candles, crucifix, and a large illuminated book of prayer. Booth's Hamlet scolded his mother sharply enough for neglecting her marriage vows to a proper man and taking a mildewed ear for a husband. That was sufficient to arouse her sense of shame. He did not have to accuse her of "honeying and making love over the nasty sty." Except to urge her to "go not to my uncle's bed" he delivered no

[3] Booth wrote this at the front of James Taylor's *Hamlet* scrapbook in 1890. The Harvard Theatre Collection.

recipe for sexual abstinence. He said nothing about the bloat king paddling in her neck with his damned fingers.

As in this scene so throughout the play the sex imagery was almost totally eliminated. Booth's Hamlet proposed to murder the King when he is "drunk, asleep, or in his rage," but not "in the incestuous pleasure of his bed." He did not threaten Ophelia with a groaning to take off his edge, or speak any of the other ribald *double entendres* to her. In the first conversation with Rosencrantz and Guildenstern he did not mention that strumpet Dame Fortune, let alone her allegorical secret parts. When he called Polonius a "fishmonger" he intended nothing more than a boyish joke; and if he were ever told that the word "nunnery" was an Elizabethan cant term for "brothel" he would have dismissed the information as the "bosh" of "some learned noodle." Booth was, in fact, as touchy about public propriety as any Comstock or Mrs. Grundy. He deplored the "French sensation dramas" in which Matilda Heron made her strongest appeal. *The Black Crook*, *The White Fawn*, and other "leg shows" of the time appalled him. He even found the Passion Play at Oberammergau "an outrage to religious sentiment" and waged a personal campaign to prevent its being imported to America. Thus, although he is not to be held alone accountable for suppressing the sex elements in *Hamlet*—for the cuts had been made ever since Garrick's time—it would have been inconceivable for him to have restored them.

Our modern Hamlets know how to ginger their performances by hurling insults into the teeth of fools and knaves in the play—but not Booth. In every passage of social intercourse Booth's Hamlet was a very perfect gentle knight. Once he had detected the treacherous intentions of Rosencrantz and Guildenstern he treated them reservedly or coolly or austerely, but always politely, showing the audience his contempt for the pair by subtly ironic tones or by a look or a gesture toward their backs as they left the room. Booth would not permit his actors of Polonius to indulge in clowning: Polonius, he insisted, was a dignified statesman and a loving, careful father. So when Hamlet has to ridicule Polonius in the antic scenes, Booth played his lines so thoughtfully, slowly, almost inwardly and utterly without virulence, that the old man never knew that he was being ragged. When in the Play scene Hamlet appears to nip Polonius with the line "It was a brute part of him to kill so capital a calf there," Booth took the line on a curving walk across the front of the stage, so that it became an aside to the audience and Polonius did not hear it. Booth handled Osric so tactfully that although the audience sensed his distaste for the waterfly, Osric's vanity was never touched, and he left the stage as well-pleased with himself as when he came.

The gentlemanly instinct was deeply ingrained in Booth, and this aspect of his Hamlet character governed his professional relations behind the scenes. He was much loved by other actors, except for the most self-seeking, not only for his charities to those in need, which became legendary, but for his never-failing kindliness to his supporting actors, down to the least of them. One of the least of them, Kitty Molony (who became Katherine Goodale), wrote a book about the tour of 1886-87 which, appearing nearly a half-century after the event, is a late love song for a dead father-figure.[4] It is worth pausing for a look at certain facts of Booth's behavior during that tour which Miss Molony never knew.

Lawrence Barrett, who was managing Booth at the time, who had arranged the tour and set up the company but did not travel with it, needed to find out which of the actors were good enough to hire for the following season, and from time to time Booth could be prodded into reluctant answers to his inquiries. Booth liked them all, he would insist, but not as actors: "You put me in a delicate position when you ask me to name such of the company that are satisfactory. You know I am easily satisfied, especially if the press does not abuse my company & thus far all has gone pretty well in that respect."[5] He was contented with most of the women, and Emma Vaders, although offstage she seemed "off her head" (eventually, indeed, she went mad), he thought the finest Ophelia he had ever seen. The men, however, were with rare exceptions nearly intolerable. Arendt was out of his element, Coleman stiff as a stick, Hanford mild and inoffensive but too fat, Sullivan hard and unsympathetic. As for John Malone, who played Claudius, "A star danced the night Malone was born—'twas far below zero and as the baby smiled at the twinkler he 'froze so,' and ever since he has smiled—he even murders while he smiles: *vide* his King Claudius.

[4] Katherine Goodale, *Behind the Scenes with Edwin Booth* (New York, 1931).

[5] Booth to Lawrence Barrett, October 10, 1886. The Harvard Theatre Collection. The further quotations are taken from subsequent letters in the same file.

This is his chief fault; he reads well & is careful, but oh, how he smiles." Charley Barron had improved his Othello by speeding it a little, and he got a genuine and deserved call each night: he "belches here & there somewhat harshly, but not often."

The one serious problem was Miss Molony. A protégée of Barrett's, she had been promised important sustaining roles in *Richard III*, Payne's *Brutus*, and *Don Caesar de Bazan*. But Booth found her "not at all capable—even for the parts she has played." She had played Jessica, the Player Queen, and Fleance, and she had expected, too, to play Osric, but Booth had tactfully displaced her in that role with a young man. "I sincerely regret it," Booth went on, "for she is a pretty and good little body; her case is hopeless." But how could he deprive her of the other roles without breaking "her aspiring heart"? There was one way, however costly. He announced to the company that he had failed to bring along his own costumes for Richard, Brutus, and Don Caesar, and that these plays would be dropped from the repertory. To such lengths Booth would go to save one individual from hurt. And he would assure Barrett, "Now not a word of this is in complaint; my intention has been all along to massacre you after the season closed, but if the press spares my warriors till then, I won't." Booth's kindly person and kindly Hamlet were cut from the same cloth.

Booth was firmly convinced that Hamlet is *not in love with Ophelia*—although he never succeeded in putting this meaning across. In his *Hamlet* Notebook there are perhaps more entries touching this subject than any other, and all are to the effect that Hamlet was *not* in love. "What a piece of work is a man," says Hamlet, and Booth appends the note: "A man. *Woman* holds a very low place in his estimation; since the very *root* of his veneration for her has been blasted by his *mother's* conduct." He describes Ophelia as "the personification of pale & feeble-minded amiability." Perhaps long ago, "in the innocence of boyhood," he had been attracted to her; or, "since virtue cannot so inoculate our old stock but we shall relish of it," perhaps she had stirred unmentionable appetites in him; but certainly he does not love her now. Laertes is quite right, Booth says, to question the reality or depth of Hamlet's supposed love, for "*Intellectuality* in him absorbed all trivial fond emotions." Polonius is right to scold Ophelia for taking Hamlet's "tenders as true pay," for Shakespeare here "endeavors to impress his readers with the fact that Hamlet does not *love*." In the final scenes, Booth notes triumphantly, Hamlet never speaks a word of regret for Ophelia's death.

On this point he convinced no one, however. The boy-girl situation which the play sets up, the romantic aura which generations of actors had cast over the relationship, Booth's inevitable gentlemanliness toward Ophelia and the profound earnestness with which he rebuked her in their one scene together convinced every spectator that he was indeed in love. At the end of the rebuking scene he worked up a careful pantomime of rejection, but this was not enough to convey his thought; he executed the pantomime so broodingly and pathetically that he only confirmed the audience's romantic prejudice: any stage hero who behaved so decently to the *jeune première* and was himself so attractive *had* to be in love.

The reason that Booth's Hamlet could not be in love was that love is a profound passion, and in Booth's reckoning Hamlet was never shaken by *any* passion which could for more than an instant disturb his command over himself or over the situation around him. Whatever our modern Hamlets make of the case, Booth's Hamlet was absolutely sane. He could break out wildly now and then, as in his convulsion at the departure of the Ghost, or in the rattle of names he hurls down to the cellarage, or in his doggerel rhymes that cap the success of the *Mousetrap*, or in his ranting at Laertes over Ophelia's grave; but these were not hysteria—they were "the very intensity of mental excitement." Booth's motto for the role and his standing answer to the question whether Hamlet is mad was "That I essentially am not in madness, but mad in craft."

Booth believed that immediately after his interview with the Ghost Hamlet coolly invents the device of the antic disposition as a cloak for self-protection. In the cryptic phrase "So be it," which he mutters when he hears his friends calling in the distance, he announces the plan to himself. At this point Booth says in his Notebook that in a brain like Hamlet's "thought requires no *time* to form its plan of action—quick as a flash his mind conceives the means of safety in pursuing his revenge." As soon as his friends arrive he tries his antic disposition on; before the scene is over he explains it to them. Whenever he uses it thereafter he does so deliberately, sanely, in perfect inner calm. His first serious use of it is his offstage appearance to Ophelia in her closet. Opposite the lines in which Ophelia describes that wild scene Booth notes that *to an actor* this is all "play-acting"; that Shakespeare, who was so well posted in actors' tricks, meant it to be so understood by the audience. To prove this, Booth says, one needs only to compare Hamlet's mad scenes to those of Ophelia or of Lear, which are genuine mad scenes, and observe the difference.

Again and again in his Notebook Booth emphasizes Hamlet's extraordinary intelligence—how he anticipates the moves of his enemies and how he hits upon any plan of action well before he puts it to work. At his first entrance in the second act, for instance, seeing the King and Queen leave Polonius, he suspects they are laying a trap for him and at once prepares to "bamboozle" the old man. He suspects Rosencrantz and Guildenstern as soon as he lays eyes on them, and "trusts them as he would adders fanged." The instant that he hears of the arrival of the Players he conceives the *Mousetrap* plan. In the scene with Ophelia he catches sight of the King and Polonius much earlier than other Hamlets were wont to do, and "*acts* the rest of the scene . . . principally for the King." At every moment in the play, except of course when he murders Polonius and except when he is under the spell of his father's spirit, he is in command of the events. Even when the King succeeds in banishing him to England, he not only executes a superb snub of the King, but marches off triumphantly, almost gaily, as if he welcomes exile or as if he is already intent upon his next objective, to delve one yard below the mines of Rozencrantz and Guildenstern and blow them at the moon. Few Hamlets have been more clear-headed, more conspicuously purposeful. Honest doubts troubled him, and the intellectualizing habit weakened his will to perform the decisive action of killing the King. But his sanity and his intelligence were perfect beyond question.

All this will suggest to modern sensibilities that there was no mystery in Booth's Hamlet, no fascinating either/or-ness, none of the subtle enchantments of ambiguity. Insofar as Booth's conscious intentions are concerned, that apprehension is correct. "Here is no riddle. Shakespeare wrote none," said Lawrence Barrett, Booth's friend and partner, who in the main shared Booth's attitudes toward the play. "Hamlet becomes a Sphinx only when some persons wish to obtain credit by solving riddles." [6] In *Hamlet,* Barrett insisted, there is only "clearness, harmony, and logical sequence,—not tortuous invention or Middle Age thaumaturgy." Booth's intention with

[6] Barrett wrote this at the front of James Taylor's *Hamlet* scrapbook.

Hamlet was not to create mystery but to dispel mystery; to make the play (or so much of it as the age could tolerate) crystal clear to every hearer.

He strove for clarity through his pace of acting, which was slow, deliberative. He gave full meaning as well as distinctive musical value to each word. He took time before he spoke important thoughts to show them in facial expression. He used illustrative gestures to point up meanings, touching his heart to indicate what *kind* of appetite when he spoke of "increase of appetite"; impersonating the weeping Niobe as he crossed the stage slowly with head on one side and fingertips touching before his breast; grasping his sword so that the upheld hilt presented a crucifix; making the sign of horns when he accused women of turning men into monsters; and so forth. During pauses at the end of certain passages he inserted gestures, looks, or little pantomimes to communicate to the audience what he had concealed from his interlocutors. If the theatre was a school, his performance was an illustrated lecture, as more than one critic in that education-minded age gratefully acknowledged. He cleared the text of obscurities as carefully as he weeded out "impurities," so that even the gallery-gods would understand it. If he intended to reduce his Hamlet-in-action to something like the good hero in contest with the bad villain—if in our latter-day view the Hamlet he strove to project was perhaps nearer to Sherlock Holmes than to Prince Myshkin—that was no obstacle to popular acceptance of what was popularly considered to be Shakespeare's most "philosophical" play.

One would not sense in Booth's Hamlet, nor in his total enterprise, that the times were in ferment, that radical ideas were already sapping the authority of the past and would revolutionize the future. If Darwin and Lord Kelvin had rewritten the Book of Genesis and Marx had laid siege to the economic establishment, if Zola was exposing the horrors of the social condition and mad painters and poets across the ocean were destroying the true and the beautiful, Booth knew little of these explosive doings, or what he had heard about them he deplored. Locked in his world of make-believe—"my own fancy world," he called it, "where I dream my life away"—[7] he was hardly aware of far-off rumbling change.

By temperament as well as by isolation Booth was of the conservative persuasion that the arts were steadily arriving at a summit

[7] Booth to F. C. Ewer, October 1, 1877. Edwina Booth Grossmann, *Edwin Booth* (New York, 1894), p. 188.

of perfection, there to be fixed, consolidated, and bulwarked against decay. Just as his friend Horace Howard Furness of Philadelphia was gathering into his New Variorum volumes all that past wisdom from the study could teach us about Shakespeare, so Booth would encyclopedize and conserve the art of theatre. The canon of his theatre was the noblest of the so-called Standard Drama. This meant, first of all, the "best" of Shakespeare. He perfected his acting versions of Shakespeare, checking the texts through the many editions back to the First Folio, trimming them then into conformity with theatrical needs and approved modern taste; and when he published them in his Prompt-Book edition, he imagined that these versions would serve the profession for generations to come. The Standard Drama included also such modern masterpieces of Bulwer and Hugo as met the prevailing tests of dignity, and he also published these. He mounted and dressed his productions according to authoritative historical and archeological research, and having found these "truths" he clung to them tenaciously and willed them to the future. When he built Booth's Theatre he was establishing a definitive institution—a perfect playhouse with a permanent repertory company where not only he but all leading actors of the time and of after generations could perpetuate the Standard Drama.

When he lost Booth's Theatre a few seasons after he opened it, his grand dream began to dissolve. Thereafter he could only wander from city to city, exhibiting his personal art in the midst of a system which was dying all around him. The days of the Standard Drama were numbered, and after him the very concept of the starring tragedian slowly faded away. Booth was not a "transitional" artist, as some have called him, for his art and his ideas did not lead beyond his own time. He was, for America, the final major artist of his kind, who brought two centuries of tradition to a culmination and an end.

It is not to belittle Booth's Hamlet to insist that his art was of his time and not of ours, but only to clarify it, and incidentally to dispel the old notion which clings about it with curious persistence that it was the Hamlet for all ages. Hogarth is not Picasso though they share a comic urge, and a Bierstadt landscape is not a landscape by Hans Hoffmann though they may be informed with the same ecstasy: we do not discard the older artists because their techniques and vision belong to the past, but gratefully relive their experiences and so enrich our own. Our directors, designers, and technicians can learn nothing from Booth or his theatre of practical use to themselves.

Yet Booth's art, framed in Victorian plush and ormolu, would be precious to us if we could see it again—beautiful in itself, a lesson in high dedication, a reliving of things long gone.

The beauty of Booth's Hamlet speaks to us from his portraits—most vividly, I think, from the well-known Sarony photograph of 1870 which is the frontispiece to this book. Just as Booth himself loved to ponder the qualities of dead actors, and seemed, he said, "to derive a more satisfactory idea of their capabilities from their counterfeit presentments than from the written records of their lives," [8] so we in our turn can "feel" Booth's Hamlet as we study the lift and turn of his head above his wide shoulders, the free tumble of dark hair above his open forehead, the set line of his lips, and above all his intelligent, lightly troubled, challenging eyes. This century-old photograph might have been taken yesterday, so near it is to a living likeness. And as we memorize its features we want to exclaim, as his father did when Booth was a boy, he "looks like Hamlet."

There is one other image of the living Booth for those who can find it. In 1890 a recording was made of his Address to the Senate in *Othello* ("To be or not to be" was recorded at the same time, but the wax cylinder was long ago destroyed in an attempt to reprocess it).[9] Through the surface noises of the primitive recording comes a low, rich, easy voice, speaking slowly, touching the words "what drugs, what charms" with gentle humor, and capable, we may be certain, of power without rant or bombast. On occasion one hears some of these Othello sentences spliced into a tape with the voices of other Shakespeareans from a lifetime ago: in that context Booth's restraint seems almost to mock the high-tragical pretensions of his early successors.

Booth's letters, too, of which only a small portion have been published, express his earnest, unaffected personality. They bring us no profound intellectual content nor star-showers of wit or imagination, but the voice one hears in them is the easy Othello voice—modest, generous, friendly, and often amused. The letters of his later years, after he had endured the worst blows that outrageous fortune could deal him, are those of "one in suffering all that suffers nothing." Booth-Hamlet became in real life Booth-Horatio, and we respond to him, as all who knew him did, with admiration and love.

[8] "A Few Words About Edmund Kean," p. 4.

[9] A re-recording of the *Othello* speech on a 78 rpm disc was made in 1939 by Frederick Packard of Harvard University. Copies of the disc are rare.

For all his gentleness, however, Booth could set the stage on fire—even in the Hamlet of his later years could sometimes make one feel "as if Jove's lightning bolts had been turned loose and were striking all about one," as Kitty Molony put it;[10] even in the quietest scenes, when his concentration was best, he could enthrall vast audiences with the spell of what Charles Clarke calls his "electric intellectuality." For all his insistence upon lucidity, there *was* mystery in his Hamlet: the beauty of his person and personality and the intensity of his thinking and feeling upon the stage created that undefinable spiritual overplus which marks the work of genius as extraordinary.

But I need not generalize further upon the style of Booth's acting. From Clarke's minutely detailed account of Booth's 1870 Hamlet, seen against the background of Charles Witham's 1870 settings, we can recapture from death and forgetfulness a theatrical experience which moved our grandfathers deeply. When the reader has gleaned the images of Booth in action which Clarke has preserved for us, he will not want generalization to understand Booth's art.

[10] Goodale, p. 180.

PART I

BOOTH'S HAMLET 1853-70

CHAPTER I

The Apprentice Years

The first person who is known to have identified Edwin Booth with Hamlet was his father, Junius Brutus the Elder. In 1852, when Booth was in his nineteenth year, he had gone with his father to California, and in Sacramento late that summer the boy was allowed to take his first professional benefit. The play he offered his patrons was *Venice Preserved*—still a popular favorite then, at least in the provinces, and well calculated to swell the box office on that occasion because of its strong billing: young Booth as beneficiary would play Jaffeir, and in Pierre his famous father would support him. When Junius Brutus saw him dressed in tragic blacks, he exclaimed curtly, "You look like Hamlet. Why didn't you play that part for your benefit?" To which the boy replied, "I will, if I ever have another." He would never forget that bit of dialogue.[1] Shortly thereafter, having stomached enough of frontier hardships, Junius Brutus set off alone for the East, leaving his son to pit his young vigor against Marysville and Downieville, Shirt-Tail Bend and Cock-Tail Canyon, the rough-and-tumble settlements of the Gold Rush world. The aging tragedian did not make it home. Sometime in December word drifted back to Booth, snowbound in one of the hill towns, that his father

[1] Booth and his father went to California at the urging of Booth's oldest brother Junius Brutus Junior, who was in theatrical management in San Francisco. Booth himself originated the legend of the "sacred pledge." It is told by Asia Booth Clarke in *The Elder and Younger Booths* (New York, 1882), p. 137, by Laurence Hutton in *Edwin Booth* (New York, 1893), p. 33, and by others.

had died along the way. The shock of it, compounded by feelings of guilt that he had let his father undertake the difficult journey unaccompanied, was almost unbearable. Tragedy, Booth suddenly knew, was something more than actors' rant and the sprawl of bodies at the end of a five-act play. His sense of loss was fierce and lasting.

Booth's First Hamlet

About the first of February in 1853 he went down out of the hills to work at the San Francisco Theatre under the management of his older brother, Junius Brutus Junior—not to play Jaffeir, however, or even lesser roles in the high drama of his father's classic repertory, but a steady round of whatever parts in light comedy, farce, and melodrama his brother thought him fit for. Twice only he managed to break out of the pattern of insignificance. Somehow he persuaded his brother to let him try Richard III, which he had played once or twice before under his father's watching in New York City. This experiment took place on April 21.[2] On April 25 he was to take his season benefit. Mindful of his father's advice—and his own response to it, which he now thought of as a "sacred pledge"—he played his first Hamlet.

His first Hamlet was no turning point in his career. His manager-brother, unimpressed, thought him no more ready to draw audiences in Hamlet than in Claude Melnotte or Dick Duberly. For the rest of the season he was put back into the trivial stuff of popular repertory.[3]

But he had fulfilled a pledge to his father and this meant much to him, for he had loved his father. Junius Brutus had been a hard man to live with, but he was a hero too, inspiring in young Booth equal parts of terror and affection. From his fourteenth year throughout his adolescence Booth had wandered the circuits with the strange,

[2] He played Richard III a second time on May 2, as a benefit for a Mr. Dumfries.

[3] Half a century afterward a veteran of the profession named J. J. McCloskey gave out numerous versions of Booth's California days which leave the impression that the Hamlet was a crashing success. Unfortunately not one of McCloskey's versions agrees in detail with any other, and all are at odds with provable history. Some of his misinformation about Booth may be found in the New York *Advertiser*, June 3, 1894; the New York *Dramatic Mirror*, August 15, 1896, December 25, 1897, December 25, 1904, December 22, 1906; the New York *Sun*, March 4, 1906; the *Green Book Album*, June, 1911.

wise, half-mad, terrible, gentle old man—partly as companion, partly as caretaker—sheltering his eccentricities; enduring his moody sulks, his drunken escapades, his occasional cruelties; worshiping his genius; admiring his erudition; triumphing in his actorship, his command over audiences; basking in his rare and brusque tokens of approval or his occasional outbreaks of paternal affection. Now that he was dead Booth need no longer fear him. Love instead, fear's counterpart, grew into a kind of Telemachan passion. He had absorbed his father's art. In time, as he grew up to it, he would play all his father's old roles. He would imitate his father's style.

With close friends he talked about his father endlessly. Once in the spring of 1859 he took his friend Adam Badeau to the deserted Booth homestead near Baltimore, and there they rummaged among Junius Brutus' relics—books, costumes, playbills—while Booth told stories about him half the night.[4] During his courtship of Mollie Devlin the presence of Junius Brutus, whom Mollie had never known alive, became almost real to her. "I am often inclined to believe in Spiritualism," she wrote Booth. "I feel frequently when alone thinking of you, that your father's spirit speaks to me, and gives me to see the true nature of his son." [5] When Mollie died in 1863 Booth himself turned to spiritualism in order to find her, and the messages which he received from his father came through as often and clearly as hers did.[6]

The Hamlet role, which so powerfully depicts a living son seeking a dead father, became for Booth almost an autopsychography; and it is little wonder that from the beginning his audiences were moved by the warm spirit of father-love which he poured into the Ghost scenes, or that in the long run the entire play became so personal to him that he seemed not to act but to be the character of Hamlet. In curious secret ways, which audiences knew nothing of, he fed his own illusion of the reality of the play. The "picture in little" of the elder Hamlet which he wore on his neck-chain was a

[4] Adam Badeau described this adventure in an essay for the *Sunday Times*, which he reprinted as "A Night with the Booths" in *The Vagabond* (New York, 1859), pp. 347-354.

[5] Twenty-seven of Miss Devlin's letters to Booth are preserved in the Theatre collection of the New York Public Library at Lincoln Center (referred to hereafter as Theatre Collection, NYPL). This one, dated "Wednesday morning," is of the summer of 1859.

[6] Booth to Adam Badeau, June 6, 1863. Printed in Edwina Booth Grossmann, *Edwin Booth* (New York, 1894), p. 149 (referred to hereafter as Grossmann).

miniature of Junius Brutus.[7] Sometimes when the play was well cast he caught inspiration by persuading himself that he heard Junius Brutus' voice through the voice of the Ghost.

Booth's First Critic

Although there was neither money nor lasting glory in Booth's first Hamlet in 1853, there was profit of another kind. The drama critic of the *Daily Placer Times and Transcript*, Ferdinand Cartwright Ewer, wrote a review of it which caught the essence of Booth's best qualities and which weighed not a little in shaping his Hamlet of the future. Ewer was a young man himself—intelligent, sensitive, educated in literature and philosophy at Harvard College, and alert to the coming spirit of the age. To a play-watcher of Ewer's temperament and training, *Hamlet* was not merely the best of all nineteenth-century melodramas and a test piece for aspiring ranters; it embodied moral complexities, delicacies of sentiment, and a code of manners which no actor in Ewer's previous experience had been able to reveal.[8]

During the preceding summer Ewer had watched Booth play lesser roles in support of his father; had sensed in Booth's dark beauty, in his "chaste and natural elegance of action and expression," the possibility of an entirely new kind of tragic acting. Indeed, as he claimed years afterward, Booth became "a hope of my life." By the end of March, he printed a bold prediction that Booth would one day rank with Edwin Forrest, who since the death of the elder Booth was unquestionably America's leading tragedian: "His school is different," Ewer wrote, "but to our mind as good as that of Mr. Forrest." On April 22 he reviewed Booth's Richard III. This was not an altogether easy assignment, for through the early acts, whether by fumbling or intention, Booth seemed tame. Richard had been his father's masterpiece, and "recollection of the consummate impersonation of the same character by that great spirit who will tread the stage no more, was vivid in the minds of all." Yet Ewer could find in the wooing scene surprisingly subtle transitions from taunting to

[7] The chain and miniature are in the Theatre Collection, NYPL.

[8] Ewer subsequently became an Episcopalian priest and in the 1870's was a storm center in the controversy over Ritualism. For further information about him, his complete reviews of Booth's Richard III and Hamlet, and his later correspondence with Booth, see my article, "Edwin Booth's First Critic," in *Theatre Survey*, VII (May, 1966), 1-14.

wheedling; and he could cry up the "blaze of genius" which broke out in the fourth act and burned hotly to the end of the play.

During the *Hamlet* performance, on April 25, Ewer became so excited that he couldn't keep to his seat. "If I darted from the audience to 'in behind the scenes,' and from 'behind the scenes' to the audience again once, I did one dozen times," he once told Booth. After the play he stopped at a popular saloon to celebrate the evening's triumph, and then, very late, went on to the *Times and Transcript* office to scribble out his long review. Booth's Hamlet, he declared, put to the blush every other Hamlet seen in California. In conception, if not in finish, it surpassed his father's Hamlet; it left far behind the "icy coldness," the "unbending iron" of the Hamlet of James Stark (the then reigning California favorite). The key word for Booth's Hamlet was "flexibility." He not only made Hamlet "philosophical," but gave to the role (here Ewer invoked a phrase of William Hazlitt's) "all the easy motion and the peaceful curves of 'a wave of the sea.' " Ewer called to mind Booth's familiarity and ease in the first meeting with Rosencrantz and Guildenstern, his sad dignity with the King and Queen, his grief at "O that this too too solid flesh would melt," the warmth and high-mindedness of his friendship with Horatio, his passionate feigning of madness in the scene with Ophelia and the "sweet sadness" of love which shone through it. The day after Ewer's review was published, an irate correspondent rebuked him for his belittlement of James Stark; in response Ewer thoughtfully capsulized his "*beau ideal*" of Hamlet: "Melancholy without gloom, contemplative yet without misanthropy, philosophical yet enjoying playfulness in social converse, a man by himself yet with ardent feelings of friendship, a thorough knower of human nature, Hamlet stands the type of all that is firm, dignified, gentlemanly and to be respected in a man." However much Ewer admired Stark in other roles, he could find nothing of this ideal in Stark's unyielding, stiff Hamlet; but Booth made it the "easy undulating, flexible thing" which Shakespeare intended it to be.

Undoubtedly Ewer read into Booth's performance much more than the unschooled nineteen-year-old had consciously acted. Booth treasured this "first *criticism* of my acting," kept it in his portfolio of credentials which he would carry back east with him three years later, and studied to infuse his later Hamlets with its principles. A quarter of a century later, having long since mislaid it, Booth applied to Ewer for a transcript.

Roughing It

Except for his first Hamlet—granted that it was half as attractive as Ewer claimed it to be—not much else happened during Booth's California years that his father could have taken pride in. He had to serve his apprenticeship and learn his craft, of course, and this meant, under frontier circumstances, playing dozens of roles in ephemeral pieces. His attitude toward the work was often more devil-may-care than professionally earnest. The scanty records provide many a hint of his laziness and indifference, of inadequate memorizing and having to "wing it," of playing while drunk, of walking through parts he did not care for. Now and then he indulged in cheap actor tricks at the expense of others. Once when he was playing Armand Duval in support of Jean Davenport's Camille, the house rose to its feet to applaud his display of grief in the death scene. Many years later Miss Davenport remembered the event affectionately, but one can only wonder what she thought of it on the spot. We observe in her account of it that between rehearsal and performance Booth discarded all her careful instructions and rearranged the death scene to his own advantage, getting himself into a favorable upstage position where his grief could steal the show.[9] An often told tale is that of his Sacramento triumph as Raphael in the American premier of *The Marble Heart:* on that occasion he played the childish prank of pretending throughout rehearsals that the role was beyond his comprehension, and then on the night, after muddling dully through the early passages, of springing the grand tear-jerking scene with all stops out. He traded shamelessly on his charm and personal beauty, which were indeed remarkable—so impressive, in fact, that Laura Keene took him to Australia as her leading man. That venture was a failure for all concerned, and it gained Booth little more than a collection of tall tales and further practice in irresponsible behavior. When he got back to California in the spring of 1855, Ferdinand Ewer lost interest in him. After a performance of Richard III, all that Ewer had to say of it in the June issue of *The Pioneer* was, "We are very fearful that Mr. Booth devotes too little time to study." He probably meant that Booth was drunk.

[9] Jean Davenport Lander's account is preserved in an unidentified newspaper clipping, "Edwin Booth in His Prentice Days," in the Booth file of the Harvard Theatre Collection.

His wild-oats sowing was deplorable. Without raking over the dubious incidents, we may take his own word for it. A decade later, after the death of his wife, he flagellated himself with black memories. "Before I was eighteen I was a drunkard, at twenty a libertine," he confessed to Elizabeth Stoddard:

I knew no better. I was allowed to roam at large, and at an early age and in a wild and almost barbarous country where boys became old men in vice very speedily; but after satiety, remorse set in like a despair, and like the devil when he was taken ill I resolved to become a saint and throw off the hoof and horns. I could not do it. Sin was in me and it consumed me while it was shut up close, so I let it out and it seemed to rage and burn more fiercely than ever. All the accumulated vices I had acquired in the wilds of California and the still less refined society of Australia seemed to have full sway over me and I yielded to their bestializing voices. I added fuel to the fire until an angel quenched it and made me, if not a man, at least a little worthier than I was. There was one spark, however, left untouched. It was merely covered, and it occasionally would ignite; still the angel kept it under. . . .[10]

As he explained to Mrs. Stoddard, his vices did *not* include "murder, robbing, and such petty offences." They were drunkenness and whoring. The "angel" he speaks of, who was Mollie Devlin, could straighten out his sex life, but not even she, except by dying, could extinguish his sick craving for alcohol. In the little that we know of his personal doings in the later 1850's there are signs enough that wild living might have been his ruin. His younger brother John Wilkes, who ran much the same course, died in infamy. Yet the greatest saints are those with a well-earned sense of sin: Booth might never have realized the spiritual insights and the emotional power of his maturest art if he had not committed these passionate self-violations during his youth.

First Bid for Stardom

In the fall of 1856 Booth returned to the East, preceded by his manager, Ben Baker, to bid for acceptance as a star. It was not easy to get a hearing. No New York manager would have him except on insultingly low terms. Laura Keene, who was opening her own theatre, would have taken him on as leading man again to support

[10] Booth to Elizabeth Stoddard, March 12, 1863. This letter was published by Dolores Bacon, with other of Booth's letters to the Stoddards, in the Sunday magazine section of the New York *Herald*, November 1, 1893.

her in *Camille*, *As You Like It*, and other "she" plays of her personal repertory; but a would-be star could not let his reputation be staled in second billing. The best engagement that Baker could secure for him was a two-week run in Boston the following spring. So Booth went on the road. All things considered, the delay was fortunate, for to emerge as a star he had to be ready in more than a dozen heavy roles, in most of which he lacked sufficient experience. On October 15 he began at Baltimore, and during the next six months he circled and crisscrossed the South, the Middle West, and the Middle East, perfecting and solidifying his repertory.

On April 20, 1857, he opened at the Boston Theatre, managed by Thomas Barry, and there for the next two weeks he exhibited himself in ten roles. Of these, six were non-Shakespearean: Massinger's Sir Giles Overreach, Bulwer's Richelieu, Sheil's Pescara, Payne's Brutus, Maturin's Bertram, and Colman's Sir Edward Mortimer. Four were Shakespearean (or what passed for Shakespearean in those days): Cibber's Richard III, Tate's Lear, Garrick's Petruchio, and Hamlet. The engagement was generously covered by the Boston press.

Boston was always kind to Booth, and from this season onward it took him for its own, seeing in him, as it were, the second coming of his father, whose London-trained perfections it had always preferred over the muscle and thunder of Edwin Forrest. Although no longer the vital center of American life, Boston complacently regarded itself as America's brain center—a suburb of London rather than of New York. It presumed to arbitrate taste in literature and the arts. Even that stepchild of the arts, the stage, once proscribed by Boston blue law, now flourished there, and audiences of "culture and distinction" petted it into conformity with Brahmin ideals of intellectualism and gentility. The newly erected Boston Theatre was held to be one of the finest playhouses in the country. The half-dozen great Boston newspapers were served by well-grounded theatrical reviewers who vied with each other in bringing in discriminating judgments.

These reviewers, although somewhat put off by "the California dramatic dictionary, noted for remarkable copiousness" (evidently Baker had made the rounds with his book of clippings), were lavish with analysis and judicious with praise. Day after day Booth could study appreciations of his work, not always flattering, but always well-informed, sympathetic, instructive, and earnest. His Sir Giles, said the *Transcript* (April 21), "brought back the most vivid recollections of the fire, the vigor, the strong intellectuality which characterized the acting of his lamented father"—and similar references to his resemblance to his father, for better or worse, recur throughout the notices. Frequently he was checked for drawling, for nasal tones, for extravagant gait, for overly exuberant displays of energy; but these were put down as faults of youth which study and experience would soon dispel.

Sometimes the reviewers were troubled by the seeming tameness of his opening acts, then surprised and gratified by the torrential energy of his later ones. As the *Courier* (April 21) put it, "he understands the secret of climax, and reserves his noblest effort for the last." And indeed his best successes in this first Boston run—Sir Giles, Richelieu, and Richard III—were roles which have such climaxes built into them. The *Transcript* (April 23) preserves vivid word-pictures of the two most "thrilling" moments of his Richard III. In the fifth-act Dream scene "he plunges madly forward and falls on his knees—his teeth chatter against each other—his eyes glare and seem bursting from their sockets—his voice gushes forth at intervals, or is lost in hurried and impotent attempts at expression." In the Death scene "he stumbles and falls on his side, and in this position holds Richmond at bay; he then by superhuman energy regains his position, and after receiving his mortal wound, lifts himself to more than his natural height, and falls at his feet." He succeeded best, said the *Transcript* (April 28), in scenes where great action is required—that is to say, in well-constructed melodramas which build to fifth-act violences, as in Cibberized Shakespeare.

This, of course, put his Hamlet at a disadvantage, for the essence of Hamlet lies in the slow, polarizing inaction of the first three acts; in the fourth act, especially as the play was cut in those days, Hamlet appears but little; the fifth contains no extended passage in which the actor can focus attention on himself alone. Accordingly, Booth did not emphasize Hamlet in his programming, playing it at Boston but once at the beginning of his second week. The choice was correct if he wished to make his first impression a blazing one.

Nonetheless, the reviewers were all watching for his Hamlet, and in their notices of April 28 they made it a special measure of his worth. He came off only moderately well. The *Journal*, the *Courier*, and the *Advertiser* settled for generalized approval, citing especially his youthful fitness for the part. The *Post* liked his natural colloquial manner in the soliloquies, through which "so many actors rant and bluster," but found many of his readings bad and regretted that he passed over many important points in seeming indifference. The *Transcript* somewhat uneasily concluded that "he did not seem to us to catch the spirit of the play," blamed him for addressing soliloquies directly at the audience and for taking liberties with the text, and reckoned his performance "hardly up to the average of the Hamlets of the theatrical stars who have performed in Boston." But then, as if to mitigate its dubious verdict, the *Transcript* appended a gushing letter signed "F.," apparently from someone who had watched Booth in another city. "F." apologizes for applying so uncritical a word as "beautiful" to Booth's Hamlet, but can find no better word. It is "the *beau ideal* of the sweet, the graceful, the gentlemanly." "F." is enraptured by the scholar's eye, the soldier's spirit, the fine severe sorrow of his face, the dark intensity of his eye, his voice replete with passion and pathos, etc., etc., and insists that Hamlet is Booth's best role.

The intellectual elite were better pleased than the professional critics, and many of them made their responses known to Booth directly. Julia Ward Howe was so delighted that she set about writing a Hippolytus play for him to perform. Benjamin Peirce, the Harvard astronomer, wrote him a note of heady praise: "Never before did this profound creation appear to me to be reproduced with so just, rich, and true imagination. Never before did I so feel the living presence of Shakespeare's Prince of Denmark." A dozen Harvard professors and prominent Cambridge citizens, including Louis Agassiz and James Russell Lowell, and fifty-one students at Harvard College sent in (too late) petitions to manager Barry to schedule a repetition of the play. For Booth, who had grown up with a learned father and hungered after education, but in the rush of living had got precious little of it, tributes of this sort were to be cherished.[11]

On May 2, at the end of the run, the critic of the *Traveller*, who had been Booth's severest critic, summed up his opinions in a thoughtful essay. Booth's measure might be taken, he wrote, by the fact that his Richard III was one of the best ever seen in Boston and his Hamlet one of the worst. The reason for this is that Richard is not a truly Shakespearean character full of fine thoughts, but only the embodiment of a common and coarse passion. Booth can play

[11] Peirce's letter and the petitions to Barry are preserved in Booth's souvenir letterbook at The Players.

Richard, but not Hamlet, because as yet he is "a mere actor, not a thinker." In the externals of his art he is excellent, and these might be detailed as follows:

> He has the charming and accurate modulations of voice, a very agreeable quality of tone, and his general average reading is quite up to the mark. He has not the condensed and withering, demoniacal passion of his father, but he has a much better general average of merit. . . . Young Booth's eye is noble and imperious, rather than charged with the basilisk glance of his father. . . . He has cultivated the same peculiar nasal twang, which his father's admirers recognize in certain passages, almost like the voice of their idol from the dead. His gait and stage address are graceful, and his movement is like the rhythmical flow of his tones. Literally, "grace is in all his steps, and in his action, dignity and love." For his cadences are delightful; however high he soars, his voice immediately drops again, and in good time. There is no ear-splitting violence. He has the magnetic, sympathizing quality in his tones. They charm you, without telling you the secret of their charm. This quality is the gift of nature. No art can catch it.

With these faults and virtues, the *Traveller* critic concludes, he is at present successful only in characters of simple mold; but assuredly years and study will fill up the framework of his mind and deepen the intensity of his person. When all is told, "he is at present, to our mind, the most attractive actor that walks the American boards."

The Forrest Rivalry

We can perceive in these early Boston reviews something working for Booth which was at the moment undefinable and which Booth could only gradually come to understand. During the years that he was roughing it in the mining towns and the antipodes, a subtle change was beginning to affect eastern society: theatrical taste was turning toward elegance; audiences were being described as "cultivated," "critical," "wealthy," "intellectual"; women were attending plays in increasing numbers; decorum and delicacy, moderation and refinement were coming to be prized above brute strength.

Booth had assumed that when he made a bid for stardom the great rival he must confront would be Edwin Forrest. To a degree this was accurate. But what Booth could not foresee was that Forrest's "old school" of tragic acting—outsized, oratorical, heavily masculine—was passing from favor. Really nice people were a little ashamed of Forrest, who for all his powerful intelligence, will, muscle, and voice had been tarnished in reputation by involvement in the Astor Place Riots and by the scandal of divorce courts. Forrest would endure, of course, and command a following for many years to come, but his giantism did not ingratiate him with the new generation of sophisticates. In the spring of 1855, when Forrest was running through his classical repertory at the Broadway, an unscrupulous writer for the New York *Tribune*—a jackal, but a cunning beast who smelt the south wind's thaw—struck dastardly but telling blows at him. This was William Stuart, né O'Flaherty, a superficially charming but wildly unprincipled fellow—a hanger-on of the theatrical world, with whom Booth would later become involved in managerial partnership, from whom still later he would endure criticism approaching slander.

Stuart described Forrest's Hamlet as "a broad-shouldered, athletic, middle-aged man, knit in coarse vigor, who seemed to writhe most uncomfortably under the load of sweet fancies and dreamy philosophic thoughts which thronged upon him." In the scene with the Ghost, he exhibited "the coarse rage of a ruffian told of a rival bully's murder, of some butchery of one of his gang, and thirsty to glut his fury." In the Play scene "he had far more the air of some huge gipsy, watching with roguish glance an opportunity to rob the hen-roost, than a highly intellectual analyzer of nature trying to descry on the human countenance the evidence of guilt." His Othello was a man of coarse, fierce passion, a Bill Sikes fixing his brute love on a fragile woman. In the Dagger scene in *Macbeth* he was a caged dyspeptic bear dreaming that a wedge of juicy flesh was dangling before his eyes. Stuart concocted many columns of such malicious stuff. The really nice people would not have said such things, but they were not reluctant to have them said; and once at least, in a review of Forrest's Brutus (*The Fall of Tarquin*), Stuart fixed the social fact so neatly that nice people might have repeated it after him: "He may have drawn many a responsive cheer from man, but has never drawn a sympathetic tear from woman." Booth, who was adored by women, would learn in time that he need not compete with Forrest on Forrest's own terms.[12]

In later years another journalist, A. C. Wheeler, whose penname was Nym Crinkle, time and again reflected upon this change of taste which occurred throughout the 1850's and 1860's and di-

[12] Stuart's review of Forrest's Hamlet appeared in the *Tribune* on March 20, 1855; of Othello on March 22; of Brutus on March 30; of Macbeth on April 3.

minished Forrest's prestige. Nym Crinkle admired Forrest without reservation, and he never ceased deploring the new "civilization" which made Booth's acting possible. In his view, Forrest, whom he called the American Titan, had forged out of himself certain roles which in their massive and crude splendor swayed the feelings of a multitude and shook the stage for a generation. His playing was never amenable, however, to the niceties of Shakespearean scholars, and was downright offensive to the prejudices of sensitive dilettantism. Independent American taste had first been infected in the late 1840's by the intellectual artificialities of William Charles Macready. By the time Booth emerged into prominence, Forrest's school of acting was held by the upper crust to belong to an outgrown condition of culture, and Forrest himself was a slightly vulgar giant who had no entrée into the exclusive school of "artists." Thus Booth's way of playing Hamlet was accepted as the correct and only way—without (in Nym Crinkle's view) Booth's contributing a single original idea to the role or really making a role of it at all. Booth never awoke the electric response, said Nym Crinkle, never touched new peaks of thought, but only passively met the new culture with the trademarks of that culture. He suppressed passion and elaborated sentiment; he substituted literary charm and nice elocution for genuine drama. He delivered an "exquisitely modulated Tennysonian transcript of Shakespeare." His sad, slight Hamlet, of the "large and melancholy sweet eyes," was nothing more than a "nineteenth century gentleman."

Nym Crinkle was never as vicious toward Booth as Stuart had been toward Forrest, but he was more persistent. From the late 1860's until after Booth's death, he labored ceaselessly to undermine the reputation of Booth's art. There are, of course, grains of truth in his hostile allegations, and his vision of the shift in social values which conditioned Booth's playing and the popular acceptance of it is acute.[13]

In the midst of that soft revolution it took a great deal of educating for Booth to understand it. The arsenal of effects which he had inherited from the past—the carpet-chewing, eye-bulging, teeth-chattering violences—would always do to blow up the gallery boys; but for gentlemen of intellect and ladies of culture upon whose favor his career would depend, he had to work out a whole new style.

[13] Two of Nym Crinkle's most telling analyses of Booth are his review of *Hamlet* in the *World*, January 9, 1870, and "A Study," which appeared in the *World* on June 9, 1893, two days after Booth's death.

Failure in New York City

On May 4, 1857, two days after his last performance in Boston, Booth made his New York debut at William Burton's New Theatre. His engagement there would run to May 28.

After Boston, New York was a chilling experience. In the first place, theatre in New York was Big Business, and Booth was immediately victimized by its crude techniques of advertising. He had instructed the Burton management that he wished to open in Sir Giles Overreach; but Burton, a master of puffing, posted him instead for Richard III, which had been Junius Brutus' favorite and most famous role, and placarded the town with signs announcing SON OF THE GREAT TRAGEDIAN and HOPE OF THE LIVING DRAMA. Every newspaper advertisement was stuffed with hyperbolic tags, culled from out-of-town reviews, about Booth's "greatness."

The puffing may have brought out a full house for the opening, but the response was cool, and thereafter the audiences diminished. The reviews, both in number and in quality, were disappointing. The New York press was far too busy in those days with murder and the marketplace to devote systematic attention to the arts, and most of Booth's roles, including his single performance of Hamlet on May 12, passed without valuable comment. By combing the reviews he might have found that he was "one of the best actors of the country," who "never outrages dramaticunity" (*sic*); that he had "a manly presence, a graceful bearing, a rich, sonorous voice of unusual compass and flexibility"; and more such platitudinous praise salted with platitudinous fault-finding. Burton's puffing fomented a rash of comparisons of Booth with his father, none of any critical worth. The reviewer for the *Morning Courier*, who confessed to being too young ever to have seen the elder Booth (whom he called "Lucius Junius"!), lectured Booth on the pronunciation of *m* and *n*, and on the necessity of ridding himself of a "gutteral" (*sic*) utterance which, he suggested, Booth had inherited from Macready!

Booth was speedily disheartened by New York and wrote to a friend in Washington, R. S. Chilton, to tell him so. On May 8 Chilton consoled him for "thin houses, newspaper critics, and other annoyances," and expressed "a little anxiety on your behalf, which has been occasioned by your note in which I thought I discovered something like despondency. . . . It appears to me that you have permitted your reception in New York (which from bad weather or some other cause appears to have been, thus far at least, less enthusiastic than you or your friends had a right to expect) to rob you of 'that pleased alacrity and cheer of spirit which you were wont to have.' " Chilton was disturbed, too, by some negative feelings Booth had expressed about Hamlet: "Depend upon it, you can easily make it your own character, and I hope you *will* do so." [14]

The remainder of the run made plain to Booth that New York was not to be his for the asking. Until he was better settled in his art and could project it with perfect certainty no really serious confrontation with the city could be gainful. He returned for a single week in the fall of 1857 and for another in the spring of 1858. Thereafter he kept out of New York for two entire seasons.

[14] Booth must have written to Chilton immediately after his New York opening on May 4. Chilton's reply is in Booth's souvenir letterbook at The Players.

CHAPTER II

An Actor's Education

Adam Badeau

Booth's education was about to begin. In mid-June, three weeks after his New York engagement ended, he received a letter which opened a new chapter of his life. One Adam Badeau—a young man-about-town, connoisseur of the arts, feuilletonist for the *Sunday Times* over the signature of "The Vagabond," and very much an exponent of what Nym Crinkle would one day label "sensitive dillettantism"—had seen every one of Booth's New York performances, had fallen in love with Booth's genius, and was determined to become Booth's mentor, guide, and friend.[1]

[1] General Adam Badeau (1831-95) is best known for his associations with Ulysses S. Grant. He was Grant's military secretary during the Civil War, and later wrote the *Military History of Ulysses S. Grant*, 3 vols. (New York, 1868-81) and *Grant in Peace* (Hartford, 1887). He assisted Grant in the composition of his *Personal Memoirs*, 2 vols. (New York, 1885-86). He also served as consul-general at the American Embassy in London from 1870 to 1881, and at Havana from 1882 to 1884. In the aftermath of his London experience he wrote a stinging, if gossipy, book about English society called *Aristocracy in England* (New York, 1886). The young Badeau with whom we are concerned suggests little, except in braininess, of the Badeau of high public affairs. In his early "Vagabond" essays he wrote brilliantly about the arts, which he genuinely loved; but in those years he also affected the dandy, priding himself on his social entrées, fancying himself a ladies' man. Physically he was quite unprepossessing—red-faced, carrot-haired, and of bad posture. Grant's first impression of him was of "a little pale, blue-eyed man, who wore spectacles and looked like a bent fo'-pence." His youthful attachment to male companions, as expressed in his letters to Booth and to his soldier-friend Harry Wilson, ranged from generous affection to maudlin and even hysterical possessiveness.

In one of his Sunday essays during Booth's run (probably May 17) Badeau had discussed Booth's tragic acting as a type of emergent American art. It is an art, Badeau says, which is vibrant with a new emotionalism. Whether we observe it in the piano music of Louis Gottschalk, who plays "poems, and dreams, and passions," or in the Camille or the Medea of Matilda Heron, which bring the sob to your throat and the blinding mist to your eyes, or in Frederick Church's new canvas of Niagara Falls, it is an art which is impulsive, erratic, and irregular, turbulent and impassioned, brimful of earnestness, stormy. It is not, of course, *uniquely* American, for it is apparent in Turner's paintings, Verdi's operas, Dumas' plays, the poetry of Tennyson, the novels of George Sand and Charlotte Bronte, the histories of Carlyle. But in our young country the artist is uniquely free to create originals rather than to copy old, effete ideas. Our painters and sculptors might take their inspiration from Indian maidens rather than from Greek slave-girls (a hit at Hiram Powers and other lingering devotees of neo-classicism).

As for actors and acting, Badeau dismisses the "clever, careful students" like Wallack and Davenport who have been trained in the intellectual school of Macready. "Give me one touch of real feeling," he cries, "one breath of absolute genius, one spark of enthusiasm before all the finish, all the elaboration, all the study in the world." In Booth he has found "the unmistakable fire, the electric spark, the god-like quality which mankind has agreed to worship." Booth, to be sure, is as yet "undeveloped, chaotic, plastic," and one may have to sit through an entire act to experience the one touch, but when it comes "it is transcendent, it goes straight home, it compensates." Given Booth's youth and beauty, his mobile face, his musical voice, and his impulsive, soulful nature, he is "all the more interesting just now from his faults; they so evidently spring from inexperience, they are so palpably negative, they are so curable, that they enlist your sympathies, while four or five times in an evening he does something that requires no sympathy, no allowance, no toleration; that commands, controls, overwhelms." The millennium of American art has not arrived yet, but "the spirit of God has moved on the waters," and Badeau has heard the stirring: "We must make haste in what we have to do, so I shall go to see Booth every night next week, and visit the Academy of Design every day." [2]

[2] Badeau reprinted this essay under the title "American Art" in *The Vagabond*, pp. 120-127.

Thus the first flutterings of this young neo-romantic around the Boothian flame. During the next few weeks Badeau read and re-read Booth's Shakespearean roles in order to recall his exact looks and tones; to fancy, moreover, what Booth "might have said, and done, and looked, and did not." He studied that passage in Churchill's *Rosciad* which celebrates the power of Garrick's eye, and recited it to a friend, who confirmed his opinion that it was exactly applicable to Booth. He re-read Hazlitt on Kean and found there described almost every excellency and every curable deficiency—uneven conception, faulty elocution, fitful performance—to be found in Booth. Then he set about a grand reassessment of Booth's genius in relation to the theatre of the day.

On June 14 the *Sunday Times* carried his essay on the imminent rebirth of tragedy. "It has been of late very much the fashion to speak slightingly of tragedy: people of taste and accomplishment decry the stilted walk of the buskin, and prefer the easy gait of the sock. Or, at any rate, tragedy must be modern and real; we must have every-day life and every-day people; Camilles and de Varvilles only, it is said, can interest us now-a-days. I confess I have been tinctured with this heresy. . . . I have leaned towards realism. *Peccavi.*" This trend of taste toward base realism is inevitable, Badeau says, when there is no tragic actor about except mouthers and ranters. Consider, for instance, Edwin Forrest. Although he is full of feeling, he never elevates nor refines by his performances. His conceptions are not intellectual; his effects are entirely physical; he moves us but does not inspire us; he excites horror, not sublime terror. His eye is the hyena's, not the eagle's. Miss Cushman is very like Forrest; and the reigning heroine of the realist school, Matilda Heron, although, to be sure, she is full of womanly instinct and great ability to express it, yet concerns herself primarily with the coarsest details of human behavior and never suggests "a higher sphere of art."

In Edwin Booth, at last, we have an actor who redeems the possibility of tragedy, who "has made me know what tragedy is," who in the moments when the divine fire is upon him recalls those highest notions of tragedy which, as we read, were known in other ages. In Booth's delivery of the last acts of Richard III, there is no "cold, debasing realism," but "the poetry of the stage, the realization of your ideas of the Richard of Shakespeare—a royal murderer, a kingly monster, a man at once magnificent in intellect and terrible in passions."

Charles Lamb to the contrary, Badeau says, the words of Shakespeare can never be so well understood in the study as when they are realized with all their concomitants by a superlative actor on the stage. There are many shades of feeling too subtle, too transient, too shaded to be expressed except through the actor's gesture, movement, and facial expression. In one passage of Booth's Hamlet, for instance, we may find a supreme example of the "originality and refined ideality" with which this young genius can illuminate the text:

> His conception of the ghost scene differs widely from any I have seen or read of. Instead of representing Hamlet as overcome by animal fear, as most, if not all, actors have done, Booth portrays him awed, of course, at the tremendous visitation, but still more imbued with a filial and yearning tenderness. The tones of his voice, especially when he falls on his knees to the ghost, and cries out, "Father!" the expression of his face, and, above all, of his eye, embody this new and exquisite conception, and seem to me more affecting even than the fright of Garrick could have been, which Fielding says made all the spectators also fear. Booth makes them share, instead, his tenderness.

If Booth can bring us such new meanings as this, it is no heresy to say that an actor gives fuller utterance to Shakespeare's ideas than do words on the printed page. When confronted by such manifestations, Badeau says, "I throw aside my books." [3]

The next day Badeau mailed Booth a copy of this essay, together with a long letter of self-introduction. He produced his credentials, declared his admiration and loyalty, indicated his reservations about Booth's work (in the most flattering possible way, by likening him to the elder Kean), and urged Booth to devote his summer vacation to hard study—"to the acquisition of a complete control of your voice, to the absolute mastery of every character you play." Finally, he insisted that Booth write him at once and visit him in New York at the earliest opportunity.[4]

Booth responded immediately. As Badeau recalled the events many years later, "at the end of a week he consented to spend Sunday with me; and from that time dated a peculiar intimacy." They passed "days as well as nights" together, and Badeau undertook to fill the chasms of Booth's mind. "I used to hunt up books and pictures about the stage, the finest criticisms, the works that illustrated his scenes, the biographies of great actors, and we studied them

[3] See "Edwin Booth" in *The Vagabond*, pp. 286-292.

[4] Badeau to Booth, June 15, 1857. This *first* letter of Badeau's is in Booth's souvenir letterbook at The Players.

together. We visited the Astor Library and the Society Library to verify costumes, and every picture or picture-gallery in New York that was accessible." [5] We have no record of their summer course of study, but it is fair to speculate on some of the books that passed between them, particularly those which are relevant to Hamlet. The titles of some of them turn up in Badeau's letters to Booth; some are mentioned in his essays as his own favorite reading; some, of which Booth shows knowledge in the near future, are simply the common furnishings of any well-read young gentleman of the time.

The volumes of theatrical biography and reminiscence through which Badeau says he guided Booth for relics of the stage effect of older actors would have included, among others, Thomas Davies' *Dramatic Miscellanies* and *Life of David Garrick*, James Boaden's *Life of John Kemble* and *Memoirs of Mrs. Siddons*, and Barry Cornwall's *Life of Edmund Kean.* Certainly they read together Hazlitt's *View of the English Stage* in order to analyze Kean's instructive successes and failures. In Hazlitt's *Characters of Shakespear's Plays* they would have lingered over the famous statement (which Ferdinand Ewer had long since applied to Booth) that Hamlet's character is "made up of undulating lines; it has the yielding flexibility of 'a wave o' the sea.'" No critic of Booth's perfected Hamlet, one suspects, ever found apter terms for it than these which Hazlitt wrote long before Booth was born:

> It is not a character marked by strength of will or even of passion, but by refinement of thought and sentiment. Hamlet is as little of the hero as a man can well be: but he is a young and princely novice, full of high enthusiasm and quick sensibility. . . . He seems incapable of deliberate action, and is only hurried into extremities on the spur of the occasion. . . . At other times, when he is most bound to act, he remains puzzled, undecided, and sceptical, dallies with his purposes, till the occasion is lost, and finds some pretense to relapse into indolence and thoughtfulness again.
>
> There is nothing of this [severity] in Hamlet. He is, as it were, wrapped up in his reflections, and only *thinks aloud.* There should be no attempt to impress what he says upon others by a studied exaggeration of emphasis or manner; no *talking at* his hearers. There should be as much of the gentleman and scholar as possible infused into his part, and as little of the actor. A pensive air of sadness should sit reluctantly upon his brow, but no appearance of fixed gloom. He is full of weakness and melancholy, but there is no harshness in his nature. He is the most amiable of misanthropes.

[5] Adam Badeau, "Edwin Booth. On and off the Stage," *McClure's Magazine*, I (August, 1893), 259.

His ruling passion is to think, not to act.[6]

The serene quietude which Hazlitt read into Hamlet had never been realized by John Philip Kemble, who played the role, Hazlitt says, "like a man in armor"; nor was it ever fully available to the irritable genius of Kean. Nor was Booth quite ready in these young days to sacrifice actors' tricks and quick applause for the Hazlitt ideal. It would take years of self-discipline to achieve that quietude, and to learn at the same time how to infuse it with dramatic fire. It would take years, too, to convince audiences, through slowly won authority, that in Hamlet they preferred quietude over more obvious theatrical excitements.

Badeau's romantic road led inevitably to *Wilhelm Meister's Apprenticeship*. Goethe's ruminations upon the character of Hamlet, though less keenly phrased than Hazlitt's, yet assume the same idealizing posture:

Pure in sentiment, he knew the honorable-minded, and could prize the rest which an upright spirit tastes on the bosom of a friend. To a certain degree he had learned to discern and value the good and the beautiful in arts and sciences; the mean, the vulgar were offensive to him; and if hatred could take root in his tender soul, it was only so far as to make him properly despise the false and changeful insects of a court, and play with them in easy scorn. He was calm in his temper, artless in his conduct; neither pleased with idleness, nor too violently eager for employment. . . . He possessed more mirth of humor than of heart; he was a good companion, pliant, courteous, discreet, and able to forget and forgive an injury; yet never able to unite himself with those who overstept the limits of the right, the good, and the becoming.

Then there is Goethe's inescapable metaphor of Hamlet's weakness—the hero without a hero's strength of nerve, who sinks beneath a burden which he cannot bear and must not cast away: "To me it is clear that Shakespeare meant to represent the effects of a great action laid upon a soul unfit for the performance of it. . . . There is an oak-tree planted in a costly jar, which should have borne only pleasant flowers in its bosom; the roots expand, the jar is shivered." [7] Three years later, as we shall see, Mollie Devlin cites this very image of the oak tree in the jar as the "clearest and most comprehensive" view

[6] William Hazlitt, *The Complete Works*, Centenary Edition, ed. P. P. Howe (London, 1930), IV, 232-237.

[7] The passages quoted from *Wilhelm Meister's Apprenticeship* (Carlyle's translation) are in Book IV, Chapters 3 and 13. Other significant passages are in Book III, Chapter 11; Book IV, Chapter 15; and Book V, Chapter 6.

of Hamlet ever offered. Charles Clarke, who may or may not have read Hazlitt or Goethe, in scene after scene of his description of Booth's performance observes Hamlet facing resolutely up to minor matters and collapsing when major matters are at hand, his fine intellect ever readying for great action but ever defeated by the weakness of his will. Booth made the Hazlitt-Goethe point crystal clear.

George Sand's *Consuelo* was one of Badeau's favorite novels. Few modern readers could easily endure its longueurs of gothic romancing, yet George Sand did know something about the art of acting, and at least one of its hundreds of pages was worth writing. The heroine, Consuelo, who began life as an orphaned street gamin, has risen to the status of prima donna of the Venetian opera. Her would-be lover, the tenor Anzoleto, has failed. "What are my faults?" he asks her. "What I have often told you," Consuelo answers:

> too much boldness, and not sufficient preparation; an energy more feverish than sustained; dramatic effects, which are the work of the will rather than emotion. You were not imbued with the feeling of your part as a whole. You learned it by fragments. You saw in it only a succession of pieces more or less brilliant, and you did not seize either the gradation, or the development, or the aggregate. In your anxiety to display your fine voice and the facility which you possess in certain respects, you exhibit the whole extent of your powers almost on your entrance upon the scene. On the slightest opportunity you endeavored after effect, and all your effects were alike. At the end of the first act they knew you. . . . They did not see the artist inspired by passion, but the actor laboring for success.[8]

This fierce little lecture is the beginning of wisdom for any serious actor, and we may be sure that Badeau passed it on to Booth.

In Badeau Booth found exactly what he most needed at this turn of his career—a devoted friend from outside the profession, sophisticated in avant-garde taste, who could help him align his art with newest modes of thought and feeling. Booth had come in from the wilderness, so to speak, where the spirit of the age was that which persisted from the 1840's—to assert, to fight, to resist, to conquer; in theatrical terms to behave like Forrest—to brandish masculinity and roar defiance. Out there he had learned from his father and his fellow actors all that he needed to know of histrionics; but of literature, languages, history, and the fine arts—the mind-stuff of the new East, the genteel culture—he was mainly ignorant. His art at the moment was part native gift, part technical craft, but it was

[8] George Sand, *Consuelo*, Chapter XIX.

raw and directionless, without significant relationship to the world beyond the green room. Badeau could teach him, or rather, lead him to understand, what the new world wanted of him.

Booth was no docile pupil, however, no scholar, no systematic thinker. He declined to take lessons methodically. Over a stretch of twenty years, for instance, he defeated every effort of Badeau and of two wives to make him learn French. At times Badeau despaired of him. As he complained once to Mollie Devlin, he "will not listen to the abstract"; or as he explained to another friend some years later, "He is a man strangely constituted, of exquisite susceptibilities. . . . His mind is not trained in any logical fashion; he is a man of genius, of perceptions and emotions, and cannot reason." [9] Booth learned things in the artist's way, absorbing what he needed by intuition, feelingly, rejecting what he did not need. Badeau's usefulness was not so much in giving him lessons but in giving him contacts, to put him at ease in the world outside the profession by guided tours, to steady his confidence in his own powers by familiarizing him with the unknown.

Thus, for instance, Badeau's enthusiasm for picture galleries led Booth into an awareness and appreciation of contemporary art, and he quickly sensed the affinity between his own work and that of the painters and sculptors. He became acquainted with many of them personally, with some perhaps through Badeau's introduction, and during the next decade he developed more close friendships with artists than with any other kind of men. He knew Eastman Johnson, whose portrait of Mollie Devlin is her best-known memorial;[10] Thomas Hicks, whose oil painting of his Iago is one of the treasures of The Players; [11] Emanuel Leutze, who provided him sketches of Venice from which the scenery of his 1867 *Merchant of Venice* was drawn. Launt Thompson, the sculptor, whose studio was a favorite gathering place of the artists, was for many years one of his dearest friends. Jervis McEntee of Rideout, an unsuccessful painter of the

[9] Badeau to James Harrison Wilson, September 12, 1863. Badeau's letters to Wilson are in the Special Collections of the Princeton University Library.

[10] In the early 1880's Johnson did oil portraits of the Booth family: Junius Brutus the Elder, taken from a miniature; Mollie Devlin, taken from a photograph; Edwina, 1883; Edwin, 1884. The portrait of Edwina has recently been acquired by Amherst College; the others are owned at present by the Adelson Galleries in Boston.

[11] Another copy of the Hicks Iago is owned by the Adelson Galleries in Boston.

Hudson River School but a gentle soul and charming correspondent, became a life-long intimate.[12] He knew well and vastly admired the great landscape luminists of the time—Albert Bierstadt, Frederick Church, and Sandford Gifford—and for many years he owned a splendid landscape of Gifford's called "The Coming Storm." [13] From watching these men at work and listening to their conversation, Booth came to understand that the function of the artist, like his own actor's function, was to feel his way into perfect identification with the objects he wished to represent. Complaining once, jocularly, to his friend Emma Cary that he lost all sense of self in the nightly round of impersonation—"it's an awful thing to be somebody else all the while"—he observed: "But I guess I'm better off than many of my artist friends, some of whom (if they are as much in their art as I am) must be bears and owls; others, trees and rocks, while my Gifford and Bierstadt must lose all sense of being save in the painted ripple of a lake, or the peak of a snow-capped mountain." [14] Which is as much as to say that the painter "acts" what he paints. Theatrical reviewers sometimes accused Booth of excessive posing, of "making statues all over the stage"; and doubtless in his affection for the arts he sometimes imitated too deliberately the images which he found in statuary and heroic or sentimental canvases. But in a higher sense he absorbed the *spirit* of his artist friends, who in the 1850's and 1860's were fixing nature's beauty with astonishing technical skill and warm emotional overglow. No more suggestive analogue to Booth's perfected Hamlet can be found than one of Sandford Gifford's luminous mountain-over-lake landscapes—exact in outline, meticulously real in every foreground detail, its distant masses glimmering serenely through a mystic haze of light.

In a memorial essay published soon after Booth's death, Badeau tells us that he worked very closely with Booth in rehearsals and practice sessions: "Often we quarrelled all day about an interpretation or a rendering, and I went to the theatre at night to be convinced

[12] Letters from Booth to Thomas Hicks and to Launt Thompson are in the Theatre Collection, NYPL. Many letters from McEntee to Booth are preserved at The Players.

[13] For a reproduction of this painting and Melville's poem about it, see *The Battle-Pieces of Herman Melville,* ed. Hennig Cohen (New York, 1963).

[14] Booth to Emma Cary, January 10, 1865. Printed in Grossmann, p. 168. See also Mrs. Thomas Bailey Aldrich, *Crowding Memories* (New York, 1920), p. 57.

that he was right and I was wrong. Sometimes he gave me a private box, and I took notes of the performance, and of the criticisms or changes that occurred to me. Next day we went over them together, and at night he would play Richard or Iago according to my suggestions—perhaps as much to gratify me as because he thought my judgment correct." [15] Undoubtedly this sometimes happened, but less often than Badeau would suggest. Booth rarely played in New York during the first years of their friendship. Occasionally Badeau followed Booth to outlying places, as far as Boston or Buffalo, but it was not until the fall of 1860, after Booth's marriage, that they were often together on Booth's working days. Their early associations were mainly in the summer holidays when Booth visited Badeau, sometimes in the city, sometimes at Badeau's country place up the Hudson.

In the long intervals they corresponded incessantly. Booth's letters have mostly disappeared, but in the first year of their friendship alone he wrote Badeau some fifty times. In October of 1858 Badeau reports that he has just re-read them all—no hasty squibs either, for he commends and even affects to be jealous of their "wit and humor, and felicities of language, and graceful style." From Badeau's letters, of which a generous handful are preserved, we can glean something of how he made himself useful to Booth.[16] As a journalist he could keep Booth's name in the air by mentioning him in the "Vagabond" essays and by taking care that his provincial doings were reported in other journalists' columns of theatrical chitchat. He could watch the New York scene, report to Booth the successes and failures of potential rivals, and advise him on the strategy of his future return to the city. He ran library and bookstore errands, looking up old plays which Booth thought might be produceable. When one G. H. Hollister offered Booth a new play called *Henry II*, Badeau helped carpenter it into shape so that Booth could stage it in New Orleans. He often wrote Booth "en pedagogue," urging him to improve his study habits, insisting that he keep up his French, encouraging him to pursue his interest in literature and art: "It means three steps forward in your career. You have the faculty of absorbing into your own genius whatever interests you."

He deviled Booth about his drinking. In April, 1859, while

[15] *McClure's Magazine*, I (August, 1893), 259.

[16] Besides Badeau's first letter to Booth cited above, about thirty-five more, written between 1857 and 1865, are preserved at The Players.

scolding Booth for not having written lately: "'Tis just as likely as not you are on a spree; it is nearly five months since any of your performances of this sort, and since I have known you, you've never missed one in that space of time. You might have waited till I could take care of you." A year later, on a more cheerful note: "You feel, you say, like an artist; and ask if it's owing to Water, Mollie, or Adam? Lest you should make a mistake, you'd better cling to all three; especially the first, who can't speak for himself, however he seems to have spoken plainly enough. For God's sake, don't desert so true a friend." He once read Booth a stern lecture against smoking, based on advice he had heard from the opera singer Brignoli. Repeatedly he fussed over Booth's medical reports, apparently with reference to a venereal disease which Booth had contracted, until at last in April of 1860 he could exclaim, "I'm delighted that you are to be free from disease. Keep so, for Heaven's sake."

Most important of all, he stoked the fires of Booth's ambition. In October of 1858 he was saying, "Your letters of this season all indicate a greater anxiety and interest in your improvement than was once the case. That's the way, Ned: you are not yet all I want you to be; but you can be it *all:* you can't be more though, than I hope for." A year later, after visiting Booth in Boston, "I was delighted to be made sure of the immense development of your genius. . . . I am sure now that you will go on, conquering and to conquer." In April of 1860: "And don't lose your interest in your profession. Your conscious genius is all that ennobles it, or you in it. It's the recognition of that which constitutes your hold on others. Do you think you improve at all? Tell me of this. And pray, stay a god." These ministrations must have been of immense worth to Booth as he wandered about the country during what we might call his second apprenticeship, gathering strength for renewed assault upon New York City.

Unfortunately the friendship was not without cost. Badeau could not keep his emotions under control. His admiration degenerated into sycophantic hero-worship; his affection into infatuation. He fixed upon Booth (as later, in the war years, he would fix upon a soldier friend) a downright sexual possessiveness. Discount as we will the queer turns of mid-century sentimentalism and neo-romantic codes of male friendship, many passages in his letters make troublesome reading. "One day you put me into blues and rages," he writes, quite in the tone of a jealous mistress; "I was fretting because any one should think themselves preferred, even though I knew they were not." He calls Booth "My Prince," "the man I love best in the world," "a god"; he refers unabashedly to "my love letters" and "my persistence in loving you." If Booth writes him in friendly tone he melts in honey gratitude; if Booth fails to answer a letter for as long as two weeks he fumes and curses. In one black sulk he cries, "I wish to God I had never seen you. It's a frightful thing to live out of one's self; to be buried alive in somebody else. To depend upon that body for your happiness." As we shall see, he encouraged and abetted Booth's marriage to Mollie Devlin, yet as the time for it drew near, his jealousy rose to fever pitch. Booth broached the notion that in a year or so he and Mollie and Badeau would do a European grand tour. Badeau, with his mastery of French and Italian and his expertise in art history, would be the ideal cicerone. On first hearing the proposal Badeau was ecstatic; but a week later, "A pretty fool I'd feel like tagging around Europe in your train, waiting for the crumbs that fell from the rich woman's table. When you could spare a moment or a thought now and then, glad to get it! Damnation, damnation, damnation, damnation. Hell!" That Booth put up with such nonsense does not seem quite believable; but he did so, and we must adjust our preconception of his character enough to include the fact.

Perhaps in those years Booth was not altogether beyond vanity, and enjoyed the "conquest" of this brilliant young man of the world. Perhaps in his preoccupation with himself he was callous to Badeau's "suffering," and simply used him because he was useful. At times, it appears, he resorted to cruel retorts, twitting him for what he called "Badeau fever" and ridiculing his womanly gush. Once he threatened to "kick" him if he did not stop using the salutation "My Prince." Once when Badeau followed him to Boston, he snubbed him throughout the visit. Yet year after year he tolerated him and kept up the relationship. He gave him presents (a cameo ring, a portrait of himself); chose him to be best man at his wedding; invited him (at least Badeau says so) to Niagara Falls to share the honeymoon vacation. In 1863 when Mollie died, Badeau being then in the deep South with the Union Army, Booth poured out his grief to him in long letters.[17] When Badeau was invalided home during the war, Booth took him into his apartment and helped nurse him. In

[17] Booth to Badeau, March 3, May 18, June 6, June 15, 1863. Printed in Grossmann, pp. 141-152.

the middle 1860's they were separated by a quarrel, and thereafter Badeau, caught up in affairs of government and in his great work of biographizing Ulysses Grant (his ultimate hero), lived away from New York, either in Washington or overseas, and no longer concerned himself professionally with literature or the theatre. Eventually, in the later 1870's, it appears that [18] their relationship was renewed, but on different terms. Now it was Badeau whose career was in doubt and who needed assistance: in 1888 he signed a note acknowledging debts to Booth amounting to $10,000.[19]

Mollie Devlin

During the season of 1859-60, while Booth was still working the provinces, it was Badeau's curious assignment to watch over Booth's bride-to-be during her "term of trial." Booth had first met Mary (Mollie) Devlin in the fall of 1856, in Richmond, Virginia, where as a sixteen-year-old actress she was the Juliet to his Romeo. That she instantly fell in love with him was no wonder to Booth, for he was accustomed to being worshiped by women. Their paths crossed repeatedly, however, and in Boston in the fall of 1858 Booth began to take her seriously. By the summer of 1859 they were engaged to be married.

This development was somewhat alarming to Booth, for his experiences with actresses had taught him never to marry one. According to the code of self-respecting gentlemen, women were either "good" or "bad," and actresses, with rare exceptions, were presumed to be "bad." Although Booth "never injured a pure woman in his life," as Badeau would sometime quaintly put it,[20] he knew all about actresses. One of them, a singing chambermaid at the Boston Theatre, was proving the code at the very time that Booth was approaching his decision about Mollie. "There is a little *sweetheart* of mine crazy to go to Cal.," Booth wrote his brother Junius. "Stark is trying to get her for his theatre, but I talked her out of it, and my p---k into her . . . can't brag on her acting so much as what we do in secret." A month after he left Boston he confessed to Junius "the premonitory symptoms of a glorious *clap*, produced I think by a strain

[18] Badeau was among the guests at a banquet in Booth's honor on June 15, 1880.

[19] This statement of indebtedness is in the Theatre Collection, NYPL.

[20] *McClure's Magazine*, I (August, 1893), 261.

only, for the woman is *virtuous* &c." [21] Gentlemen did not marry actresses without taking careful stock of the situation.

Mollie Devlin was the rare exception. She had "all the qualities of heart, and mind, though undeveloped, which I most need to make life cheerful to me," he wrote to some older friends. "The few years she has passed on the stage have not been detrimental to her in the least." He had never observed in her "the slightest indication of coarseness or vulgarity so common among persons in the profession." [22] All the same it was necessary that she be, so to speak, decontaminated. He set her up in residence in Hoboken with books and a piano (Badeau gave her a guitar also), hired her a French teacher and a music teacher, and instructed her to forget the stage and improve her mind. Badeau was to keep her in good cheer by frequent visits, while Booth went off to the South and West to improve his craft and pile up money—and incidentally to cure himself of the aftereffects of the singing chambermaid.

He shouldn't have worried about Mollie. "You need never tell me, Edwin," she protested, "what your motive is for having me seclude myself this one year—I know . . . that it is for me, for *me* alone, that your bounty gives so much." [23] With the dedication of a nun she abjured "the busy world, of which I was *once* a member," and she would not "mix again with the world until I am your wife." She mastered French (as Booth himself could never be made to do) with schoolgirl celerity, practiced the piano days on end, and although "my weak fingers can't pace my ambition," she perfected guitar accompaniment to tender lyrics, against the "many, many evenings we will while away in peace rendered more delightful by Apollo's gift."

Fervently and selflessly she devoted herself to the cause of Booth's art and well-being. "My future ambition will be to see you great and good and if devotion of mind and intellect, but what is more influencing, an absorbing affection, can accomplish it, you shall be everything that the world has predicted." And gradually but surely

[21] Booth to Junius Brutus Booth Junior, October 31 and December 12, 1858. These letters are in a folder of Booth letters in the Harvard Theatre Collection.

[22] Booth to Dr. and Mrs. Beale, July 26, 1859. The Folger Shakespeare Library, Y.c. 215 (29).

[23] All the following quotations from Mollie Devlin's letters are taken from the manuscripts in the Theatre Collection, NYPL, by permission of the New York Public Library, the Astor, Lenox, and Tilden foundations.

she assumed the role of counselor, as wise through instinct as Badeau could be through sophistication, and probably, with love in the balance, much more persuasive.

The improvements you have made in the "Cardinal" charmed me: you must not forget to tell me of your studies; they interest me alike with the movements of your heart—*my heart;* for 'tis *mine*, you tell me.

The conversational, colloquial school you desire to adopt is the only true one, Edwin, for the present day, but as you very reasonably add, too much is "dangerous": for example, Miss Heron (don't shudder, I will make no comparisons) in the beginning of her career was praised for her "naturalness," and deservedly so; and while she "used it" in moderation was successful. But *now* could you see her! She gives you too much of "Mrs. John Smith,"—and endeavors,—or labors rather to be so very commonplace that 'tis simply ridiculous, and even her greatest admirers can find no mind in her now. Acting is an imitation of Nature, is it not? Then 'tis Art; and the Art must be seen too, for nature upon the stage would be most ridiculous.

In moral idealism (and likewise in her esthetics), Mollie was downright puritanical, fiercely uncompromising. One night in January of 1860 she went into the city to see Miss Heron's newest play, *Lesbia*, "intensely French and horribly dramatic." Miss Heron acted in her "usual 'grotesque' manner." Mollie heard afterward that the play was a failure, and she was glad that it failed.

Camilles, Medeas, and Lesbias are fit only for the French stage: the atmosphere of *Lesbia* is unhealthy—and can produce no good. Society is sufficiently corrupted without being taught immorality from the Stage—where it is seen in its most dangerous and seductive form too! Women without principle in virtue—represented in gold and jewels—and pearls and diamonds falling from their laps—enlisting the sympathy of an ignorant audience. To see an Art as *holy* as the drama so desecrated and perverted—is it not outrageous? How glad I am, dear one, that the branch you were fitted for has not been disgraced, for though unappreciated now—the day will come, when "Gorgeous Tragedy" will have its sway! You are held as its only representative in this day—and you can, if you will, change the perverted taste of the public by your truth and sublimity, and you *must study* for this! Dear Edwin, I will never allow you to droop for a single moment. . . . Oh, you do not know how close a *critic*, I will be of your "Genius"—a child, who requires more nursing than the helpless babe, at the mother's breast!

If he was to save the Art, he must do so here in the city, and she would never let him forget the test that lay ahead: "I want you to be 'au fait' when you come to play before the great Moguls."

From the tiny cluster of Mollie's letters that were saved it is obvious that Booth had found his captain's captain. Of course, she said, she could never be as clever as Mr. Badeau, for "a brilliant education has never fallen to my lot"; but all the same she counted herself "sufficiently well informed to appreciate the good and beautiful." At the insistence of her French teacher she gave up reading Victor Hugo, for, as he told her, "my mind was too youthful and too ardent to read this author without being intoxicated"; she must be, he told her, "learned and intellectual, but retain with it all the simplicity of a child!" A cunning child!

In one of her last letters before Booth came home to her in 1860 she called attention to something in her French readings which she believed Booth would find enormously useful: one of the most respected philosophers of the day had vividly postulated the exact esthetic principles from which Booth's art depended. Here was both authority and inspiration for her "bien aimé." "What a pity you do not read French fluently! And this regret shall be of short duration—you must acquire it immediately; at least as soon as I am permitted to sit by your side and instruct you! There is one single discourse of Cousin's that will more than repay you for your study—'tis a pity that you are not able to read and profit by its instructions ere donning your Hamlet dress again. . . . I will be the . . . most tyrannical of 'professors' until you can read Cousin!" The work she refers to was Victor Cousin's *Du vrai, du beau, et du bien*, which had been published in Paris in 1853.[24] Several passages in Lecture VIII, "On Art," corresponded perfectly to her image of Booth. The first of these distinguishes the creative artist from the mere man of taste (Badeau?). The man of taste, says Cousin, endowed with imagination, sentiment, and reason, is capable only of feeling, judging, and analyzing. But the artist, the man of genius, has within him the irresistible need to create what he feels. Socrates calls this driving power his "genius"; Voltaire calls it "the devil in the flesh." Give it what name you please, this *je-ne-sais-quoi* torments the artist until his reveries become living works. The artist imitates nature, of course, but he does not servilely copy nature. (Here Mollie would be reckoning the distance between Booth and actors of the Matilda Heron kind.) The true artist finds out the *ideal*, the moral beauty, in nature, and hungers to see that ideal realized. As Raphael once wrote

[24] Mollie did not know that Cousin's book was available in English. A translation by O. W. Wight was brought out in London immediately after the French publication in 1853. A New York edition appeared in 1855.

to Castiglione, "Since I am destitute of beautiful models, I use a certain ideal which I form for myself."

Further (and here Cousin descends directly to the theatre for his illustration), the artist aims for something more than mere illusion. The end of art is not *trompe l'oeil;* the masterpiece of art is not the curious grapes of Zeuxis which birds came to and pecked at. The theatrical piece must, to be sure, persuade us that on the stage are real men speaking and moving and endowed with passion, and not pale phantoms of the past. But in the magic light of the stage these figures are ennobled, lifted above ordinary miseries, transported to regions where the imperfections of reality give place to a certain perfection, where the language is elevated above common language, where the persons are made beautiful, where the ugly is not admitted.

In the interests of illusion, theatrical men have taken great pains in these latter times to secure historical accuracy of costume. This is all very well; but it is not the important thing. Had you found, and lent to the actor who plays Brutus, the very costume that of old the Roman hero wore, it would touch true connoisseurs very little. . . . If I believed that Iphigenia were in fact being immolated by her father at a distance of twenty paces from me, I should leave the theatre trembling with horror. . . . It is said that the aim of the poet is to excite pity and terror. Yes, but at first in a certain measure; he must mix with them some other sentiment that tempers them, or makes them serve some other end. If the aim of dramatic art were only to excite pity and terror in the highest degree, art would be the powerless rival of nature. . . . The first hospital is fuller of pity and terror than all the theatres of the world.

Finally, art is not to be understood as the mere servant of religion and morals. Rather, it is a separate religion in itself, the religion of beauty, which by its own means perfects the soul and by its own pathways leads to God. Every work of art, whatever its form, small or great, figured, sung, or spoken—every work of art throws the soul into a reverie which elevates it toward the infinite.

Cousin's lecture may seem to us a commonplace popularization of the philosophical idealism by which the "best of all possible worlds" blinded itself to the sordid brutalities of the real world over which it floated in serene ease. But Mollie Devlin aspired to that best of all possible worlds, and so too in his art did her "bien aimé." Here was high authority for her abiding faith, and if it bastioned Booth's determination to create a more ideal Hamlet, her French lessons had been worth their candles.

Badeau lived up to his promise to watch over Mollie. Weather and affairs permitting, he was faithful to her Thursdays, gave her sound advice about Booth's mind and character, and even, in his curious way, came to "love" her too. He praised her to Booth, garnered recommendations of her from the "ladies of Richmond," and urged on the marriage, however much it agonized him to lose first place in Booth's "heart." In the beginning, Mollie was unaffectedly fond of him, mainly because of his devotion to Booth. "He has made me feel, darling, more truly the responsibility for the precious life and heart entrusted to my care, and gave me advice which shall never be forgotten or neglected by me; and in the happy, blissful time to *come*, when that life shall be mine forever, his love for you will I hope be only more closely cemented by the knowledge that there is another heart beating in unison with yours. . . ." Eventually, however, she came to distrust him, even to despise him a little. When he told her once that he expected to make a marriage of convenience with a lady who had been "educated in finely French style, and knows nothing of the heart," she was outraged. For all his talent "he is very weak in many respects," she wrote Booth: "The goddess Fashion he must blame for that though." And she begged Booth that they two should never abandon "primitive nature" or know "the torments of the blasé." On another occasion she regretted that Badeau was "not like other men," and urged Booth to "tutor him, or he will continue through life an intolerable bore—a second Boswell—I fancy that is what he most desires to be."

In the long run, secure in her marriage, she could accept Badeau for Booth's sake—could share her box with him at the theatre and sometimes leave the two men to enjoy their theatrical shop talk far into the night. Yet one suspects that she did not lament much, when the time came in 1861 for the long-awaited trip to Europe, that Badeau could not accompany them. He had just been sent south by his newspaper to report the war. And if Booth let her read Badeau's letters from the battlefield she must have been relieved to know that he had found "real and exquisite happiness" in conferring his "profound and tender and anxious love" upon a young soldier.

In the autumn after their marriage, when Booth took up his work again, Mollie began to compile a notebook of criticism of his acting.[25] Dated "Baltimore, Oct. 4th, 1860," the volume is pathetic-

[25] Mollie's book of critiques, a red leather notebook, 5¼ x 7¾, is in the Theatre Collection, NYPL. In the 1870's Booth reported that his second wife, Mary Runnion McVicker, also worked up a book of "how and why I do certain things in the course of my performances." By 1878 she had carried it far enough to contemplate publishing it, but probably it was destroyed after her death. See Grossmann, p. 192.

ally incomplete, but its fragments, "which I dedicate with deep affection to his service," glow with love. The following sentences about Hamlet clearly reflect Booth's own intimations of the character in this season when his Hamlet began to emerge as his own.

Of this play, Goethe says "that Shakespeare's intention was to exhibit the effects of a great action, imposed as a duty upon a mind too feeble for its accomplishment," "an oak planted in a china vase," &c; a view that to me seems the clearest and most comprehensive of any that have been offered and thrust upon us by the 'meddlers' of our immortal bard. After reading their several commentaries, do we not return to the work itself confused and unenlightened? Their endeavors to seek after and explain the truth lead them almost invariably into a mutilation of nature that is unpardonable. All that has been said about it—and written too, can never, to my mind, throw a light comparable to that that the intellectual and spiritual power of an actor of genius can inculcate. In the person of 'mon cher ami' we have an ideal of Hamlet—"the glass of fashion and the mould of form." The closely critical and primarily analytical might quarrel with our estimate, finding him too tame, too passionate or conventional in such and such a place. But the musical and poetic ones will not allow their soothed senses to be distracted by the material standard of these carping critics. Who but those too entirely encrusted with mortality to receive the images of fancy—could resist the pale, spiritual beauty of his face and form when he first apears upon the scene? . . .

It is but a beginning, the impromptu outpourings of a twenty-year-old girl. But there are shrewd things in it. "Dear, dear Soul!" Booth wrote on the packet of her letters. "I was unworthy so much goodness." Not only goodness but a part of his artistic conscience was lost to Booth when this wise child died before her time.

CHAPTER III

The Emergence of Hamlet

1860-61. First Season at the Winter Garden: Hamlet Fails

By the autumn of 1860 Booth at last felt himself, as Mollie would say, "au fait" for the decisive assault upon New York City, and he reckoned Hamlet his strongest card. He had now made "copious restorations of the original text," including such major units as the King's Prayer scene in the third act and Hamlet's narrative of his sea-adventures in the fifth act; during his out-of-town engagements he polished these.[1] In Boston the Howard Athenaeum advertised "New Scenes! ! Novel Effects! ! !" and there on September 10, after a week of other roles, he opened *Hamlet* for a six-night run. The demand for seats was so great that one reviewer complained that after several attempts he had not yet got within seeing distance of the stage. Three extra performances had to be added to satisfy the public.

"In no character has this accomplished tragedian so nearly touched the sympathy of the Boston public as in this," declared the *Advertiser* (September 12), and it praised the "delicacy and refinement of his conception," his "exquisite emphasis," his intense but never noisy passion, the subtle expressiveness of his "ever-changing eye and countenance." The *Post* (September 20) contrasted the "subdued power and natural grace" of his Hamlet with the "far-fetched fury and unnatural grimaces" of his Richard III; acknowledged that

[1] These restorations are cited in the New York *Dispatch*, December 1, 1860. The narrative of the sea-adventures does not appear in the 1866 acting version, but Booth used it again in 1870.

at twenty-seven he was exactly the right age for Hamlet (whereas Forrest was by now a quarter of a century too old for the part); admired his filial veneration of the dead father and the boyish delight with which he greeted his old school friends; observed gratefully that he never lapsed into tragical rant where "simple colloquial talk was required." On September 21 the critic of the *Advertiser*, having by now seen Booth's more vigorous Macbeth, reviewed Hamlet a second time. He admired Macbeth well enough, but its principal value was to throw into relief "the admirable *tone* of his picture of Hamlet": after the more violent method of Macbeth one could appreciate that Hamlet's quietude was not merely "natural" but was carefully controlled art.

Armed with such praises, he was ready for his first major stand in New York City, a four-week engagement at the Winter Garden. On November 26 he opened in *Hamlet*, undoubtedly with the highest expectations. As the *Tribune* critic announced the next day, at the end of a glowing review, "Hamlet will be acted every night till the public countermand the order by staying away from the theatre, which we believe they will not soon be willing to do." That was a bad calculation. The first-night audience, though enthusiastic, had not been numerous. The second and third audiences dwindled. Something had gone wrong.

For one thing, as Booth had to learn from hard experience, the approval of Boston was no guarantee, then or ever, of the approval of New York. "New York does not believe in Boston, nor in what Boston discovers," as George William Curtis put it, reviewing the event in *Harper's* (April, 1861). For another thing, Booth's impact was diminished by competition. It happened that the two most celebrated American tragedians of the old school—Charlotte Cushman and Edwin Forrest—elected this season for reappearance, both of them having been absent from the city for three years. Miss Cushman preceded Booth at the Winter Garden, and although she was gone before he came, after eight weeks of her powerful Bianca, Lady Macbeth, and Meg Merrilies, Booth's gentle Hamlet must have seemed very pale fire indeed. Forrest was drawing the crowds to Niblo's with a formidable display of his old might. He had already given nine Hamlets and nine Lears, and was now at the end of November in the midst of his nine Othellos; in December he would put up Macbeth and Richard III.

In any case the Hamlet of Booth's reading was too fragile a

vessel for the rough metropolis in its present temper. In the wake of the presidential election (with four candidates in the field a minority of the electorate had put Abraham Lincoln in the White House), in the midst of social angers which were about to erupt into war between the states, the New York public craved theatricals, but what it wanted was broad comedy to distract it, broad tragedy to indulge its boiling emotions, or the heroics of melodrama to spur it on. It was in no mood for the "philosophical strain," for meditation, for the tragedy of indecision.

Booth had to bow to circumstance. Instantly he dropped *Hamlet* and reverted to the repertory pattern of his accustomed openings. On November 29 he played Pescara, on the 30th Richelieu. On Monday, December 3, according to pattern he should have done Macbeth, but Forrest was starting Macbeth that night, so Booth passed on to Richard III. By that time he realized that his Richelieu had made a "ten-strike," as the *Spirit of the Times* put it; on December 5 he returned to Richelieu and kept it for an eight-night run, the hit of his season.

Richelieu was all melodrama and flashy histrionics, of course, in manner as remote as could be from Hamlet, and it exactly suited Booth's need to catch attention. At the "curse of Rome" speech, we read in the *Spirit of the Times* (December 15), the audience was at first stunned into silence, then it broke out in a torrent of applause: "The men stood up and gave vent to cheer upon cheer, the ladies waved their handkerchiefs, and every man in the theatre helped to swell the violence of applause that greeted this unequalled gem of the player's art." Cheap words for cheap goods, one might think. Yet we must bear in mind that Bulwer's masterwork, which in 1860 was just over two decades old, enjoyed extraordinary esteem with the mass of playgoers, who saw no difference between its fustian and Shakespeare's poetry, between its trivial, jerry-built action and the organic plot of a really good play. Its auspices were impeccable: the famous Bulwer-Lytton was its author, the role had been created by "the eminent" Mr. Macready, the play was in the repertory of every first-line tragic actor. Its recipe was infallible, and perhaps never more appropriate than to America on the brink of war: a high-colored historical melodrama, stalking in blank verse, with something like Virtue disguised as something like a Superman, rescuing a tottering state from greedy, evil, dissident politicians. Booth reveled in its histrionic trickishness, and to the end of his days it was at least his second favorite role: on nights when he felt like "acting," it was his first. Considering his status in the early 1860's we must acknowledge that without his Richelieu he might never have got a proper hearing for his Hamlet. He had to make the mob listen before they would hear.

On the strength of Richelieu and, incidentally, of Iago, which now too began to emerge as one of his most apt roles, his autumn engagement at the Winter Garden was immensely successful, leading to another four-week stand in January and February, and to a final two weeks in April. Only here and there through the ten weeks did he dare sprinkle in performances of Hamlet.

The critiques of his Hamlet that were published this season were not, on the whole, unfavorable, but they are streaked and muddled with odd cross-purposes, hostilities, and irrelevancies. Sometimes the writers seem less interested in Booth than in other issues. Sometimes they squabbled with each other.

The supporting company took a good deal of abuse. Manager Jackson's stock actors, with one or two exceptions, were probably not up to Shakespearean work. In roles like Richelieu, Booth could obscure them, but in Hamlet their ineptitude was all too conspicuous. William Hurlburt of the *Albion* (December 15) invoked against them the rule of Horace, *nec deus intersit nisi dignum vindice nodus*, rendering it clownishly as, "Let us have no leading actor driven mad by a noodle—much less by a company of noodles." [2] The same cry against bad support would echo through hundreds of notices during the next thirty years. When Booth rose to managership he himself was quite unfairly blamed for it.

Those critics who were outright partisans of Forrest savaged Booth or dismissed him with contempt—as for example the writer for the *Daily News* (November 27): "He played with his former general carelessness and fugitive flashes of genius. He has neither improved nor deteriorated; and, we should imagine, is as far as ever beyond the influence of correction, and as remotely removed from anything like a first class position as when he performed here three years ago." Some critics of this stripe made light of him because he was only a pale imitator of his father; some blamed him for not resembling his father at all.

A curious case is the reviewer for the weekly *Dispatch*, a crotch-

[2] *Ars Poetica*, l. 191. The sense is "a god must not be introduced unless there is a difficulty worthy of such a deliverer."

ety old gentleman who prided himself that he had known more years of playgoing than Booth had years on his back. He had warmly admired the elder Booth, and at first (December 1) he was warmly disposed toward the young one. With some acuteness he observed Booth's emphasis on Hamlet's "weakness and moody irresolution," and he declared this Hamlet "the most satisfactory which we have ever seen." He pointed out faults, and sharply too, assuring his readers that Booth was the sort of actor who would profit from instruction. Two weeks later, outraged to find the public running after Richelieu, he declared that Richelieu required "not one fiftieth part of the study and thought which he has so prodigiously lavished upon his Hamlet." By the following February, however, he completely reversed his stand. Booth is merely a good actor, he now declared, certainly not a great one. If his name were Smith instead of Booth he would pass unnoticed. "His Macbeth is atrocious, his Sir Giles Overreach fair, his Hamlet a clever specimen of stage tact acquired by long practice." He has abandoned that energy and fire with which four years ago he showed himself a worthy son of his father, and "degenerated into the unenergetic and so-called intellectual school. This will never do." He is now but a "spoiled favorite," ruined by the "injudicious praise" of "neophyte critics."

Henceforth the *Dispatch* reviewer devoted himself to passionate advocacy of Forrest, and for the next five years never once printed Booth's name. Whatever else provoked his perverse turnabout, surely the everlasting war between the generations had much to do with it. He saw at first enough in Booth's manner to gratify his nostalgia for the "old school." But as Booth, hot in pursuit of modernity, multiplied his "faults," and as "neophyte critics" praised him for them, the old man could only vent his wrath and look another way.

The Booth partisans were more numerous than the Booth enemies, and like "neophytes" in any age, more intemperate. They used Booth to club down Forrest. "Mr. Booth," said Hurlburt of the *Albion* (December 8), "is as unlike Mr. Forrest as Mr. Forrest is unlike Hamlet": the taunt was sufficient—Hurlburt did not bother to explain it. "Unquestionably the greatest actor we have now upon the American stage is Edwin Booth," exclaimed the *Spirit of the Times* (December 8), and lest anyone should miss the comparison the writer added that when Forrest plays Hamlet he "loses all the tenderness and all the dignity . . . destroys every feeling save that of violence." The *Evening Post* (November 27), by way of praising Booth's earnestness and pity in his interview with the Queen, spoke of the "insolent brutality" shown by most actors in that scene. A long eulogy of Booth in the *Tribune* (November 27)—"what gigantic strides he has taken toward the highest tragic excellence"—makes its strongest impact by hardly veiled sarcasms about Forrest. Booth is

> the first Hamlet for many a day who, in the closet scene, does not consider it necessary to rave and rant at the Queen like a drunken potboy—he is the first Hamlet for many a day whose conduct in the same scene would not justify the interference of third parties, on the supposition that he intended to commit an assault and battery upon his mother—he is the first Prince of Denmark for many a year who has dared, in this same scene, to conduct himself like a gentleman, and not a blackguard.

This sort of left-handed work was not to Booth's taste. His only concern was to win his own way, not to provoke disparagements of Forrest or any other rival. In scheduling his roles throughout this season he scrupulously avoided confrontations with Forrest which would invite such attacks.[3]

The most illuminating review of his Hamlet was perhaps that of E. G. P. Wilkins in the *Herald* (November 29). Wilkins' tone was by no means adulatory. The Hamlet is "a very clever performance," the result of "complete mastery of the tricks by which actors tickle the fancy of the public." With a flick of the whip he suggested that Booth abandon the classics and turn to French sensation dramas, "where, in his redundancy of gesture and action—the result, we presume, of a temperament highly charged with mental electricity—he would add to the effect of the performance." So much for belittlement. On the other hand, Wilkins appreciated Booth's natural qualities—his youth, handsome person, and very sympathetic and musical voice. He understood Booth's efforts at absorption and quietude: "Mr. Booth's prime quality—and we wish all actors and actresses would note this—is that he appears perfectly unconscious

[3] Booth always treated Forrest respectfully, even to the point of inviting him to play Othello for the opening of Booth's Theatre in 1869, which Forrest refused to do. Forrest nursed grudges, and there are many anecdotes which illustrate his vindictiveness toward Booth. William Winter says in his *Life and Art of Edwin Booth*, p. 142, that Forrest never forgave Booth for acting in support of Catherine Sinclair, Forrest's divorced wife, in California. In January of 1861, when Booth returned to his second engagement at the Winter Garden prepared to resume *Richelieu*, Forrest scheduled the same play on the same nights; Booth broke off his run and turned to noncompeting roles.

that there is any audience before him. He seems to us to possess the very important power of losing himself in the play." When he urged Booth to strive for a more "level, natural, off-hand manner" of speaking dialogue, and called for "more repose," he was but echoing Booth's intentions, charging him with falling short of his own aims.

If in this first season Booth had not persuaded the mob to accept his Hamlet, he had at least given a shake to the critics and taken a hold on the New York stage which would never be broken. In a backward glance at the end of December Hurlburt wrote in the *Albion:* "I leave Mr. Booth in the very height and ardor of his new and most legitimate success. Once more we see the eyes of old critics kindling with new fire in the presence of an unexpected dramatic future. We hear once more the great words of Shakespeare married to the passion of an actor on whose lips they glow with life. We have genuine qualities to delight in, genuine faults to quarrel with." When the season was over, Booth could confidently turn his back upon New York City for an entire year, and bend his thoughts toward Europe.

1861-62. A Season in London: The Example of Charles Fechter

Booth had originally meant his trip abroad to be simply a refreshment, a vacation, and an education. As he had explained to his friend Richard Cary a year earlier, he was already well enough set in his profession to make all the money he could ask for—"but money is not what I want—nor position either, unless I can feel within the consciousness of deserving it. Fortune has placed me in (for my years) a high, and, many think, an enviable position, but I feel the ground tremble beneath my feet, and I'm perfectly well aware that unless I am at a larger circumference than the rim of the 'almighty dollar' (which one can't help in America) I'll go down 'eye-deep' in the quicksand of popular favor." [4] In America, it seemed to Booth, theatrical art was sinking below the standard of a trade, and by merely continuing to act without new ideas, he would dwindle into insignificance. "My taste is becoming vitiated; my love of it is dying out; and I need the recuperation." His goals were Italy and France, where he would study art in its native atmosphere, thereby

[4] Booth to Richard Cary, 1860. Printed in Grossmann, p. 132.

to "vivify my future productions with something of the true and beautiful."

It did not work out that way. When he and Mollie sailed on the *Arabia* in August of 1861, his destination was the Haymarket Theatre in London, his aim to prove his art to the English. Since he did not play Hamlet there, we need not linger over his London engagement, which was rather a disaster. The Haymarket was the wrong theatre, J. B. Buckstone's company of comedians gave him grossly inappropriate support, and he chose the wrong vehicles. His Shylock, Sir Giles, and Richard III were scorned by the press. His Richelieu succeeded, but it came too late in the run to turn the tide in his favor. In any case, it was an ugly time for Americans of the Union to be in England. England was siding with the Confederacy, and anti-Yankeeism was rampant. On December 9, when Mollie suffered her confinement in London, Booth stretched an American flag above her to signify that the infant Edwina belonged to America and was not born under the hated English monarchy. As soon as Mollie was able to travel they decamped to the more hospitable atmosphere of Paris, where they enjoyed a spring and summer vacation before sailing home.

That Booth did not play Hamlet in London was probably the better part of valor, for London was in thrall to the French actor Charles Fechter, whose "new" Hamlet had just finished its long run. Booth did not see Fechter's Hamlet, but he saw his Othello and quite disliked it.[5] It was for him an object lesson in how not to play Shakespeare.

The Fechter method, which consisted in a new look at the classics and a certain kind of actor-inventiveness, was to be the wave of the future. Spreading down the years through the work of Henry Irving and Beerbohm Tree, abetted too by the rise of the modern drama of realism, it wrought fundamental changes in the acting and producing of Shakespeare which affect our stages to this day. Out of principle, training, and temperament, Booth resisted the Fechter method, and herein lies the reason why, when he visited England a second time twenty years later, the London critics dismissed him as old-fashioned, stagey, rhetorical; why even in his own country, after Henry Irving had given us a taste of his quality, certain American critics grew restive at Booth's seeming to fall behind the times.

[5] Booth to William Winter, June 4, 1878. The Folger Shakespeare Library, Y.c. 215 (282).

Fechter, who had created Armand Duval in *La Dame aux camélias*, undertook to make Shakespearean heroes as much like Armand Duval as possible. Insofar as he sought to root out of Shakespearean acting all that was stilted, inflated, declamatory, and falsely solemn, even Booth might have applauded him; but in domesticating classic heroes to the drawing room and boudoir, in imposing upon them the everyday minutiae of human behavior, and in restless pursuit of novelty, he often overdid it. Someone compared him to the pre-Raphaelite painters, who "would copy every leaf in a tree and every pebble in a landscape." [6] He produced startlingly new interpretations of character and bits of stage business hitherto undreamed of. His Hamlet had nothing about him of the melancholy or the introspective, but was a bustling, dashing, cheery man of the world. He was a blond or saffron-haired fat Dane—not so much because Goethe had once suggested that he ought to be, but because all previous stage Hamlets had been slender brunettes. His Horatio did not cross the Ghost's path at "I'll cross it though it blast me," but like a good Catholic made a sign of the cross. His Ghost did not simply walk off the stage when his work was done, but by a modern magic-shop arrangement of lights and gauzes vanished on the spot. Fechter read "To be or not to be" at great speed, with his sword drawn, as if he were deciding to commit suicide then and there. At the climax of the Play scene he ripped pages from the manuscript he was holding and hurled them into the air. In the words of one hostile critic, "He chatters in the graveyard as though he had no thought but of bagatelles, rattles through his soliloquies like problems in metaphysics, and wears lofty passions like temporary annoyances." [7]

His Hamlet was immensely successful in London. His Othello aroused objection, but its profusion of surprising little realisms continued to enchant Charles Dickens and the ever-increasing number of devotees of curious and quaint detail. As Othello he lolled on chairs and sofas, pawed Iago with school-chum affection, shook hands with every comer. Upon meeting Desdemona at Cyprus he did not embrace her, but like a modern gentleman kept her at a discreet distance and gallantly kissed her hand. When in the privacy of their quarters Desdemona insisted on having Cassio to dinner, he toyed with her curls. While Iago planted the seeds of suspicion in him,

[6] Boston *Daily Advertiser*, November 26, 1862.
[7] *Ibid.*

he busied himself with a feather pen, doing paperwork at his writing table. At "I took by the throat the circumcised dog," he manhandled Iago, as if about to murder *him*, and then, ever so astonishingly, stabbed himself. In all this sort of thing George Henry Lewes saw the danger clearly: "In his desire to be effective by means of small details of 'business,' he has entirely frittered away the great effects of the drama. He has yet to learn the virtue of simplicity; he has yet to learn that tragedy acts through the emotions, and not through the eye."[8]

Booth in his own way was determined to free his acting from the sterilities of convention, to act from motive rather than from precedent, and to "naturalize" the tragic heroes, at least to the extent of investing them with parts and passions which were recognizably human. But he could not follow the Fechter method. He was a man of feeling, not of wit. He was not inventive. His way was to strip a role to its essentials, to seize upon the ideas in it which as a child of the mid-century he believed to be valid Shakespearean ideas, and to project them directly, without distracting clutter, to the mind of his audience. It is true that, like Fechter, he introduced a "free use of chairs" into his playing, sometimes to the wonderment of older critics who would rather have confined their tragic heroes to the stalk-and-stand; but no one ever accused him of "lolling." He used the handshake, though only when intimacy called for it. He hung upon Horatio remarkably much, but here the business was proof of credible affection. Some details in his performance one wishes he had avoided. At one time in the early years, when he said "make Ossa like a wart," he fingered an imaginary wart on his left hand—but he soon abandoned that silliness.[9] When he spoke of his mother's "increase of appetite," he touched his heart "to indicate what kind of appetite"; but that gesture, in itself perfectly unobtrusive, was only for decorum's sake, to prevent lewd minds from straying lower. One wearies of his insistent presentation of the sword-hilt as crucifix, and of other obvious pieties. Sometime in the 1870's he contrived the utterly unintelligible device of peering into the King's eyeballs to see reflected there the "cherub" (himself) who sees Hamlet's "pur-

[8] George Henry Lewes, *On Actors and the Art of Acting* (London, 1875), p. 130. Details from Fechter's acting are taken from Lewes's Chapter XI, "Foreign Actors on Our Stage"; Kate Field's *Charles Albert Fechter* (New York, 1882); an article on Fechter in the *Galaxy*, IX (April, 1870), 554-561; Booth's Notebook at The Players.

[9] The *Albion*, September 26, 1863.

poses." In closed-mind advocacy of the text of the First Folio, he insisted upon calling Hecuba "inobled" (meaning "rendered ignoble") instead of "mobled." Such details, however, were mere pendantries, dull but honest, and they nowise define his essential method. He worked up characters from inside out, so to speak, and never sought in Fechter's way to make Shakespeare "our contemporary" by an overlay of ingenious tricks and contemporary references. When he got home from Europe, numerous critics speculated on how much his Hamlet had been influenced by Fechter's (which he had not seen). Fechter's real influence was to teach him what not to do, and to drive him back upon his instinctively simplistic approach.

1862-63. Return to the Winter Garden: Triumph and Disaster

Booth's autumn season in 1862 began with a seven-week stand at the Winter Garden. He opened on September 29 with four nights of Hamlet; then after single performances of Othello, Payne's Brutus, Shylock, and Iago, he settled into two weeks of his well-perfected Richelieu. Forrest was playing at Niblo's, but not in overlapping roles, so that the competition did not degenerate into interference. On November 24 Booth began his month at the Boston Theatre with two nights of Hamlet.

Public and critics of both cities welcomed him home. He had been missed; and the simple fact that he had braved out a season in London boosted his prestige, especially with the social elite. The first audience at the Winter Garden was "one of the most fashionable that we ever saw assembled," said the *Herald* (September 30), "and there was not a seat unoccupied." In the vast Boston Theatre, "from parquette to amphitheatre the house was crowded by one of the most fashionable audiences that ever attended a dramatic performance in this city." Everyone observed that his Hamlet had been altered, and according to most of the critics, for the better: it was much quieter. The *Evening Post* (September 30) praised him for "rendering that which was natural still more natural," and for "imparting additional grace to what was always graceful."

The critics of Boston praised him with unstinting eloquence. According to the *Courier* (November 25): "His conception of the character seems riper—more natural—the result of deeper study. There is no claptrap—no false excitement—for the purpose of producing an effect upon the audience; but every word and gesture will bear the closest criticism and most searching analysis." The Boston *Post* (November 29), in attempting to quash the imputation of influence by Fechter, declared:

> He has changed materially, and his stage business in *Hamlet* is to a great extent refreshingly novel. It has been said that he imitates Fechter. We do not believe it. Mr. Booth is no imitator. He acts from, by, and through the genius born in him, and it is to that very impulsiveness of genius he is indebted for certain peculiarities which some people have termed faults. Formerly he was one of the most uneven of the great actors that we had ever seen. Now he is one of the most consistent and steady. He no longer listlessly waits for special points at which great effects may be made, making you forget that you are seeing a brilliant artist, until by some sudden burst he startles you into a recollection of it, but presents a thoroughly complete, if not an unblemished picture.

Young William Winter, formerly of Boston and long since one of Booth's admirers, who had brought into the New York critical scene the seeding germs of Bostonian idealizing elegance, described Booth's improvement succinctly in the *Albion* (October 4). "Time, foreign travel, experience and study have matured his judgment and polished his style," Winter wrote: "From first to last, he not only does not make points where points are usually made, but he does not make a point at all. He is natural, simple, impressive—winning the honest and earnest admiration of all who honor the dramatic art." Nothing could more cleanly distinguish Booth's method from the Fechter method than the implication of those words, "he does not make a point at all."

The death of his father a decade earlier had been Booth's most personal experience of tragic loss. In the fall of 1862, his friend Richard Cary had died in battle. Now the cudgel was raised in darkness for the worst of all possible blows, the death of his wife. Mollie was consumptive. When Booth went down to New York to play in February of 1863, he left her in a rented house in Dorchester, out of Boston, under the care of an expert physician, Dr. Erasmus Miller. Sick with worry, he was drowning his worry in drink. At his opening in Hamlet on February 9 he played wretchedly. He was "suffering from a severe cold and from the fatigue of a long journey," the *Herald* reported the next day, "and was not, therefore, in his best mood." That was to put it charitably. During the next ten days his drinking and his acting worsened, and hostile critics abused him.

Meanwhile Mollie caught a cold, which turned swiftly into pneumonia. Dr. Miller felt that he was controlling it. On February 18 and 19 Booth received six separate messages that she was "improving" and "comfortable." [10] But abruptly on the evening of the 20th she passed into a crisis, and long before Booth could arrive home on the 21st, she was dead.

From Dorchester Booth poured his grief and remorse into long frenzied letters to friends. He could not accept death as an ending. Mollie's spirit seemed real and immediate. "I think she is somewhere near me now," he wrote to Adam Badeau two weeks later; "I see her, feel her, hear her, every minute of the day. I call her, look for her, every time the door opens; in every car that passes our little cottage door, where we anticipated so much joy, I expect to see the loved form of her who was my *world*." [11] This was not conventional prosing. He meant that he felt her presence literally. When he closed the Dorchester house and moved to New York with his year-old daughter, his fevered imagination drove him into pseudo-religion, and he sought out the well-known spiritualist Laura Edmonds to try to communicate with Mollie. For some weeks he was nearly convinced that he received messages from her, and from his father also.[12]

What is interesting in all this is not the folly of his belief in the unbelievable, but the tremendous emotional pressure which compelled his faith. Although he eventually gave up the services of Miss Edmonds, he continued psychic experiments of his own. Badeau, who was with him in the late summer of 1863, described one of these events to his soldier friend Harry Wilson:

> I sat up on my couch one night at Booth's house in a circle, or *seance*. No one of us was a spiritualist; all were friends and knew nothing of the peculiar methods of producing the results. Nothing was produced until we touched each other's hands as they lay on the table. I sat next to Ned, and our fingers met. I instantly felt a strong nervous influence pass from him into me, such as I never experienced before. In a few minutes

[10] Biographers of Booth are wont to heighten Booth's guilt and shame on the occasion by telling how on the evening of February 20 a rush of warning telegrams arrived which Booth was too drunk to open. The six messages of encouragement, now in the Theatre Collection, NYPL, have not hitherto been noticed. In the last of these Dr. Miller assures Booth that although Mary would be delighted to see him, she prefers that he stay in New York and finish his engagement.

[11] Booth to Adam Badeau, March 3, 1863. Printed in Grossmann, p. 142.

[12] Booth to Adam Badeau, June 6, 1863. Printed in Grossmann, p. 149.

my right hand and arm were seized with an involuntary motion which I could not control, and shaken more rapidly than any human being can shake his own arm; so rapidly that you could not see my hand. I inquired if this were spiritual; if so that the motion should be renewed; it was violently; then I asked for the motion to be changed; I did not say, and did not think Ned; and my hand was struck up and down on the table until it hurt me. Afterwards it assumed the position of a hand in writing, and was shaken to and fro; they put a pencil in my hand, for I could not stop its motion, and marks were scratched on a paper laid beneath it; but they amounted to nothing.[13]

This went on for an hour. The next night they tried again, and it all happened again in the same pattern. Badeau could make nothing of it, and indeed his report is underlined with a sort of skepticism. "I suppose," he says, "'twas a sort of nervousness." The point is that it was Booth who made this happen. He was certainly not a knowing hypnotist, and in ordinary social life he was a quiet, shy, almost recessive person, but given this highly wrought situation, the wild excitement which ran through him could produce these wildly involuntary responses in another. In the theatre, when he willed it, something of this "psychic electricity" passed into his acting. It blazed from his eyes; it compelled audiences; it marked him out from the herd of "mere actors"; it was the unique component of his genius.

Mollie's gentle goodness was a living reality to Booth. From the day of her death he was set free of his craving for alcohol. The memory of his drunkenness during those last weeks filled him with self-loathing, and for many years he did not drink at all—nor ever, perhaps, to excess.[14] She lived, too, in his work. As he wrote to a friend in 1865, "I feel that all my actions have been and are influenced by her whose love is to me the strength and wisdom of my spirit. Whatever I do of serious import, I regard it as a performance of a sacred duty I owe to all that is pure and honest in my nature—a duty to the very religion of my heart." [15]

[13] Badeau to James Harrison Wilson, September 12, 1863. Special Collections of the Princeton University Library.

[14] In London in 1882 Booth seems occasionally to have taken a glass too much—once at a midnight supper given in his honor at the Lyceum by Henry Irving. In subsequent letters to William Winter, who was present at the supper, Booth regrets his "poor brain, like Cassio's" for drinking. Booth to William Winter, July 8, August 7, September 24, 1882. The Folger Shakespeare Library, Y.c. 215 (422, 425, 426).

[15] Booth to Mrs. Richard Cary, February 9, 1865. Printed in Grossmann, p. 169.

1863-64. Third Season at the Winter Garden: *Hamlet* in the Wrong Key

In the fall of 1863, Booth began a series of New York engagements in what appears to have been renewed vigor and a new attack upon his roles. He opened with *Hamlet,* as everyone now expected him to do, on September 21, and gave it a stronger thrust than usual by keeping it on for six nights. Apparently, too, he attempted at this time to energize the role somewhat more than in the preceding season, to brighten its steady quietude with moments of "acting." At any rate, the *Herald* (September 22) blamed him even more than it had in 1860 for doing too much: his "greatest danger is to overact, to gesticulate too much, to twist his body into unnatural shapes." The *Herald* concluded that he must be playing to the galleries and insisted that he abandon these false histrionics and address himself solely to the intellectual part of the audience.

That the objection was not merely a continuing quirk of the *Herald* is proved by the fact that in the *Albion* four days later William Winter, Booth's champion, addressed himself to the same objection: "I have, on former occasions, seen reason to consider his ideal of the character as truer than it seemed to be in the performance of Monday. . . . Prior to the arrival of the Ghost, and during its presence, he was all instinct with awe, and dread, and shuddering madness. But, after its departure, he recovered instantly, and thenceforward to the end played on with wholly inadmissible firmness of purpose and style." One does not expect adverse criticism of Booth from William Winter, but it is only out of context that the words seem hard. Unquestionably Booth was overplaying in an untoned, raw-edged manner, and Winter knew it. But instead of blaming Booth he concocted a long sophistry-ridden essay (from which these sentences are taken) in which he blamed the *play.* The role of Hamlet, he says, is for the study only; for the stage it is a downright impossibility. If played ideally it would be merely tiresome. "It involves no sensual excitements, no sensuous delight, no gorgeousness of color, no celerity of movement. Its passion—if that be the right word—is that of intense intellectuality." But what is an actor to do, Winter asks, when he confronts audiences who are no more fit to receive the ideal Hamlet than those notorious bushels of beans who make up the Sunday congregations in New England churches are fit to listen to a good sermon? All that theatre audiences can understand is physical sensation. That is why so many admire the Hamlet of Forrest, which is artistically "as bad as bad can be." Other actors are not to be blamed if they follow Forrest's example, since they must win success with "the general." Surely Winter did not mean that Booth was imitating Forrest. It is rather that in those days he would write anything to cover for Booth's errors.

A matter of pride and inspiration to Booth in this season was the completion of Launt Thompson's splendid bronze bust of his Hamlet (now at The Players). Booth had been much excited by the bust while Thompson was working on it. Speaking of it to Badeau—"selfishly, as I ever think and speak of all things"—he declared that it was "worthy of Michelangelo." [16] When it was done he assured Thompson that because of it he had "lost all my old sensible 'don't care a d----tiveness' " and had "grown as idiotic and vain as any of my tribe." [17] He had the bust displayed in theatre lobbies and art-shop windows, and he proposed to write into his will arrangements for a bronze replica of it to be set on a granite pillar at the head of his grave. As the Boston *Courier* (November 12) observed when the bust was first exhibited there, it made Booth look older than he then was; and being larger than lifesize it gave him a dignity and solidity which he probably had not yet achieved. It was the sculptor's inspired prevision of what Booth's Hamlet would become a few years later when energy and quietude would become perfectly fused—a model for Booth to emulate.

During the 1863-64 season he did not use Richelieu so often as heretofore, but began introducing other roles of similarly "actory" kind. In October he gave five performances of Victor Hugo's passionate and tragical lover Ruy Blas. In March and April he showed to New York audiences a role he had been playing out of town since 1860, that agonizing monster Bertuccio in *The Fool's Revenge*—his own revision of Tom Taylor's adaptation of Hugo's *Le Roi s'amuse*. Both these innovations succeeded, and they nicely fattened his repertory. Bertuccio—the deformed jester whose scene of broken-hearted dancing before the scoffing courtiers was remembered by the late G. C. D. Odell as "one of the most stupendous effects ever achieved by an actor"—was a mainstay nearly to the end of his career.[18] A

[16] Booth to Adam Badeau, May 18, 1863. Printed in Grossmann, p. 148.

[17] Booth to Launt Thompson, July 30, 1863. Theatre Collection, NYPL.

[18] G. C. D. Odell, *Annals of the New York Stage*, VII (New York, 1931), 562.

third effort of the kind, a revival of his old California triumph of Raphael in *The Marble Heart*, came to nothing.

In May, during an eleven-night resumé of his favorite roles, he returned to Hamlet, and in the *Spirit of the Times* (May 21) we learn from "Bayard," an admirer of Booth, that several additional performances of *Hamlet* were added to answer popular demand. Bayard renews the old complaint against the wretched supporting actors: "The jewel in the center was surrounded by California diamonds, home-made paste, bits of old looking-glass, and Coney Island pebbles—an atrocious conglomerate that would puzzle a geologist to classify." But Booth was steadily experimenting, refining, improving his own part: "You see it today, and pronounce it perfection; go next week, and you find that he has gilded refined gold, shaded a little here, touched with sharper color a point here, evoked a new meaning from some apparently meaningless phrase, and all with that reverent regard for the author which all true Shakespearian actors must ever feel."

1864-65. Winter Garden Management: The Hundred Nights *Hamlet* and the Assassination

By the summer of 1864 Booth could claim mastery of some half-dozen Shakespearean roles (Hamlet, Othello and Iago, Shylock, Richard III, Macbeth), and of non-Shakespearean roles a slightly larger number. His pre-eminence as an actor was unquestioned, save by diehard partisans of Forrest, an occasional currish penny-a-liner, or an occasional young Booth partisan who was simply impatient with him for not advancing his romantic-realist art more rapidly. The time had come for a bold decision. He could go on merely acting, like his father before him, or Forrest at present, polishing and perfecting old roles, now and again perhaps adding a new one, as long as the public demanded his personal art. The alternative was to emulate such major English actors as Macready and Charles Kean, both of whom, after years of starring, had gone into management and gained transcendent reputations by mounting splendid productions.

Booth already had a bit of experience in management as a purely commercial venture. In partnership with his brother-in-law, the comic actor John Sleeper Clarke, he had taken over the Walnut Street Theatre in Philadelphia, and it had paid off so well that in a single year they were able to retire $50,000 of their $80,000 mortgage.[19] But art and control of the profession, more than money, was his ambition. Mollie had envisioned him as a true theatrical leader, and even before their marriage had lectured him on theatrical governance:

> The society of Artists in all countries but our own, is said to be more charming than of all other classes—for art, with all save us, is religion. We shall see this when we go abroad. 'Twill encourage and assist you, darling, in the mission you are to perform toward your sinking art here; and if you will only choose to follow the course which my judgment prompts me is the direct and proper one. . . . I would never have you inculcate a spirit of haughty pride and a contemptuous regard for all those who toil beneath you—as our friend Mr. B. would have you—and which is neither good nor proper—but the dignity and gentleness of a worthy Chief towards his subjects . . . for 'tis glorious to have the power to rule, when swayed benignantly.[20]

His increasingly intimate association with the studio artists at this time—with Gifford, McEntee, Thompson, Bierstadt, and others—excited him about the possibilities of *mise-en-scène*, of surrounding his personal creations with worthy pictorial effects.

Thus it came to pass that in the summer of 1864 he and Clarke and the popular, if unscrupulous, William Stuart took over the Winter Garden. Stuart fronted for the triumvirate, served as business manager, and took public responsibility for the Winter Garden's affairs. Clarke's contribution was to open the season with some three months of comedies and farces, from August 18 to November 24. Booth meanwhile worked up his grand plan "to bring out several of the Shakesperian plays in a superior style." [21] The first would be *Hamlet.* Booth hired a skilled scene painter, John Thorne, to prepare the three exterior scenes, and a twenty-two-year-old newcomer, Charles Witham, to do the seven or eight interiors. The printed program, in emulation of Charles Kean's London practice in the 1850's, would carry full acknowledgment of these artists, of Robert Stoepel the music director, and of all those principally responsible for costumes, properties, machinery, and lights. In mid-October Booth was telling Badeau that "The tragedy of Hamlet, by Wm Shakespeare, is being 'done' in the paint-room, the wardrobe & the property rooms

[19] Booth to Adam Badeau, September 28, 1864. The Folger Shakespeare Library, Y.c. 215 (15).

[20] Mary Devlin to Booth, May 10, 1860. Theatre Collection, NYPL.

[21] Booth to Emma Cary, August 26, 1864. Printed in Grossmann, p. 164. See also footnotes in Winter's *Life and Art of Edwin Booth*, pp. 82 and 112.

of the Winter Garden for me.—I shall be called upon to be genteel & gentle—or rather, pale & polite, about the 27th November. . . . Every scene, every dress, every chair & table—and nearly all the actors will be new. Some of the pictures in the play will be what has never been used on any stage in America & I doubt if Kean did anything like it." [22] The new *Hamlet*, to be known eventually as the "Hundred Nights *Hamlet*," opened on November 26.

The acting version which Booth settled on in 1864 is represented in the edition which Booth allowed Henry Hinton to bring out in 1866. The cuts, which amounted to about 1,380 lines, were the traditional ones which I have described in the Introduction (see above, pp. xvi-xvii). The one major restoration was the King's Prayer scene and Hamlet's attendant soliloquy in the third act. Minor restorations were made *passim*. One restoration *not* made in 1864 is that passage in which Hamlet addresses comical nicknames to the Ghost in the cellarage. This omission vastly gratified a correspondent to the *Spirit of the Times* (December 24). No one, he exclaimed, who truly comprehends Hamlet's character could believe that Shakespeare ever put into Hamlet's mouth such terms as "Ha! boy," "truepenny," and "old mole." These are the intrusions of "vile tamperers": "Is it not horrible! most repulsive, to have such words set down for Hamlet to speak to his dear Father's Spirit? I need not say Booth ignores them entirely, and such as these." The text was of course cleansed everywhere of vulgarity and bawdry.

The press was much taken by the beauty and completeness of the production, recognizing that for the first time in America the play was brought out "with due regard to external effect." Few of the reviewers, however, were attuned to the descriptive art, and it would be difficult to imagine the *mise-en-scène*—its prevailing Romanesque or Norman architecture—from the niggling details they give us.[23] On one minor technical novelty, the treatment of the "tormentors," the reviewer for the *Tribune* (November 28) sustained his excite-

[22] Booth to Adam Badeau, October 14, 1864. The Folger Shakespeare Library, Y.c. 215 (16).

[23] Booth may have got the idea to decorate *Hamlet* in Norman style from news of Charles Fechter's sumptuous revival of the play at the London Lyceum six months earlier (May 22, 1864). Fechter's Norman settings, designed by the veteran scene painter William Telbin, were said to be extremely beautiful, and the London critics hailed their "historical accuracy" as an innovation. Curiously, none of the American reviewers of Booth's production, either in 1864 or 1870, seems to have seen or heard of Fechter's.

ment long enough to preserve a curious fact. These scenic units, set at the sides just upstage of the proscenium to frame the successive settings, had hitherto been permanent installations, painted to match the decoration of the auditorium, "so that the ridiculous spectacle has night after night been presented of ladies and gentlemen entering a wood, a hut, an open landscape, or whatnot, through gilded and painted doors." Now for the first time these permanent tormentors were replaced by units appropriate to each set: "hinged pieces at the front of the stage, which, after the rising of the curtain, are pushed forward so as to enclose the scene." This innovation, said the *Tribune*, should never be abandoned.

Despite the inadequacy of the reviewers' accounts, we have fair access to the principal scenes through the engravings published in Henry Hinton's edition. As the Hundred Nights wound out their slow length, Stuart, who was ever on the lookout for a new publicity dodge, urged Booth to prepare a "book of the play" for sale in the lobby; and Hinton, a minor actor in the company, offered his services as editor. The notion pleased Booth, for in the 1850's Charles Kean had published *his* acting versions (with elaborate critical apparatus, but without illustrations). By adding sketches of the play in progress he might outdo Kean. He foresaw in the course of time a series of ten or a dozen plays in cheap format, and eventually a more elegant edition. He readied the text of *Hamlet* (of *Richelieu* also), got Charles Witham to draw up six *Hamlet* scenes exactly as they were staged, and converted these drawings into engravings. When a year later he finally gave Hinton *carte blanche* to proceed, he was satisfied that the text, the stage business, and the illustrations of *Hamlet* were accurate. His only caution to Hinton was not to move too fast with the series —not, that is, to bring out acting versions of further plays until the sets and costumes had been realized upon the stage: "I think the illustrations to such a work should be exact copies of the scenes as they are represented when I act, or in other words—as they are produced at the Winter Garden, where scenery & costume are expressly gotten up for me." [24] The 1866 illustrations (see Plates XVI-XVIII),

[24] Booth to Henry L. Hinton, January 15, 1866. The Folger Shakespeare Library, Y.c. 215 (118). Many details of Booth's involvement with Hinton are contained in sixteen letters to Hinton in this Folger file (nos. 118-133). Booth could not restrain Hinton as he wished. Hinton published at least eight "Booth plays," several in highly irresponsible texts. A decade later, in proposing that William Winter edit the Prompt-Book series of his plays, Booth vented his wrath upon "the stupid mess" which Hinton had made of

however crude, are correct. From the notes and groundplans in a newly discovered Winter Garden promptbook, marked for use in Philadelphia and elsewhere, it is clear that when Booth took *Hamlet* on the road he expected local stage managers to imitate these illustrations in preparing their sets. The ultimate interest of the illustrations is that they show the beginnings of the far more elaborate *Hamlet* settings at Booth's Theatre in 1870.

With this production of *Hamlet*, Booth firmly implicated the American stage in the greatest theatrical heresy of the century—the subversion of Shakespeare to scenery of the "historically accurate" kind. Two decades earlier Charles Kean had attempted as much at the Park Theatre with *Richard III*, *Two Gentlemen of Verona*, and *King John*—to attain "the utmost of historic illustration," from "accredited authorities"—but the effort had been disastrously expensive, and Kean had gone home to London, where in the 1850's he realized his historico-pictorial dreams at the Princess's. Booth's 1864 *Hamlet*, his 1866 *Richelieu*, and his 1867 *Merchant of Venice* at the Winter Garden were the first serious and successful efforts by an American actor-manager to imitate Kean's practice. Later, at his own theatre, Booth would refine upon these first efforts and extend the program to many other plays.

In fairness to Booth it must be recognized that he did not permit scenic embellishment to wreck the plays, but aimed only at what he took to be "fit illustration." He did not, like Kean, displace great chunks of the plays with elaborate processions and pageants; nor did he, like the later Augustin Daly and Beerbohm Tree, chop and dislocate the texts to accommodate them to cumbersome, inflexible settings. He wasted no performance time on scene changing: whether under the old wing-and-groove system at the Winter Garden, or his improved rise-and-sink system at Booth's Theatre, the changes were instantaneous. However we may condescend to his acting versions, their shortcomings were imposed by other necessities than those of scenic arrangement.

Nonetheless, the pursuit of "historical accuracy" appears to us

his books: "They are useless & not at all correctly cut or marked." Even the *Hamlet* book, which Booth had prepared himself, had become an annoyance, mainly because of the cover-portrait, which "represents me as a drunken *Dumas*—(or some other nigger) & excites the indignation of my wife." Booth to William Winter, April 18, 1878. The Folger Shakespeare Library, Y.c. 215 (232).

now a grand delusion and a dangerous one. When one reads, for instance, that in Booth's *Romeo and Juliet* of 1869 the backs of the chairs were embossed and the table linen embroidered with the monograms of the Montague and Capulet families,[25] we can only conclude that a downright anti-Shakespearean pedantry was the informing spirit. Booth did not invent the heresy. It was in the air, and when he turned producer he could not have avoided it—not even if he had remembered Victor Cousin's warning about the "grapes of Zeuxis which birds came to and pecked at." [26] Not until William Poel made his obscure experiments with platform staging and Shaw praised him for them, not until Craig and Granville-Barker brought in their unifying simplicities after the turn of the century would the theatre be set upon its track again. Not indeed until the art of the cinema took "historical accuracy" for its special province would the theatre be able to put its whole mind upon its proper kind of art.

Few critics of the Hundred Nights *Hamlet*, however, would have dreamed of objecting to Booth's scenic method. To most of them it meant only that Kean's ideal method was at last being realized in America. But one critic writing a valedictory notice in the *Evening Post* (March 22) was adamant in opposition to it. In the first place, he said, certain of the scenic elements fail on their own terms. The costumes, for instance, appear to be fifteenth-century Flemish or Italian and in no way suggest the imaginary Danish court in Elsinore. The ceilings of the palace rooms show massive blocks of stone laid over the heads of the inhabitants in the manner of rafters, apparently held aloft by nothing but plaster. This is architecturally unbelievable. But these are mere details. The entire scenic effort is a vast irrelevance. "The inherent depravity of stage decoration is such that when it is best it is worst, and among the agonies of the scene-painter one always sighs for a barn, or the golden days of Shakespeare himself, when actors moved in the sumptuous costume of the time among scenes that merely suggested the situation, without dividing attention with the text."

All that really matters on the stage, says this critic, is Booth.

[25] The *Galaxy*, IX (January, 1870), 132.

[26] In London in 1881 Booth became quite embittered against the arts of production. He wrote to William Winter on January 22, "The actor's art is judged by his costume and the scenery. If they are not 'esthetic' (God save the mark!) he makes no stir . . . Chas Kean, Fechter, & Irving have feasted the Londoners so richly that they cannot relish undecorated dishes." The Folger Shakespeare Library, Y.c. 215 (380).

He admires Booth's initiative in carrying the production through its hundred nights ("the great Shakespearian event of the century"), and admires Booth's personal art immensely. He praises Booth's appearance throughout—the "long succession of poses remarkable for their originality, strength, and grace, gestures of astonishing meaning and brilliancy, and facile movements extraordinarily expressive and flexible." He praises his tremendous emotional climaxes: the "mask of horror, wet upon forehead and lip with the beads of fright" while he listens to the Ghost; the will-destroying hysteria he falls into at the end of the Play scene, so that "Claudius, in the moment of his utmost danger, has escaped, because Hamlet has nearly died." He works up a capsule image of Booth's Hamlet as we see it first and last which is a prose poem of considerable power:

> He is first seen sitting under the great Raven of Denmark, which hangs above him on a standard; among a gaudy court, "he alone with them alone," easily prince, and nullifying their effect by the intensity and color of his gloom. He is last seen with the same court disturbed around him like a thresher's grain, himself fallen across the arms of Horatio, and as the curtain lowers, his face seems suddenly to break from the shoulders and welters on the floor in a pool of inky hair.[27]

At the start of the run (for no one was aware that history was in the making) few of the critics took a fresh look at Booth's performance or added any distinctive opinions to their earlier records. Only in the *Herald*, which for once seems to have found another pair of spectacles to view the occasion, we find a surprisingly positive affirmation of Booth's *clarity:* "The performance of Hamlet by Mr. Booth is a continual elucidation of Shakespere. There are no inconsistencies, no knotty incomprehensible points in the part as Mr. Booth plays it. We may burn our hundred volumes of commentaries if we will go often enough to the Winter Garden. All is as clear as daylight. To see it inevitably excites the wonder that this part should have been so misunderstood by so many able writers."

No one could have foreseen the Hundred Nights. Booth did not. As the weeks dragged on, he referred to it as "this terrible success," [28] and years afterward he recalled how it distressed him: "I was heartily sick and wearied of the monotonous work, and several times during it suggested a change of bill, for I felt that the incessant repetition was

[27] Compare Richard Grant White's similar opinions in 1870, below, pp. 80-82.

[28] Booth to Emma Cary, January 10, 1865. Printed in Grossmann, p. 167.

seriously affecting my acting, as at that time I was unused to such a thing. But Stuart, wild with his (!) wonderful success, would exclaim, 'No, not at all, my dear boy! Keep it up, keep it up! If it goes a year, keep it up!' And so we kept it up." [29] Stuart loaded his advertisements with puffs. At the Christmas season he recommended it as a family play to bring children to. Later he worked up vaunting comparisons of this run with the lesser runs of Kean, Fechter, and other famous actors. The reviewer for the *Spirit of the Times* this season—a jocular fellow who called himself Touchstone, a former actor who was on hail-fellow terms with "dear boy" Stuart—was annoyed by what seemed to him crude advertising stunts. Week after week he posted such flippancies as, "I can't be expected to go to see Hamlet more than half a dozen times in one season"; or, "*Toujours perdrix*—always Hamlet—Edwin Booth still as the melancholy Dane." When the last nights were finally being announced, Touchstone reserved "doubts of the veracity of the advertising impressario."

About the time the run ended, *Harper's* (April, 1865) brought out a charmingly personalized notice of it. George William Curtis, the witty proprietor of the "Editor's Easy Chair," usually took a *de-haut-en-bas* view of native theatricals (like all art lovers who had been adults in New York in the 1850's he had of course adored Rachel), but gradually he had succumbed to the charm of Booth: "A really fine actor is as uncommon as a really great dramatic poet. Yet what Garrick was in Richard III or Edmund Kean in Shylock, we are sure Edwin Booth is in Hamlet." Boston has approved him long since, Curtis says, and in New York he has latterly become first the fashion, then the passion. And rightly so. Although our ideal vision of Hamlet derives from Sir Thomas Lawrence's famous painting of the preternaturally tall, black-clad Hamlet of John Philip Kemble, yet this "sad, slight Prince" of Booth, in his "small lithe form with the mobility and intellectual sadness of his face, and his large melancholy eyes," satisfies us that he "is Hamlet as he lived in Shakespeare's world."

His playing throughout has an exquisite tone, like an old picture. The charm of the finest portraits, of Raphael's Julius or Leo, of Titian's Francis I or Ippolito di Medici, of Vandyck's Charles I, is not the drawing nor even the coloring, so much as the nameless, subtle harmony which is called tone. So in Mr. Booth's Hamlet it is not any particular scene, or passage, or look, or movement that conveys the impression; it is the consistency

[29] Winter, *Life and Art of Edwin Booth*, p. 78.

of every part with every other, the pervasive sense of a true gentleman sadly strained and jarred. Through the whole play the mind is borne on in mournful reverie. It is not so much what he says or does that we observe; for under all, beneath every scene and word and act, we hear what is not audible, the melancholy music of the sweet bells jangled, out of tune, and harsh.

There is a kind of art, Curtis says, in poetry or any other form, which may be admirably finished but does not satisfy us because we can see so easily how it is done. And so in the theatre, "if the acting is merely in the mouth or on the back, it is like the Western wines, which have so delicious a bouquet, but are sharp and thin to the taste." By reference to three or four moments in the performance Curtis demonstrates Booth's rendering of Hamlet's morbidity, intellectual superiority, and ultimate bafflement by life's mystery. "The 'cumulative' sadness of the play was never so palpable as in Mr. Booth's acting. It is a spell from which you cannot escape. . . . The curtain falls. The audience rises and departs. We move out with the chatting crowd. The street sparkles and roars. The old life receives us at the portal. But on the old life a new thread is woven; the golden thread of a fresh vision of beauty." Curtis' writing is, of course, but esthetic impressionism at its daintiest. It tells us little more than that the performance inspired him to make up charming sentences about it. To Booth, however, it meant that he had won the unqualified approval of the most fastidious of public connoisseurs.

After the close of the Hundred Nights at the end of March, Booth took himself to Boston. As usual he was received there warmly. But here and there in the press one could detect a certain snappishness. For once it was Boston's turn to reject what New York had approved of. The critic of the *Advertiser* (March 28) found little to praise, and much deterioration to carp at. Booth, he said, used a "choked, weary, broken utterance" on lines that ought to be spoken pluckily. He had become careless of significances: having just complained that the air bites shrewdly, he took off his cap and spoke bareheaded. He stood through passages of listening with his back to the audience. He had let inaccuracies into the text—omissions and mispronunciations. He was seduced by tricky lighting effects, as in that scene with the Ghost when the ray of moonlight obligingly illuminated only the few square feet where Hamlet stood. All in all, said the *Advertiser*, Booth had better forget his famous Hundred Nights, lay by the role until he could give it a thorough rethinking, and return to it fresh in the fall.

There would be plenty of time for rethinking, if that was truly in order. On April 15, 1865, Booth's brother John Wilkes assassinated President Lincoln. For many months it appeared that Booth's career had ended.

1866. Fifth Season at the Winter Garden: Return to Management

Booth's resiliency under the heaviest misfortune was amazing. However crushing the disaster—Mollie's death two years earlier, now the assassination, two years hence the Winter Garden fire, later still his bankruptcy and the loss of his theatre, his near death in a carriage accident in 1875 and again in 1879 from a madman's bullet, his second wife's slowly developing lunacy and her death—he rebounded always with increased determination and initiative. In April of 1865 the very name of Booth was so vile a word that his life was threatened and he dared not walk the streets in daylight. Yet nine months later he was Hamlet at the Winter Garden once more, his art deepened, his professional intentions strengthened, his hold upon the public stronger than ever.

On January 3, 1866, when the second scene of *Hamlet* opened and Booth was discovered sitting with bowed head, "The men stamped, clapped their hands, and hurrahed, continuously; the ladies rose in their seats and waved a thousand handkerchiefs; and for full five minutes a scene of wild excitement forbade the progress of the play." Thus the *World* (January 4). Bayard of the *Spirit of the Times* (January 13) counted nine cheers, then six, then three, then nine more, and recorded not only the weeping of women but "tears rolling down some cheeks where whiskers are wont to grow." Booth rose, came forward, and bowed repeatedly until the tumult died down. At the end of the first act he was called back for a shower of bouquets. At the end of the third act someone called for "groans" for James Gordon Bennett's *Herald*, which alone among the newspapers had denounced Booth's return to the stage: howls and hisses filled the air. At the end of the performance the audience awarded "three groans" to Bennett personally. In the streets outside, a platoon of police "preserved the utmost good order that could be expected under the circumstances." Booth kept *Hamlet* on for four weeks: on February 1 he displaced it with a long-planned and equally splendid production of *Richelieu*.

In May of 1866 his reputation was flattered by a full-dress essay in the *Atlantic Monthly*. The author was E. C. Stedman, the then renowned poet, and the *Atlantic* was the Brahmin monitor of American culture. Stedman's writing is a little overstuffed, but a couple of his points are worth paying attention to. For one thing he neatly marks out the difference between Booth's Richelieu and his Hamlet. In Richelieu we never think of Booth, for the man is concealed in the role: at every moment of it he is *acting*. In Hamlet we see and think of Booth constantly, for in this role he does not act but *be*. Every quality of Hamlet ("for our Hamlet is both gentleman and scholar") finds its precise equivalent in Booth's own person. "He is in full sympathy with it, whether on or off the stage. We know it from our earliest glance at that lithe and sinuous figure, elegant in the solemn garb of sables,—at the pallor of his face and hands, the darkness of his hair, those eyes that can be so melancholy-sweet, yet ever look beyond and deeper than the things around him." His extraordinary grace of movement, by which he "makes statues all over the stage," creates unforgettable pictures—as when he makes Horatio and Marcellus swear on the cross-hilt of his sword, or in the fencing bout with Laertes, or in his sitting attitudes on quaint lounges of the period. He never forces attention by "elocutionary climaxes or quick-stopping strides," but rather, as Betterton is said to have done, "courts rapturous silence than clamorous applause."

In one line of roles, says Stedman, Booth can never excel: those towering figures of action, giants in emotion, kings in repose—Othello, Coriolanus, Virginius, Macbeth. These figures "are essentially *masculine*, and we connect their ideals with the stately figure, the deep chest-utterance, the slow, enduring majesty of men." Booth's genius has a *feminine* quality; he is rather Corinthian than Doric; he is limited to roles which call for subtlety, tunefulness, mobility. In roles of his proper range, he "has every resource of taste and study at his command; his action is finished to the last, his stage-business perfect, his reading distinct and musical as a bell. He is thus the ripened product of our eclectic later age."

Stedman's recognition of the femininity of Booth's Hamlet is perhaps unique—except for Booth's own words on the subject. Some fifteen years later, in a little book called *The Mystery of Hamlet*, an American Shakespearean named Edward Vining suggested that Shakespeare's original plan was to write *Hamlet* as a story of a woman in disguise—a sort of Rosalind (or Portia, or Helena) at Elsinore.

Booth was much excited by Vining's book and tried to interest William Winter in it. Its theory was absurd, of course, but that did not matter. What pleased Booth was the vast number of details of "womanliness" in the character which Vining had marshaled to support his theory. "I have always endeavored," he wrote Winter, "to make prominent the femininity of Hamlet's character and therein lies the secret of my success—I think. I doubt if ever a robust and masculine treatment of the character will be accepted so generally as the more womanly and refined interpretation. I know that frequently I fall into effeminacy, but we can't always hit the proper key-note. You must see the book—it will amuse & I think it will interest you too." [30]

What Stedman most desired for Booth in 1866 was another role of more cheerful temper in which Booth also need not *act*, but as in Hamlet, need only *be*. "We should like to see him, ere many winters have passed over his head, in some new classic play, whose arrangement should not be confined to the bald, antique model, nor yet too much infused with the mingled Gothic elements of our own drama; but warm with the sunlight, magical with the grace of the young Athenian feeling, and full of a healthful action which would display the fairest endowments of his mind and person." In this wish Stedman would be disappointed. Julia Ward Howe had once written for Booth a Hippolytus play, but nothing came of it. The romantic Eugene de Morny in Falconer's *Love's Ordeal*, which Booth tried in Boston in 1868, proved worthless. Booth had never liked playing lover's parts, and as he grew older he became more and more disaffected from them. His Romeo, for instance, which once charmed Mollie Devlin and multitudes of girlish susceptibles, by 1869 took a turn toward the ridiculous. Hostile reviewers made savage fun of it, and Booth dropped it from his repertory. For a while he clung to Bulwer's Claude Melnotte, but that was too slight a confection from which to create anything enduring. He tried Richard II in the latter 1870's, but although the role was right for him, the play was too still-life to prosper in a melodramatic age. Thus he came more and more to depend upon the old standbys—Hamlet and Richelieu, Iago and Bertuccio, Shylock and Petruchio, occasionally Macbeth, Lear, and Richard III, and in later years Shakespeare's Brutus.

[30] Booth to William Winter, February 9, 1882. The Folger Shakespeare Library, Y.c. 215 (412).

1866-67. The Winter Garden Fire

In the fall of 1866 Booth gave Boston a new production of *Hamlet*, the scenery by a painter named Heister, and played it there for three weeks. On November 27 he opened the Winter Garden, where after a week of *Hamlet* he spun off over a dozen roles in repertory pattern. On January 22, 1867, nearly two years after the event, a committee of distinguished citizens (including half a dozen of Booth's artist friends) presented him a Hamlet medal in commemoration of the Hundred Nights.[31] On January 28, he opened his third great Winter Garden production—*The Merchant of Venice*, with scenery by Charles Witham taken from Venetian sketches by the late Emanuel Leutze. Then, during the night of March 23, the Winter Garden burned. Scenery, costumes, properties, books—the accumulated work of three seasons—were destroyed in a few hours. For the next year and a half Booth did not act in New York at all but resolutely took to the road—as far west as St. Louis, as far south as New Orleans, all though the Middle East and New England—piling up capital to build his great new theatre at Sixth Avenue and Twenty-third Street.

1869. Booth's Theatre: First Season

We need not be concerned here with the follies that went into the building of Booth's Theatre, neither the senseless financial miscalculations which would in five years plummet Booth into bankruptcy, nor the oppressive gawdiness of the so-called "Renaissance" style of decoration. As a machine for showing plays, however, Booth's Theatre had many splendid features. The size of the auditorium was not excessive: seating for 1,750, standing room for some 250 more. A powerful fan system provided the best heating and cooling arrangements then available in any public building. The gas lighting of the auditorium, controlled by electric spark, could be taken down to almost perfect darkness, so that fine subtleties of stage illumination could be achieved. The orchestra was sunk below stage level so that the part of the audience seated in the parquet did not have to view the action through a forest of fiddle bows. The stage was flat, not raked, and the old lateral, split-scene, wing-and-groove system of scene change was replaced by a new vertical system. Sets flew down

[31] Winter, *Life and Art of Edwin Booth*, p. 75.

from a ninety-six-foot fly-loft, or rose up through the stage floor from a thirty-two-foot-deep cellarage. In excavations extending under Twenty-third Street, huge engines powered the scene changes by means of hydraulic rams. The dimensions of the stage house are moot, for no one account of them published at the time quite agrees with any other. The following figures are probable: depth from curtain line to back wall, 55 feet; width from wall to wall, about 74 feet; height to fly-gallery, 65 feet; height of fly-loft, 96 feet. For the width of the proscenium arch, which is of course one of the most significant dimensions, the lack of information is exasperating: the best guesses now put it at about 45 feet. The proscenium height, according to the style of the time, was considerably greater, but the actual playing height was reduced according to need by border curtains.[32]

Booth opened his theatre on February 3, 1869, with a spectacular production of *Romeo and Juliet* which ran for ten weeks, and followed it on April 12 with an equally handsome *Othello* which ran another ten weeks, down to May 29. Neither play was ideally cast. Booth was a poor Romeo and too small of stature for Othello. When he changed over to Iago in late April, that one role at least was in expert hands. His new leading lady, Mary Runnion McVicker (presently to become the second Mrs. Booth), was too hard, sharp, and midwestern to please anybody as Juliet or Desdemona.[33] Nonetheless the novelty of the new house and the splendor of the mountings brought in audiences, and the enterprise prospered.

It was not Booth's policy for his theatre to fill it with his own work only, but to make it a home for the finest actors in the best of classic and modern drama. Through June and July, his leading man, Edwin Adams, kept the house open, first with *The Lady of Lyons* and other stock plays, then with a much-praised dramatization of Tennyson's *Enoch Arden*. In August Booth gave his friend Joseph Jefferson a superb new mounting of *Rip Van Winkle*, and Jefferson played nightly down to September 18. The autumn brought a series of visiting stars—Kate Bateman in *Leah the Forsaken* and *Mary Warner*, the famous James Hackett in the Falstaff plays, and Emma Waller as Meg Merrilies in *Guy Mannering*. By January, 1870, Booth was ready with his definitive production of *Hamlet*.

[32] I am indebted to Professor Gerald L. Honaker of Catawba College for advice upon these dimensions.

[33] On June 7, 1870, Booth and Miss McVicker were married. After that, of course, she did no more acting.

CHAPTER IV

Hamlet at Booth's Theatre, 1870

Hamlet opened on Wednesday, January 5, 1870. It played five nights and a Saturday matinee each week for a total of sixty-four performances, and closed on Saturday, March 19. From first to last it was immensely popular. Seats were booked two weeks in advance, and except on extremely wintry nights the sign "Only Standing Room Left" was regularly hung up at the box office. "Not to have seen *Hamlet* will be an unenviable distinction," observed a reporter to the *Telegram* (January 29); [1] during this 1870 run well in excess of 100,000 persons did see it.

The only serious competition that turned up seems to have done it no harm at the box office—the appearance of Charles Fechter, whose "modern" Hamlet had delighted London nine years earlier. His American visit had been heralded for months. The August issue of the *Atlantic Monthly* had carried a glowing introduction of him by Charles Dickens, as if his coming were a cultural event of extraordinary importance, and the New York critics anticipated hungrily the contest of "the actor who has taken the first rank in the Old World with the one who holds so securely the esteem of the new." Booth, who did not care for contests, had invited Fechter to play at Booth's Theatre—even to play Hamlet there on alternate nights in Booth's

[1] The first reviews (daily newspapers) appeared on Thursday, January 6. Reviews in the weeklies appeared on January 8 and 9, and a vast number more appeared throughout the run. When quoting the reviews I have regularly given the date of issue except for the morning-after ones. When the date is not given, it may be assumed to be January 6.

own settings; but Fechter, more cunning than wise, declined the invitation on the grounds that he was committed to perform at Niblo's.[2] There during his first four weeks he confined himself to modern plays —Hugo's *Ruy Blas* from January 10 and Brougham's *The Duke's Motto* from January 26. Rumor persisted that he might yet go to Booth's for *Hamlet*, but nothing came of it, and beginning on February 14 he gave a single week of *Hamlet* to conclude his Niblo's engagement. His performance attracted ardent partisans, of course, but in limited numbers; the bulk of critical and popular support remained with Booth, whose reputation and profit were rather enhanced than diminished by the unsought-for competition.

Another sort of competition which sprang up was flattering and delightful. As *Hamlet*-fever swept the town, the clowns came forward with *Hamlet* burlesques. The best of these was George Fox's at the Olympic. Fox made up his face to resemble Booth's, and the more exactly and earnestly he imitated Booth's melancholy, the more hilarious was the effect. Booth's production had been much paragraphed for its "wintriness," especially as reflected in its heavy costumes, so that Fox garbed himself in a gigantic fur-collared overcoat, enormous mittens, and Arctic overshoes. His First Actor was a stage Irishman. His Actress was a fat blond woman six feet tall. The duel was fought with parasols. Booth himself always enjoyed Fox's burlesques, and his daughter Edwina recalls his particular delight in this spoof of *Hamlet*.[3] Other burlesques included Tony Pastor's at his theatre in the Bowery; Dan Bryant's minstrel-show version featuring the perennially favorite silly song "Shoo Fly, Don't Bother Me";[4] and a pair of theatrical pugilists, Jem Morse and John Heenan, who performed the duel as a boxing match.

That Booth withdrew *Hamlet* in mid-March was something of a puzzler to the town, for its popularity had not at all abated and it could obviously have outlasted the old record of a hundred nights, and probably have run to the end of the season. Booth gave out the excuse (obviously specious) that he was committed to producing certain other works. To William Winter he confided his real reason: "I do not wish to surfeit the *dear pub* with it—as it is my standby &

[2] A letter from Fechter excusing himself from the invitation is in Booth's souvenir letterbook at The Players.

[3] Grossmann, p. 15.

[4] A folksong or minstrel-show song which had been popular from Civil War days. See Vance Randolph, *Ozark Folksongs* (New York, 1946-50), II, 352.

must be done a little each season." [5] The nightly expenses were very high too, he noted, and if he could bring in full houses to less costly performances the profit would be greater. He was still under the illusion that he could one day pay for Booth's Theatre.

First Testimonials, Including Some Words from William Shakespeare

The audience on the opening night was enormous, and no one present could have failed to be aware that the event was a historic one. Crowds swarmed through the aisles and lobbies before curtain time, and once the play began the *Evening Post* reporter counted standees seven rows deep. "Beauty and fashion mingled and glittered in the brilliant crowd," according to the *Tribune*, and a correspondent to the *Atlas* (January 8) reckoned from the vast number of high-polished bald heads that "intellect" was well represented too. Fechter and his leading lady Carlotta Leclercq, who had just arrived in town, were guests in Booth's own box; Fechter applauded generously and often, and the audience, who recognized him, were pleased that he was pleased. When Booth appeared at the opening of the second scene, he was greeted with the expectable ovation. "It was many moments before he could make his voice heard," said the *Home Journal* (January 12); "he stood, with pale face and glowing eyes, clad in the mourning garb of the Danish prince, inclining his head slightly with stately grace, but not for an instant separating himself from the part he had assumed." He was summoned for applause at the end of every act, and finally a speech was called for, but he gave none. The performance lasted past midnight.

To celebrate the event the reviewers spared no hyperboles. "In the production of Hamlet last night," said the *Post*, "the most admired actor and manager on the American stage achieved the greatest triumph he has yet known." To the *Herald* critic, it was "a genuine feast of reason, of beauty . . . of histrionic intelligence and splendor. . . . It was, in fact, just such a treat as 'professionals' and critical old playgoers would almost risk the shortening of their span of life to enjoy." The boldest writers favored an international gambit. "Outside the Grand Opera House of Paris," said the critic of the *Globe*, "we may well doubt if the world has seen the equal of that which

[5] Booth to William Winter. The Folger Shakespeare Library, Y.c. 215 (212).

thousands had the pleasure of seeing last night." The *Home Journal* declared it "a magnificent honor, not only to the American stage, but to the drama of the entire civilized world," and, overleaping time as well as oceans, found it "doubtful if any future attempt can greatly surpass it." Sentimentality and self-gratulation united to produce this pretty whimsy in the *Spirit of the Times* (January 8): [6] "For us there was but one drawback to the pleasure of the occasion—this was a regret that Shakespeare in his life could not have seen his play so produced; the resources of the stage in his day were bare indeed. Yet if his spirit did not hover delightedly over the battlements of the castle scene, and walk among the trees and tombs of the churchyard when the body of Ophelia was given to the earth, 'tis only because a sad tyranny is exercized in the other world."

But Shakespeare *was* there, wonderful to relate, and the *Leader* (January 8), achieving a first-rate scoop, published a long statement from him, dated "Dramatic Sphere, Spiritual World, Jan. 7th," and communicated by way of a medium identified as "O.K." [7] The statement was addressed to Booth, and its burden is Shakespeare's insistence that "from the rising of the curtain until the going down thereof, you are *my* Hamlet. . . . You are my young, quick-witted, ready-tongued, psychical, impassioned, emotion-swayed Prince. Of whom it may be said as an elegy—I quote from my brother Gray—'And Melancholy marked him for her own.' " Often before this, Shakespeare says, he has wanted to communicate with the living world, but he has waited for the proper time and the proper man. He wishes the modern public to understand that when as "a member of the most worshipful fraternity of player folks" he had worked over the play of *Hamlet*, it had *not* been one of his favorites. It was not an original work. He had not given it much thought, had not even looked into its documentary backgrounds—indeed, in those days he had never heard of Saxo or Belleforest. He was in fact only re-carpentering an old play of Thomas Kyd's. But as the generations

[6] The *Spirit of the Times* carried two major reviews, both perhaps guest-written. This one of January 8 praises the production in nearly every point; the one of February 5, almost certainly written by Nym Crinkle, though beginning with an acknowledgment of the "beautiful and artistically exact presentment," is mainly hostile (see below, pp. 83, 92).

[7] Apparently this letter from Shakespeare to Booth was updated from an earlier psychic transmission. William Stuart quoted a scrap from it in his advertisements for the Winter Garden *Hamlet*. See the *Times*, December 24, 1864.

have passed until the present time, when one can find so many young Hamlets at the Cambridges of England and Massachusetts, he has come to appreciate how much of humanity is caught up in it, so that he thinks better of it now than he used to do.

Shakespeare has a very low regard for most of the closet critics of *Hamlet*, past and present: "Many of my so-called beauties have been only the complacencies of writers who wished to wrap themselves in the habiliments of my fame." The moguls of criticism, from Johnson to Guizot, he dismisses as pretentious obfuscators or deifiers of self. He mentions articles in nine or ten contemporary magazines which he thinks may have amused Booth, but are worth no more. He does approve of two writers, William Maginn and Richard Grant White, whose scholarship is sane and whose heartiness and affinity to the theatre match his own. But the Hamlet of the closet is not, for the most part, *his* Hamlet.

He allows that Hamlet on the stage has fared somewhat more successfully: Betterton and Kemble, at least, came close to the mark. But most stage Hamlets, too, have been all wrong: "I have seen men essay acting their own Hamlets; but they were monstrously bothered with my words. They were perpetually kicking with rhetorical gyves on!" The worst of them all was William Charles Macready, who was "freaky," a sort of elocutionary rope-dancer. Whatever else may be said of Edwin Forrest, Shakespeare is indebted to him for having hissed Macready's Hamlet at Edinburgh. He thanks Booth, in passing, for the scenic production. The play has been "equally well propertied on the stage in England, but never better." And, of course, "in my day, all the machinery of scenic effect, this variety of property and the combinations of science which on the modern stage come to aid my illustrations of men and manners, were utterly undreamed of."

The Production: Arthur Matthison's Brochure

The pleasure which Shakespeare's ghost took in the modern "machinery of scenic effect" qualified him as a very knowledgeable, up-to-date ghost, whose opinions would win an approving nod from every up-to-date New York theatre-goer—except, as we shall see, that very Richard Grant White whose writings the ghost claimed to admire. For weeks in advance of the opening, news columnists teased their readers with hints of the pictorial delights to come. Settings and dresses had been in preparation for many months (or a year, or more than a year), they said, "and all that lavish expenditure can do to make this revival the grandest of the age, has been done."

Propaganda for the *Hamlet* scenery took on even a moralizing tone, as we may read in the *World* on the day of the opening:

It is safe to say that tonight will begin a new era in the history of the legitimate drama. Henceforth Shakespeare will receive a setting that has heretofore been reserved only for the cheap and pasty gems of Farnie. The attraction of the meretricious drama has consisted solely in the magnificence with which its meaningless balderdash has been lavishly arrayed. It receives its death-blow when the legitimate drama rivals or surpasses it in its one attractive feature. This blow Mr. Booth strikes surely and splendidly tonight.

The "Farnie" upon whom the *World* critic unloads his scorn was H. B. Farnie, the author of a burlesque extravaganza of *The Forty Thieves*, in which Lydia Thompson and her British Blondes had lately exhibited their wit and limbs; beyond this "cheap and pasty gem," and indeed beyond the pale for all pure-hearted theatregoers, lay the notorious *Black Crook*, in which (to gather together some of the metaphors applied to it) scenic art and sin had built a path to hell through a wilderness of roses. Booth's scenery for *Hamlet*, then, was to redeem the theatre from the profanations of its vulgar abusers.

If Booth himself did not proclaim so extremely reformist an intention, at least he intended his theatre to be an institution for educational uplift. He had taken great pains to make this *Hamlet* production "historically accurate," and in the manner of Charles Kean at the Princess's in London he wished to share with his audiences some of the erudition which had gone into it. He had commissioned Arthur Matthison, a talented member of his company who had also a bit of literary gift, to prepare a brochure called *Booth's Theatre: Hamlet* for distribution at the theatre. In the first half of his brochure Matthison likens the play to a symphonic composition ("for it is music"); and by standard quotations from Schlegel, Goethe, Hudson, Lamb, and Mrs. Jameson he declares that the play can rouse us "from the narrow sphere of our daily lives into a loftier, grander region, whose atmosphere perforce shall purify and exalt our souls . . . shall infuse some of its own precious metal of nobility, honesty and courage into our own lives, glorifying our too mundane souls with some of its higher, more heavenly attributes!" Matthison defines Hamlet as a transcendentally virtuous character. He insists emphatically, too, that Hamlet is *never mad*, but that his antic disposition is always assumed. We are thus advised to trust Hamlet and to take his every utterance unsalted.

In the second half of the brochure Matthison calls attention to the staging and the scholarship which justifies it. The period and place of the play is tenth-century Denmark, and this will be the first time the play has been so set and dressed in any theatre in America. (Here the argument seems to forget the once proud scenic decoration of *Hamlet* at the Winter Garden.) Matthison mentions, and in some instances briefly describes, ten of the sets—including, by the way, two which did not appear and omitting three which did. He calls attention to the armorial significance of the lion-leopard and the Danish raven; gives us the technical terminology and the published authorities for the dresses; identifies the principal musical compositions to be played by Edward Mollenhauer's orchestra.

The brochure proved a considerable aid to conscientious reviewers, and one or two of them reprinted the whole of it in their columns. Until the discovery of Charles Witham's 1870 scene designs, the brochure has been our principal authority for what Booth's 1870 *Hamlet* looked like.

The Costumes

The costumes, which bespoke wintriness, were a novelty, and they aroused much delighted comment. They were entirely new in design and material—"rich and elegant," said the *Globe*, and "of a different pattern from those the public has heretofore seen in this play." In all earlier productions, even at the Winter Garden, the play had been dressed either in Flemish or Renaissance Italian or theatrical nondescript style—"entirely forgetful," said the *Sunday News* (January 30), "that the thermometer in Denmark not infrequently falls twenty-two degrees below zero. A scene in Denmark peopled with princes and courtiers in the summer costumes of Italy, was a palpable incongruity." For the patterns Booth now drew upon what was known of north European, or Saxon, dress of the tenth and eleventh centuries—not unlike what is shown in the Bayeux tapestry. During the next few years he would model the dresses for *Macbeth* and *Lear* upon the same patterns.[8] The men wore knee-length tunics, long-

[8] So Booth explains in a letter to William Winter, July 1, 1878. The Folger Shakespeare Library, Y.c. 215 (289).

sleeved shirts, mantles buckled from their right shoulders, fleshings cross-banded from instep to knee, and low shoes. Armor was called "mascled"—we should call it "chain mail"—and it covered the upper body but not the arms, which were clad in long sleeves. Mascled hoods were worn, covering the head, throat, and jaws, and over these hoods were metal helmets with broad nose guards. The women wore floor-reaching gowns, knee-length tunics over these, mantles, and head veils. No velvets or silks were used, for these materials were held to be anachronistic, but only fine woven woolens. Both men's and women's dresses were embroidered and decorated with broad gold trimming.

Matthison does not speak of the colors, but we are to imagine a wide range of hues. The courtiers in the first Court scene, in robes of "spotted lilac or saffron," were likened by one observer to the figures in the frescoes at the Campo Santo at Pisa. The recorder-players that Hamlet calls for after the *Mousetrap* wore "flame-colored robes." The background of the Play scene was crowded over with "living groups in the most softly-vivid dresses." The spectrum set against the gray stone walls of the sets was broad and brilliant.

All the characters but one were wigged as blondes. Charles Fechter had long since given stage life to the Goethean notion that Hamlet was a blonde, and throughout the 1860's it had become axiomatic in the world behind the scenes that *all* Danes are blonde. Booth maintained, however, that there was one important exception. The beard of Hamlet's father had been "a sable silvered," so that Booth as Hamlet, true son of a brunette father, wore his own flowing black hair. The compromise was a cunning one, especially in 1870. It permitted Booth to appear in the role as he was used to appearing and as was most becoming to him. It set him off in strong visual contrast to the rest of the company. It embraced "truth" and yet it precluded any seeming imitation of Fechter, who would be exhibiting *his* blonde (actually saffron-haired) Hamlet at a rival theatre within a few weeks.

Apparently in later productions, away from his own theatre, Booth did not impose the blonde rule upon his companies. The actors at McVicker's in Chicago in 1873 (see Plate X) were certainly not so wigged. And at least one of his many later Horatios, who closely resembled Booth, reports that Mrs. Booth once compelled him to wear a blonde wig so that the audience would not confuse him with her husband.[9] But the blonde effect was maintained in 1870, apparently to the delighted approval of the literal-minded beholders.

The Scenery

The settings were mostly designed by Charles Witham (1842-1926), the young artist who had been Booth's favorite and principal scene painter ever since the Hundred Nights *Hamlet* of 1864. Witham was assisted in this production by the then well-known landscape painter Russell Smith (1812-97), who was also a specialist in scenic act drops and had in fact a year earlier created the act drop of Booth's Theatre; by John Thorne, who had shared in the Hundred Nights *Hamlet;* by Henry Hillyard (b. 1806), whose career began in London and who had long since brought to America his training in the Marinari-Stanfield-Grieve tradition; and by a lesser-known scene painter named Minard Lewis. The copies of the designs that come to us in the 1870 promptbook were executed by Witham.

The scenery aroused all but unanimous delight. According to the *Brooklyn Union*, everything scenic that had been accomplished during the preceding year at Booth's Theatre was as nothing in comparison with that of *Hamlet*, "which may be set down as the most perfect display of scenic art, combined with dramatic talent, ever before presented on the stage either in this country or elsewhere." The critic of the *Metropolitan* (January 15) recalled that the *Hamlet* scenery at the Winter Garden had seemed "the acme of perfection"; but this new *Hamlet* "is as much superior to its representation at the Winter Garden four years ago, as are the stage facilities of the present day to those which pleased and sometimes surprised the last generation of playgoers."

Much of the delight seems to have been stimulated by the new stage facilities of Booth's Theatre—the rise-and-sink system of scene changing, which now, perhaps for the first time, was being exploited to its utmost degree of effectiveness. The frequency and the magical precision of the scene changing prompted this enraptured outburst in the *Spirit of the Times* (January 8):

> Never before in this country has a play been so set upon the stage. . . . Never before Booth's have we had a theatre possessed of a stage where the play could be so set, a stage within the limits of which the little kingdom

[9] James Taylor in an interview, "Booth on *Hamlet*," in the Philadelphia *Public Ledger*, September 15, 1893.

of Denmark might be comfortably packed away, and still leave room for an additional principality or power if it were necessary for the general effect. For the first time in our experience we found it possible to give ourselves almost wholly up to an illusion, and deem that reality which was only acting. Nothing broke the pleasing spell; so carefully had the piece been rehearsed that there were no awkward "waits," no catching of scenery; everything moved—not like clock-work, for the impression was rather that of magic than of machinery.

The *Sun* praised the scenery for its unity, coherence, and restraint: everything that stage carpenter and scene painter could do was done, and all was controlled by conspicuous good taste, so that no one scene stood out from the rest or degenerated into mere spectacle, and every appointment served to illustrate, not overwhelm, the text. The *Courier* critic (January 9), whose memories went back a quarter of a century to Charles Kean's famous productions at the Park, thought that Kean's stage decorations may have equaled these in point of "historical fidelity," but under the old wing-and-groove system it had been impossible to produce such extraordinary effects as now were possible at Booth's.

The critic of the *World*—he who had promised that Booth's *Hamlet* would wipe out with one blow all meretricious uses of scenery for vulgar extravaganzas—measured "the prodigious advance Mr. Booth has made in scenic illustration" by inviting comparisons with Charles Kemble's *Hamlet* at the Park Theatre *forty* years ago! The marvelous illusionism of the settings gratified his highest expectations:

There were no makeshifts, no expedients, no omissions, to suddenly recall the mind from the fanciful realm represented to the ungrateful theatric reality. In so perfect a combination of mechanical and artistic resources, the actors seemed for the time being to be impressed by the illusion about them. That new sense of reality which the witchery of paint had evoked in the spectators, seemed to lend a new freedom to the performers. They were in no danger of mistaking pasteboard boxes for battlements and carved oak panels for doors. The massive stone stairways they seemed to know would bear the tread of a regiment, and that distant blue above them got to be in their minds the very "brave o'er-hanging firmament" itself, "fretted"—so far as anyone but the high ensconced deity of a stage carpenter could see—"with golden fire."

Most, if not all, of these reviewers must have seen Booth's 1864-67 *Hamlet* at the Winter Garden, yet not one of them mentions what to us is most obvious, that the 1870 settings were not fundamentally new at all, but were adaptations and elaborations of what they had seen before. One need only compare the illustrations in the 1866 acting edition (and the groundplans in the 1866 promptbook) with the 1870 watercolors to recognize that the new settings improve upon the old ones only in terms of expansion and refinement of detail (see Plates XVI-XVIII). In the opening scene, for instance, we find in both productions the castle, moon, and ground-level battlements presented in the same spatial relationships. The Graveyard scene of the fifth act is much prettier in Witham's 1870 version, but the grave, the church, and the tomb where Hamlet centers his action are in the same positions that they had been at the Winter Garden. The interior sets all exhibit the same Romanesque architecture—walls of stone block, and heavy columns supporting elaborately decorated round arches. The huge set for the second and fourth acts, called the Hall of Arches, has seven arches in the 1870 version instead of five, and a triple-vaulted ceiling instead of a flat one; yet the fundamental plan is the same; and as a matter of fact the positioning of the characters in the 1866 illustration (Hamlet conversing with the Actors) is exactly the same as that which Charles Clarke describes in 1870. The great staircase set of the third act was invented for the Winter Garden, though it was not then given the colonnaded facade across the gallery nor the vaulted ceiling. The Queen's Chamber was improved in 1870 only by increasing the number of blind arches across the back wall from two to three. Unquestionably the 1870 sets were bigger, better finished, more subtly lighted, more "beautiful" than the earlier ones, and with the rise-and-sink machinery they worked better. But as we stare at the flat pictures of the two productions we are astonished at the conservatism of idea, and as we pore over the masses of critiques we can only wonder that no one remarked on it at the time. Apparently the judgment of the critics was dazzled by their own expectations, by the greater size of the new stage, and by the glamor of the occasion and the surroundings. As the *Home Journal* (January 12) put it, "it is, indeed, difficult to write of it in temperate language, because ordinary words seem inadequate to a proper expression of its positive grandeur."

To this extravagant praise we must demur on another count. When we compare these sets with the best work then being done by scene painters in England, we must declare them stiff, confining, and some three or four decades behind the times. In every one of them except the "Wood and Cut Wood" of the fifth scene and the Graveyard of the fifth act we find repeated the old-fashioned or "classical" pattern of center focus and symmetry, whereas by 1870 we should expect sophisticated use of the "romantic" pattern of side focus and asymmetry. Time was when the inevitable position of a principal entrance (the doors of a great hall, the city gates, the entrance to a castle), or of a focal object (a throne, a tomb, an altar, a banquet table, a gallows) was exactly at upstage center. When a king entered attended by a dozen courtiers, the king took center stage and his followers ranged themselves exactly six to a side. The old wing-and-shutter scenery, which divided stage pictures into neat halves, had invited, if it did not compel, such rigid balance. But when, for instance, in the 1830's William Charles Macready realized that Lear's throne could be set at a quarter-angle at stage left and Lear's audience could group themselves freely across the stage, bulking toward stage right, the new romantic mode of stage composition was well under way. By the 1850's Charles Kean not only set Lear's throne to one side but turned the whole court room at an angle, so that the spectators looked both into it and across it, thus receiving an enhanced impression of its vastness and mystery. Kean's stage architecture was always remarkable for off-centering of focus, for diagonal house fronts, streets on a bias, canted great halls, vistas of farther rooms seen through and to one side of colonnaded near rooms. In such settings stage movement itself became easier, freer; action became, so to speak, more colloquial. The stage center position lost its strength, and positions away from center were found to yield subtler and more suggestive emphasis. It became esthetically desirable for the actor to do what in fact Booth loved to do: turn one's back on the audience, make curved and diagonal stage crosses, play about with furniture, deliver soliloquies sitting on a chair.

What happened in this instance was simply that Witham got trapped by his beginnings. In 1864 when as a novice he had designed *Hamlet* for a wing-and-shutter stage, he had of course obeyed its symmetrical imperatives. He, and Booth too, then lived for years with those first settings and became thoroughly accustomed to them. In 1869 when they moved into the new theatre and Witham began preparing the 1870 revival, it was only natural that he should adhere to his old, well-proved ideas, only elaborating and expanding them to fill up the vast width, height, and depth now available. Until he had some experience with the new spaces, his imagination was not ready to exploit the new freedoms which they afforded. Thus his 1870 *Hamlet* sets, however gorgeous in laid-on detail, were basically conventional and constrictive because they had been conceived in old-fashioned circumstances by a novice who had not yet discovered a modern style.

Witham was quick to learn, however. In the collection of his designs preserved at the Museum of the City of New York we observed that his *Richelieu* and *Julius Caesar* which followed at Booth's, and his later designs for the Harrigan comedies and other modern plays are marvelously free, colorful, and "modern" in their arrangements. Professor Thomas F. Marshall, who has studied the whole of Witham's known work, has in fact concluded that it is the notable tendency of his compositions to be "asymmetrical, with a strong off-center slant." [10]

The Scenery Criticized

At the time of the Hundred Nights *Hamlet* only one reviewer had condemned the new fashions in stage decoration of Shakespeare —declaring that "when it is best it is worst," wishing it all away.[11] In 1870 there were two—Nym Crinkle, who had lately come onto the staff of the *World*,[12] and the well-known Shakespeare scholar Richard Grant White. Nym Crinkle was an entertaining writer, but as a critic he is difficult to follow. On one day he is a sentimental bleeding heart (or a champion of dramatic realism?), assuring us that what the public wants, and naturally and rightly responds to, is not Shakespeare at all but honest dramas of modern domestic life, like Tom Taylor's *Mary Warner*. On another day he sturdily deplores the loss of those golden giants of the stage, the great actors of the past who gave us Shakespeare unadorned. There was a time, he says—and since, as a man of thirty-five, he was looking back upon the 1850's when such stalwarts as Forrest and Cushman and Davenport ruled the roost, and Gustavus Brooke and Barry Sullivan passed through town, we are willing to grant him his premise—there was a time when we took our Shakespeare straight, contented with "the truth that lay like diamonds

[10] Professor Marshall of Kent State University discussed Witham's scene painting before the International Theatre Conference at Amsterdam in 1965.

[11] See above, Chapter III, pp. 58-59.

[12] The *World* had two theatre critics at this time. The one whose opinions of Booth's scenery have been quoted above wrote for the daily paper. Nym Crinkle's lengthy feuilletons appeared on Sundays. In their opinions of this *Hamlet* the two squarely opposed each other on every point.

under the pure stream of poetry." But the current taste runs toward *realism*. So far as acting goes, the public "harbors a secret contempt for those demonstrative displays of grief and hate and love which once constituted the very *anima* of the tragic stage." Nowadays the public cares only for archeology, for the "marvellous accuracy with which the chausses and helmets, and tunics and gowns of the circumambulating nobodies are reproduced." It is the spirit of our times, he says, to "localize and particularize," to subdue whatever is spiritually significant to "historical decoration," to reduce "poetic truth" to the "accuracy of a chronicle." The stage abandons idealism and busies itself with reproducing "trivial contemporaneous customs and habits," and the result is "a marvellous pre-Raphaelite picture of fire which neither warms nor illumes."

If we cannot get a new insight into the problem of Hamlet's mind, he goes on, we are "assured of the exact cut of the Danish soldier's breeches . . . and the style of furniture and decoration in Polonius's house." As an audience we have "outgrown the sentimentalism of the ancient stage, and not wishing to be wrung, or touched, or moved," we are "delighted to be virtuosi and antiquaries, and talk learnedly of the historical truth of the stone walls and the recurring fidelity of the armorial bearings, and the exquisite reliability of the new clothes."

Nym Crinkle's sarcasms about stage decoration are at once telling and amusing, but, as he somewhere says of himself, he is often "assertive rather than argumentative," and he probably spun off these sentences as much out of the sheer joy of flailing about as out of principle. At any rate, at the end of his essay, as if he had forgotten the beginning of it, he cancels his whole attack with a tribute to the "beauty" of the production—to "the harmony, the smoothness, the illusion, the general effect, the interdependencies, the delicacy of interwrought art, the magnificence, the abiding result of the whole work . . . the most amazing combination of all the arts that our stage has ever seen."

Richard Grant White's attack is much more interesting, because it is reasoned rather than visceral and is grounded on solid knowledge of Shakespeare, history, and current esthetics. It was published in the March issue of the *Galaxy*, which came out about mid-February, some five or six weeks after Booth's *Hamlet* opened. The title of the article is "The Clown's Real Pigling," and White begins his argument by recounting the story of the ancient actor Parmenon, famous for his imitation of the squealing of a pig. One day a rival actor came on the stage with a real pig concealed under his cloak, and produced the squealing by twisting the pig's tail. The audience preferred Parmenon.

The usual moral read into the story is that audiences are too stupid to know the truth when it is set before them. White contends, however, that the ancient audience was right, for in matters of art the *ideal* is preferable to the *real.* "Real art," he says, "is always low art. It may be excellent in itself, and admirable in its kind; but its kind is inferior." In a painting by Raphael or Correggio an expert modiste cannot tell what stuff the drapery is made of: it is simply drapery. It is all very well in *genre* pictures to have satin and velvet and lace and leather "really" painted; but the beauty of *genre* pictures is not "noble beauty," and "the age or the school which can produce only *genre* pictures is a declining age or school."

Thus, the more Booth labors away at convincing us of the *reality* of his scenes and dresses, the more he defeats the purpose of his calling. "When Hamlet comes before us, we should not care where Hamlet is or what he wears. Only let his surroundings not attract our attention, either by their careless unfitness or their elaborate fitness."

> "Just to think," said a lady to me, radiant no less with delight than with beauty, as she came from seeing the life and death of the Prince of Denmark—"Just to think, the grave-digger must dig a real grave every night. I never saw more than a shovelful of earth taken up before, but at Booth's he takes up a whole barrelful. It's perfectly splendid."

The point White is making is identical with Nym Crinkle's, though White makes it more winningly. It is identical, too, with Victor Cousin's, which Mollie Devlin had told Booth of a decade earlier. But Booth had long since caught the plaguey notion that truth lay in surfaces. His personal art—his acting—was more profound than that, but as long as he was a producer, responsible for the total image of the play, the delusion had to run its course.

White had yet another line of argument. Let us, he says, grant the pictorial beauty of scene after scene of the production, "which in spirit, keeping, and composition, and even in effects of color, few living painters could hope to rival," yet the production as a whole is "a splendid blunder." It is supposed to be historically accurate. But this it cannot be, for "*Hamlet* is, from beginning to end, in its external conditions and in its very structure and spirit, one monstrous anachronism." Its period is utterly indeterminable, ranging from the depths of the Dark Ages to the time of Shakespeare himself. Why should we trouble ourselves about tenth-century Danish architecture, furniture, and dress, when we must listen to fifteenth-century cannon fire and witness a duel with sixteenth-century rapiers, hear a conversation based upon terms of an English coroner's inquest, and watch a funeral ceremony conducted by Roman Catholic ritual?

The greatest anachronism of all, says White, is Hamlet himself. Nowhere in the great epics of rude times—the *Nibelungenlied*, the *Chanson de Roland*, the Norse sagas—do we find a hero possessed of "the speculative habit and power of mind" which Hamlet exhibits in an extreme and even morbid form. Hamlet's philosophizing is as impossible to the tenth century as are Polonius' references to French fashions. "To Amleth the Dane, the soliloquy 'To be or not to be,' and the musings in the churchyard, the reflections on man, indeed almost every thought uttered by Shakespeare's prince, were as inconceivable as a discourse on the electric telegraph or a discussion of the law of nations." To attempt to present the play in terms of historical realism is simply preposterous. The sole artistic aim that should govern the mounting of this play is that scenery and costume be inconspicuous.

White's article stirred up flurries of resistance. In the *Weekly Review* (March 19), William Winter reaffirmed Booth's "conscientious regard of an antiquary and scholar for the chronology, manner, and dresses of the periods represented on his stage"; and declared that "there never was a more mistaken or more sordid theory than that advanced by some writers of the time, that elegance and complete exactitude of scenery, dresses, and appointments are unworthy of high tragedy, and detrimental to its simplicity and spiritual effect." The critic of the Philadelphia *Morning Post* (undated clipping), no friend to Booth, argued that whether White was right or wrong Booth did wisely to surround himself with fancy stage trappings, for he was not a good enough Hamlet to get along without them; and in any case it is better to lavish these scenic splendors on *Hamlet* than on *The Black Crook*.

Booth himself, triumphant in his enterprise, was simply bewildered by the attacks. One evening in early March a trio of friends called upon Booth and his wife in his apartment in the theatre while he was taking his fourth act meerschaum and rest, and a few days later there appeared in the *Globe* (March 11) an account of the interview, called "Hamlet Behind the Scenes." One of the visitors asked Booth what he thought of the idea that his production was too realistic. "What am I to do?" Booth responded warmly. "If I read *Hamlet* as I read *Manfred*, it is simply a poem. The intellectual few will appreciate it, and probably after I have read it two or three times, the interest will die out, because the people who would be interested in a mere reading are comparatively few." The dilemma which Booth here set up was quite false, of course, for no one had proposed that he abandon the stage for the elocutionist's podium; but Booth was cornered and desperate. "I play it as it is written," he went on, "and put it on the stage according to every authority. There is not a costume, a decoration, or painting, that I have not some reason for introducing. . . . There is not an attitude nor situation that is not an effort to express what I regard to be the meaning of Shakespeare." His "every authority," White would contend, is no authority, and his defense only runs in circles.

To one of White's points in which he touched upon Booth's acting, Booth quietly submitted. White had good-humoredly ridiculed the extravagant stage fall Booth took after the Ghost's exit in the fifth scene, and according to Charles Clarke's account Booth cut out the fancy work and took the fall quite simply. White was genuinely fond of Booth and enjoyed his acting. In his next *Galaxy* article, in April, he described Booth's Hamlet as a "thoughtful, sensitive, graceful, and courtly impersonation," and rated it the foremost Hamlet of the day.

The Supporting Company

The supporting company, all drawn from among the stock actors of Booth's Theatre, was held to be either reasonably good or very bad according to the whim of the reporters. "The cast is a very even one," said the *Globe*, "and all the parts are well sustained." The *Leader* (January 15), on the other hand, dragged up the old canard that Booth tolerated such poor actors around him because he knew the public would flock to his own Hamlet no matter how weak the support. A reviewer for the *Spirit of the Times* (February 5)—on this occasion apparently Nym Crinkle—paid Booth a queerly left-handed compliment. In the course of proving that Booth was no genius but only a technical expert, he found evidence in "the precision and smoothness of the business of the entire corps." Individually, he said, the actors are untalented, but in no other company has such lack of talent been so "splendidly compensated by drill and management." Booth understands as well as the Germans do that "the real excellence of a dramatic entertainment consists in the contribution by every member of the company, no matter how trivial his part, to the sum total of the action."

The cast was as follows:[13]

CLAUDIUS, King of Denmark	Mr. THEO. HAMILTON
HAMLET, son of the former and nephew to the latter	Mr. EDWIN BOOTH
POLONIUS, Lord Chamberlain	Mr. D. C. ANDERSON
HORATIO, friend to Hamlet	Mr. AUGUSTUS PITOU
LAERTES, son to Polonius	Mr. W. E. SHERIDAN
ROSENCRANTZ (courtiers)	Mr. THOMAS J. HIND
GUILDENSTERN (courtiers)	Mr. NELSON DECKER
OSRIC (courtiers)	Mr. CHARLES NORRIS
PRIEST	Mr. WILLIAM DRUMMOND
MARCELLUS (officers)	Mr. HENRY L. HINTON
BERNARDO (officers)	Mr. A. MATTHISON
FRANCISCO, a soldier	Mr. HENRY HOGAN
GHOST OF HAMLET'S FATHER	Mr. D. W. WALLER
1ST ACTOR	Mr. A. W. FENNO
2ND ACTOR	Mr. T. F. BRENNAN
ACTRESS	Master WILLIE SEYMOUR
1ST GRAVE DIGGER	Mr. CHARLES PETERS
2ND GRAVE DIGGER	Mr. CHARLES ROSENE
GERTRUDE, Queen of Denmark, and the mother of Hamlet	Miss FANNY MORANT
OPHELIA, daughter of Polonius	Miss BLANCHE DE BAR

Of the five or six actors mentioned most often, Fanny Morant (1821-1900), who played the Queen, was praised on all hands. Of English origin, she was well known to New Yorkers, having played leading roles at Wallack's through most of the 1860's. She had joined

[13] Photographs of many of Booth's supporting actors are accessible in Odell's *Annals of the New York Stage* (New York, 1927-49); Augustus Pitou, IX, 8; W. E. Sheridan, IX, 8, X, 176, X, 216, XII, 460; T. J. Hind, VII, 388; Nelson Decker, X, 380; D. W. Waller, VII, 16; A. W. Fenno, VI, 546; Willie Seymour, X, 316; Charles Peters, VII, 132; W. S. Andrews, VIII, 18; Charles Rosene, X, 208; Fanny Morant, VI, 294, VII, 548, IX, 544, X, 24, X, 204; Blanche de Bar, VIII, 426.

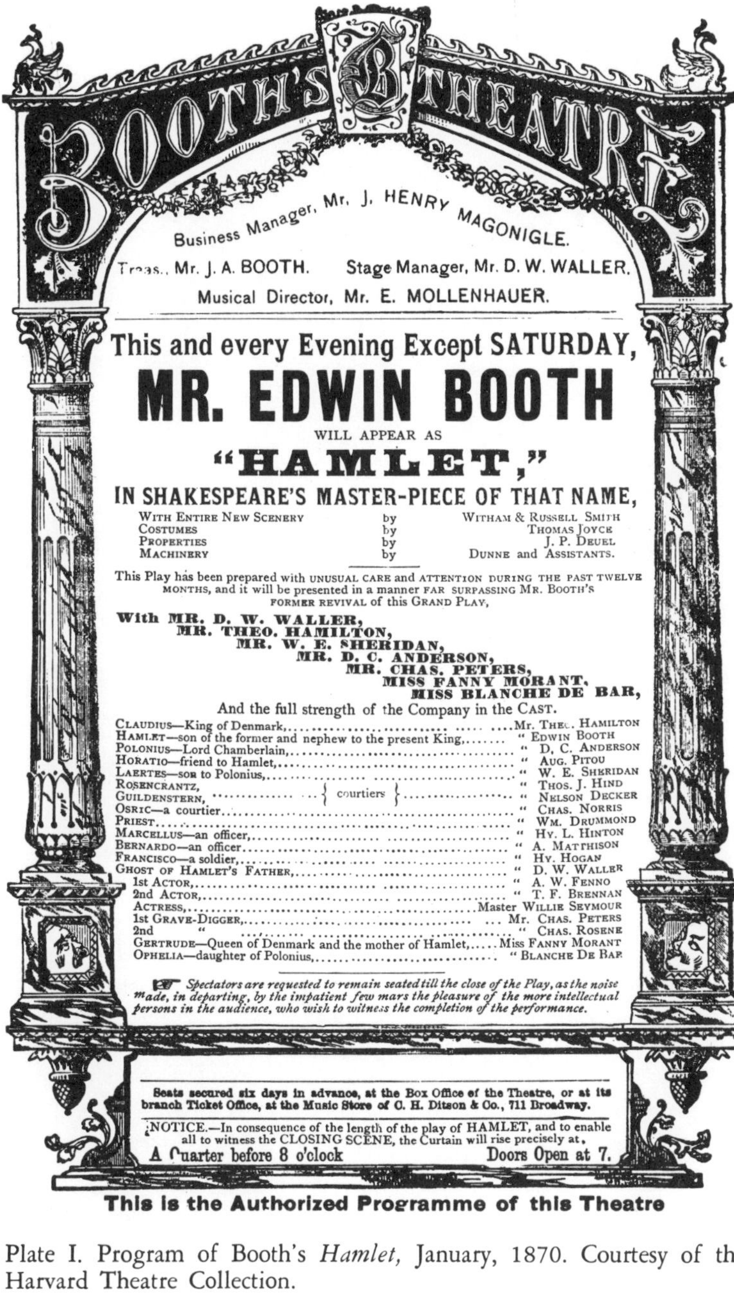
BOOTH'S THEATRE

Business Manager, Mr. J. HENRY MAGONIGLE.

Treas., Mr. J. A. BOOTH. Stage Manager, Mr. D. W. WALLER.

Musical Director, Mr. E. MOLLENHAUER.

This and every Evening Except SATURDAY,

MR. EDWIN BOOTH

WILL APPEAR AS

"HAMLET,"

IN SHAKESPEARE'S MASTER-PIECE OF THAT NAME,

WITH ENTIRE NEW SCENERY	by	WITHAM & RUSSELL SMITH
COSTUMES	by	THOMAS JOYCE
PROPERTIES	by	J. P. DEUEL
MACHINERY	by	DUNNE and ASSISTANTS.

This Play has been prepared with UNUSUAL CARE and ATTENTION DURING THE PAST TWELVE MONTHS, and it will be presented in a manner FAR SURPASSING MR. BOOTH'S FORMER REVIVAL of this GRAND PLAY,

With MR. D. W. WALLER,
MR. THEO. HAMILTON,
MR. W. E. SHERIDAN,
MR. D. C. ANDERSON,
MR. CHAS. PETERS,
MISS FANNY MORANT,
MISS BLANCHE DE BAR,

And the full strength of the Company in the CAST.

CLAUDIUS—King of Denmark,	Mr. THEO. HAMILTON
HAMLET—son of the former and nephew to the present King,	" EDWIN BOOTH
POLONIUS—Lord Chamberlain,	" D. C. ANDERSON
HORATIO—friend to Hamlet,	" AUG. PITOU
LAERTES—son to Polonius,	" W. E. SHERIDAN
ROSENCRANTZ, } courtiers	" THOS. J. HIND
GUILDENSTERN, } courtiers	" NELSON DECKER
OSRIC—a courtier	" CHAS. NORRIS
PRIEST	" WM. DRUMMOND
MARCELLUS—an officer,	" HY. L. HINTON
BERNARDO—an officer	" A. MATTHISON
FRANCISCO—a soldier,	" HY. HOGAN
GHOST OF HAMLET'S FATHER,	" D. W. WALLER
1st ACTOR,	" A. W. FENNO
2nd ACTOR,	" T. F. BRENNAN
ACTRESS,	Master WILLIE SEYMOUR
1st GRAVE-DIGGER,	Mr. CHAS. PETERS
2nd "	" CHAS. ROSENE
GERTRUDE—Queen of Denmark and the mother of Hamlet,	Miss FANNY MORANT
OPHELIA—daughter of Polonius,	" BLANCHE DE BAR

☞ *Spectators are requested to remain seated till the close of the Play, as the noise made, in departing, by the impatient few mars the pleasure of the more intellectual persons in the audience, who wish to witness the completion of the performance.*

Seats secured six days in advance, at the Box Office of the Theatre, or at its branch Ticket Office, at the Music Store of C. H. Ditson & Co., 711 Broadway.

NOTICE.—In consequence of the length of the play of HAMLET, and to enable all to witness the CLOSING SCENE, the Curtain will rise precisely at,

A Quarter before 8 o'clock Doors Open at 7.

This is the Authorized Programme of this Theatre

Plate I. Program of Booth's *Hamlet,* January, 1870. Courtesy of the Harvard Theatre Collection.

Plate II. Booth's Theatre at Twenty-third Street and Sixth Avenue, 1869-83. From *Harper's Weekly*, January 9, 1869.

Plate III. The interior of Booth's Theatre on the opening night: a scene from *Romeo and Juliet.* From *Frank Leslie's Illustrated Newspaper,* February 27, 1869.

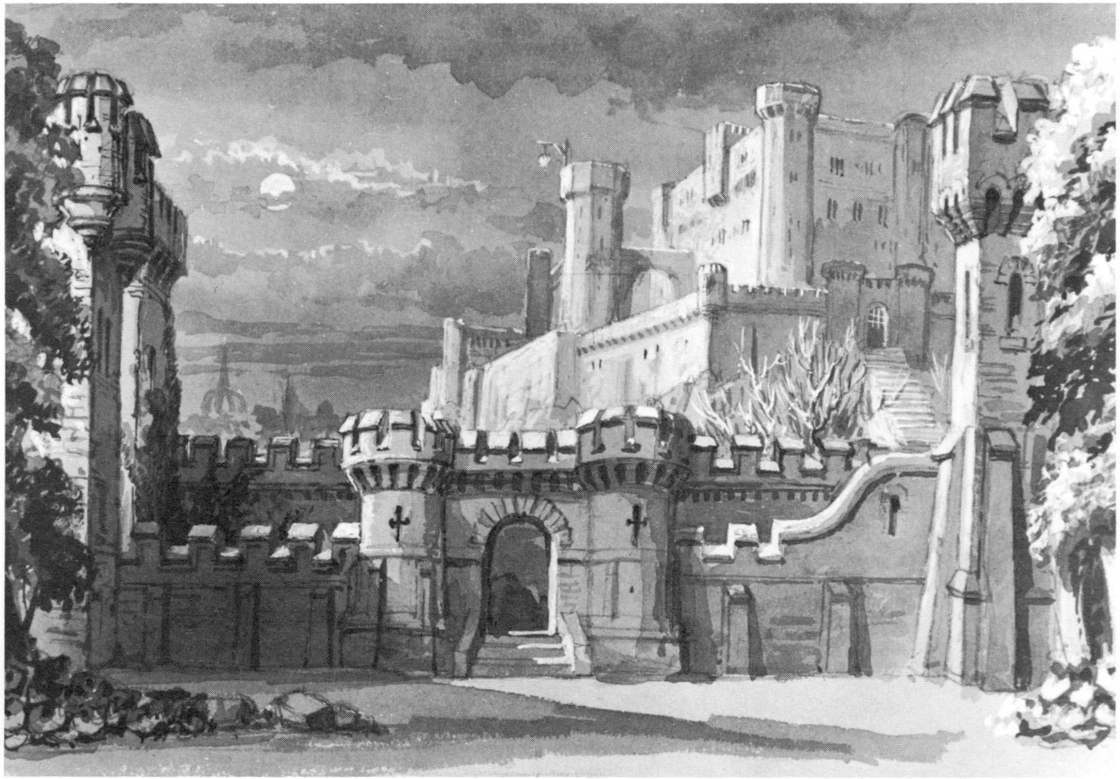

Plate IV. *A Platform before the Castle,* Act I, 1 and 4. Charles Witham's watercolor in the 1870 promptbook. Courtesy of the Harvard Theatre Collection.

Plate V. *A Room of State in the Castle,* Act I, 2, and Act V, 3. Charles Witham's watercolor in the 1870 promptbook. Courtesy of the Harvard Theatre Collection.

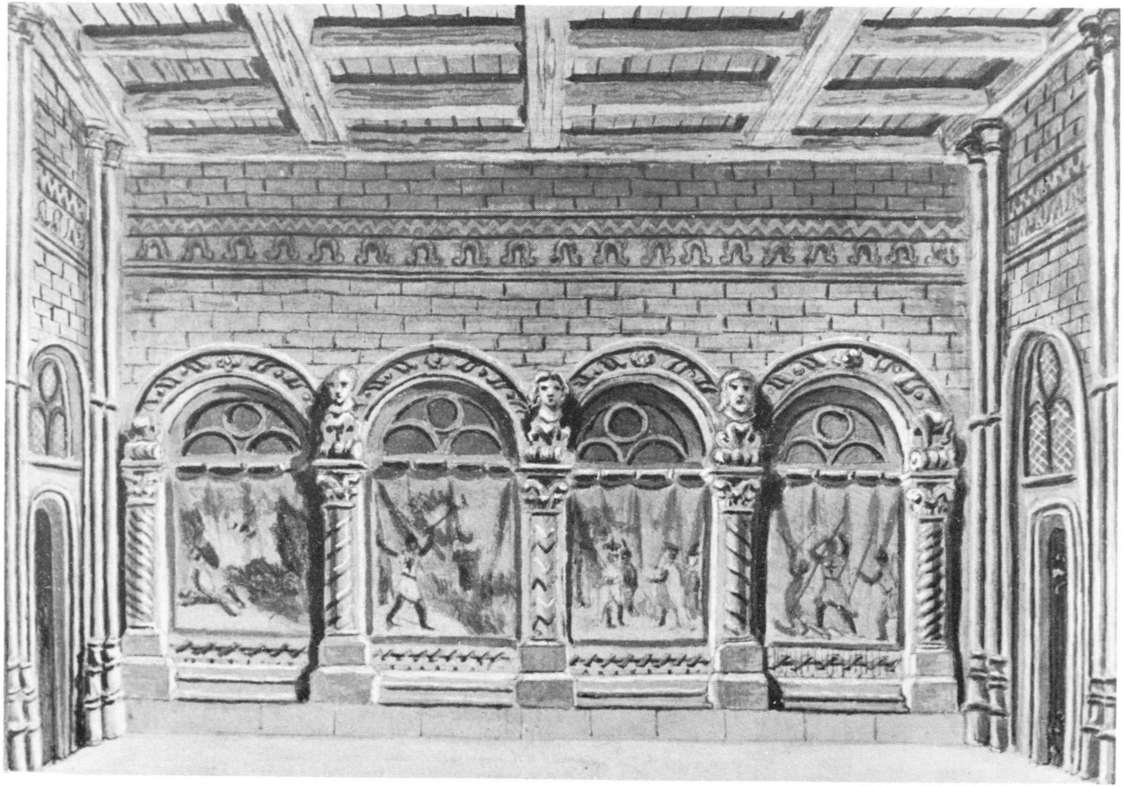

Plate VI. *A Room in Polonius' House,* Act I, 3. Charles Witham's watercolor in the 1870 promptbook. Courtesy of the Harvard Theatre Collection.

Plate VII. *A Grove Adjoining the Castle,* Act I, 5. Charles Witham's watercolor in the 1870 promptbook. Courtesy of the Harvard Theatre Collection.

Plate VIII. *A Room in the Palace, called the Hall of Arches,* Acts II and IV. Charles Witham's watercolor in the 1870 promptbook. Courtesy of the Harvard Theatre Collection.

Plate IX. *A Room in the Palace, called the Grand Hall of Audience,* Act III, 1 and 3, and Act V, 3. Charles Witham's watercolor in the 1870 promptbook. Courtesy of the Harvard Theatre Collection.

Plate X. *The Play Scene* at McVicker's Theatre, Chicago, 1873. Courtesy of the Harvard Theatre Collection.

Plate XI. *"To be or not to be."* Watercolor by William Wallace Scott. Courtesy of the Harvard Theatre Collection.

Plate XII. *The King's Closet,* Act III, 4. Charles Witham's watercolor in the 1870 promptbook. Courtesy of the Harvard Theatre Collection.

Plate XIII. *The Queen's Private Apartment,* Act III, 5. Charles Witham's watercolor in the 1870 promptbook. Courtesy of the Harvard Theatre Collection.

Plate XIV. *A Churchyard,* Act V, 1. Charles Witham's watercolor in the 1870 promptbook. Courtesy of the Harvard Theatre Collection.

Plate XV. *A Portico of the Castle,* Act V, 2. Charles Witham's watercolor in the 1870 promptbook. Courtesy of the Harvard Theatre Collection.

Plate XVI. a. *A Platform before the Castle,* at the Winter Garden. b. *The Hall of Arches,* at the Winter Garden. From the Booth-Hinton edition of 1866. Courtesy of the Folger Shakespeare Library.

Plate XVII. a. *The Grand Hall of Audience with a Theatre,* at the Winter Garden. b. *The Queen's Private Apartment,* at the Winter Garden. From the Booth-Hinton edition of 1866. Courtesy of the Folger Shakespeare Library.

Plate XVIII. a. *A Churchyard,* at the Winter Garden. b. *A Room of State in the Castle,* at the Winter Garden. From the Booth-Hinton edition of 1866. Courtesy of the Folger Shakespeare Library.

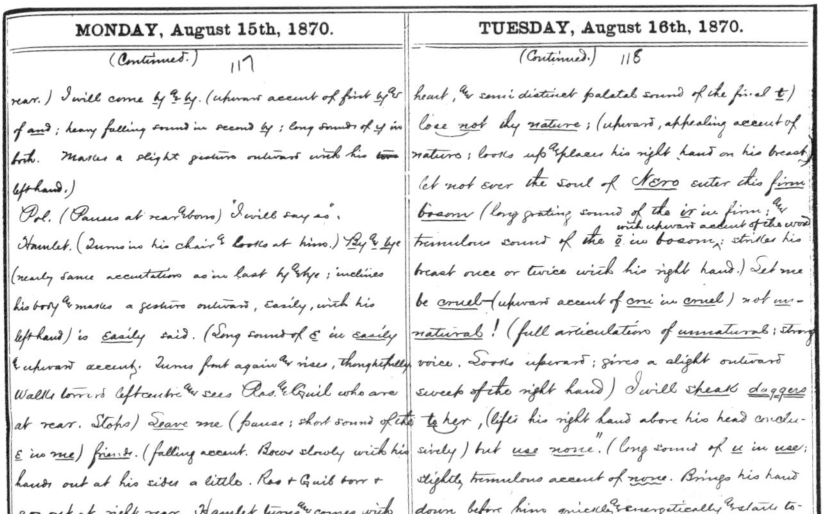

MONDAY, August 15th, 1870.

(Continued.) 117

rear.) I will come by & by. (upward accent of first by & of and; heavy falling sound in second by; long sounds of y in both. Makes a slight gesture outward with his ~~two~~ left hand.)

Pol. (Pauses at rear & bows) "I will say so".

Hamlet. (Turns in his chair & looks at him.) By & bye (nearly same accentuation as in last by & bye; inclines his body & makes a gesture outward, easily, with his left hand) is easily said. (Long sound of e in easily & upward accent. Turns front again & rises, thoughtfully. Walks toward left centre & sees Ros. & Guil. who are at rear. Stops) Leave me (pause; short sound of the e in me) friends. (falling accent. Bows slowly with his hands out at his sides a little. Ros + Guil bow + go out at right rear. Hamlet turns & comes with moderate, reflective walk down to left front where he leans against the wall at the corner of the left front exit or passage way & seems to be looking out into the evening.) 'Tis now the very witching time (turns, faces front) of night when (faces centre) churchyards yawn (broad sound of yawn; slight, upward accent. Moves slowly toward left centre) & hell itself breathes out contagion to this world. Now could I drink hot blood (stops at left centre facing right rear) & do such bitter business (looking down sternly) as the day would quake to look on! (Brings down his clenched fist before his breast in a threatening stroke with earnest determined manner. Then pauses briefly & drops his hand as if to ponder his feeling, but immediately keeps on) Soft — now to my mother. (Takes a step toward rear.) oh! heart, (upward ~~sound~~ accent of

TUESDAY, August 16th, 1870.

(Continued.) 118

heart, & semi distinct palatal sound of the final t) lose not thy nature; (upward, appealing accent of nature; looks up & places his right hand on his breast) let not ever the soul of Nero enter this firm bosom (long grating sound of the ir in firm; & tremulous sound of the o in bosom with upward accent of the word; strikes his breast once or twice with his right hand.) Let me be cruel — (upward accent of cru in cruel) not unnatural! (full articulation of unnatural; strong voice. Looks upward; gives a slight outward sweep of the right hand) I will speak daggers to her, (lifts his right hand above his head conclusively) but use none." (long sound of u in use; slightly tremulous accent of none. Brings his hand down before him quickly & energetically & starts toward rear. As the next scene shuts him from sight, he is walking toward the right rear ~~slowly~~ with both hands on his fore head, evidently thinking intently) —

In this scene Hamlet's resolution in minor matters, & irresolution & involuntary shrinking from the great business in his hands were well shown.

In his entrance Booth ~~he~~ was consciously meditative, walking to the front with purposed abstraction of demeanor, but losing much of this gravity, & seeming more attentive to surroundings as he walked back from the front to the temporary stage. The gradation from this abstracted mood to a perceptive one was adroitly effected. When the King spoke to him he replied in an easy informal way, & carried himself with an unconventional freedom of movement & attitude

(over)

Plate XIX. A page from Charles Clarke's manuscript description of Booth's Hamlet: the end of Act II. Courtesy of the Folger Shakespeare Library.

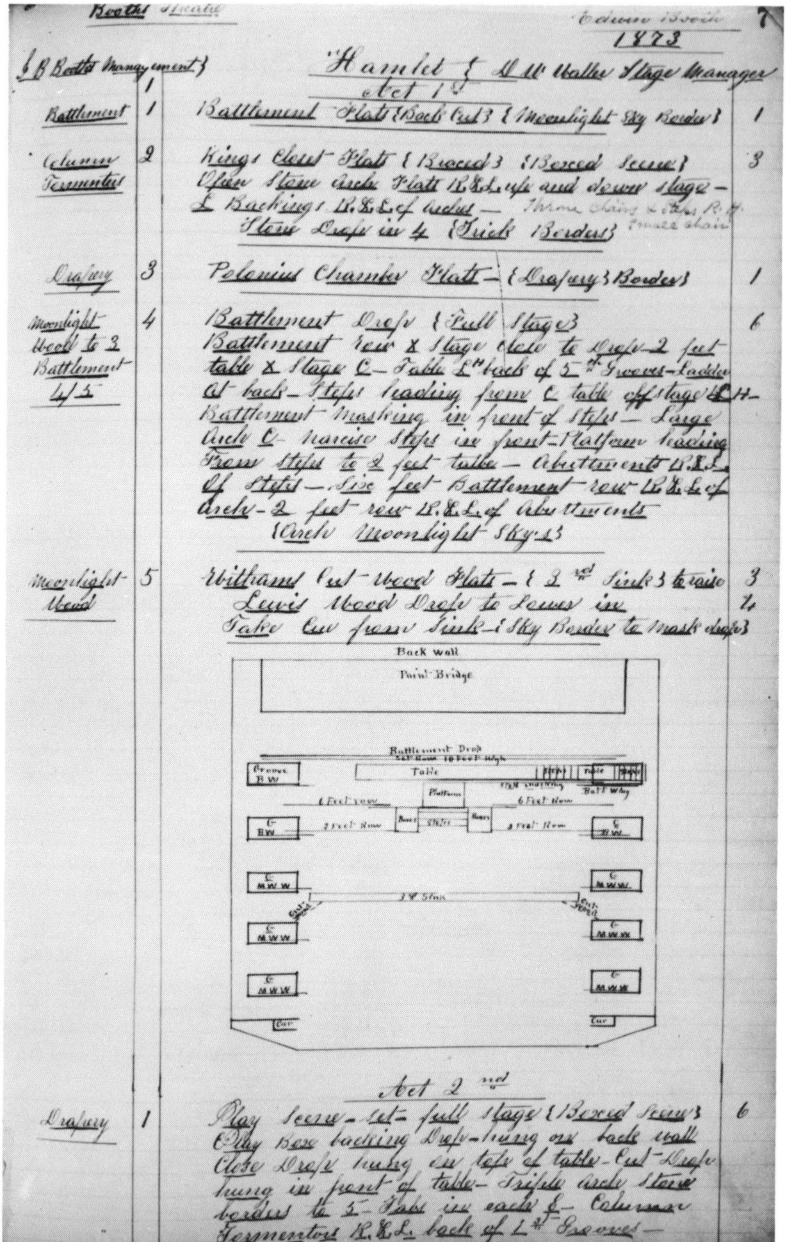

Booths Theatre — Edwin Booth — 1873 — 7

{J B Booths Management} — Hamlet {D W Waller Stage Manager}

Act 1st

Battlement — 1 — Battlement Flats {Back Cut} {Moonlight Sky Border} — 1

Column Tormentors — 2 — Kings Closet Flats {Braced} {Boxed Scene} — 3
Open Stone Arch Flats R.&L. up and down stage —
L Backings R.&L. of Arches — Throne Chairs & Steps R.H.
Stone Drop in 4 {Trick Border} — 2 small chairs

Drapery — 3 — Polonius Chamber Flats — {Drapery} Border} — 1

Moonlight Wood to 3 Battlement 4/5 — 4 — Battlement Drop {Full Stage} — 6
Battlement row X Stage close to Drop 2 feet
table X Stage C — Table L'th back of 5th Grooves — Ladder
at back — Steps leading from C table off stage L H —
Battlement Masking in front of Steps — Large
Arch C — narrow steps in front — Platform leading
from steps to 2 feet table — Abutments R.&L.
of steps — Six feet Battlement row R.&L. of
Arch — 2 feet row R.&L. of Abutments
{Arch Moonlight Sky 1}

Moonlight Wood — 5 — Williams Cut Wood Flats — {3rd Sink} to raise — 3
Lewis Wood Drop to Lower in — 4
Take Cut from Sink — {Sky Border to mask drop}

Act 2nd

Drapery — 1 — Play Scene — set — full stage {Boxed Scene} — 6
Play Box backing Drop — hung on back wall
Close Drop hung on top of table — Cut Drop
hung in front of table — Triple Arch Stone
borders to 5 — Flats in each E — Column
Tormentors R.&L. back of 1st Grooves —

Plate XX. A page from Bensen Sherwood's "Stage Plans, Booth's Theatre." Courtesy of the Theatre Collection of the New York Public Library.

Booth's Theatre at its opening, and played the Nurse in *Romeo and Juliet.* As Gertrude she was credited with queenly beauty (though a brunette, she wore a blonde wig with long braids), dignity, and precision. The *Times* (January 9) praised her unusually sympathetic response to the play going on about her ("so rare as to deserve particular mention"); her exhibition of voluptuousness, feminine vanity, and the "syren-like fascination" with which she lured Claudius; and her magnificent display of "remorse, terror, and passionate grief" in the Closet scene. Nym Crinkle in the *World*, although somewhat put off by her hanging about her husband's neck on all occasions, credited her rather more than Booth for the powerful effect of the Closet scene.

Theodore Hamilton (1836-1916), the Claudius, although a comparative newcomer to New York, had a popular following. Born in Baltimore, he had played in amateur theatricals with Booth when they were boys together. After some fifteen years as a stock actor, broken by service in the Confederate Army, he had arrived at Booth's Theatre at the start of its second season. Before coming to Claudius he had played in *Leah the Forsaken*, *Enoch Arden*, *Mary Warner*, *Henry IV* (Prince Hal), *The Merry Wives of Windsor* (Page, and *Guy Mannering*, and he would go on to Macduff, Beauséant in *The Lady of Lyons*, and other roles to the end of the season. William Winter said in the *Tribune* that Hamilton was the best Claudius he had ever seen, credible as lover to the Queen, and with mind and dignity enough ("neither a low knave nor a blustering ruffian") to be credible as the King. The critic of the *Globe*, though a little startled to find Hamilton concealed in a blonde wig and moustache, thought him "to the manner born" and liked the way he "doted on the Queen with loving eyes and tender caresses." The *Era* (January 8) ranked him second to Booth in the company, though it complained of his occasional indistinctness of speech; and the *Citizen's Round Table* (January 8) had never seen a more artistic representation of the guilty but sometime noble Claudius. Only the *Sunday News* (January 16) took serious exception, finding him "too dapper for a Danish monarch, whom we should expect to find of a more rugged type, and of an age better fitting him to mate with Hamlet's mother."

D. Wilmarth Waller (1823-82), who played the Ghost, was Booth's stage manager, and he would continue to hold that position until Booth lost his theatre in 1874. A classical tragedian of long experience but no great reputation, he had spent most of his career in the far West, where Booth had acted under his management in the 1850's. His wife Emma, a much stronger actor than he, also belonged to Booth's company, and on the Saturday nights when *Hamlet* did not play, she was starring as Meg Merrilies and as Bianca in *Fazio*. Waller's Ghost, tall and black-bearded, armored and gauze-clad, appears to have done his spiriting in typical nineteenth-century *ore rotundo* style, dividing the critics down the middle. William Winter, of course, praised "the fine and solemn dignity of the character, and the awful halo of mystery surrounding it," and declared that "the text was read with fervid meaning and simple beauty." Half a dozen other reviewers joined in the praise. Inevitably, however, the less reverential found him a figure of fun. The *Dispatch* (January 9) bade him divest himself of the "Presbyterian sing-song style." Nym Crinkle sarcastically referred him to Andrew Jackson Davis, the notorious spiritualist: "It was in all respects a model ghost, stepping out like a pedestrian, holding its mace over the left shoulder in statuesque dignity, vocalizing with all Mr. Waller's music of intonation, strong in the traditional dolefulness upon one note."

Blanche de Bar (1844-1930), the daughter of Booth's brother Junius Brutus, was the Ophelia. Booth had brought her into his stock company in the spring of 1869 to make her New York debut as Pauline in *The Lady of Lyons*, and she had continued to play leading ingenues. Though William Winter spoke of the "true and winning sweetness" of her Ophelia, most of the critics put her down as colorless, uneven, lackadaisical, and stagey. Several of them allowed that her mad scenes were effective, and there are signs that she strengthened her playing during the course of the run. One or two found her to be too much the modern Miss to stand as Polonius' daughter, and the daily critic of the *World* objected to her "flaxen wig of most bewitchingly modern frizzle."

D. C. Anderson (1813-84), the Polonius, was a dear old "dogan" [14] who had first gone on the New York stage about the year Booth was born, had never amounted to much as an actor, but had been Booth's closest companion during the San Francisco days and the Australian adventure in the early 1850's. Booth hired "Uncle Dave" about the end of 1869 specifically to play Polonius, and he would keep him in money and sometimes in employment as long as

[14] "Dogan" was Booth's word for a professional actor of no great competence.

he lived. Anderson's forte, if anything, was old men. Rather surprisingly Nym Crinkle saw in him "an actor of strong good sense and much experience," but most of the critics passed him over as lacking dignity, or too senile, or simply not up to the part.

Augustus Pitou (1843-1915), the young man who played Horatio, had made his stage debut under Booth as the Priest in *Hamlet* at the Winter Garden in 1867. He belonged to the Booth Theatre stock company for about two years, playing such parts as Escalus in *Romeo and Juliet*, Louis XIII in *Richelieu*, and Florizel in *The Winter's Tale.* He somewhat resembled Booth, and years later in an interview with the *Dramatic Mirror* he recalled that on the opening night of Booth's Theatre when he came on as Escalus the audience mistook him for Booth and gave him an embarrassing ovation. The resemblance was noticed, even under his blond wig, when he played Horatio. Most of the critics called him "sympathetic" or "correct." But Nym Crinkle could not endure him: "His sharp, shrewd precision of manner and utterance . . . sets the teeth on edge. Mr. Pitou is not, nor can he be, the attached, the philosophic, the unpretending Horatio. . . . He is a martinet, a slightly waspish second Hamlet, whose whole life has been a struggle with consonants and inflections and emphasis."

William E. Sheridan (1839-87), the Laertes, was a versatile young actor whose previous experience had largely been in melodrama. His Laertes struck some observers as melodramatic. During his three years at Booth's Theatre his Shakespearean roles would include Ford, Banquo, Claudio, and Polixenes.

A. W. Fenno (1815-73), the First Actor, is an interesting case of the superfluously lagging veteran. In the 1840's he had starred in countless melodramas, specializing in nautical heroes. In the 1850's he had acted the standard drama in support of Forrest, Cushman, Brooke, Couldock, Davenport, and other stars of the time. In the 1860's his career seems to have disintegrated, but when Booth put together his stock company in 1869, Fenno was ripe for dignified old men's parts: Capulet, the Duke in *Othello*, Duncan, Leonato, the Soothsayer in *Julius Caesar*, etc. A stalwart, handsome man, with high forehead, eagle eyes, and Forrestian beard and moustache, he brought authority and a touch of palmy-days flamboyance to the First Actor.

Henry Hinton, the Marcellus, a minor actor with Booth at the Winter Garden as well as at Booth's Theatre, is more to be remembered for his work as a theatrical editor and publisher. His acting editions of Booth's plays, which he brought out in the 1860's and early 1870's, have been discussed above (pp. 55-57).

Arthur Matthison (1826-83), the Bernardo, was likewise a more interesting figure than his small part in *Hamlet* would suggest. Of English origin, he was a professional singer and in a minor way a man of letters. From 1866 on he appeared on New York stages in musical concerts, or reading a lecture on Dante, or reciting original poems. At Booth's Theatre in the 1869-70 season he won conspicuous praise for his acting and "sweet" tenor singing of Henry Bertram in *Guy Mannering;* and, as we have been, Booth was indebted to him for composing the souvenir pamphlet, *Booth's Theatre: Hamlet.* He also dramatized Tennyson's *Enoch Arden* for the Booth's Theatre production during the preceding summer. After another season or two of performing in New York, at Daly's, Booth's, and Niblo's, he returned to London, where he was a popular club man and wit. In the last decade of his life he wrote about twenty plays.

Thomas J. Hind (1815-81), the Rosencrantz, was also English, and during his early London career in the latter 1830's he had shared with a brother in the publication of *Hind's English Stage.* From 1849 on he had been a reliable small-part actor in many New York theatres.

Of the rest of the company Nelson Decker (fl. 1864-84), the Guildenstern, and Henry Hogan (d. 1905), the Francisco, were small-part actors who had been with Booth at the Winter Garden; Charles Norris (1846-89), the Osric, later played in support of Mary Anderson and Julia Marlowe; T. F. Brennan, the Second Actor, and William Drummond, the Priest, were undistinguished minor actors; Charles Peters (fl. 1854-71), the First Gravedigger, had been a popular comedian at several New York theatres in the 1850's and 1860's, and W. S. Andrews, who stood in for Peters on the opening night, had dug graves for Booth previously at the Winter Garden; Charles Rosene (fl. 1869-89), the Second Gravedigger, was a younger comedian who wandered sporadically through various New York theatres during the next two decades. Master Willie Seymour (1855-1933), the Actress, was the son of the actor James Seymour and had been on stages since the age of seven. He served as callboy at Booth's Theatre and afterward enjoyed a long and distinguished career as a stage manager and director. At Booth's Theatre (but not afterward) Booth assigned the role of the Actress to a boy in order to preserve the historical point that in the Shakespearean theatre women did not act.

Booth's Hamlet and the Critics

The Ghost of William Shakespeare, speaking through the columns of the New York *Leader* (January 8), declared to Booth: "From the rising of the curtain until the going down thereof, you are *my* Hamlet." In that season the New York critical fraternity for the most part needed no ghost from the grave to tell them this. Review after review triumphantly proclaimed that Booth was the very Hamlet of Shakespeare, America's only Hamlet, the Hamlet of the century.

There were dissidents, of course, and the most articulately virulent of these, Nym Crinkle of the Sunday *World*, shall speak his piece presently. It is best, however, to examine first the critic of the *Times*, whose evaluation of Booth's Hamlet on this occasion seems of them all the least partisan, the most scrupulous and judicious. The review is unsigned, of course, and there are no clues to break the anonymity. The writer was plainly no novice, but a man of middle age with much experience in playgoing on both sides of the Atlantic; and whether by choice or by commission, he undertook his assignment with unusual care. He did not, in the way of ordinary reviewers, spin off a post-midnight effusion, keeping barely a hundred words ahead of the typesetters, but divided his task into three parts and worked up each part with due deliberation. On January 6 he released a very brief notice only to acknowledge the over-all success of the production. His major statement, delayed until January 7, is a learned and considered essay devoted entirely to Booth's performance. On Sunday, January 9, he added thoughtful notes on scenery and costume together with criticism of the principal supporting actors.

His critique of Booth acknowledges at once that Booth's Hamlet is the best that the present generation has seen—perhaps the best that an American has ever offered. He only wishes in saying this that it signified more; there have been no Bettertons, Garricks, or Kembles in our time against whom Booth might be tested. He mentions briefly the shortcomings of those major actors—Forrest, Macready, Charles Kean, Junius Brutus Booth, and Brooke—who have played Hamlet in New York within living memory. Then he reviews Booth's career: how after unpromising beginnings he caught attention—"as swift and bright things always do"—by his rapid bound up the professional ladder. For several years now Hamlet has been the source and test of his fame, and the first reason for this has been the peculiar rightness of his physique and temperament. "His spare and almost attenuated frame, his thoughtful, and, indeed, habitually mournful expression; his hollow, low-pitched voice; his splendid dark eye; his jetty, disheveled locks, and a certain morbidness that is suggested by his whole look and bearing, carry conviction to the mass of beholders that in him they see as near an approach as possible to the Hamlet of Shakespeare." If Hamlet should indeed "have yellow hair and sunny blue eyes, be 'fat and scant of breath' " (here the critic is thinking of the oncoming Hamlet of Charles Fechter), the public does not think so, and quite justly it clings to the image which Booth gives them.

Booth's Hamlet, he says, "is in truth a remarkably well-studied and harmonious piece of acting. It is a product of much patient thought, and of a rigid determination to achieve in the character the utmost that nature and art will permit." He declines the tedious exercise of discussing new readings and points of stage business, mentioning only two or three which appear to be improvements. It seems to him that in general Booth is too intent upon introducing novelties whether or not they are strictly appropriate (but he does not prove this charge with instances).

Booth's temperateness of vocal display, although praiseworthy for its rejection of "robustiousness," sometimes disappoints us by causing him to fall short of the expected passion of the scene. For "it is undeniable that . . . there is a want of fire and *electricity* in the great test scenes of Mr. Booth's *Hamlet* which is inconsistent with the requirements of the part and with the artist's own reputation." He excepts the Nunnery scene and the Ghost scenes from this stricture, but again he insists that "in passages of violent declamation, Mr. Booth appears to lack power."

Booth's more successful moments are those of "subtle and complicated indications of character." In these, however, his body somewhat betrays him. He is languid rather than easy. His gesticulation is angular. He has "an unpleasant habit of sinking the head between the shoulders, of *crouching*, as it were," in attitudes better suited to Richard III than to Hamlet. He keeps his upper lip too stiff, uses the lower lip and shows the under teeth almost exclusively, in a manner that produces excessive sibilance and gives him an air of "virulent ferocity." If these are small faults, still they are worth correcting in order to improve a performance already notable for care to minutiae.

Altogether he finds Booth's Hamlet a very interesting and very fine performance. "If it fails to excite our enthusiasm by the force of unquestionable genius, it commands our respect by its fidelity, its self restraint, its obvious reverence for art, and the admirable influence of its example." It is not like reading Shakespeare by flashes of lightning, but rather "by a steady light which illumes the beauties of his magnificent poetry, and reveals the intricacies of his teeming imagination with an equable and instructive ray." For close study of the text Booth must be awarded the heartiest praise; and for the over-all splendor of his production he deserves "the honor and gratitude of the community."

These opinions of the *Times* critic reflect a conservative taste, molded by the more muscular and musically bolder school of acting of the past generation. He would not willingly surrender the old criterion of "power." When he speaks of "fire and electricity," he is thinking of those storms from heaven which Forrest and Booth's father could bring down. Yet he is generous toward Booth's new naturalness and toward Booth's "reverence for art."

Nym Crinkle, of course, is *not* generous. His review in the *World* (January 9), from which I have already culled his observations on the scenery and costume, is a tumultuous rumble of attack. Booth's Hamlet, he says, is "the perfect expression of the artistic taste of our times," but the taste of our times is for "the substitution of finish for feeling, elaborateness for earnestness, accuracy for emotion." Our theatre-going public "leans strongly toward realism. It is inclined to look upon tragedy as overdone weakness." Granted that Booth is the greatest *artist* in the American theatre today, yet "I question whether he ever had a positive and well grounded conviction sufficient to cover the entire role of Hamlet." The trouble with Booth, paradoxically, is that he is "a purely intellectual man." The great actors of Hamlet in the past did not apply to the role the "microscopic eye of reason"; they seized upon the character "with their instincts or their feelings." They may have got it wrong, but they knew what they meant and they expressed it unmistakably. Their audiences, too, knew what they meant, because from season to season they were always the same Hamlets, altering their performances only to sharpen or deepen their first conceptions with improved techniques of expression. But Booth, who "never grasped the whole of the work with the assimilative force of sympathy and understanding," is forever altering his Hamlet. When he came back from London in 1862 he played it so differently that everyone concluded he had been studying Fechter. He has now changed it in many further ways—some of them improvements, some merely inexplicable novelties. He is now less brutal toward Ophelia, but his flashes of tenderness have no apparent motive. His tenderness toward the Ghost is "superlatively fine" and a vast improvement over the superstitious terror invoked by all our other Hamlets; but his sardonic bantering of the Ghost at "Ha, ha, boy, sayst thou so," etc., is painfully at odds with the tenderness which he has just exhibited; and later, when he confronts the Ghost in the Closet scene, he unaccountably reverts to superstitious terror.

At times he "forces the language into declamatory *tours de force*" when he ought to be natural. Passages that ought to be meditative and melancholy are overwrought and intense. At moments of strong action, as at the killing of the King, Booth belies Hamlet's habits of indecision by "impetuous recklessness."

The trouble with Booth is that he is merely eclectic, repeating in bits and pieces what other actors have done before him. Thus the utmost compliment Nym Crinkle can offer is that Booth's Hamlet is "the most splendid Mosaic that I have ever seen upon the stage, and for that matter, I believe the most splendid ever executed anywhere."

A week later he returns to the subject briefly. He has taken a new measure of Booth by observing the response of his audience. Since all Booth has to offer is technical perfection, "intelligence sits primly up in front and weighs him by sentences, and gravely acquiesces in his points without a ruffle of emotion or a thrill of enthusiasm." For contrast one should observe the audience at a play like Taylor's *Mary Warner* or Tom Robertson's *Ours*. There one is "out of the pedantry and priggishness of *technique* at once into the warm atmosphere of expectation, with a human interest glowing in all faces, and every man, woman, and child content to leave his and her foot-rule and scales at home, and for an hour or two give themselves up to an illusion which looks like life."

On February 5, as guest critic for the second full-dress review in the *Spirit of the Times*, Nym Crinkle reiterates his main objections with toughened assurance. By now he declares that *no competent critic at this day* "claims that the actor impersonates the character with a deep inner conviction of its meaning." He has picked up the major reservation of the *Times* critic, which he now calls *the oft-repeated charge* "that Mr. Booth's Hamlet lacks electricity or fire." At Booth's hands the role is merely "ornamented . . . with the refinements of what may be called stage culture"; dressed up with "superadded embellishments, selected with much searching from all that is good in many generations of Hamlets." Booth is an "Edward Everett of tragedy."

Nym Crinkle was manifestly out of sympathy with Booth, and he would assume any posture, seize upon any evidence, false or fair, to cut Booth down. In giving so much space to his roughneck opinions I do not intend to convert anyone to his attitude toward Booth, which was hostile, destructive, and all but malign. In fairness to Nym Crinkle, though, it should be recognized that he was after bigger game. However bumptious and dogmatic he was, he aimed his attacks at the general cultural softness which was seeping through the country. Like a minor Aristophanes he hurled blows and roars against the genteel ivory-towerism, the false estheticism, the romantic nostalgia, the cult of prettiness and preciosity which governed "official" art in America during the last third of the nineteenth century. No one reads Thomas Bailey Aldrich any more, that faint-hearted apostle of Beauty, that "twilight poet, groping quite alone": from time to time, though, we ought to read him, in order to be reminded that in those days the likes of Aldrich, not Walt Whitman, was the going American notion of a poet. It was against the same sterility of mind and spirit that produced the Aldriches that Nym Crinkle was battling. In attacking Booth, at whatever expense of truth, he was attacking a growing cultural effeteness and loss of morale.[15]

Perhaps it was the theatrical reviewing of William Winter as much as Booth's acting that set Nym Crinkle's teeth on edge. Winter was Booth's most loquacious champion, and in the world of theatrical criticism (in poetastery, too) he was an Aldrich counterpart.

The ink which William Winter always wrote with was literally purple, and the style which he affected when he "loved" something was purple too. Or it used to be. By now it has faded to an obfuscatory murk. Unfortunately he loved Booth, and he gushed buckets of

[15] For all his hostility to Booth, Nym Crinkle is a long cut above such jackals of the trade as William Stuart, John Moray (August R. Cazauran), and Joe Howard, who wrote about Booth abusively. What Crinkle wrote was criticism, however prejudiced; those others dealt only in sneers, scandal-mongering, and personal attack.

purple ink to celebrate the "informing charm," the "beautiful spirit," the "liveliest imagination," the "heartiest feeling," the "loftiest magnanimity," the "most sweet and gentle refinement," the "mysterious halo of romance and pathos" which he found in Booth's Hamlet. These terms are drawn from a single sentence of his morning-after review in the *Tribune,* and they do not quite exhaust that treasury.

The *Times* critic saw only Booth's outsides, so to speak, set down coolly what he saw, and judiciously measured the effect it had upon him. We are informed. Winter presumes to see Booth's insides, to identify with Booth's mind, to become Booth, to play the Hamlet role with his pen. We lose all sight of the actor in a rush of purple words. Having expectably declared that "the Hamlet of Mr. Booth seems, in our thought, to be the literal Hamlet of Shakespeare," he piles up a sentence over a hundred words long to develop this mighty theme. To ease the reader's attention I shall set up this sentence clause by clause, as if it were a passage from *Leaves of Grass,* of whose style, indeed, it may be taken as a sort of flowery parody. Hamlet is

> a princely gentleman, exquisitely sensitive in
> temperament and delicate in manner;
> whose fond and faithful heart has been broken by
> affliction and grief;
> whose imagination has been o'erfraught, and whose
> reason has been dazed by communion with the
> spiritual world;
> whose nervous organization, strung to the highest
> pitch, is tremulous as a lily-leaf to every breath
> of feeling and circumstance;
> whose sad-eyed wisdom sees the futility of everything
> on earth;
> whose mind, oppressed by all-sufficient motive and
> necessity for action, yet saturated with the sense
> of human nothingness, is perplexed in the extreme;
> and
> whose soul, carrying the mortal life as the weariest
> of burdens, gropes darkly toward immortality.

The problem is to find the actor—or even to find the character, since Winter has assured us that they are one and the same—under the smoke of words.

Winter had a second style—the rasping or shrewish—which he used when he needed to thrash opposition. It served him in a pseudonymous notice in *Turf, Field and Farm* (February 18), soon after the debut of Fechter's Hamlet, when he wanted to declare that "carping criticism loses its point when ninety-nine hundredths of the best minds of the country have endorsed Mr. Edwin Booth's Hamlet as the true Hamlet of Shakespeare"; to denounce "the utter folly of any critic in assuming that Hamlet . . . was three or four inches taller than Edwin Booth, and that because the ancient Danes were a tow-headed people, the representative of the Prince of Denmark should wear a carrotty wig, with eyebrows to correspond, and have blue or gray eyes"; to defend Booth as "neither a brawler, a bully, nor a prize-fighter, nor one given to the folly of 'tearing a passion to tatters.' " This is spunky, and though it drops toward Nym Crinkle's level, it keeps one awake. But his proper style was the inflated idealizing. In a valedictory review in the *Tribune* (March 21), having asserted once more, tirelessly, the absolute identity of Booth's Hamlet with Shakespeare's, he soars again:

He is inexpressibly gentle. No leaf of lily was ever finer or purer than Hamlet's instincts of courtesy are to his fellow men. His youth has been noble and manly. He has honored father and mother with that beautiful filial affection which is rooted in the soul, and which shows the angel in man. . . . This is that Hamlet which we see in Mr. Booth's representation, and that seems to us admirable because—among other reasons—it is Shakespeare's creation. To lose it is to lose a joy and a benefit.

Over the years Booth's performing inspired Winter to many, many thousands of words of such "faultless prose," under which, as under a floral blanket, Booth's features have been concealed. Any page or two of the boyish but sharp-eyed reporting by the novice Charles Clarke helps us now, more than ever Winter can, to see Booth's acting as it really was.

The less conspicuous critics approved of Booth's performance in an enthusiastic chorus. Here and there, to be sure, someone took exception to what seemed to him artificial elocution or misplaced emphasis or the staginess of certain bits of business: in notes accompanying the reconstruction of Booth's Hamlet in Part II of this book, I have cited the more interesting of these exceptions where they fall relevant. A dozen or more reviewers expressed delight at how much Booth had improved the role since they had last seen him at the Winter Garden. Criticism laid by its knives and turned to affirmation, to celebration, to prophecy. "It seems to us, then," said the *Sunday Times* (January 9),

of secondary importance whether, at such and such a point, Mr. Booth stands or sits, whether he crouches or lies prone, whether his readings correspond with the traditional vernacular of the stage, or with the ingenious wrestings of some tiresome commentator. . . . It is as true that every great actor has some one role which will be representative of him to posterity, as that every great poet will rest superlative claims to remembrance upon some one poem. Hamlet is such a role with Mr. Booth.

The *Sun* confessed that "most of us have surrendered our judgments, accepted his idea as final, and have ceased to think of Hamlet as other than the man that this great actor has pictured him to us." For most of its beholders, Booth's Hamlet was beyond argument.

What Booth's Hamlet Meant to Charles Clarke

Certainly it was beyond argument for Charles Clarke, the youthful spectator from whose recording of Booth's Hamlet my description of it mainly derives. Clarke had no doubt about the meaning of the performance, and though no master of generalization, he did not hesitate to define Booth's conception. As he put it most succinctly at the end of his account of the Prayer scene, Booth shows us a Hamlet who is "a man of first-class intellect and second-class will." As he explained repeatedly—at the end of the Play scene, at the end of the last act, and elsewhere—this Hamlet is capable of innumerable *small* determinations. He can confront a ghost with courage; can ridicule Polonius, entrap Rosencrantz and Guildenstern, or lay out a plot to catch the King's conscience with perfect efficiency; on a stroke of impulse he can thrust his sword into a spy behind a curtain. But every time the *great* challenge confronts him—to kill the King—his will boggles. And at the end of the play, when almost by accident, without thinking, he has done the deed, he staggers from the throne irresolute and bewildered: "His conscientiousness was outraged. His will was appalled, for it had overdone itself."

This is refreshing. Here is none of Nym Crinkle's theatrically sophisticated but niggling complaint about "electicism," none of William Winter's maudlin poetizing about the "mysterious halo of romance and pathos." It is the response of a sensitive and sensible young man who approached the performance with an uncluttered mind and studied it with extraordinary care. Remarkably, Clarke had never laid eyes on Booth until he saw him as Hamlet, so that his first impression was quite free of prejudgments or irrelevant associations. The impact of the experience was overwhelming. "I went away that night awestruck," he writes, "with every faculty in my brain intensely active; with my heart in a whirl and my very soul wondrously aroused." Before he was to write his account of the performance he would see it, all told, eight times.

Clarke's reading of the character is a moral reading—this "man of first-class intellect and second-class will"—but a much tougher moral than the idealizing, hearth-and-home critics of the day could have entertained. For them, it would seem, the play, staled by repetition, hardly worked any more as a dramatic experience, and its hero was only a still-life study of good behavior, the model-book of a gentleman. For Clarke the play was a deeply moving tragedy—not a mere illustrated lecture nor merely a sweet-sad picture of a pathetic situation. It was a *caused* tragedy, and he coolly set down the cause as it appeared to him, without abstracting little lessons from it.

The effect which the tragedy, and Booth's performance of it, exerted upon Clarke was strong, and it worked as probably Aristotle's remark about catharsis meant it should work: it released new energies in him, awakened his powers of perception. The experience was exhilarating, and literally, as we shall see, health-giving. In a charming aside near the end of his task of writing—a "rhapsody" he calls it—Clarke speaks of "all that Booth has done to drill my mind, and put an edge upon my sensibility; and instruct my emotions, and inform my imagination." Whenever he thinks of these things, he says, "my first impulse is to arise and reach up my arms and cry with vague longing and admiration and humility, Oh Booth! Booth! as if his identity and power were somewhere just overhead and I was looking up toward them as to some source of mental health and light." This is confessional talk; said aloud it would sound naive. But a century later it seems a finer tribute to Booth's Hamlet than many a thousand words of official encomium that were published in Booth's time.

Beyond this, months after the experience and at the close of his labors in recording it, Clarke would essay a general definition of Booth's art in the role:

> Booth's Hamlet is not natural. Shakespeare's Hamlet is not natural. Shakespeare's Hamlet is full of art, full of rhetoric, full of versification. Booth's Hamlet is full of art, full of mechanical rhetoric, full of that poetry of way and method which in the actor is akin to the versification of the poet. Both are ideal—too ideal for life. Yet both are full of human nature.
>
> It is unsafe and false to play Hamlet *practically.* I did not like Fechter, because he played it in a realistic way. No piece that is written

in poetry can be played prosaically. It must be expressed in a higher form than the literal and commonplace expression of matter of fact. It represents possibility—not reality. It appeals to one's sense of what might be—it does not represent actual occurrence.

Booth's Hamlet is poetical; essentially lifelike, but life elaborated and thrown into rhythmical shape.

In an age of periphrastic prose, only an unschooled youth talking to himself could say so much so simply. How he arrived at such a phrase as "life elaborated and thrown into rhythmical shape" is one of those miracles of the innocent imagination working without fetters.

✠

PART II

BOOTH'S HAMLET RECONSTRUCTED

CHAPTER V

The Documents

Twice during his thirty-eight-year career in *Hamlet* Booth was able to give the play total production—that is, to cast and direct his own company of actors in it and to present them in dresses and scenery especially designed under his own supervision. The first of these occasions was at the Winter Garden in the autumn of 1864, when he launched what came to be known as the "Hundred Nights *Hamlet*." The second, in January of 1870, was at Booth's Theatre, which he had lately designed, built, and equipped for the perfect exhibition of all that was best of American theatre art.

The Winter Garden *Hamlet* has always claimed the attention of historians and biographers. It was the first time that *Hamlet* had been "produced" in America; it was the first time in America that any Shakespeare play had been given so long a run; it put the capstone on Booth's early career and fixed his reputation as America's leading tragic actor. Yet the 1870 *Hamlet* at Booth's Theatre, although it made no "firsts" and broke no records, was intrinsically the more important of the two. In 1870, at the age of thirty-six, Booth as an actor was at the peak of his energy and ambition. Having deepened his art since the "Hundred Nights" with several more years of experience, and having built his own theatre, he was at the peak of authority too. And even if, as we have seen, the 1870 *mise-en-scène* was rather a revival than a new conception, yet the scene painters could exploit the vast spaces and the wonder-working stage machinery of Booth's Theatre so that all seemed to the audiences not only new but beyond imagination to improve upon.

The public and critical reverberation was far greater in 1870 than in 1864. The Winter Garden *Hamlet* came out at a time when the public was distracted by the seemingly endless years of war; and although they responded to the production in sufficient numbers to keep it going, it appears to have been as much by William Stuart's ingenuity in publicizing as by popular demand that it reached its record run. The critics at first treated it as a notable, but "only another," Booth *Hamlet;* and not until the statistical hundredth night had been achieved was it ticketed as an event for the history books. By 1870, on the other hand, the public, released from care and swept up into confidence on the wave of postwar expansionism, was disposed to indulge in "culture." Booth's pre-eminence, not only as an actor but as a popular cultural agent, was all but universally recognized. To applaud him was to applaud one's self; it was almost, too, an act of patriotism. Fascinated by his person, his reputation, and his marvelous theatre, the public crowded to *Hamlet* nightly. The press was now ready for him also. I have counted nearly seventy substantial reviews and analyses of the 1870 production, most of them glowing appreciations, and the journalists' news notes, announcements, and lesser mentions run into the hundreds.

My description of Booth's *Hamlet*—his production and his performance both—is that of 1870. Significant differences in his earlier and later treatments of the play are recorded in the running notes. This description derives from the following primary documents.

1. The Charles Clarke Manuscript.[1]

In the summer of 1870 a twenty-one-year-old admirer of Booth named Charles W. Clarke, not an actor nor otherwise affiliated with the theatre, but a "mere playgoer," wrote out a massive recording of Booth's performance of the Hamlet role. In this amazing work Clarke endeavored to capture every one of Booth's movements, gestures, looks, and vocal effects which could be expressed in writing. As Murray Bundy observed when he first called attention to Clarke's

[1] The Clarke manuscript, which is in the Folger Shakespeare Library, is listed in my *Shakespeare Promptbooks: A Descriptive Catalogue* (Urbana, Ill., 1965) as HAM, 86.

manuscript in the *Shakespeare Quarterly*,[2] it is perhaps the fullest record of any Shakespearean performance before the advent of the motion picture and the sound track. Clarke's work provides, of course, the main bulk of the ensuing account.

Clarke was a native of Forestville, Connecticut, born there on December 31, 1848. At the age of eighteen he went to work for the commercial firm of N. B. Phelps and Company in New York City. He attended an evening school in New York, and also pursued his juvenile literary career, which had begun when he was seventeen with the acceptance of a story for Frank Leslie's *Chimney Corner*. On January 18, 1870, he went to *Hamlet* at Booth's Theatre, and there for the first time saw Edwin Booth. The experience moved him profoundly.

Determined to make the most of it he plunged into an intensive study of the play. To begin with, he memorized it: "I learned the play of Hamlet word for word from beginning to end, until I knew it so thoroughly that, any person reading off to me four consecutive words in it, I could immediately take up the matter at the end of the four words and recite with absolute accuracy to the end of the scene, act, or play as might be desired." He repeated passages to himself to test the meanings of the lines and determine in his own judgment the correct accents and inflections. He read reviews of Booth's performance and studied every criticism of the play that he had access to. "Then I went to see Booth. I saw him eight times."

During that spring Clarke's health was failing, so that about the end of May he gave up his job in the city and rejoined his family—first, briefly, at Forestville, and then, since the "old homestead" was being sold, at the farm of a brother-in-law at Bushnell's Basin near Rochester, New York. Clarke was eager to continue his education in the fall, but his health was so poor that everyone counseled him against it. His spirits were good, however, and his hopes high. "The future—" he wrote, "that is for me. It is full of promise." Throughout the summer he busied himself putting his notes and memories of Booth's Hamlet in order. He must have written the whole of it (nearly 60,000 words) more than once, for the manuscript we have is "fair copy," with very few strike-outs, insertions, or corrections.

[2] "A Record of Edwin Booth's *Hamlet*," *Shakespeare Quarterly*, II (April, 1951), 99-102. The following information about Clarke is partly taken from Murray Bundy's account and partly from Clarke's obituary in the *Spokane Review*, January 1, 1941.

This labor of love proved a restorative. "I never had a study that I enjoyed more than I did the study of Booth's Hamlet," he wrote at the end of it; "never one that repaid me better for the time and attention bestowed. . . . It increased my faculty of judging character, my power of appreciating art, my understanding of Shakespeare, my understanding of myself."

When fall came he was sufficiently recovered that he could enroll, as he had hoped to do, at the Rochester Free Academy. By the time he was graduated, three years later, his budding career as a writer seems to have given way before the tough demands of existence. He married in that year, and in the words of his daughter Emma, "the task of earning a living for his family prevented him from carrying out his literary ambitions."

In 1886, accompanied by two brothers, he took his wife and children (eventually there were eight children) to the Pacific Northwest, where he went into the cattle business on the Moran prairie near Spokane, founded the town of Post Falls, Idaho, operated a match factory there, became commissioner of Kootenai County. In 1893 he moved to Spokane, where for ten years he was engaged in the real estate business and later in a security company and a fruit company. From 1920 to 1940 he and a son operated the Bonded Adjustment Company of Spokane. During his fifty-four years in the West, according to his daughter Emma, he made and lost several small fortunes. He died in Spokane on the last day of 1940, his ninety-second birthday.

Sometime after his death Emma Clarke discovered his Booth manuscript, hitherto unknown except in the family circle, and gave it to the Folger Shakespeare Library. It is written in a large journal book ($9 \times 10\frac{1}{2}$ inches) manufactured for use in the year 1870. The pages, of unlined paper, are double-columned, with a calendar date printed at the top of each column. Clarke's tiny, graceful, regular, and extraordinarily legible handwriting fills 214 of these columns (see Plate XIX).

Clarke prefaces his work with two and a half columns explaining the circumstances under which he first saw Booth and his decision to write this account; two columns of remarks about Booth's Theatre, its scenic appointments, and the audience; and four columns about Booth's mind, manner, and physique. Then he begins the play. Since Hamlet does not appear in the first scene, Clarke disposes of it in a very few lines; the second scene, which is 210 lines long as Booth played it, he describes in twenty columns, or about 5,600 words. His method throughout is to mention sets and surroundings only briefly, but to describe the appearance of Booth's Hamlet exhaustively; to report the words of other characters only enough to give Hamlet his cues or to keep the sense going, but to record every word of Hamlet's speeches and to explicate them with succinct notations of sound and accompanying action. At the end of each scene or important passage he pauses in his recording to reflect upon what has passed—to generalize upon Booth's acting, to interpret the larger meanings of the scene, to express its effect upon himself, sometimes to enter an objection.

He underscores words once, twice, or (rarely) thrice to indicate degrees of stress: these stresses I have reproduced by the usual italics, small capitals, and large capitals. Sometimes he underscores with a wavy line, by which *perhaps* he means a vibrato—but since he nowhere explains this mark I have not differentiated it from ordinary italic stress. By curving lines underneath pairs or groups of words he indicates that the words were phrased together; I have expressed this effect with hyphens: "And yet, to *me*, what-is-this *quintessence* of *dust?*" On rare occasions he writes a word uphill or downhill to indicate rising or falling inflection (or, to use *his* common terms for it—"upward accent" or "downward accent"): this device being typographically impractical I have translated the effect into his own usual verbal formulae.

Having quoted a word or phrase or line and marked it, Clarke then inserts between parentheses whatever needs to be recorded: such vocal effects as upward or downward accent, pause, pitch, length or quality of vowel, and tempo; the emotional coloration; such physical effects as facial expression, gesture, and movement. These parenthetical units become troublesomely crowded at times as Clarke sets them down, and in the interest of readability I have assumed a good deal of liberty in reproducing them. Apparently Clarke intended regularly to give the vocal effects first and the physical effects afterward: where he has reversed or jumbled these I have corrected the order. He has mixed his grammatical forms rather wantonly, often dropping a pattern of phrasal constructions and turning to independent sentences: for the sake of smoothness I have usually regularized the patterns and the punctuation. The greatest liberty I have taken, and perhaps a dangerous one, has been to lift out of the parentheses whole statements, especially those reporting physical effects, and to present them in the form of running narrative.[3] If the action is a simple one and seems to happen *on the word or closely after it*, I have left it in the parentheses following the word: thus, "I am *too much* (raising his left hand with the palm toward the King), i' the *sun*." If it is a comparatively elaborate action or one that seems to precede the word, I have removed it from the parentheses and set it out in advance of the word: thus, "He bends a little forward, casting his right hand a trifle toward her, the arm raised, the hand hollowed with palm upward, the index finger half pointing upward: ' 'Tis not *alone* my inky cloak, good mother.' " This pair of rules is much easier to state than to follow, and now and then I have probably misjudged the timing which Clarke had in mind but did not express. But not by much: an extremely deliberate actor, Booth took plenty of time to *show* his thought (as Clarke himself assures us) in eye, face, and hand, and often in advance of his utterance. With these observations in mind the reader should rely upon his own sense of histrionic rightness to adjust the action to the word, the word to the action.

The key words which Clarke uses to report sounds and actions always say exactly what he means, and in tinkering with his constructions I have carefully preserved those words which bear the message. His passages of general commentary, however, are often best conveyed in summary or indirect discourse and with considerable trimming. For all his keenness as a reporter, his discursive style is wobbly, and one must frequently distill his meaning out of labored or crooked wording. In his analysis of the first soliloquy, for instance, after he has said vividly and in several different ways that Booth's Hamlet would never fly into an abrupt rage, it is better not to let him flounder on into a swamp of pseudo-language: "There is always an intermediate phase shown that gives the effect of uprise and makes the passions seem either the natural ascendant rebound from a circumstance, or the climax reached by a legitimate procession of emotions." [4]

There is a certain charm in Clarke's boyish imperfections, a vitality in his very ineptitudes, and I regret that these qualities do not always survive in "translation." But this is not the main business.

[3] In recording positions and movements to the "right" or "left," Clarke always means to the right or left of the spectator. I have reversed his terms, in conformity with standard practice, so that they mean to the right or left of the actor.

[4] For an example of Clarke's most successful generalizing, see above, pp. 97-98.

It is through the information which Clarke gives us, not his style, that we can realize Booth's Hamlet.

2. The Harvard 1870 Promptbook

As recently as the summer of 1965 there was reason to doubt the reliability of Clarke's account. When I first attempted to match it with the then known promptbooks of Booth's *Hamlet* (all of later vintage), at too many important points it simply did not square. Act and scene divisions were different. Contradictions in scenic arrangements, which in turn affected stage action, seemed impossible to resolve. In the second scene, for instance, did a rising curtain discover the King and Queen seated on thrones (as in the promptbooks)? or did the King and Queen walk onto the stage, preceded by their entourage, and play the scene standing (as in Clarke)? In giving his Advice to the Players did Hamlet stand about mid-stage, somewhere near the special platform erected for the *Mousetrap* (the promptbooks)? or was this passage treated as a separate scene played well downstage in a sort of hallway or anteroom (Clarke)? Did Hamlet enter his mother's chamber through an upstage center archway (the promptbooks)? or from a door at one side of the stage (Clarke)? Was the final scene played on a fairly simple one-level stage (the promptbooks)? or in the great staircase set, its upper levels crowded with courtiers and attendants (Clarke)? On the one hand, Clarke's honesty of intention seemed unimpeachable; yet if he erred in such major matters, his entire document was put in question. The late Pat Carroll, custodian at The Players, who knew the promptbooks well, was convinced that Clarke's account was not to be trusted.

In December of 1965 the key to unlock the mystery came to hand. The Harvard Theatre Collection acquired Booth's own souvenir promptbook of 1870, with text cut as the play was then performed, with the stage manager's notes of scenic arrangement and basic stage business recorded in official, no-nonsense manner, and with watercolors of ten sets. The first value of this promptbook is that in nearly every point which had been moot it validates Clarke, defining a production upon which Clarke's description comfortably rests.

That such a promptbook once existed was known. Opposite page 1 of Edwina Booth Grossmann's volume of her father's letters is printed the final quatrain of Bulwer-Lytton's "Talent and Genius," ending with a line which Booth was fond of quoting: "And fools on fools still ask what 'Hamlet' means." This quatrain, Mrs. Grossmann says, was written in Booth's *Hamlet* promptbook "by himself." On the flyleaf of this new-found book, in purple ink and in Booth's own hand, are the very lines.

The text on which the 1870 promptbook is founded is pages 139-196 (double-columned) from volume II of the Kenny Meadows illustrated *Shakespeare* (7 × 10¾ inches). This *Shakespeare* was first published in 1843, but the copy from which the promptbook sheets were extracted was evidently of a later printing. The interleaves of the book are of blue-lined white paper, trimmed flush with the pages. The binding is brown leather boards with gilt borders front and back; with title gilt on the spine, and title and Booth's name gilt on the cover; with brown and white mottled end-papers. The prompter's annotations, written in a bold, clear hand (though not always perfectly spelled), are not generously detailed, being no more than the necessary directions for setting the stage, running the show, or instructing a new company. We find cuts, act and scene divisions, property lists, numbered calls for actors, actors' entrances and exits and major crosses, basic business of the supporting actors, frequent maps or groundplans showing where the actors are to stand, and cues for music and curtains. For Booth's distinctive stage business we must look to other sources, especially, of course, to Clarke.

This is *not* the promptbook which was used in the theatre—it shows none of the random scribbling, thumb-grease, tearing of edges, or other deterioration of an actual working copy; it was made up (and put into its fancy binding) during or after the 1870 run as a souvenir of the production. Possibly it was intended as a model for later productions in other theatres. The depth of some of the sets—for example, the opening scene before the castle—has been drastically reduced, as if to accommodate to shallower stages than that of Booth's Theatre.

The most conspicuous feature of the book is its watercolors of ten sets, the only one omitted being the hallway in which Hamlet delivered his Advice to the Players. Charles Witham, Booth's favorite scenic artist, who painted these pictures, showed no color in them, but confined his palette to black, gray, and white, with here and there a streak of brown. He did not thereby sacrifice much, nor is much more lost in black-and-white reproduction, for Booth's *Hamlet* was predominantly nocturnal (Ophelia's burial took place by moonlight!) and even in the interior scenes only sober tapestries, often dimly lighted, and a few banners and displays of armor warmed up the gray walls. This being a post-production book, in one or two scenes we catch Witham "improving" his pictures over what was actually shown on the stage. But by and large, with these watercolors before us, and with our imaginations supplying the warm colors of the costumes, we can for the first time in nearly a century visualize the total *mise-en-scène.*[5]

3. The Bensen Sherwood Stage Plans [6]

Bensen Sherwood (d. 1894), a stage manager of Booth's generation, obtained from another stage manager named Sheridan and transcribed into a huge workbook (12 × 18½ inches) the stage plans of fifty-five productions which were played at Booth's Theatre during the years 1873 and 1874. Ten of Booth's own are included, of which the first is *Hamlet.* Each set is precisely defined, every unit of it and its exact position on the stage identified in the abbreviated jargon used by stage managers to communicate with each other. By 1873 the *Hamlet* scenery had diminished somewhat: the great Hall of Arches of the second and fourth acts had been replaced by simpler makeshifts, and other economizings are to be noticed. Bensen Sherwood's principal contribution to our reckonings is his large clear groundplans of three full-stage sets—the Platform before the Castle (see Plate XX), the staircase set for the Play scene, and the Graveyard. These enable us to understand how Booth used the great depth of his stage, and how the sets were put together.

4. Edwin Booth's *Hamlet* Notebooks [7]

Preserved at The Players is an interleaved copy of the Booth-Winter edition of *Hamlet* (1878) in which Booth wrote about 230

[5] Five of Witham's watercolor scene designs done in advance of the production are preserved at the Museum of the City of New York: the first Court scene; the staircase set, called the Hall of Audience, for the Play scene (two renderings); the oratory for the Prayer scene; the Queen's Chamber.

[6] This volume of stage plans is in the Theatre Collection of the New York Public Library. It also contains plans for 135 plays staged at the Fifth Avenue Theatre from 1878 to 1884, including a Booth *Hamlet* done there with drops.

[7] These are listed in *The Shakespeare Promptbooks* as HAM, 109 and 76 respectively.

"Rough *mems* for future use. To put into proper shape at leisure." These are Booth's private notations of his own stage business, motivation, emotional colorings, pronunciations, his ideas about the secondary characters, his comments on other actors of Hamlet, and so forth. Booth made these notes late in life, probably after he retired: in 1890 he told the actor James Taylor that for the last twelve years he had had at home an interleaved book reserved for this purpose, but had never put pen to it. The book is of great use in confirming Clarke's observations and in revealing Booth's thoughts about the play.

Another notebook at The Players, based on the Booth-Hinton edition of 1866 and written up in the 1860's or early 1870's, contains similar but far fewer notes.

5. E. T. Mason's Record of Booth's Stage Business [8]

Sometime after Booth's retirement, Edward Tuckerman Mason, a literary critic and devotee of the theatre, compiled in an interleaved copy of the Booth-Winter *Hamlet* (1888) a record of all Booth's most notable stage business as Mason had observed it from 1862 to 1891. There are 234 notes, many of them supplemented by stage maps. This book is at The Players. A transcription of it, done on a 1909 issue of the Booth-Winter *Hamlet*, is at the Boston Athenaeum. Mason's especial use to us is that he dates the principal innovations in Booth's stage business.

6. The Players 1876 Promptbook [9]

At The Players is a well-marked and much-used promptbook which served Booth on tours during the 1870's down to 1877. It is based on the Booth-Hinton edition of 1866, and presumably it ceased to be used after the Booth-Winter edition came out in 1878. As a stage manager's working book, it does not add to our knowledge of Booth's personal performance, but it is useful to check certain alterations in the staging.

[8] *The Shakespeare Promptbooks*, HAM, 110 and 111.
[9] *The Shakespeare Promptbooks*, HAM, 87.

7. James R. Pitman's 1884 Promptbook [10]

In the fall of 1884 Booth joined the Boston Museum Company, and in 1885 he brought them to New York. At that time, I assume, the company's stage manager and prompter, James R. Pitman, compiled a book according to Booth's way with the play. A transcription of this in Pitman's elegantly flowing hand, autographed by Booth, is at The Players. It is one of a set of souvenir Booth promptbooks, bound in black limp leather, which Pitman made up for A. Russ Whytal, a Museum Company actor. Another Pitman book, which shows signs of use, is in the Furness Collection at the University of Pennsylvania. Both books are made on the Booth-Winter edition (1879).

8. The Harvard 1890 Promptbook [11]

This is a fully though crudely marked promptbook, based on the Booth-Winter edition (1890), which served Booth during his final season. Several pages are missing from the end. It records Booth's arrangement of the play after he went under the management of Lawrence Barrett.

9. James Taylor's 1890 Promptbook [12]

By far the fullest records of Booth's final arrangements and performances of the play were made by the actor James Taylor, who had sometimes been Booth's Horatio in the late 1860's and early 1870's and was Horatio again in 1889-90. First Taylor compiled a sort of scrapbook of the play in an interleaved Steevens edition, pasting in portraits of actors, articles on the stage history of the play, and assorted critical material, and writing into it many descriptive notes on Booth's performance. He gave this to Booth, who was delighted to have it and who added notes of his own. Lawrence Barrett an-

[10] *The Shakespeare Promptbooks*, HAM, 103; Pitman's book at Pennsylvania is HAM, 104.

[11] *The Shakespeare Promptbooks*, HAM, 107.

[12] Taylor's scrapbook is listed in *The Shakespeare Promptbooks* as HAM, 108; his promptbook owned by John Cranford Adams is not listed. Taylor described his scrapbook in an interview with the Philadelphia *Public Ledger*, September 15, 1893.

notated it further. This book is now in the Harvard Theatre Collection.

Later on, probably after Booth's death, Taylor made up another interleaved book on a Clarendon Press (Clarke and Wright) text, transcribed into it all the manuscript matter from the first book (his own notes, Booth's, and Barrett's), recorded all the cuts, entered all the standard stage manager's directions, and added many more notes on Booth's specific stage business. This book is owned by Professor John Cranford Adams. It is the Adams copy which I refer to by the rubric "Taylor 1890." Taylor was an accurate if not sensitive or imaginative reporter, and his work is a reliable anchor to Booth's final Hamlet.

10. E. T. Mason's Record of Modjeska's Stage Business [13]

In the season of 1889-90 when Booth toured with Helena Modjeska, Edward Tuckerman Mason made notations of Modjeska's business in the principal Ophelia scenes. These have nothing to do with the 1870 production, of course, but since Clarke omits the Ophelia scenes, and since Modjeska was an ideal nineteenth-century Ophelia, I have drawn upon them to fill out the record. The notes are in the Boston Athenaeum.

11. The Harvard 1866 Promptbook

In the summer of 1968 the Harvard Theatre Collection acquired a promptbook, once the property of Booth's assistant Henry Flohr, which was prepared in 1866 for touring use in Philadelphia and elsewhere. This is the earliest promptbook of Booth's *Hamlet* which has come to light, and it is the most authentic representation we are ever likely to find of the Winter Garden production of 1864-67.[14] Its text is the then newly published Booth-Hinton edition. Its interleaves, double-columned to correspond to the double-columned text, carefully instruct stage managers how to set up and run the show. An immense scene plot ($7\frac{5}{8} \times 35\frac{1}{2}$ inches) breaks down each set into structural units. A note at the head of the third act insists that local scene painters imitate the Winter Garden staircase set exactly. Al-

[13] *The Shakespeare Promptbooks*, HAM, 106.

[14] All promptbooks which were actually in use at the Winter Garden in 1867 were presumably destroyed when the theatre burned.

though I have not made many references to this promptbook in the ensuing description, it has served to confirm certain assumptions about the relationship of the Winter Garden *Hamlet* to that of 1870.

12. Other Marked Copies [15]

I have examined but not used several other marked copies which are related to Booth's work with the play before or after 1870:

a) A Tauchnitz edition of 1862 inscribed "Found by me at Winter Garden during my 'Hundred Nights' and marked for reference" (at The Players).

b) A rehearsal copy of the Booth-Winter edition given by Booth to Charles Dunphie in 1880 (at the Folger Shakespeare Library).

c) A promptbook based on the Booth-Winter edition, made up in the twentieth century by the actor Hallam Bosworth, who intermingled Booth's stage directions with those from other traditional sources (in the Theatre Collection of the New York Public Library).

d) A copy of the Booth-Winter edition (1896) containing photographs, autographs, and some notes by William Winter (at the Folger).

e) A promptbook-notebook-rehearsal copy based on the Booth-Winter edition (1878), of mixed and uncertain provenience (in the Harvard Theatre Collection). This book was sometime used by the actor or actors who played the Ghost and Rosencrantz. Someone, perhaps an orchestra leader, systematically entered every music cue. It was later used by E. T. Mason to plot out his record of Booth's stage business. Many of its notations are certainly relevant to Booth's practice, but many others, unconfirmed by other documents, are doubtful. During a part of the first soliloquy Hamlet is shown to wander up to the throne and sit on it—a very natural and suggestive business which one might wish Booth had used, but not one recorded by any other observer. During "To be or not to be" Hamlet is made to *sit* at the precise moment when according to other records he *rises*. Hamlet is uncharacteristically given to throwing things: in the scene with Ophelia he throws the "box" of remembrances up left, and in the Recorder scene he gets rid of the pipe by throwing it upstage.

[15] The following books are listed in *The Shakespeare Promptbooks* respectively as HAM, 75, 102, 112, 113, and 101.

These and many other unique notations in this book may be proved by further investigations to be valid for Booth, but since they are undatable and apparently out of keeping I have not incorporated them.

CHAPTER VI

The Performance

Act I

Act I, 1. *Elsinore. A Platform before the Castle. Moonlight.*
(Globe edition: Act I, 1. 175 lines cut to 104.)

The house lights dim, the Overture plays (the music is Gluck's Overture to *Iphigenia*), a great bell tolls midnight. On the eighth stroke of the bell the curtain rises on a scene of mystery—a moonlit view of the Castle of Elsinore (see Plate IV).[1] In the background we see, mounting in tiers toward stage left, the massive Norman castle with square keep and octagon beacon tower; toward stage right the full moon hangs low behind a drift of clouds. Downstage of the Castle its outer defenses—two crenellated walls—cross the stage. The low forward wall connects at right and left with very tall watch towers; and at the center of this wall, three steps up from ground

[1] The curtain time on Wednesday, January 5, was 8:00. A week later, as announced in all the papers, it was moved back to 7:45, "in consequence of the great length of *Hamlet,* which Mr. Booth's artistic and conscientious regard has not permitted him to abbreviate of any of its length or beauty" (*Sun*). The playing time seems to have been about four hours. The house lights (gas jets) were very much lowered, if not completely extinguished, so that in the Ghost scenes the nocturnal effects made their point. A reporter to the St. Paul *Dispatch* (February 26) tells his provincial readers, as if it would be news to them, that "while the play proceeds the audience sit in twilight, all the light as well as all the interest being concentrated on the stage." Clarke complains that all the Ghost scenes were in fact too dark: when he sat in the gallery he could make out in the fourth and fifth scenes only the outline of Booth's person.

level, is a stone portal whose arched opening is flanked by low gate towers. The second defense wall rises several feet higher than the forward one, and at stage right it too terminates at a watch tower. Downstage of the defense walls the scene is bordered at right and left with leafy trees. All is bathed in an eerie glow from green footlights, and white light of low intensity pours down from stage right.

The set is much deeper than it appears in the watercolor or than is indicated in the stage directions of the 1870 promptbook. Charles Clarke's first note on the performance is, "Scene 1st opens with nearly the whole depth of the stage in use." In the Bensen Sherwood "Stage Plans" (see Plate XX),[2] the scene is labeled "Full Stage," and the scenic units are placed as follows. The "Battlement Drop" (the tiered Castle and the moonlit sky) is hung at the sixth grooves—that is, some 42 feet beyond the curtain line.[3] In front of this drop, and just upstage of the fifth grooves, is "Set Row 10 Feet High": this is the second defense wall. Just above the fourth grooves is "Six Feet Battlement Row R & L of Arch": this is the low forward defense wall with its center portal, which is about 30 feet beyond the curtain line. In the fourth and fifth grooves at either side are "Battlement Wings" (marked "BW"), which appear in the watercolor as tall watch towers.

Crossing the stage between the first and second defense walls is a two-foot-high "Table" (that is, a platform) along which the actors pass to make their entrances at the center portal. At the stage left end of this table a flight of steps rises to a higher table concealed behind the watch tower, so that entering characters appear to be coming down from the high ground of the Castle. Fronting the center portal is a three-step unit labeled "Narcise [*sic*] Steps" (pre-

[2] The following details are taken from the account of the *fourth* scene in the Sherwood "Stage Plans." In 1873, according to the "Stage Plans," the opening scene was played in a very shallow "front set," consisting only of "Battlement Flats" at the first grooves backed by a "Moonlight Sky Border." Why this was the arrangement in 1873 I do not know. In 1870 and in all the promptbooks of later date the opening was unquestionably "full stage."

[3] The use of the term "grooves" at Booth's Theatre is merely figurative. Since Booth had now supplanted the lateral, sliding shutter system of scene changing by the vertical, rise-and-sink system, the stage floor was not literally grooved. Even the wing pieces, which did not rise and sink, appear to have been free-standing or held in place by stage braces. Yet the term "groove" persisted as a measurement of stage depth. From groove to groove was about seven feet.

sumably it was first made for Booth's 1869 production of Tom Taylor's *Narcisse*). These steps are flanked by "Boxes" or "Abutt-ments" (that is, stone railings), and from the downstage ends of these, very low walls called "2 Feet Row" run right and left to the watch towers. (These lowest walls do not appear in the watercolor and their significance is not apparent.) Down the sides of the stage at the third, second, and first grooves stand "Moonlight Wood Wings" (marked "MWW"), and supplementary "Cut Wood" pieces partly close across the third entrances.

The effect of spaciousness, of distance, in this setting astonished the beholders, as well it might. Even the arithmetic is impressive. The width of the proscenium in Booth's Theatre can only be conjectured, but such evidence as we have suggests at least 45 feet; the height of the trim was about the same figure. The distance from curtain line to the center portal was some 30 feet, and to the back-drop a dozen feet farther. The first reviewer for the *Spirit of the Times* (January 8) could exclaim that the stage was big enough to contain all Denmark "and still leave room for an additional principality or power." The vastness was enhanced by soft gas lighting, which, as Clarke says, pervaded the air "with haziness and gloom." The *Evening Post* reviewer (March 16) pays special tribute to "that unseen functionary who manages the lights. He succeeds in giving to the ghost scenes a ghostly glimmer which is peculiarly befitting the occasion, and most happily reproduces the 'pale glimpses of the moon.' By this subdued light the individuals on the stage seem as if but shadowed forth in outline, and even the two friends of Hamlet, who 'hold the watch tonight,' partake of the supernatural element which invests the whole scene."

The beauty of the scene was praised on all hands. In the *World* (January 9), Nym Crinkle found it "matchless," and he was especially charmed by "the surpassingly beautiful bit of cloud and its apparent distance and fleeciness." The *Albion* (January 8) declared that "this set for breadth, beauty and a quite super-scenic substantiality, althogether surpasses any yet placed upon the stage even at this theatre." The words "even at this theatre" were in New York in 1870 the most honorific comparison that could be bestowed.

Since Hamlet himself does not appear in this first scene, Clarke dismisses it with a few perfunctory sentences. The following account of the basic movements is derived from the Harvard 1870 prompt-book, with occasional augmentation from other sources.

1-38. "Who's there?"

On the eighth stroke of the midnight bell the rising curtain discovers Francisco as sentinel, in mascled armor and cone-shaped helmet, pacing from stage left to right across the mid-stage area. He disappears into the trees for an instant, then returns. When he has crossed again just past center, he hears a call of "Who's there?" from behind the left watch tower, as if someone were approaching from the castle. He swings round to face the portal, lowers his spear to the guard position, and challenges the comer. We see a flash of light on armor as Bernardo appears from behind the left watch tower and comes swiftly down the steps and along the platform behind the forward wall; on the words "Long live the King!" he enters through the portal and crosses down into the shadows at the right. Francisco follows him there, hands him the spear, whispers the password to him, and goes up into the portal.[4]

At about line 12, "If you do meet . . . ," the voices of Horatio and Marcellus are heard behind the left tower and at a distance, growing stronger as they approach. At "Stand, ho! Who's there?" Francisco disappears up the steps to meet them. A half-dozen quick lines are heard from offstage, and Francisco's final "Give you good night" sounds faintly as he seems to retire toward the castle. At "Holla! Bernardo!" Marcellus comes through the portal, followed by Horatio, or, as he says jestingly, "a piece of him." Bernardo advances to the center to greet Horatio and receive his handshake. Marcellus, who has gone down into the shadows at the right, introduces the business of the scene ("What! has this thing appeared again tonight?") and explains that he has brought the skeptical Horatio to be a witness.[5] Bernardo invites Horatio to "sit down awhile" to hear again the story of the Ghost's nightly visitation; and, Horatio agreeing, the two of them move upstage center and sit on

[4] *4.* Booth argues in his Notebook that the passwood is not "Long live the King!" but the responses given by Horatio and Marcellus at line 15: "Friends to this ground. And liegemen to the Dane." Francisco's business of handing over the spear and whispering the password is spelled out in the Taylor 1890 promptbook; it may have been invented later than 1870.

[5] *21.* Booth was sensitive to the skeptical overtone in the question about "this thing." In his Notebook he calls the line "contemptuous," and suggests that it "better fits Horatio's mouth, who does not believe in it." But so far as I know he always let Marcellus speak it.

the stone steps.[6] Marcellus stands to the right of them, and Bernardo begins his tale.

38-175. "Peace, break thee off; look, where it comes again!"

Marcellus is the first to see the Ghost as it appears from behind the left watch tower, and he cries out. Horatio and Bernardo leap up and break away to the left as the Ghost, helmeted and bearing a truncheon, steps into the portal. The Ghost's figure is veiled in blue-green gauze. "Every art has, of course, been used to make the apparition as unsubstantial as possible," notes a correspondent to the *Evening Post* (February 28); "the 'very armor he had on,' in color and texture, looking as if forged of cobweb; the footfall noiseless." It stands in the portal looking at the friends as they call to each other,[7] but at the end of Horatio's challenging interrogation it moves down the steps and to the right, and goes offstage right into the trees.

The troubled partners gather at center stage in a triangle—Bernardo at center, Marcellus at right, Horatio at left—and marvel at what they have seen.[8] The long matter of Fortinbras and the Norwegian wars (lines 70-125) being cut, they do not wonder long: about a minute after the Ghost's exit, it comes again—this time along the platform behind the *right* wall and again through the portal. Horatio, being at the left, is the first to see it. He drops back toward the downstage left corner. As the Ghost advances toward him, he cries out, "I'll cross it, though it blast me." [9] There

[6] *34.* The business of "sitting" at this point had not been used since the seventeenth century. Booth would want to restore it because under his principles of stage realism, sitting was a natural and welcome thing to do. He was able to restore it in 1870 because his stage arrangements provided a place to sit. In his 1878 edition, however, he suppressed the dialogue references to sitting, presumably because under touring conditions appropriate sitting places could not always be counted on.

[7] *42.* In a note he added to the Taylor 1890 promptbook, Booth justifies the traditional suppression of Marcellus' line, "Thou art a scholar; speak to it, Horatio," with the curious argument that Marcellus too is a scholar: "Hamlet presently calls him one" (I, 5, 141).

[8] *52-69.* In the latter 1880's Booth reduced this scene by having the Ghost appear only once. Thus in the Taylor 1890 and Harvard 1890 promptbooks these lines of commentary on the Ghost's behavior are transposed to follow line 139, after what is properly the Ghost's *second* exit. A penciled cut in the Winter Garden 1866 promptbook suggests that Booth sometimes used this economy in early years too.

[9] *127.* At "I'll cross it" the actor of Horatio in Charles Fechter's production made the sign of the cross. Booth scorned this. In a copy of the play

is room for him to do so—to cross its path, that is—once; but the Ghost passes on steadily toward the trees down left, and Horatio circles behind it to the center of the stage. The Ghost waits at the left exit, hears out Horatio's four-part invocation, starts as if to speak, and then disappears into the trees.[10] Horatio rushes to the exit and falls upon his knees.

After a moment of silence, Bernardo, who is at center, says, "It was about to speak when the cock crew." Horatio rises and returns to the others, and as the lights gradually work up he discourses on the legendry of cockcrow.[11] He notes the coming on of dawn, and invites the companions to carry the news with him to Hamlet, for "this spirit, dumb to us, will speak to him." All three go up through the portal, pass to the left, and climb the steps as toward the castle.[12] The orchestra strikes up flourishes to cover the scene change.

The text of Act I, 1 (line-numbering of the Globe edition).

The extensive cuts in this scene (71 lines) are traditional. These

marked in the 1870's (at The Players) he scribbled "Fechter's *cross!*" and in his Notebook he explains that the expression means "to cross the path of the ghost, which was considered fatal to him who did so."

[10] *138-146.* The dignity and mystery of this moment was not disturbed by an offstage sound of "cockcrow." The *New Variorum Hamlet*, I, 22, quotes Alexander Dyce to the effect that in Garrick's time the cock crew, "but now-a-days managers have done wisely in striking the *cock* from the Dramatis Personae." Booth tried it once when an inventor named Buggles provided him a "remarkable instrument" for imitating the sound, and, according to Thomas Bailey Aldrich, it threw the audience into convulsions of laughter. On New Year's Day, 1882, Booth sent the "instrument" to Aldrich as a plaything for his children (C. T. Copeland, *Edwin Booth* (Boston, 1901), pp. 125-127). For much the same reason—the preservation of dignity—Booth could not possibly have used the lines about striking at the Ghost, or " 'Tis here. 'Tis here. 'Tis gone," which imply that the Ghost darts about nimbly. Booth's conception of the Ghost was simply that it was majestical and awesome, to be treated with fear and respect.

[11] *158-164.* Booth restored Marcellus' lines about the cock crowing on Christmas Eve, but always gave the lines to Horatio to speak, presumably to be sure they were handled by a worthy elocutionist.

[12] After Booth left his own theatre and lost the advantage of his deep stage and rise-and-sink machinery, he had to use the act-drop here to cover the scene change. In later promptbooks (Pitman 1884, Taylor 1890, Harvard 1890) scene 1 is called "Act I," and what follows is called "Act II." There was "No Wait" here (that is, no entr'acte), but the orchestra played a march while the Court scene was being readied. The Taylor promptbook ends this "Act I" with a tableau: Horatio is at the top of the center steps and Marcellus and Bernardo are standing below, all three looking offstage where the Ghost has gone.

are: 42, 43b (the appeal to Horatio to speak to it because he is a scholar); 70-125 (Fortinbras and the Norwegian wars); 139b-146 (striking at the Ghost); 155b-157; 165; 172-175 (the "flat" ending).

There are two alterations: 65, "jump" > "just"; 158-164, Marcellus' lines are given to Horatio.

The restorations (12 lines) are as follows: 30b, 33b (directions to "sit"); 56a ("Before my God"); 62-64 (the sledded Polack); 158-164 (cockcrow on Christmas Eve).

Act I, 2. *Elsinore. A Room of State in the Castle.*

(Globe edition: Act I, 2. 258 lines cut to 210.)

The design for the Room of State (see Plate V) shows a large square hall (a box set) with walls of gray stone block much broken up by openings and heavily dressed with architectural detail. Each side wall is pierced at center by a tall round-arched entrance flanked by engaged columns which support a wide chevron (zigzag) molding framed by two roll moldings with outside dentils; in the downstage section of each side wall is a smaller arch containing a wooden door. At the center of the back wall, dominating attention, is a large round-arched entrance some nine or ten feet wide, through which we have a limited view of a farther room.

This central arch is richly ornamented in four fanciful orders. The innermost order is a cable molding; the next is a broad flat band containing medallions of three heads (the King? the Queen? Hamlet?); the next is a narrow concave molding, beaded. The outer order is a wide double chevron, framed by a roll molding with outside dentils. The arch rests upon a plain entablature, which runs across the back wall and down the side walls as far as the side arches. The entablature is supported at either side of the rear entrance by three engaged columns of fanciful design. The columns appear to be about nine feet tall.

The lower walls, beneath the entablature, are hung with tapestries depicting coats of arms and military scenes. At each upper corner of the back wall is a large wheel pattern—the rim consisting of black and gray stones, the face of the wheel pierced by round holes. At the top of the walls a chevron frieze runs straight around the three sides of the hall. Above this frieze in the back wall is an arcade of tiny blind arches. The flat ceiling is supported by heavy decorated beams running crossways of the stage, with curved buttresses at their ends.

In various details the design as given in the watercolor is inaccurate for Act I, 2. First, the two throne chairs, the dais they stand on, and the half curtain behind them are intended for the final scene of the play.[13] They are not used in the present scene, and in fact when the scene begins, the central opening is closed with double doors. Second, the arched entrances at either side should be closed with curtains. Finally, according to Charles Clarke's account, somewhere high and prominent in the set is "a coat of arms and a shield containing a raven, which is used in theatres as the insignia of The Dane." This raven motif appears in most of the other interiors of the production, and we must accept Clarke's word that it was used in this first interior also.

The change of scene, which took place in full view of the audience, was accomplished in a matter of seconds, and by all accounts it was magically effective. Happily we have an eyewitness account of it. In mid-December, 1871, soon after a revival of the production at Booth's Theatre, the Philadelphia *Evening Bulletin* published an article from a New York correspondent who signs himself "Perdu," entitled "How to Set a Great Play on the Stage." It is Perdu's intention to communicate to Philadelphians what marvels have eluded them if they have seen this *Hamlet* only when restaged in

[13] But see Act V, 3, for discussion of how the final scene was actually staged in 1870. It is a distinguishing feature of the 1870 production that this first Court scene was played *without thrones*, and the characters entered and stood rather than being seated and "discovered." The "original" design for the Court scene, which is preserved in the Witham Collection at the Museum of the City of New York, contains *no* furniture. (This original design differs from the promptbook design in two other details: the ceiling is a plain affair of planks and straight crossbeams; the side arches are closed with diamond-patterned curtains.)

The obvious reason for the "thronelessness" of the scene is that in the rise-and-sink system of scene change it was not practicable at this point to introduce furniture. The appearance of such nondramatic agents as stage carpenters, who would have to set furniture in place, was unthinkable. Even after he lost his theatre, Booth clung to the notion that the scene be played without thrones: in his 1878 edition the characters are still directed to "enter." But in all his later stagings for which we have promptbook records, the arrangements are altered. The scene change is covered by the act-drop and the scene is "discovered," the King and Queen being seated on thrones mounted on a dais upstage center, Hamlet on a stool somewhat forward of the dais and toward stage right, Polonius and Laertes at left center, and crowds of extras dressing the sides. Mason mentions that the dais was four steps high. The presence of raised thrones in these later stagings of course altered and enriched the stage picture and movements: Laertes knelt to the throne, the Queen and King spoke from the throne or came down from it to speak, etc.

the old-fashioned facilities of the Walnut Street Theatre. At Booth's Theatre, he writes:

After the initial scene displaying the moonlit ramparts at Elsinore, the first surprise is occasioned by seeing a chamber wall come rising up out of a long slit across the stage, steady, with an easy gliding motion, with nothing unsubstantial or tottering about it, but mounting to its destiny like a wall of Ilium to the harp of Orpheus. . . . The flat is met by side wings, enclosing them [*sic*] almost at right angles, and, in effect, building a real chamber on the stage, as is now the practice in all first-class theatres of Europe; a great improvement on the old-fashioned coulisses, which allow you to look between them at the carpenters and the actors waiting for their cues.

Perdu has enjoyed special privileges in Booth's Theatre: he takes us now for a rare visit behind and beneath the stage to observe magic's machinery at work:

The influence . . . which causes the scene to lift is very far from magical. Down in the cold and cavernous cellar a row of Mr. Booth's hydraulic rams, supplied from tanks near the roof, which are pumped full by Mr. Booth's subterranean steam-engine, do the business. On the stage the effect is an enchanting instance of the repose of even motion. Down below, thirty feet beneath the stage, it is a sort of Dantean pandemonium. There is a rush and stir of water, a turn of huge wheels like wings in the dusk, great pistons move, and the proper scene separates from the collection of ruins, temples, and forests stored away there, and delicately rises into the flood of stage lights and the admiration of the audience.

The audience's pleasure at this novel mode of scene changing, Perdu says, continues progressively throughout the play.

The "long slit" through which the chamber wall rises cuts across the stage immediately downstage of the third grooves, so that we can estimate the depth of the Room of State at about 20 feet. The room, one should note, stands well forward of the architectural units of the preceding Castle set, which can therefore remain undisturbed for their reappearance in scene 4. No one tells us how the downstage wood wings of the Castle set are cleared away, nor how the long side walls of the Room of State are brought into place to meet the back wall; presumably these are manual operations occurring at stage level. Bensen Sherwood's "Stage Plans" adds the following details: "Column Tormentors," which are probably "returns" to finish off the downstage ends of the side walls; "Backings" for the arched entrances at right and left; "Stone Drop in 4," which is a cloth lowered behind the central entrance to show the vista of a farther room; and "Trick Borders," which fly down to meet the chamber walls and create the ceiling. The Room of State is assembled in the hazy half-light of the preceding scene: when the transformation is completed, footlights and border lights come up to full.

The orchestra is sounding a run of flourishes during the change and while the Court is making its massive entrance.[14] The great center doors are swung open (away from us) by two wand-bearing Chamberlains, who then enter and stand at right and left of the archway. "The archway reveals a throng of courtiers," Perdu tells us, "that appear to have stepped out of the frescoes of Orcagna at the Campo Santo at Pisa; ladies with slender, long-necked elegance, their hair cushioned and draped, knights with narrow robes of spotted lilac or saffron, reaching to their feet; all coming in backwards, to prepare for the king and queen." The Courtiers, with Polonius, Laertes, and Osric among them, divide into two groups and, bowing toward the entrance, move to either side of the stage. Next comes Hamlet, who advances to right center.[15] The King bearing a truncheon, with the Queen on his right, comes forward and stands at the center. A pair of Pages stand behind them. A troop of Soldiers, two with banners and the rest with shields and axes, guard the entrance. The music stops as the King speaks. Hamlet stands toward the right, motionless, with arms folded and lips compressed, facing partly toward the audience and partly toward the King.

Hamlet is dressed in a black court suit, the skirt of which comes nearly to his knees. His legs, in fleshings, are bound with strips of dark pink cloth in crisscross pattern from the slipper to above the knee. A black furred cloak hangs from his shoulders. Around his neck hangs a steel chain to which is attached a miniature of his father.[16] A pouch and a dagger are suspended from the left side of

[14] Clarke says, "A march is sounded." The promptbook says only, "A Flourish."

[15] *1.* According to the 1878 edition, Hamlet did not enter until line 63, at the conclusion of the Laertes affair. In *Appleton's Journal* of November 20, 1875, O. B. Bunce mentions this as a recent innovation. Critics objected to the delayed entrance as an improper device for catching applause for the star. Kitty Molony reports that Booth had abandoned it before she joined his company in 1886. See Katherine Goodale, *Behind the Scenes with Edwin Booth* (New York, 1931), p. 176.

[16] The miniature was of Booth's own father (see Chapter I, footnote 7). Clarke says that Booth's costume was velvet, but presumably like the rest it was fine wool. For a full-length view of it, see the portrait by W. W. Scott (Plate XI). In the great Oliver Lay portrait at The Players, the color is deep purple. Another costume, preserved at The Players, is a floor-reaching

his girdle. "His bearing," says Clarke, "is that of one borne down with dejection. His face is sober and sorrowful. His walk is a monotread, without variety, that seems to bring him on in sullen obedience to the courtesy of the occasion. His head is bent forward and his looks are downcast."

1-63. "Though yet of Hamlet our dear brother's death. . . ."

The King speaks of the death of the elder Hamlet and of taking Gertrude to wife; he expresses his thanks to the Court. He addresses Laertes, who on his cue to speak steps in and kneels to him. At this Hamlet turns his eyes and looks at them, dropping his right hand to his side and his left hand to his dagger hilt; then he again lowers his eyes to the ground. Laertes rises when his petition to return to France is granted, and goes up into the crowd at the left.[17]

64-86. "But now, my cousin Hamlet, and my son. . . ."

When the King addresses him, Hamlet starts and comes a little toward the front, giving his aside with solemn scorn: "A little *more* than kin—and *less* (slight pause) than kind." He turns and makes a slow bow to the King. When the King asks why the clouds still hang on him, Hamlet advances his left foot one short step toward the King. His voice is soft and courteous, yet firm: "Not *so* (prolonged), my lord. I am *too much* (raising his left hand with the palm toward the King) i' the *sun*." There is a pause. Still facing the King he lowers his head and drops his hand to his side.

The Queen, who stands between him and the King, advances and begs him to give up his mourning. When she utters the word "common," he raises his head and looks meaningfully at her. When he responds he joins his hands at his girdle, lifts his head, and speaks with the air of one who is heavily burdened by reflections but

black gown. This costume, worn only in the second and third acts, seems to have been adopted in the 1880's. The Viennese critic Johannes Meissner mentioned it in the *Deutsche Zeitung* (April 8, 1883): "So tragt er ein langes schwarzes Scholarenkleid, an der Seite geschlitzt." A reviewer in the New York *Mirror* (January 31, 1885), speaking of it as a recent innovation, thought it picturesque when the actor was in repose, but awkward when he moved in it.

[17] *63.* In later stagings, according to the promptbooks, when Laertes was dismissed he rose, crossed to Hamlet at the right center, shook his hand or kissed his hand, and went out immediately at stage right. In the 1878 edition he is directed to go out at line 86, when his father goes to assist the King down from the throne.

is obliged because of position to pay attention to her and give a polite answer: "*Ay, madam*, it is (short pause) *common*." The word sounds final. He lowers his head slowly, releases his hands, gives them a slight outward motion, and drops them to his sides. But she demands why then it seems "so particular" with him. At the word "seems," he starts a little and draws in the fingers of his right hand, ready to speak. "*Seems*, madam!" He raises his right hand. "Nay (slight pause), it *is* (a special emphasis on *is*)." He bends a little forward, casting his right hand a trifle toward her, the arm raised, the hand hollowed with palm upward, the index finger half pointing upward: " 'Tis not *alone* my inky cloak, good mother, nor customary suits of *solemn* black (drawing up the hem of his cloak a little with his left hand), no, nor the fruitful river in the *eye* (giving his right hand a passive backward toss, the finger motioning toward his eyes), nor (lowering his right hand toward his girdle and looking at her reproachfully) the dejected 'havior of the visage, together with all *forms, modes, shows* of grief (the tone mournful but monitory; reaching his arms out a little at either side with the hands open) that can denote *me* (dropping his left hand to his girdle and raising his right hand to his breast) truly. *These* indeed (lifting his left hand) *seem* (faintly contemptuous tone; he is bending slightly forward, holding his hands spread wide but toward her, the palms upward and his elbows close to his sides). For (dropping both hands, the left one to his dagger hilt) they are actions that a man might play (giving his right hand a slight outward movement at his girdle). But I have that *within* (striking his breast gravely with the joined fingers of his right hand) which *passeth show; these* but the *trappings* (raising his cloak a little with his left hand) and the *suits* of woe."

The many gestures in this ten-line speech, Clarke says, are delivered so easily and naturally that, although it takes much space to describe them, in action one scarcely gives them especial notice. They are langorous, without vivacity, and perfectly consonant with Hamlet's meditative, mournful demeanor.

87-128. " 'Tis sweet and commendable in your nature, Hamlet."

When the King speaks, the Queen returns to him, and Hamlet stands alone, facing front with eyes cast down and his left hand resting on the hilt of his dagger. When he hears the words "And think of us as of a father," he starts and looks at the King, expressing repugnance with his eyes. Then he folds his arms and looks down again until the King is finished. The Queen approaches him to make her final plea. He turns toward her, drops his arms to his sides, and looks at her quietly. When she concludes, he bows slightly, and moving his hands outward says, "I shall, in all my *best* obey you (slight pause), madam."

The King accepts his seeming submission. At the King's words "Be as ourself in Denmark," Hamlet makes a partial bow, turns upstage, and goes to the back wall with both hands on his forehead. When the King says, "Madam, come," the two Chamberlains leave the center entrance, cross to the archway in the left wall, and draw apart the curtains. Meanwhile, at the back, Hamlet turns, dropping his left hand to his dagger and his right hand to his side, and listens while the King builds up his noisy exit speech. At "Come away" there is a grand flourish from the orchestra. Hamlet lowers his head. The King and Queen go out at the left, followed by their Pages, Polonius, the ladies and gentlemen of the Court, and last of all Laertes. All bow to Hamlet as they go. The music ceases.

129-159. "Oh, that this too, too solid flesh would melt. . . ."

Hamlet is alone. He comes to the front of the stage with his left hand raised. He turns and goes to the back again with both hands on his forehead. He turns and speaks: "*Oh* (prolonged), that this too (raising his right arm) *too* (prolonged) *solid* (giving his upheld hand a shake) *flesh*[18] (dropping his hand to his breast) would melt! *thaw*—and resolve itself into a *dew* (prolonged)." He is holding out his right hand, palm upward, the arm inclining toward the ground, and he drops his eyes groundward; his left hand is on his dagger: "Or that the Ever*last*ing had-not fixed (throwing his head back and raising his arm, he points with his hand and looks into the top gallery of the auditorium) his canon 'gainst *self-slaugh*ter! *Oh* God! *Oh* God! (striking his breast with his closed right hand, his head lowered and his eyes looking down, his countenance drawn together with emotion) how *weary* (prolonged)—*stale*—*flat*—and *unprofitable* (*un-* in a low wailing tone, *prof-* rising in volume and sonorousness, *-itable* in a deep bass declining again to a wail; he

[18] *129.* The image of "solid flesh" prompted Booth to enter in his Notebook that Hamlet was *not fat.* He thought that the Queen's line during the fencing scene should be "Our son is *hot* and scant of breath." In performance, however, this line of the Queen's was simply omitted.

stands looking down with his closed hand on his breast) seem to me *all* the *uses* of this life! Fie on't! (raising his right hand from his breast) oh, fie! (he strikes lightly in the air before his face, shaking his head a little, and starts down to the front, dropping his hand to his side) 'tis an unweeded garden, that grows to seed."

He pauses at the front of the stage: "Things *rank* (holding out his right hand palm upward) and *gross* in-nature (turning his hand over and looking down, beyond it) *poss*ess it, merely." He drops his hand: "That it should come to *this!*" He takes two steps toward upstage left, clasping his hands: "But *two months* dead!" He keeps on toward upstage left: "Nay (prolonged), *not* so *much*, not two." He stops up left and shakes his right hand above his head: "So *ex*cellent a king (dropping his hand and looking upward) that was to *this* (contemptuous tone; prolonged; reaching his right hand energetically toward the curtained archway) Hyperion (raising his hand somewhat, then lowering it) to a *Sat*yr!" He strikes upward with his hand and nods his head toward the archway: "So loving to my *mother* (crossing to upstage center, his hands hanging down) that he might not beteem (speaking quickly; turning and coming forward toward the left) the winds of heaven (stopping at left center, holding out both hands, his eyes up) visit her face *too* (prolonged) roughly."

He raises his hands outward a little higher than his face, closes his fingers, and strikes once a little upward. He speaks with strong emotion: "Heaven and earth! must I re*member?*" He drops his hands, looking down toward the left front. He raises his right hand and places it on his left breast: "Why, she would *hang on him* (deep, coarse tone) as if *increase* of appetite had *grown* by what it fed on." He smites his breast lightly several times:[19] "And yet (the *yet* is isolated, the *t* heavily sounded) within a month—" He raises his right hand with fingers drawn together, and raises his left hand not quite so high with fingers spread apart: "Let me *not* think on't!" He looks up bitterly, raising his right hand with a stroke in the air and dropping his left hand to his dagger: "*Frailty* (deep voice; prolonged; turning toward the left archway, he throws back his head and right arm, and putting out his right foot he stands very nearly as a boy stands to throw a stone), *thy* name (prolonged) is *Woman!*

[19] *144.* This smiting the breast is explained by Booth in his Notebook. He tells the actor to "touch your heart to indicate what kind of appetite."

(very deep, heavy sound; sweeping his right arm forward toward the left archway and shaking his head at the same time.)"

He turns and comes quickly down to the right front, his hands clasped at his girdle. He turns at the right front: "A little month, or ere those *shoes* (prolonged) were old (crossing toward the left front) with which she followed (changing his direction toward up left) my *poor* father's body, like *Niobe*,[20] *all* tears, she married (he stops abruptly up left) with mine uncle (releasing his hands from his girdle and reaching them out before him, held apart), my father's brother (slight tone of detestation; raising his arms to shoulder level and reaching out); but (a deep sigh) no more *like* (warm tone; prolonged; raising his hands higher) my father (tender tone; prolonged; he clasps his hands and draws them back almost to his face, then lets them fall apart) than I (raising his hand) to *Hercules!*[21] (impressive but not loud sound)." He raises his hand above his face, and looking up strikes with it once, then drops it to his side: "*It is not, nor* it *cannot come* to good." He turns to face the stage right archway and puts his right hand on his breast: "But BREAK, my *heart* (full, impassioned tones; striking his breast with his right hand), for I *must—hold*—my tongue." He drops his hand to his side, lowers his head, and crosses to the right archway.

Throughout this soliloquy, Clarke says, there is no sudden vehemence, bluster, or violent transition from one mood to another. Booth's Hamlet is too well tempered for that. It is the Hamlet of a gentleman and a scholar, of a man not apt to fly into a passion abruptly. When he does rise to lofty heights of passion, as in the Closet scene or the Graveyard scene, the passion is either built up gradually through a procession of successive emotions, or is clearly the response to strong provocation. In this soliloquy the fitfulness of delivery, though very great, is never savagely abrupt but is always gradated—the passion of one accustomed to self-control. He is restless and energetic, yet also phlegmatic; and the shadow of his sadness falls constantly across the activity of his thought and motion.

160-183. "Hail to your lordship!"

As Hamlet puts his hand on the curtain of the right archway, Horatio,

[20] *149.* Mason says that here he "personates Niobe, pacing slowly left, with hands raised to height of breast, fingertips touching."

[21] *153.* Booth glosses "than I to Hercules" with the remark that "Burbage was undersized." Booth himself was about five feet seven.

followed by Bernardo and Marcellus, enters from the left and calls out to him. Hamlet turns with a look of partial displeasure, as at an intruder, and comes down toward the front of the stage, saying vaguely, as if still deep in his own thoughts, but politely, as if constrained to courtesy, "I am glad to see you well." [22] Then, as if recalled to the present, he looks more closely at the visitor (who has crossed the stage toward him), starts back a little, and then steps quickly down to him, crying joyously, "*Horatio!* or I do *forget* myself!" [23] The greeting is cordial but not lighthearted, tempered still with his grief. He takes Horatio's hand in both of his and shakes it warmly: "Sir, my good *friend* (still holding Horatio's hand in his right one, he puts his left hand on Horatio's shoulder), I'll change *that* name with you. And what make you from Wittenberg, Horatio?" He draws back a little on the inquiry, and in so doing he notices Marcellus standing with Bernardo toward the left. He steps out a little to the front, though without removing his hand from Horatio's shoulder: "Marcellus?" [24] Nothing, says Clarke, could be more superbly gracious than his pronunciation of that name or his bearing as he says it. He looks at Marcellus with kindly recognition and subtle courtesy, yet we cannot forget his underlying sorrow. "I am very glad to see you." To Bernardo he says, "Good even, sir," with a polite bow though not a low one.

He returns his attention to Horatio: "But what, in faith, make you from Wittenberg?" Horatio pleads jestingly his truant disposition. "I would not hear your *enemy* say so (moving his left hand from Horatio's shoulder to his breast), nor shall *you* do mine-ear that violence to make it truster of your *own* report against *yourself* (slight upward inflection). I *know* you are no *truant*." He shakes Horatio's hand with both of his: "But what is your affair at Elsi-

[22] *160.* Booth spoke the words "I am glad to see you well" in 1870, but in the 1878 edition and ever afterward he assigned the remark to Horatio. As he wrote in Taylor's promptbook, "Why should Hamlet say so to one whom he hardly recognizes?" Lawrence Barrett added "No!" to this note and sensibly corrected Booth's interpretation.

[23] *161-258.* Along the margins of the text in Booth's Notebook are jotted about two dozen adverbs of manner: cheerfully, heartily, bitterly, incredulously, nervously, etc. I have not attempted to incorporate all these, but Clarke's account implies most of them.

[24] *165.* In later stagings, when Hamlet had shaken hands with Horatio and went on to recognize Marcellus, he "puts Horatio across"—that is, he moved Horatio to his right and took center stage himself. This gave him a much more advantageous position from which to act. In 1870 he does not take the center position until line 212.

nore?" He lets go Horatio's hand, folds his arms, and looks into Horatio's face: "We'll teach you (pause) to *drink deep* (soberly, in a tone implying disapprobation) ere you depart." Horatio replies that he came to see Hamlet's father's funeral. Hamlet steps forward and puts his right hand on Horatio's shoulder, his left hand on Horatio's breast. His countenance is very sad. "I pray thee, do not *mock* me, fellow student. I-think (he draws back, faces front, and folds his arms; his eyes grow cold, his face becomes stern and gloomy, and his voice catches in his throat) it was to see my-*mother's* wedding."

Horatio agrees that it followed hard upon. Hamlet gives his left hand an outward toss: "Thrift, thrift (he speaks these words shortly, almost in an undertone, and with severe irony, and he looks with derisive assurance into Horatio's face), Horatio! the funeral baked meats [25] (reaching out his left hand toward Horatio, the index finger a little apart) did coldly furnish forth the marriage tables (each of these words is made prominent and full, and spoken in a deep sarcastic tone). Would (the voice drops and becomes tremulous) I had met (raising his left hand) my dearest *foe* in *heaven* (catching his breath, raising his left hand above his face) or ever I had seen that *day*, Horatio." He drops his hand and gives a brief glance at Horatio.

184-220. "My father, methinks I see my father."

Hamlet faces front and a little to the right, clasps his hands before him, and looks up: "My *father* (the voice impassioned and trembling), methinks I *see* my *father* (upward accent;[26] prolonged; moving a little forward, his lifted face intense with longing and recognition)." The others start in astonishment, and Horatio, springing forward, cries, "Oh where, my lord?" Hamlet turns his head toward Horatio with a surprised and perplexed look: "*In* (deep sound) my *mind's* (upward accent) eye, Horatio (rising inflec-

[25] *180.* Booth was fascinated by "funeral baked meats," which he took to be an exclusively English custom. He had encountered it, he notes in the Taylor 1890 promptbook, in 1861 when he was served a luncheon after the funeral of his maternal grandmother at Reading near London. Lawrence Barrett assures him in an added note that the custom of funeral feasts is common throughout Europe; he instances Irish wakes.

[26] *184.* Here for the first time Clarke uses the term "upward accent," which he will use with great frequency hereafter. The term is not easily intelligible, but obviously it indicates some kind of lift of pitch. In his final notes on Act II (see p. 180) he comments briefly on the phenomenon.

tion)." He stares at Horatio and Marcellus wonderingly and a little reprovingly. He stands a little back. At Horatio's words "I saw him once," Hamlet looks at him quickly, gives a nod as much as to say, "You saw a man then for once," and turns as if to go to the back of the stage. At the words "He was a goodly king," Hamlet turns sharply around and reaches out his left arm toward Horatio with hand open and palm upward; his right hand is on his breast, and his back is a little arched and chest lifted: "He was a MAN (upward accent; pause), take him for *all* in *all*, I shall *not look* (drawing back his left hand toward his face) upon *his* like again (the voice drops sadly)."

He folds his arms and comes down to the right front; then he turns toward Horatio but with his eyes lowered in sorrowful thought and his shoulders stooping. At the words "I saw him yesternight," Hamlet raises his head a little and looks at Horatio in mild surprise. Then he lets go the surprise, draws up his shoulders, shifts his weight as if about to move, but does not move: "Saw who? (his voice is between earnest and indifferent curiosity)." Horatio says, "The king —your father." Hamlet repeats, "The King—" He draws back a little, raising both hands with fingers closed: "—*my* father!" He sounds confused. His brows drop, and he stares at Horatio, drawing back his upper lip so that the wings of his nose are raised.

Horatio offers to tell him, with witnesses, what has happened.[27] Hamlet takes two steps toward Horatio, his body bent forward, his hands raised above his girdle: "*For-God's* love, let me hear! (upward accent)." [28] He listens without motion to that part of the narrative which tells of the Ghost's appearance to the two soldiers. At the words "This to me . . . impart they did," he takes a step toward Horatio and stands half turned away from the audience, his head sinking between his shoulders. When Horatio says that on the third night he too kept the watch, Hamlet steps to him and takes his hand excitedly. He looks alternately at Horatio and the soldiers, grasping Horatio now by the shoulder, now by the wrist or hand, until he

[27] *192-211.* Booth records in his Notebook valuable directives to Horatio: "Now that the ice is broken speak with animation"; and, "As Hamlet's interest becomes more intense, speak somewhat rapidly—yet distinctly. Let your *feeling* keep pace with Hamlet's."

[28] *195.* Later promptbooks show that at "For God's love, let me hear!" Booth went downstage center and listened to Horatio's recital with his back to the audience. This full-back position was one which he favored and used with increasing frequency in later years.

hears that the apparition did indeed come: "But *where was this?* (tone of amazement)."

Now for the first time he breaks past Horatio to the center and confronts the soldiers. Marcellus answers that it was upon the sentry's platform. Hamlet turns sharply and grasps Horatio's left arm: "Did *you* not speak to it?" As Horatio describes the Ghost's silence and its departure at cockcrow, Hamlet stares into his face in extreme agitation, his breath coming short, and a movement of his lips or throat hinting of a tremor running through his whole body. At last he draws his clenched hands up to the sides of his face: " 'Tis *very* (deep, trembling voice) strange." He turns and goes a few feet toward the back of the stage.

221-243. "As I do live, my honored lord, 'tis true."

At Horatio's insistent assurance Hamlet wheels about to face the audience for an instant, then looks at Horatio, makes a slight forward motion of the head, and with his *eye* expresses his belief in Horatio's word. Then he turns and goes a few steps farther upstage, his head thrown back, both hands on his forehead, his elbows lifted higher than his shoulders. He turns suddenly at the rear and drops his hands from his forehead, holding them out a little at the sides of his face: "*Indeed, indeed* (drawing in a breath with each word, the second *indeed* prolonged, the voice strong but trembling; his face is rigid with lines of emotion), sirs, but this *troubles* me (short sound of *me*)."

He lowers his hands and clasps them at his girdle; he comes down to Marcellus and Bernardo, speaking as he comes: "*Hold* (as if he were swallowing something) *you* the watch tonight?" On their answer he turns to Horatio, reaching out with his right hand, his left hand at his side: "*Armed* (full, rough-edged voice), say you? (softer, supplicating voice)." Horatio repeats the word. "From *top* to *toe?* (prolonged; manly but plaintive voice)." His hands are clasped before him and he looks at Horatio in pained expectancy. At the response "from head to foot," he stands back and his hands fly up: "Then *saw*-you not his face? (a trace of disappointment)." He reaches forward with his right hand eagerly. Horatio tells him that the Ghost wore his beaver up. "What!" Bending back his body, he draws his right hand up higher than his head and backward over his shoulder; his left hand reaches up before his breast; both hands tremble perceptibly. His eyes are intensely active and doubly black:

"Looked he *frowningly?* (great emphasis on *frown-*, and the syllables are separated almost too distinctly)."

At Horatio's reply that the Ghost looked more in sorrow than in anger, Hamlet drops his hands and clasps them at his girdle, and his eyes lose something of their energy: "*Pale* or red? (a soft, feminine voice, full of stops, eager almost to anguish; had a woman spoken it so, Clarke says, one would have thought tears were close behind)." At the answer, "Nay, very pale," he raises his clasped hands a little: "And fixed his *eyes* upon you? (his voice rises a little, but is still full of anxiety)." "Most constantly," says Horatio. "I *would* I had been there (the *I* sounds almost like *O*; the voice is all vibration, expressing wonder and regret)." He drops his head and covers his face with his hands. Horatio says it would have much amazed him.

Hamlet lifts his face, which is troubled with quick inquiry, drops his hands, and holds them out at either side with fingers closed. He turns toward the back of the stage again. Then he looks round at Horatio and says in a voice softened by its burden of feeling and idea, "Very like, very like." He nods, turns away again, puts both hands to his forehead, and walks three or four steps upstage; then he wheels about suddenly, keeping his left hand still on his temple but reaching toward Horatio with his right hand, and takes a step forward: "*Stayed* it long?"

As the witnesses dispute the answer, Hamlet looks quickly from Horatio to the soldiers as if perplexed by the discrepancy of their estimates. He takes a step backward, then comes eagerly forward, his left hand raised to breast level but reaching out toward Marcellus, his right hand extended toward Horatio. He jogs his left hand as he puts the question to Marcellus, "His beard was grizzled?"; then draws it back trembling to his lips as he turns and addresses to Horatio the long-drawn-out, hesitating "*No?*" The question is enormously important, and his whole body trembles as if he dreaded that the Ghost's identity be either denied or confirmed. Horatio assures him that it was grizzled—"a sable silvered." [29] He darts forward in great excitement and takes Horatio's right hand in both of his: "*I* (full, lung-thrown voice; a slight shrug of his shoulders, as if to cast off some-

[29] *242.* That the beard was "a sable silvered" meant for Booth that "Hamlet (pere) was not a *blonde*." Hence, he would argue, Hamlet himself was not a blonde; hence actors like Charles Fechter who assumed a blonde wig were in error.

thing which throbs in his throat) will watch tonight. Perchance 'twill walk again (upward accent; the whole sentence strong and eager)."

244-258. "If it assume my noble father's person. . . ."

He stands on a level with Horatio, facing the audience, grasping Horatio's right hand with his own right hand, his left hand raised with the index finger projecting: "If it assume my noble *father's* person, I'll speak to it, though hell itself should GAPE (pointing down with his left hand, leaning back a little, looking impetuously into Horatio's face) and *bid* me (lets go Horatio's hand and raises his right hand toward his own shoulder) *hold* (prolonged) my peace." He strikes down with his right hand.

He crosses downstage of Horatio and walks to the right front with his hands on his face. He turns there, and Horatio joins him. He takes Horatio's left hand in his own left hand: "I *pray you* all, if you have hitherto (moving toward center, with Horatio walking backward before him) con*cealed* (prolonged; the voice rises a little) this *sight*, let it be tenable in your silence still (upward accent)." He is standing at center, his left hand grasping Horatio's, his right hand pointing across at the soldiers: "And whatsoever *else* shall *hap* tonight, give it an understanding but no tongue (upward accent and no recognition of a period)." He looks from the soldiers to Horatio, takes Horatio's hand in both of his and shakes it: "I will *requite* your loves. So fare-you-well." He lets go Horatio's hand. Horatio and the soldiers walk backward toward the left archway, bowing as they go. "Upon the platform, 'twixt eleven and twelve, I'll *visit* you." He stands at center, holding out his right hand toward them in a friendly manner. When Horatio says, "Our *duty* to your honor," Hamlet crosses to him quickly, takes his hand again, and shakes it: "Your *loves*, as mine to you." He lets go Horatio's hand and bows to them as they go out.

When alone he turns toward upstage right, his hand on his forehead, and takes two or three slow steps. "My *father's* spirit! (thin, sharp voice) in *arms!* [30] (more resonant)." He starts back: "*All* (prolonged) is not well! (deep doubting tone; he raises his face). I doubt some *foul* play." He strikes up slowly with his right hand. He turns to the left: "*Would* the *night* were come! (a little impatiently).

[30] *255.* Booth says in his Notebook that he prefers Garrick's reading of "My father's spirit! in arms!" to the unbroken interrogation of the First Folio, "Else it would seem that spirits were no *uncommon* sights."

Till then *sit* still, my *soul* (striking his breast with his right hand)." He takes a step toward the left archway, stops, reaches out his right hand and points downward with it, the fingers closed: "*Foul deeds* WILL rise (lifting his hand higher than his head and outward toward the audience), though all the *earth* o'er-whelm them (his voice dropping from the sonorous tone to one of lesser force, but quite as earnest; bringing down his arm energetically in a rounding sweep) *to* men's eyes (slight upward accent, but final recognition of the period)." [31] He goes out through the left archway.

Clarke ends his account of this scene with an acknowledgment that many of Booth's means of expression are untellable. Booth's eyes, he says, "glance in and out of his gestures, completing the significance of an attitude or the meaning of a motion, in ways that the pen cannot portray." As he received from Horatio the facts about the Ghost, his eyes "helped wonderfully to translate his feelings at each successive item of information." Then too there are the innumerable "minute posturings of the body and limbs and features" contributing to the meaning, which can hardly be remembered and which "the pen cannot describe without dropping into intolerable garrulity."

He stresses Booth's comparative stillness of body throughout the scene. Though his body is full of energy, "thought always overweighs his actions" and "he is not physically vehement in expressing his surprise." His face expresses "deep philosophical and emotional perplexity, while his body is comparatively immobile." Clarke defines this aspect of Booth's Hamlet with the curious term "top heavy," by which he means "more intellectual by far than passionate."

Owing to his "spirituality," Booth's Hamlet is not so astonished at the news about the Ghost as another actor's Hamlet might be. Though amazed at the narration, he trusts Horatio's word completely. He is bewildered and excited, but is neither skeptical nor too credulous in accepting the tale.

The text of Act I, 2 (line-numbering of the Globe edition).

The cuts in this scene (48 lines) are traditional. These are: 11-13; 17-41 (Fortinbras matter and the dispatching of Cornelius and Voltemand); 79 ("Nor windy suspiration of forced breath"); 96-106a (part

[31] *258.* Booth's annotation of the last line is, "Of all the hateful rhyming exits this is the worst."

of the King's argument against mourning); 110-116 (the King's direct reference to Hamlet's going back to school in Wittenberg); 149b-151a (the "beast that wants discourse of reason"; these lines are not cut in the promptbook, nor in Booth's 1878 edition, but Clarke does not record them); 156c-157 ("incestuous sheets"); 211b-212a.

There is one minor alteration, which may in fact be but a slip of the pen: Clarke records Hamlet's "all the uses of this world," at line 134, as "all the uses of this life."

The restorations (13 lines) are as follows: 44-50a (the larger part of the King's address to Laertes); 58b-60; 78 ("Nor customary suits of solemn black"); 127; 153b-156a ("Within a month . . . wicked speed"; Booth would cut this bit in his 1878 edition).

Act I, 3. *A Room in Polonius' House.*

(Globe edition: Act I, 3. 136 lines cut to 94.)

The Room in Polonius' House (see Plate VI),[32] which is a shallow box set, is consistent in decoration with the preceding Room of State. The back wall, which runs straight across the stage, is of gray stone block in its upper third; its lower two-thirds is divided by twisted columns into four round-arched niches. The lunettes of the arches are decorated with circle patterns, and hanging from poles beneath the lunettes are tapestries depicting scenes of war. Each of the three central columns supports a bust—male, female, and male (Polonius? Ophelia? Laertes?). The side walls are pierced by identical round-arched doorways surmounted by round-arched lunettes. At each corner of the room stands a pair of very slender engaged columns extending to the ceiling. A double frieze, the upper one of chevrons and the lower one of inverted U-forms, runs straight around the upper walls. The planked ceiling is supported by plain square beams running crossways of the stage, and these are notched into heavier square beams running toward the audience.

As the side walls of the preceding Room of State are drawn away, the back wall of this set rises out of the floor at the first

[32] In Booth's 1878 edition this scene was not assigned a separate setting, but was to be continued in the Room of State. As Hamlet went out at stage left, Laertes and Ophelia came on through the center. In most later promptbooks, however—e.g. the Harvard 1890 book—we find "Chamber in 1st G." or the equivalent. The reason for restoring the separate setting is that whenever the Room of State contained thrones and dais the present scene had to be played forward, as a "carpenters' scene," so that the dais could be removed and the following set prepared.

grooves, the end walls swing into place,[33] and a ceiling border drops down to complete the picture. The lights remain at full.

While this scene is being played, the Room of State of Act I, 2, is disposed of and the "Moonlight Wood Wings" of the Castle set are readied for the scene to follow.

Since Hamlet does not appear in this scene, Clarke does not describe it. The essential movements as given in the 1870 promptbook, with augmentation from later sources, are quickly reported.

1-136. "My necessaries are embarked. Farewell."

Laertes draws Ophelia into view through the stage right entrance, speaking as he comes. They cross just past center and stand near the front. Laertes' fears that Hamlet is not in love with Ophelia are quite correct, says Booth in his Notebook, for Hamlet's "*intellectuality*" has already "absorbed all 'trivial, fond' emotions." At line 52 Polonius enters from the door at the left and comes above and between them. To receive his father's blessing and advice, Laertes kneels a little downstage and to the left of Polonius, with his back somewhat to the audience.[34] At line 82 Laertes rises and goes toward the left door; and at his "Farewell, Ophelia," Ophelia crosses near to him. He goes out left. Ophelia then returns to Polonius at center for the discussion of her relations with Hamlet. "All that Polonius says to Ophelia," Booth wrote in Taylor's promptbook, "should be spoken tenderly—not testily or with reproach: 'Use all gently,' most fatherly." [35] At the end of the scene Polonius goes to the right entrance, there turns and sees Ophelia still at center looking downcast. He stretches out his arms to her, she rushes to him, and they go out the door. The lights darken and the scene changes.

[33] When I say "the end walls swing into place," I am guessing that in these shallow, first-groove sets (see also III, 2, and V, 2) the narrow end walls were hinged to the back walls, rose with them in the long cuts which crossed the stage parallel to the footlights, and then were swung forward to their proper angle.

[34] The trio was variously arranged for the "advice" scene in order to give center position to one actor or another. In 1870, Polonius (Booth's old friend Dave Anderson) was at center. In Modjeska's arrangement in 1889, Ophelia was at center. In the Taylor 1890 promptbook, Laertes (probably Lawrence Barrett) was at center with Ophelia slightly above and behind him.

[35] Occasionally Polonius was allowed a brusque touch. At the end of the scene, in the Pitman 1884 promptbook, Polonius sees that Ophelia is paying no attention to him but is looking off left after Laertes. He repeats "Come your ways" angrily. She turns toward him pouting. He repeats the line pleasantly. She crosses to him and they go out fondly together.

This drab account tells nothing of the emotional life of Ophelia in the scene, although Booth probably expected little enough from his young niece Blanche de Bar, who played the role in 1870, or from most of the dozens of actresses who sustained for him what he calls in his Notebook "the personification of pale and feeble-minded amiability." In 1889, however, the lovely Helena Modjeska was his Ophelia, and as co-starring actress she was of course permitted to build up the scene in her own manner. Her business in this scene was recorded by E. T. Mason, and it is appropriate here to let the scene come to life through her vivid touches.

When at the first Laertes begs her to write to him during his absence, she responds with "a smile of sisterly love." When he tells her that Hamlet's affection is but "a toy in blood," she says "No more but so?" in a "half-playful tone," turning her face away, smiling, and dropping her eyes. As he bids her to fear Hamlet and to "keep in the rear of her affection," she does not look at him, but faces front, her eyes somewhat raised as if in thoughtful attention to his words, her face showing sadness and anxiety.

The entrance of Polonius is neatly arranged to give Modjeska the center position. Laertes and Ophelia have got a little to the left of center, and Polonius, entering from the right, stops at right center. Ophelia runs across to meet him. Polonius embraces her with his left arm, and she leans against him, resting her head upon his breast. Laertes, then, to receive the blessing, crosses to them at right center and kneels there. Throughout the "advice" speech, Ophelia continues to rest in Polonius' arm, her eyes generally on Laertes; but occasionally she lifts her face to Polonius, as if especially interested in some parts of his advice. At the mention of costly dress, she looks critically at Laertes, then lifts his cloak slightly and drops it again with a look of approbation.

When she has followed Laertes to the left entrance for their farewell embrace, she does not return to Polonius, but stands near the door, facing front, listening with head lowered and clasped hands hanging down before her. She does not look at him during her responses, and she speaks in a low tone and with a hesitating and troubled manner. At "I do not know, my lord, what I should think," she drops her hands to her sides, raises her eyes, and gazes vacantly forward. She listens with growing trouble until she hears the words "Tender me a fool," at which she starts, draws herself up in dignified protest, and speaks the words "importuned me in honorable fashion" in a tone of earnest self-assertion, in defense of her maidenly dignity.

When she speaks of Hamlet's "holy vows of heaven," she delivers the line with upraised eyes and a happy smile, as if recalling past scenes and rejoicing in the memory of them. At "This is for all," Polonius crosses to her at the left and takes her right hand; she turns her face away from him and hides it with her left hand. When he forbids her any more to talk with Hamlet he drops her right hand and strides across nearly to the right entrance. She raises her right hand to her face and stands weeping for a moment. At "Come your ways," she pauses a moment, then crosses to him quickly, kisses his hand, lays her head upon his breast, and says in a sorrowful voice broken by weeping, "I shall obey, my lord." Polonius leads her out, his left arm around her, she in tears.

The text of Act I, 3 (line-numbering of the Globe edition).

The heavy cuts in this scene (42 lines) are traditional. These are: 7-18, 22-28, 31b-32, 38-44 (all these from Laertes' advice to Ophelia; in the 1878 edition Booth restored the first of these cuts); 83; 117b-131a (from Polonius' advice to Ophelia).

The restorations (29 lines) are: 3; 53-54; 57b-81 (the whole of Polonius' advice to Laertes); 108-109a.

Act I, 4. *The Platform.*

(Globe edition: Act I, 4, 91 lines cut to 60.)

As the Room in Polonius' House slips down through the stage floor at the first grooves and the lights are again lowered, we see once more the deep scene of the Platform before the Castle with which the play began (see Plate IV). It is bathed in green light from the foots and a flood of white moonlight from the right.[36] Marcellus is on guard upstage center, just to the left of the portal.

1-38. "The air bites shrewdly."

Hamlet and Horatio are seen coming down from behind the stage left watch tower as from the castle.[37] They pass through the center

[36] In the 1878 edition the scenic direction gives "Dim Starlight" for this scene, as against "Moonlight" for Act I, 1. But this is probably a poetical touch by William Winter, the editor, rather than a stage fact. In 1870 there is surely no change of skycloth, and the same moon shines on both scenes.

[37] *1.* In later stagings Booth did not always enter from up left. On the road, according to the Taylor 1890 promptbook, "the business is transposed according to Mr. Booth's dressing room."

portal, descend the steps, and advance toward the front. Hamlet rubs his hands as he comes and says, "The air bites *shrewdly;* it is very *cold.*" [38] He wears his black furred cloak and a bonnet of matching furred stuff. The dagger he wore in the earlier scene is now replaced by a sword. Horatio, at his right, speaks of the eager and nipping air.

As Hamlet asks, "What hour now?" he turns and starts slowly back toward the portal. When Horatio remarks that it is time for the spirit to walk, Hamlet is standing at center with arms folded, looking to the left. Marcellus has crossed to upstage right. Suddenly from far off, as from the castle, is heard a flourish of trumpets and drums and a round of ordnance. Hamlet starts at the sound, looks up a little and raises his left hand, shakes his hand mournfully two or three times at the left side of his face, and folds his arms again. His head sinks between his shoulders and he looks down as if in painful thought. Horatio asks what the noise means. Hamlet looks up and raises his left hand again: "The *King* doth *wake* tonight and takes his rouse; and as he drains his draughts of Rhenish down, the kettle-drum-and-trumpet thus *bray* out (tossing his left hand up a little) the triumph of his pledge." He folds his arms again and looks down as before. Horatio asks if it is a custom. Hamlet turns front and looks up: "*Ay, marry*-is't; but to my mind—though I am *native* here and to the manner *born*—it is a custom more honored in the *breach* (slight pause) than the observance." He raises his left hand to his head thoughtfully. All this while he has stood in calm expectancy, showing no excitement, and speaking to Horatio as if to beguile the time as tranquilly as possible.

In the passage which now follows, and throughout the fifth scene, Booth put his whole art and energy into what he took to be Hamlet's grand motivation—love for his father. He had been working up this exhibition of filial affection since his earliest studies of the role, and as early as 1857 Adam Badeau had exclaimed upon the "originality and refined ideality" with which Booth substituted "yearning tenderness" for the traditional "supernatural dread." [39] In

[38] *1.* At the Winter Garden at the time of the Hundred Nights *Hamlet*, Booth commenced the scene very differently from the restrained, tranquil manner which Clarke describes for 1870. A note of Mason's made in 1865 shows that "He enters upon the scene with a nervous uneasiness of manner, and in apparent fearful anticipation of some strange occurrence. He takes off his cap, as if for coolness. Every action shows his feverish excitement."

[39] See Chapters I and II, pp. 4-6 and 21, for Badeau's review and for notes on Booth's identification of the Ghost with his own father's spirit.

1870 the critics were still rewriting Badeau's recognition and appraisal. The author of "Table Talk" in *Appleton's Journal* (February 5) observed warmly that these two scenes are the best in Booth's entire performance: "It is doubtful whether the fearful conflict of emotions that agitate Hamlet, in the first interview with the mysterious presence—the awe, the grief, the wonder, the filial tenderness—were ever better expressed than by Mr. Booth. . . . It is emotional rather than intellectual, but it captivates and subdues every listener, and, more than any other feature of the play, wins for the actor the popular identification of his name with the character." This was O. B. Bunce, a critic who would later develop a considerable hostility to Booth's Hamlet. Nym Crinkle, who thought most of the performance "merely vacuous rhetoric," yet found this first address to the Ghost "superlatively fine." In the *World* (January 9) he analyzed the series of appellations, "Hamlet, king, father—royal Dane," as follows: "The 'Hamlet' is an articulate sigh of loyalty; that of 'father' is the yearning of filial affection; and 'royal Dane' swells roundly and grandly into the pride of lineage and pomp of power." Nym Crinkle would give Booth no credit for originality in the matter, for he recalled that Edmund Kean's Hamlet was long since famous for tenderness toward the Ghost; but in Booth's use of the idea, even though he borrowed it, the scene became "superior in refined ideality to nearly all else in the play, as we now have it, and so much better than the superstitious terror of all our other Hamlets." If Garrick frightened his audiences by the display of his own terror, "Booth has improved on Garrick."

38-57. "Look, my lord, it comes!"

The Ghost has entered from behind the watch tower and passed through the portal, and it comes down to the left of Hamlet.[40] Hamlet, rapt in thought, does not see it, but Horatio starts back, crying, "Look, my lord, it comes!" Hamlet rouses himself as if from

[40] *38 ff.* In later stagings we find in the promptbooks that the Ghost occupied stage right rather than stage left, so that the action of the major part of the scene was exactly reversed from that of 1870. The reversal was effected as follows: when Hamlet had said, "More honored in the breach than the observance," he went upstage left and stood with his back to the audience; the Ghost then entered from the right wings; Horatio saw it, cried out, and ran up left to Hamlet, who turned, stepped forward a little, and began "Angels and ministers of grace." The reversed arrangement would have been more comfortable and effective for Booth: at the exit, for instance, he would be carrying the upraised sword in his right hand rather than his left.

some idea that has laid hold of him, and turning, confronts the Ghost, which stands quite near him; he staggers back to the right, raising his left hand swiftly as if to clear his eyes; in so doing he throws off his bonnet so that it hangs down his back. He sinks into Horatio's arms at right center, and says in a fearful whisper, "Angels and ministers of grace defend us!" [41] The Ghost moves to just below left center.

Hamlet leans against Horatio, staring at the Ghost and breathing hard. "Be thou a spirit of *health* (thin, clear voice, just above a whisper) or goblin *damned* (rising tone), bring with thee *airs* from *heaven* or *blasts* (shrinking tenor voice that rises to height of volume in *airs* and continues so to *blasts*) from *hell* (*from* in a rounder tone, *hell* deepening toward bass), be thy intents wicked *or* (heavier sound on *be*, high tenor sound on *intents wicked*, marked and full pronunciation of *or*) charitable (the voice sinks a little), thou com'st in such a *questionable* shape that I *will* speak to thee (upward accent; the voice becomes gradually natural, full of pathos and entreaty). I'll *call* thee *Hamlet* (strong emphasis on the name and heavy sound of *H*; rising on tiptoe, though still supported by Horatio, and reaching out both arms toward the Ghost), *King* (taking a step forward, with Horatio keeping his hands on him lightly), *Father!* (deep, tender, appealing tone)." [42]

He sinks to his knees, still reaching out his arms; he bows his head and pauses for an instant: "*Royal* (prolonged) Dane (looking up; his face seems to throb with feeling, and his hands tremble so violently as to be noticeable in all parts of the theatre), oh *answer* me! (upward accent of *me*). Let me not *burst* in ignorance (he drops his hands and clasps them at his girdle), but tell why thy canonized [43] bones, hearsed in *death*, have burst their *cer*ements! why (pathetic interrogation) the sepulchre wherein we *saw* thee quietly in-urned, hath oped his *ponderous* and *marble jaws* to *cast* thee *up again!* (the

[41] *39.* In 1865, according to Mason, Booth's response to the Ghost was more explosive. The instant he saw it he raised both hands, cried out, "Angels and ministers of grace defend us!" and fell wildly back with his whole weight into Horatio's arms.

[42] *45.* As Booth told H. H. Furness, he (and his father before him) rejected the Folio punctuation which puts the four appellations in a series climaxing in "Royal Dane," and took on the amended punctuation which climaxes in "Father" (*New Variorum Hamlet*, I, 90).

[43] *47.* Booth puzzled over the accenting of "canonized," and eventually elected to stress the second syllable, wondering in his Notebook, "Has anyone else given this accent?" In 1870, it seems, he pronounces it "cánonized."

word *again* sounds interrogatory rather than like an exclamation). What *may* this *mean?* (both stressed words are prolonged) that *thou*, dread corse, again in complete *steel*, revisit'st-thus (low, shaking voice; supplicating tone) the-glimpses of-the-moon, making-night *hideous* (upward accent; prolonged; raising his hands and looking piteously at the Ghost), and we *fools* (low voice; prolonged) of nature, so-horridly-to-shake-our-dispositions (upward accent continuing from *so* to the end of the question) with thoughts-beyond-the-reaches of-our-souls? (downward accent). Say (upward accent), *why* is this? *wherefore?* what *should* we do?"

Throughout this speech, Clarke says, his voice is very low, yet distinct and clear. The speech is delivered slowly, with marvelous pathos, fear, and longing. From the moment he cries "Father!" which he does with deep reverence and tenderness, he keeps upon his knees. At the end of the speech the Ghost beckons with its truncheon. Hamlet starts back, and his arms fall to his sides but with hands held up palm outward. His lips fall open. His eyes glare with fear. His bonnet hangs down from his shoulders, and one or two dark locks of hair fall across his temples. His meager, sad countenance is lighted up with dread interest.

58-91. "It beckons you to go away with it."

The Ghost beckons; the friends forbid Hamlet to go with it. Hamlet, intensely conscious of the Ghost's motionings, seems only half attentive to their talk. He is still on his knees, his body quivering, his hands held open and outward at his girdle: "It will not *speak* (low voice; long thin sound); then I will *follow* it (long, mellow sound of the final *o* in *follow*)." Horatio bids him not to. Hamlet watches the Ghost intently, and he speaks as if only incidentally responding to his companions while he makes his own decision: "Why, *what* should be the *fear?* (low voice as before; upward accent). I do not set my life at a *pin's* fee; and for my *soul*, what *can* it do to *that* (broad, full sound), being a thing immortal as itself?" The Ghost beckons. "It *waves* me *forth*, *again; I'll* follow it (slight upward accent)." He clasps his hands and trembles violently.

During Horatio's half-dozen lines of reasoned warning,[44] Ham-

[44] 72. In this speech Horatio warns Hamlet that the Ghost may assume "some other horrible form" and drive him mad. Booth's instruction to the actor, which is recorded in his Notebook, prevents him from the "mistake" of stressing "*other*." He notes that earlier (I, 1, 47) Horatio referred to the

let watches the Ghost intently as it continues to beckon him. He is violently agitated. His body trembles and his breath is hard-drawn. His hands are clasped and dropped down: "It (deep, tremulous voice) *waves* (long, thin sound) me still." He lifts his left knee and puts his foot on the ground: "*Go* on (upward accent)." He rises: "*I'll* follow thee." He reaches out his arms toward the Ghost, which again beckons. Horatio and Marcellus seize him by the arms. "*Hold off—your hands.*" They struggle with him and draw him back several feet toward the right. Horatio has forced Hamlet's right hand high above his head; Marcellus pins his left hand down at his side. "My *fate* cries out (upward accent) and makes each petty *artery* in this body (upward accent) as *hardy* (both vowels prolonged) *as* the Nemean *lion's nerve* (upward accent; strong, resolute voice throughout)." He has got hold of the scabbard of his sword with his left hand and tilted it, and gradually he forces his right hand down toward the hilt. The Ghost beckons in the foreground. "*Still* am I *called* (upward accent). *Unhand* (long, hard sound) me, gentle*men. By* (prolonged) *Heaven* (gritting his teeth, he strives to wrench free), I'll make a *ghost* of him that *lets* me." He grasps the sword and draws it: "I say *away!*"

He throws off the friends and darts quickly toward the Ghost, panting, holding the sword point forward. When within a few feet of the Ghost, he stops abruptly, draws back, stares affrightedly, and then bends his body slowly forward.[45] He lowers the sword, takes it by the blade in his left hand, and lifts it again hilt upward and broadside toward the Ghost, so that it appears a crucifix. In a low voice, greatly in contrast to the energy of his voice when he was struggling, he says, "*Go* (prolonged) *on; I'll follow* thee (slight upward accent)." [46]

Ghost as a "fair and warlike form." Here therefore the actor should pause before the word "horrible" and give it distinguishing emphasis: "some other —*horrible* form."

[45] *86.* A correspondent to the *Leader* (January 8), who signs himself J. K. K., says that he observed several points "of surpassing excellence" which he took to be original with Booth: "Of these, are his *pause* after breaking away from his friends and advancing to follow the ghost; in his violent efforts to disengage himself from his friends, he has approached the ghost more nearly than he anticipated; and his natural start and pause were very striking and artistic."

[46] *86.* Mason records that in earlier years at the Winter Garden, the exit being made to the left, Booth stretched out his left hand toward the Ghost and with his right hand trailed his sword behind him. A silver statuette of Booth in this pose was made by the sculptor John Rogers. Exactly when the

The Ghost slowly withdraws into the trees downstage left, still beckoning Hamlet with its truncheon. Hamlet follows, holding the sword-hilt high before him, so that light from stage right throws his own shadow and the shadow of the sword as a *cross* upon the ground. Near the exit he stops doubtfully and takes one step backward. Horatio and Marcellus run to him and are about to seize him, but he puts out his right hand with fingers spread and motions them two or three times to stay back. He goes out slowly, and after a moment's pause Horatio and Marcellus silently follow him.

In reflecting upon this scene, Clarke is again impressed by Booth's imaginative temperament, or what he earlier called his "spirituality"—by his unquestioning recognition of the supernatural, and his reverence and obedience to it. This Hamlet is not in the least infected by nineteenth-century skepticism.[47]

After the Ghost appeared, he never once turned his eyes upon his companions. . . . All his observation and thought was centered on the Ghost; and the fear, interest, and longing which he manifested when knowing or seeing it to be his father's spirit were superbly blended and wonderfully expressed in voice, looks, and action. The distance at which he kept from the spirit; the nearness to the spirit which he seemed to effect in mind by the intensity of his appeal to the Ghost; the shiver which crossed him when the Ghost first pointed at him with its truncheon; the start of the eyes with which he first saw it motion him to go away with it; the dread which fell across his soul at the first thought of going off alone with the Ghost and the process of quick reasoning and of gradual

sword-as-crucifix business was invented is unknown, but in his Notebook Booth records the circumstances of the invention: "By an awkward movement on the part of Horatio I once lost the blade. I availed myself of this lucky accident and held the weapon up as a moral guard against the spirit—the hilt and handle forming the sign of the cross." He adds that Charles Fechter saw and applauded this business, and subsequently adopted it himself: "I was accused of imitating him—although I had for many years made the exit in this manner."

[47] Nym Crinkle, himself a belligerent skeptic, congratulates Booth for avoiding "superstitious terror," but Clarke is surely correct in crediting Booth with total belief in the supernatural (see Chapters I and III, pp. 5-6 and 48-50). A smug writer for the *City of Brooklyn* (January 25, 1872) absurdly out-Crinkles Nym Crinkle in "modern thought." He assures us that Booth could not possibly display any fear of the supernatural because he is a man of advanced intellectual development, and he therefore addresses himself to the "superior intelligence and culture" of the modern audience; we moderns may not know so much Latin and Greek as the eighteenth-century audience did, but whereas they "trembled and suffered with Garrick and Mrs. Siddons . . . we are content to *analyze* and " 'make no sign.' "

resolve by which he decided to go with it, were all accomplished by the most wonderful pantomime of eyes and face and attitudes.

Booth's exit with the sword held up as a cross appears to Clarke to be "very poetic and beautiful." It was, he says, "one of the most commanding situations of the whole play; and during his exit the whole theatre was in such a hush that it seemed as if even to wink would have made a noise audible throughout the place. He was always loudly applauded after this exit; and from the time he struggled with his friends until he went off the stage . . . I do not believe I breathed. It did not seem as if I did, and I know I always had a strong physical relaxation the instant he went out of sight."

The text of Act I, 4 (line-numbering of the Globe edition).

The cuts in this scene (31 lines) are traditional. These are: 9 ("Keeps wassail and the swaggering upspring reels"; this line is not cut in the promptbook, nor in Booth's 1878 edition, but Clarke does not record it); 17-38a (the "dram of eale" speech); 74b-78a; 87-91 (the dialogue after Hamlet's exit).

At line 52, "dead corse" is altered to "dread corse." At line 55, Clarke records "horribly" instead of "horridly," but this is probably a slip of the pen. At line 49 Booth uses the Folio's "enurned," pronouncing it "in-urned," rather than the Quartos' "interred."

The only restoration is line 71, "That beetles o'er his base into the sea."

Act I, 5. *A Grove adjoining the Castle.*

(Globe edition: Act I, 5. 190 lines cut to 170.)

Hamlet's interview with the Ghost was played not on the traditional "remote part of the Platform" (as in the *Modern Standard Drama*), nor on the "battlements" (as Booth had formerly staged it at the Winter Garden), but in a clearing of a dense grove (see Plate VII).[48] The ancient, twisted trees, of which we can count the trunks of at least eight, are in full leaf. The sky is visible above them, and moonlight streaming through an opening at stage right brightens the ferny undergrowth at the back and the leafage at the left. As in the preceding scene, the footlights are kept very low.

[48] In most of Booth's later stagings, at least those after 1878, the scene was again given an architectural treatment: in the 1878 edition it is called "Another part of the platform." According to Mason's notes this was effected simply by letting down a drop depicting another view of the castle.

For both novelty and romantic mystery the woodland setting seems appropriate, but it cannot be credited altogether to artistic planning. Alongside the design in the promptbook Booth penciled a note that "this was used as a substitute for a 'remote part of the platform,' having no time to paint the latter." What we have then is a sort of happy error: a stock set of "Wood and Cut Wood" pulled from storage to cover an emergency.[49]

As Clarke reports, and as the mechanical realities of the stage compel, "but half the depth of the stage was disclosed." From Bensen Sherwood's "Stage Plans" we can reconstruct the exact operation of the scene change. As Marcellus and Bernardo follow Hamlet off stage left, "Witham's Cut Wood Flats" rise up through the slit at the third grooves, and "Lewis Wood Drop" (with a "Sky Border" to mask the top edge of it) flies down behind the "Cut Wood" at the fourth grooves. The "Moonlight Wood Wings" which have framed the downstage area of the preceding scene—bright at stage left and shadowed at stage right—simply stay in place to become part of the Grove.

The critics' pleasure in Hamlet's response to his father's spirit spills over from the preceding scene into this one. The *Metropolitan* (January 15) pays especial attention to Booth's pantomime of listening: "In the scene in which Hamlet listens to, rather than holds converse with, his father's ghost, voice, face and hands play their part so perfectly that the mastery of the subject by the artist is at once established, and every auditor knows that the performance will be perfect to the end." The *Sunday News* (February 6), defending Booth from a charge which had been made in its own columns that he was incapable of exciting sympathy, cites this listening passage as sufficient to prove his appeal: "His effective simulation of nature during the recital by the ghost, and the varied expressions he displays while being wrought up to a high state of nervous tension, and the transition from intense interest to overpowering prostration, as he falls to the ground, are manifestations of art rarely equalled."

[49] The use of the woodland setting was probably not by such a last-minute decision as Booth's note suggests; for Arthur Matthison's souvenir pamphlet of the production, *Booth's Theatre: Hamlet*, printed for distribution at the theatre, tells us that the scene was played in "a grove adjoining the Castle." That the pamphlet was printed *in advance* of the opening night is indicated by the fact that it fails to record a genuine last-minute decision about the setting of the final scene (see V, 3).

1-8. "Whither wilt thou lead me?"

The Ghost enters through the "Cut Wood" trees at upstage left, beckoning with its truncheon as it comes.[50] It walks backward to the center, then moves down into the shadowy area toward stage right. Hamlet follows doubtingly, still holding his sword up like a cross with his left hand. After two or three steps he pauses to lean back against a tree trunk at the edge of the clearing, his right hand to his head. Then, as the Ghost comes to rest, Hamlet takes a step forward into the light: "*Whither* (heavy sound of *wh;* passionate tone, full of appeal) wilt thou *lead* me? (short sound of *me*). *Speak!* (prolonged)." He comes forward earnestly to the center and stands where the moonlight from the right falls across his face but not his body. The sword-hilt is now dropped downward, his fingers grasping the middle of the blade. "I'll *go—no further.*"

The Ghost's first words are "Mark me"; and Booth comments in his Notebook: "A shudder at this—the first sound of his father's voice. Such delicate touches may be lost upon the audience, but no matter—give them, if you *feel* them." Hamlet responds, "*I will* (rising accent on *I*, falling on *will* with the top sound on the *w*)," and he slowly reaches out his right arm toward the Ghost. He listens to "My hour is almost come . . ." with a look of pity, almost of pain. "Alas, *poor* (low, quavering tone; prolonged) ghost!" When the Ghost bids him to lend his serious hearing, he reaches out his right arm to full length, the palm upward: "*Speak* (upward accent). I am *bound* to hear (long, rising sound of the *e*, but then the voice falls)." The Ghost tells him that he will be bound also to revenge. "What? (upward accent; and long, thin, pathetic sound). He asks not in the sense of "What do you say?" but "What am I to revenge?" with a pitying and earnest intonation. He keeps his eyes fixedly on the Ghost.

9-40. "I am thy father's spirit. . . ."

When Hamlet hears the words "I am thy father's spirit," he draws a long breath, his body inclines a little backward, and he sinks slowly

[50] In later stagings the blocking of this scene was reversed. At the end of the preceding scene (see above, footnote 40), the Ghost led Hamlet off to the *right;* therefore the entry here was also from the right. The Ghost then took his position at about left center, somewhat upstage, facing front; Hamlet took a lower position at center or a little right thereof, standing and kneeling with his back toward the audience. The Ghost then made his exit to the left.

and reverently to his knees. The point of his sword rests on the ground at his left and toward the audience, and both his hands are on the butt of the hilt. As he listens he turns his head down and somewhat away from the Ghost, as if afraid of what he hears; but his eyes, looking askance, are still fixed upon the Ghost. He raises his right hand a little as if to shield his ears from the terrible words. Presently he seems to grow more stouthearted, and he again lifts his face toward the Ghost. At "knotted and combined locks to part," he raises his right knee and puts his foot on the ground before him; he reaches out toward the Ghost with his right hand.

At "If thou didst ever thy dear father love," he draws back his hand quickly to his breast and cries softly, "*Oh* (long, quivering sound) heaven! (low tone)." At "Revenge his foul and most unnatural murder," he starts to his feet. He drops his sword and his hands fly up to his shoulder. "Murder!" he cries.[51] The rising accent of the word conveys at once amazement, fright, and the corroboration of a fearful surmise. At the Ghost's words, "Murder most foul," he emits a long breath, but stands motionless; at "this most foul, strange, and unnatural," he takes a half-step forward and reaches out with his right hand, his left hand grasping his cloak. "*Haste* me to know it," he cries, "that I with *wings*-as-swift-as-meditation, or the *thoughts* of love, may *sweep* (prolonged; a brief circular movement of the right arm) to my revenge (slightly increased emphasis on *revenge*, but the voice then falls)." As the Ghost says "I find thee apt," Hamlet reaches out his right arm imploringly; then gradually he lowers it as the Ghost speaks on. He listens with open lips and staring eyes. His neck is a trifle sunken between his shoulders, his left hand held out at his side, palm downward and fingers spread. At "The serpent that did sting thy father's life," his chest rises, his body advances, his right hand lifts again, his eyes peer intently at the Ghost. At "Now wears his crown," he starts back into the shade and his hands fly up.

40-91. "Oh, my prophetic soul! My uncle!"

Hamlet begins his recognition line in a strong whisper: "Oh (prolonged), my prophetic (considerable volume but still not voiced) *soul!* (the voice emerges into full sound and makes the exclamation

[51] *26.* According to Mason and the Taylor 1890 promptbook he dropped his cloak when he cried "Murder!" But Clarke records the dropping of the cloak at line 136.

point)." His left hand fingers his throat as if his cloak choked him, and his right hand rises slowly: "My (short sound of *my*) *un*cle! (the first syllable is strongly voiced, but the ending drops away as if he were scarcely able to speak the word; with his raised right hand he is pointing backward and to the left, as if toward the castle)." At "Ay, that incestuous, that adulterous beast," Hamlet breathes hard once or twice. He drops his head wearily to one side, listening, but soon raises it again. Throughout the Ghost's speech, he stands with his legs bent, one a little forward. His hands are drawn up before him, his eyes fixed intently on the Ghost, his face full of pity, awe, and resolution. When he hears "with all my imperfections on my head," he moves his head sorrowfully and breaks in: "Oh, *horrible!* oh, *horrible! most* horrible! (low voice and thin, quivering tones; his hands are at his breast)." [52] As the Ghost continues, he remains motionless, but at the words "against thy mother aught," he takes a step forward and reaches toward the Ghost with his right arm.[53] At "Adieu, adieu. Remember me," the Ghost turns to the right and goes out into the trees. Hamlet follows a little to the center, reaching ahead with hands clasped together, and drops to his knees.[54] An instant after the Ghost has disappeared, he falls prone on his right side, fronting the audience, his face hidden by his extended arms. The moonlight is now fading, and the footlights are gradually working up.

Booth liked to experiment with this falling business, finding various ways to gratify his histrionic appetite; but on the present occasion he let himself be lured into something too much. In earlier

[52] *80.* In his Notebook Booth cites Mrs. Jameson as authority for taking the Ghost's "Oh, horrible" line for Hamlet to speak, and claims also that such was Shakespeare's intention. The stage tradition of this goes back to Garrick. After the word "horrible" Booth adds: "I sometimes fancy it to be as applicable to the performer of the Ghost as to the tale he tells."

[53] *86.* Booth notes that the Ghost's injunction not to harm the Queen is evidence that she was ignorant of the murder: "Hamlet should express great relief at this—by a deep sigh and a partial relaxation of his hitherto rigid muscles."

[54] *91.* In later stagings Booth introduced here a special business with the sword. Instead of dropping it at line 26 ("Murder!") he continued to carry it until the Ghost's exit. Then, as he fell to his knees at about left center, he would lean heavily on it, forcing the point into the floor of the stage. When he fell prostrate, it would stand alone like a crucifix. At line 148 he would retrieve it for the oath-taking. Booth records in the Taylor 1890 promptbook that other actors subsequently adopted the same business.

years at the Winter Garden, according to Mason, he had already made the fall extremely elaborate:

> He falls upon his knees as the Ghost begins his farewell, stretching out both hands toward the Ghost, as if begging it to stay—then, as the Ghost exits, Hamlet follows it with his body (still upon his knees), until it disappears, when he falls forward. After a moment's pause, he raises himself upon his elbow, and, looking upward, says: "Oh, all you host of of heaven!" Then, looking down: "Oh, earth!" and then, as though struck by the association: "What else? And shall I couple hell?"

Now in 1870 he extended this into what Richard Grant White called "perhaps the most extraordinary combination of attitude and elocution ever seen on the stage." He not only fell flat, with his head toward the audience, but rolled over upon his back, tossed and writhed for a moment in a tumult of emotion and exhaustion, and uttered the opening words with his face to the sky. Nowadays, of course, we should take such a bit of stage business unblinkingly, but in 1870 it ruffled the nerves of Richard Grant White, who, though a devoted playgoer, an admirer of Booth, and by no means a pedant, yet felt there were limits beyond which stage realism did Shakespeare absolute disservice. In an essay in the March *Galaxy*, called "The Clown's Real Pigling," he denounced Booth's fall and gyrations as a harmful extravagance. Such a way of delivering the speech, he said, is exactly what might happen in real life if such a man were prostrated by such a vision, and just as certainly Shakespeare had no such delivery in mind when he wrote the speech: "For there is so great an incongruity between the realism of the actor's treatment and the ideal and romantic conception of the scene as to void the performance of all dignity, and to make it approach as nearly to the ridiculous as is possible in the hands of an artist of Mr. Booth's histrionic power." Booth was not wont to take instruction from the "crickets," as he called them, but so sensible a rebuke so generously turned in its ending was irresistible. He retained the fall, Clarke tells us, but in deference to White's opinion he modified it to a simple cross-stage fall.[55]

92-112. "Oh all you host of heaven! Oh earth! What else?"

He begins his soliloquy lying on his side, his hands upon his head

[55] The March *Galaxy* came out about mid-February, and White's article was widely noticed. On February 19 the *Leader* reprinted it, together with a rebuttal. Thus Booth's changing of this stage business probably took place in the third week of February.

and covering his face: "*Oh*-all you *host* (prolonged) of heaven! (tremulous tones). Oh *earth!* (short sound, with a guttural push). *What else?* And shall I couple *hell?* (downward accent; he begins to rise). *Hold*, *hold*, my heart (lifting from the ground a little, he supports his body with his right hand), and you (prolonged), my sinews (long sound of *ew;* he rises almost to a sitting posture), grow not instant *old* (prolonged), but *bear* me *stiffly* up." Rising further, he puts his right foot forward on the ground and rests upon that and his left knee: "Re*mem*ber thee? *Ay*, thou poor (prolonged) ghost, while memory holds a *seat* in this *distracted globe!* (laying his hand heavily on his forehead). Re*mem*ber thee? Yea, from the *table* of my memory I'll wipe away *all* trivial fond records,[56] *all* saws of books, all (upward accent) forms and pressures past that youth and observation *copied* there (upward accent), and *thy* commandment all alone (rising inflection) shall *live* (upward accent; pause; the voice then deepens) within the book and *volume* of my *brain* (slapping his forehead) *unmixed* (rising sound) with *baser* matter. Yes, by heaven! (deep voice again; raising his right hand toward the top gallery of the auditorium). I have sworn it (his voice sinks almost to a whisper; he drops his face upon his hand)."

112-132. The entrance of Horatio and Marcellus.

The voices of the friends are heard calling "My lord! my lord!" from up left beyond the trees. At "Lord Hamlet!" Hamlet starts up with one hand to his head, goes excitedly to the rear edge of the clearing, and comes forward again, drawing out a handkerchief. He hears someone cry, "Heaven secure him!" and says, "*So be it!* (low voice, falling inflection)";[57] and he walks toward the rear, wiping his face swiftly with his handkerchief. As he answers their call with "Hillo,

[56] *99.* Among the "trivial fond records," Booth says in his Notebook, was "the remembrance of his boyish fancy for Ophelia." Booth made the most of every suggestion that Hamlet was no longer in love with Ophelia.

[57] *114.* Booth recognizes in his Notebook that "So be it!" may be understood as an "Amen" to "Heaven secure him!" Histrionically, however, he thinks it better taken as a sudden resolution to play the madman: "In such a brain thought requires no *time* to form its plan of action—quick as a flash his mind conceives the means of safety in pursuing his revenge. He had the older Brutus for a model too. Besides, Horatio had given him his *cue* when dissuading him from following the ghost." The likeness of Hamlet to the "older Brutus" is mentioned in Belleforest's *Histoires tragiques* and in *The Hystorie of Hamblet.* The character of Lucius Junius Brutus was one of Booth's favorite acting roles, the play being John Howard Payne's *Brutus; or, The Fall of Tarquin* (1818).

ho, ho (the *o*'s prolonged), boy! *Come*, bird, *come!*" he waves the handkerchief over his head once or twice; and as they enter through the trees up left, he comes forward again, putting the handkerchief into his bosom. They follow down at either side of him, grasp his arms, and Horatio, at his right, demands the news.

"Oh, *wonder*ful!" cries Hamlet quickly, on a long, sonorous, rising note. He can hardly control his excitement. Again Horatio begs to be told. "No," says Hamlet, crossing Horatio to the right, "you will *reveal* it (short, admonitory tone)." The friends protest that they will not. Hamlet turns, places his left hand on Horatio's right arm: "*How say* you then? Would *heart* of *man* (slight upward accent) once think it? But (lower voice and speaking quickly) you'll be *secret?* (falling inflection)." He raises his right hand to suggest an oath-taking. They agree "by heaven." Hamlet draws back a little, raises his right hand higher, looks at them earnestly, and says in a loud, deep voice: "There's *ne'er* a *villain* dwelling in *all Denmark* (his voice then drops a little) but *he's* (prolonged) an arrant *knave*." [58]

He brings down his right arm conclusively, lets go Horatio's arm, and walks a few steps to the right with his hand on his head. Horatio protests that it needs no ghost from the grave to tell them this. Hamlet faces them: "*Why, right* (upward accent). You are in the *right;* and so, without *more circumstance at all* (upward accent), I hold it fit that we *shake hands* and *part;* you as your business and desire shall *point* you (upward accent), for every man *hath business* and *desire*, such *as it is* (upward accent), and for *my own poor* (prolonged) *part* (falling inflection), I will go *pray* (slight upward accent)." He crosses Horatio and goes between him and Marcellus to the back of the stage, his head bowed.

133-149. "These are but wild and whirling words, my lord."

Horatio takes exception to these wild and whirling words. Hamlet, at the back, partly turns to look at him: "I am *sorry* they offend you, *heartily;* yes, faith, *heartily*." There is no offense, says Horatio. Hamlet throws his cloak to the ground: "*Yes*, by Saint Patrick, but

[58] *123.* Booth explains, partly in the Taylor 1890 promptbook and partly in his Notebook, why he checked himself and broke his speech after "There's ne'er a villain dwelling in all Denmark." He supposes that Hamlet "is about to say—'greater than the King thereof,' but remembering that would be treason, which even *he* must not *utter*, he turns the current of his speech with a jest. Already he begins the practice of that antic disposition he afterwards assumes."

there *is*, Horatio, and much *offense* too." Marcellus and Horatio move slightly to the left, and Hamlet comes down to stand just above them. "Touching this *vision* here—" he says in a confidential tone, and he lays his right hand on Horatio's shoulder and his left on Marcellus', as if he were about to tell them what has passed.[59] But he pauses, and then says shortly, "It is an *honest* ghost (with a nod), *that let* me tell you. For your desire to know what is *between* us (rising accent), *o'ermaster*-it as you *may* (falling accent). And *now*, good friends, as you are *friends*, *scholars*, and *soldiers*, give me one *poor* request." He drops his hands from their shoulders and stands a little back. Horatio asks what the request is to be. Hamlet raises his right hand: "*Never make known* (upward accent; slowly and earnestly) *what you have seen tonight*." They say they will not.

His sword lies on the ground before him, and he stoops between Marcellus and Horatio to take it up: "*Nay*, but *swear* it." They decline to swear. Kneeling between them, he holds the sword by the blade in his right hand, hilt upward, his left hand on the cross of it: "*Upon* my *sword*." [60] When Marcellus protests that they have sworn already, Hamlet shakes his head in agitation and looks up at Marcellus both appealingly and commandingly: "*Indeed*, upon my *sword*, *indeed* (upward accents)." As the two friends move their hands toward the sword, the Ghost calls from under the stage, "Swear!"

150-162. "Ah, ha, boy! say'st thou so? Art thou there, truepenny?"

The friends recoil, and Hamlet starts up and steps backward quickly, both hands held up to his face, the sword being in his right hand.

[59] *137.* Clarke appears to have missed a significant bit of business here. At "Touching this vision," according to the 1870 promptbook, Horatio and Marcellus "both rush up to him eagerly." The eagerness, especially on the part of Marcellus, checks Hamlet and prevents him from telling them what happened. The 1878 edition, later promptbooks, and Booth's notes confirm the business for later stagings. Hamlet's sharp suspicion of Marcellus, though nowhere provable from the text, is an actor's device which, as A. C. Sprague tells us in *Shakespeare and the Actors* (Cambridge, 1945), p. 145, goes back to Henderson and Kemble in the 1780's.

[60] *147.* In his Notebook Booth observes that oaths are commonly sworn upon the *blade* of a sword because the word *Jesu* was traditionally inscribed there. But for obvious stage reasons he chose to swear his friends upon the cruciform hilt. He notes with mild grievance that when Mounet-Sully used this bit of business in Paris in 1886, he was much lauded for it; but that no one (except a single London critic) had ever remarked on his own use of it over the past twenty years.

"Ah, *ha*-boy! say'st thou *so?* (upward accent; prolonged). Art thou *there*, truepenny? (prolonged, trembling sound of *truepenny*, ending in almost a groan or a rattling wail)." [61] He lifts his face and clasps it in his left hand, looking upward toward his raised right hand. He breathes heavily, looks about at Horatio and Marcellus, and holds out the sword again: "Come on. You hear *this fellow* in the *cellarage*." He tears these words out with great feeling and agitation, as if from his very lungs; and he points down behind him.

He starts forward then, with his left hand on his breast, holding the sword up, and says rapidly in deep tones, "*Consent* to *swear!*" Horatio asks for the words of the oath. Regrasping the sword below the hilt, and looking from one to the other, he says again, "*Never* to *speak* of *this that you have seen* (he holds out the sword once more) *swear by my sword*." Again from under the stage the Ghost cries, "Swear!" Hamlet steps swiftly backward, staring at the ground. He grasps the sword at both ends and holds it down at his girdle: "Hic et ubique? *Nay* (prolonged), *then* (rising accent on both words; looking down affrightedly), we'll shift our *ground* (low voice; prolonged)."

He looks about stealthily, and walks almost on tiptoe to downstage right, beckoning the friends two or three times to follow him, but without looking back at them, his eyes being fixed on the place where the Ghost had left the stage. He turns and whispers, "Come *hither*, gentlemen." They cross down right to him, and Hamlet turns toward them, his back to the audience: "And (low tone) lay your *hands again upon* my *sword*. *Never* to *speak* of *this that you have seen* (holding up the sword), swear by my sword (earnest voice)." Again the Ghost cries. Hamlet turns front swiftly and points the hilt of the sword downward, his left hand on his breast: "Well *said*, old mole! (upward accent). Canst work i' the *ground* so *fast?* A *worthy* pioneer! (upward accent)." He throws his head back and covers his face with his left hand. In this attitude he takes a couple

[61] *150.* The comic name-calling was one of Booth's 1870 restorations. It proved dangerous. Although Booth intended the lines "not as unfeeling levity, but the very intensity of mental excitement" (Notebook), critics objected to them. Nym Crinkle in the *World* (January 9) found the "bantering tone . . . conspicuously, if not painfully, opposed to the ineffable tenderness with which he has just addressed the dread visitant." In the 1878 edition Booth retained "boy" and "truepenny," but suppressed the other comic terms. As he explained to William Winter at that time (Folger, Y.c. 215 (282)), he could not trust supporting actors to behave properly during the passage.

of steps backward, then turns slowly to face the rear, saying slowly, "*Once* more, *remove*—good friends (low voice)."

164-180. "Oh day and night, but this is wondrous strange!"

Horatio remains down right as he makes his exclamation. Hamlet, shifting his sword to his left hand, comes down to Horatio and grasps his left hand with his own right. He bends forward a little so that their faces are close together: "And therefore *as* (upward accent) a stranger give it (slowly, in a mellow but sad voice) *welcome*." He stops for an instant. He partially closes his lips, and there is a peculiar play of the nostrils: "There are *more* things in *Heaven* and *earth*, Horatio (raising his hand), than are dreamt of in your *philosophy* (slight upward accent)." [62] He clasps Horatio's hand again, then drops it.

Taking the sword by both ends, he holds it horizontally before him: "But come. *Here* as before, *never* (first syllable prolonged), so help you *mercy!* how *strange* or *odd* (motioning up and down a couple of times with the horizontal sword) *soe'er* I bear myself, as I perchance hereafter shall think *meet* (upward accent) to put an antic *disposition*-on,[63] that *you*, at such time *seeing* me (short sound of *me*) *never* shall with *arms* encumbered thus (folding his arms, the sword kept in his right hand and pressed against his left breast, the hilt rising above his left shoulder), or this *head* shake (shaking his head), or by pronouncing of some doubtful *phrase* (holding his left arm out a little from his breast), *as*, '*Well*, *well* (slowly), we *know* (long falling sound),' or—'If we list to *speak* (nodding lightly),' or, 'There *be* an if they *might*,' or such *ambiguous* giving out to note that you know *aught* of me (short sound of *me* and upward accent) —*this* do ye *swear* (upward accent; he holds up the sword perpendicularly, hilt upward), so *grace* (upward accent) *and* (downward accent) *mercy* (upward and then downward accent) at your *most need help* (upward accent) *you* (upward accent) —*swear* (prolonged) by my *sword!*" He holds the sword out, the friends put their

[62] *167.* Some actors of Hamlet apparently bore down heavily on "your" in "your philosophy," thus accusing Horatio of skeptical materialism. Booth notes that "your" should be "rather indistinctly uttered than emphasized." He would prefer the word "our."

[63] *172.* Booth observes that the words "shall think it meet to put an antic disposition on" are "undoubtedly the key-note to the character": are unexceptionable evidence that Hamlet's madness is always a matter of role-playing and never reality.

hands on the guard of the hilt, and he gradually lowers it.[64] Again the Ghost cries.

181-190. "Swear."

During the Ghost's final long-drawn-out cry,[65] Hamlet continues the downward movement of the sword until the point touches the ground. He kneels, and at either side of him the friends kneel. He says reverently, "Rest, rest (low, solemn tone), perturbèd spirit! (almost a whisper on *spirit*)." He lowers his head until his forehead rests upon his right hand on the butt of his sword-hilt. His left hand hangs at his side. All three remain silent and motionless a moment. Then Hamlet slowly rises, drawing up the sword, but the others stay on their knees. He stands back, looking at them with sad and sober gratitude, feeling for his scabbard: "*So*-gentlemen (low voice), with *all* my *love* I do *commend* me to you (upward accent), and what as poor a man as *Hamlet*-is may do to *express* (upward accent) his *love* and *friending* to you (upward accent), Heaven *willing*, shall not lack (his voice falls)."

The friends rise and stand down right. Hamlet advances to Horatio, who turns up to him, and takes his right hand: "Let us go *in* together. And still your *fingers* on your *lips* I pray." He lets go of Horatio's hand and raises his right hand to his own lips: "The *time* is *out of joint*." He raises his right hand: "Oh *cursed* spite! That ever *I* was *born* to set it right!" [66] He drops his hand to his forehead, then lowers it, and puts his left hand on Horatio's shoulder. Marcellus starts to go off by himself toward the left. "*Nay*, come (upward accent), let's *go together*." He beckons Marcellus. All three go up left toward the opening between the trees. The curtain falls slowly to end the first act.[67]

[64] *180.* On one occasion of the final swearing, Booth recalls, he accidentally dropped his sword and it stuck upright in the light in such a way as to cast a cruciform shadow on the ground. He then made the friends take their oath upon the shadow. "I in vain tried to repeat it; the sword would not stick."

[65] *181.* The Ghost's last "Swear," Booth says, "should be given as a long-drawn, far-off sigh till it fades into Hamlet's 'Rest, rest, perturbed spirit,' which should be spoken in the same key."

[66] *189.* The couplet, Booth says, should be spoken as to himself: " 'Tis the groan of his overburthened soul."

[67] *190.* Although Hamlet threw his cloak off at line 136, neither Clarke nor the Harvard 1870 promptbook mentions the retrieval of it. Later promptbooks show the retrieval being worked up into a stage picture. Hamlet and Horatio, going arm in arm, pause at upstage center; Marcellus picks up the cloak, kneels to Hamlet, and presents it. On this tableau the curtain falls.

Throughout this scene, Clarke says, Booth "never forgot that he was the student prince and that he was vastly different from practical, realistic men of the nineteenth century"—that is, his belief in the Ghost is untroubled by modern skepticism. He showed great power under very great control: during his colloquy with the Ghost he was at once impassioned but physically very still. He never forgot that he was representing a man of "phlegmatic temperament."

The departure of the Ghost left him "in a state of high excitement. His wonder and fear were fresh upon him. His new duty bewildered him by its solemn magnitude." With the friends he was barely able to maintain coherence. "He was restless, secretive, wild, only bent on securing the silence of his friends regarding the spirit. He appealed to them with fitful eagerness. . . . There was a ghastly levity in his reception of his friends and in his delivery of 'You hear this fellow in the cellarage.' He gave a most perfect representation of whirl and complexity of feelings—of pity for the Ghost; of dread of its presence, of horror at its tale, of strong intellectual resolution of revenge but faintness of will. . . ." As he went from the stage he displayed "head-resolve but heart-doubt, despair, aching memory, and gloomy self-reliance." He was determined to avenge his father, yet hated the task and went about it with "the most thorough discontent of soul."

The text of Act I, 5 (line-numbering of the Globe edition).

The few cuts (20 lines) in this scene are traditional. These are: 44-45a, 53-57, 68-73a (all these from the Ghost's narrative); 105-111 (Hamlet's writing in his "tables"; this cut is not made in the promptbook, but Clarke does not record the lines and they are cut from Booth's 1878 edition); 176b.

The following alterations appear in Clarke's recording: 24, "Oh God!" > "Oh heaven!"; 93, "Oh fie!" is omitted; 99-100, "All saws of books" comes ahead of "all trivial fond records"—but here Clarke has had to interline two phrases and he may simply have got them in the wrong place; 136, "Horatio" > "my lord" (Folio reading); 162, "earth" > "ground"; 179, "this do swear" > "this do ye swear," and after 180 Booth inserted a final "Swear by my sword"; 184, "so poor a man" > "as poor a man"; 186, "God" > "Heaven."

The restorations (22 lines) are as follows: 32-34a (the Ghost's metaphor of the fat weed on Lethe wharf: not printed in the 1878 edition); 77; 92-93a (Hamlet's appeal to heaven, earth, and hell); 100-101; 145-152a, 156-163 (Hamlet's repeated commands to swear, the Ghost's first and third cries, the comic name-calling); 190.

Act II

Act II. *A Room in the Palace, called the Hall of Arches.*
(Globe edition: Act II, 1 and 2. 120 lines cut to 33; 634 lines cut to 463; total: 754 lines cut to 496.)

The setting for the second act, which is played through without change of scene, is a great hall of marvelous vastness (see Plate VIII).[1] The lights are up full. The ceiling of the hall gives it the appearance of a Romanesque church, its huge central vault defining the nave and the two lesser vaults covering narrow aisles. The vaulting is not quite consistent: although the nave is barrel-vaulted in Norman style, the side aisles combine barrel-vaulting with the pointed arches of Gothic style.

The lower portion of the set, where the audience's attention would mainly rest, is emphatically Norman, matching the other interiors we have seen. It consists of a tall stone screen, which cuts across the near ends of the side aisles, runs up the nave under the bosses of the pendant ceiling arches, and curves across the back somewhere short of the back wall, making a sort of U-shaped room-within-a-room. The screen is opened up by seven round arches with chevron molding: one across each side aisle, fronting us; one at each side of the nave, at right angles to the footlights; three across the U-curve at the back. The arches are supported on heavy columns. A chevron frieze runs straight around the top of the entire screen.

Beyond the screen are vistas of the enclosing room, a huge rectangle as wide as the proscenium and perhaps 45 feet deep. The far end of it is hung with tapestry, and high up, beyond the top of the

[1] Comparison of this Hall of Arches with the corresponding set in the Winter Garden production of 1864-67 (see Plate XVIb) affords an especially vivid demonstration of how the greater stage spaces of Booth's Theatre permitted Booth and Witham to elaborate upon their original scenic ideas. The simple rectangular center room bounded by three archways becomes a deep U-shaped room bounded by five archways; the low, flat ceiling becomes a majestically vaulted one. The changes, however, are merely decorative, not fundamental. Stage actions as blocked in 1864 could still be used in 1870. The early sketch of Hamlet conversing with the actors in 1864-67 conforms exactly to the arrangement which Clarke describes for 1870 (line 546) when the First Actor bows to take his leave. Handsome as this Hall of Arches was, it did not survive long, even at Booth's Theatre. By 1873, according to Bensen Sherwood's "Stage Plans," the Act III Play scene set was erected at the first intermission and served both the second and third acts. When Booth toured the play even simpler expedients were used. The Taylor 1890 promptbook, for instance, specifies "same scene as preceding interior," by which is meant whatever Room of State had served in Act I, 2.

U-shaped section of the screen, are three small round-arched windows. Through the arch at stage left we see a farther arch which leads offstage into other parts of the castle. Through the arch at stage right is a glimpse of outdoors—a bit of low crenellated wall and beyond it bright sky or distant landscape. Light pours in from this stage right opening, touching up the architectural details of the interior.

Downstage at extreme right and left, brief side walls run forward toward the proscenium, each containing a small archway closed with a wooden door. Furled banners are mounted at the corners of the stone screen where it turns up the nave; and above the stage right arch which fronts us is displayed a raven painted on a shield.

The action calls for furniture. None is shown in the watercolor, but a groundplan in the Harvard 1870 promptbook indicates a table with books on it upstage in front of the center arch, and four "Hamlet" chairs: one at the right of the U-shaped room, just below the side arch; one near the left side arch; and one (for decoration only?) upstage right and left in each of the "outer rooms." [2] Clarke's account of the action implies at least one more chair somewhere close to the table.

Since this set was erected between the acts, out of sight of the audience, and will not be changed until the act-drop falls again, the manipulation of its parts need not concern us. The apparent solidity of the ceiling and the fact that, as we shall see, it will hang in place for three consecutive acts might tempt one to suspect that it was a three-dimensional construction. But the note in Bensen Sherwood's "Stage Plans" is decisive: the words "Triple Arch Stone Borders to 5—Tabs in each E" can mean only that the ceiling was created by perspective painting on a series of five border cloths, hung one above each of the five grooves, with side cloths (tabs) to close the spaces between them.

74-120 (of Globe edition Act II, 1). *"How now, Ophelia! what's the matter?"*

The Polonius-Reynaldo scene being deleted, the brief interview between Ophelia and Polonius is simply tacked onto the long second scene of the act. Ophelia is telling her father of Hamlet's lunatic

[2] These "Hamlet" chairs, which are used in most of the interior scenes, are constructed with side arms but no backs, so that they can be sat in from either direction.

behavior in her closet, and Polonius decides to report it to the King.[3] Since Clarke does not record the passage, there is nothing to illuminate it but the sparse notations of the Harvard 1870 promptbook. Polonius enters "L. U. E."—that is, through the left arch at the back; Ophelia enters "R. 2. E."—that is, through the right side arch of the U-shaped room; and they meet at center. At the end of their interview they go out through the first entrance left—that is, by way of the downstage wooden door. From the Taylor 1890 promptbook we glean only obvious details: that Polonius takes Ophelia's hand as he addresses her, and that at line 100, at the end of her narrative, she falls on his shoulder.

1-170 (of Globe edition Act II, 2). "*Welcome, dear Rosencrantz and Guildenstern!*"

As Polonius and Ophelia disappear at the left, the King, followed by Rosencrantz and Guildenstern, enters through the archway at up right of the U-shaped room.[4] At line 10, as he is saying, "I entreat you both . . . ," the Queen enters to him from the left side arch, attended by two Pages who take their posts just inside the arch.[5] After line 37, when she says, "Go you, and bring these gentlemen where Hamlet is," the Pages lead Rosencrantz and Guildenstern away into the castle through the left side arch. Simultaneously Polonius comes hurrying on through the upstage left arch, bearing a "Written

[3] *77-100.* Booth, who was always being pestered by queries as to whether Hamlet was "mad," and who was determinedly convinced that he was sane, left several notes on Ophelia's report of Hamlet's offstage mad scene. In an early workbook (at The Players) he calls Hamlet here "a skillful gamester" who begins "the game of antics . . . where it is most likely to win the first trick." In his Notebook he writes, "To the actor this is all 'play-acting,' and Shakespeare—so well posted in the actor's tricks, as is plainly shewn throughout this play, intended it to be so understood by his audience. 'Tis enough to scare a girl—but not a *sound* physician: 'tis stage-madness only. Compare it with *Lear's* real lunacy, or indeed her own."

[4] *1-10.* In later stagings, according to the Pitman 1884 and the Harvard 1890 promptbooks, the King was attended by four or five extra Lords, the Queen by four Ladies. Although not called for in the Harvard 1870 promptbook, there were probably at least this many extras in the 1870 production. They would all leave the stage with Rosencrantz and Guildenstern at line 37.

5-7. The King's line about the change in Hamlet's appearance is cut, but Booth says in his Notebook that " 'Tis plain his dress should be disordered—as indeed Ophelia has described it to be. My father and others of his early day observed this." Booth, of course, did not observe it.

[5] *19-21.* The Queen's assurance to Rosencrantz and Guildenstern that Hamlet loves them is, Booth says, "mere flattery"; for Hamlet, in fact, "suspects them from the first and trusts them as he would 'adders fang'd.' "

Scroll," to explain "the very cause of Hamlet's lunacy." The King and Queen stand at about center to hear the beginning of his garrulous prattle, but at line 95, as the Queen says, "More matter with less art," she crosses Polonius and sits in the chair near the left side arch.[6] When his tale is finished and commented upon and the plan is laid to "loose my daughter to him," [7] the Queen sees Hamlet coming from the right; she and the King go out through the left side arch and disappear into the farther rooms of the castle.

171-227. "How does my good Lord Hamlet?"

Hamlet enters at line 167, so that we see him as the Queen says, "But look where sadly the poor wretch comes reading." [8] Clarke says he enters at the "front," which would mean by way of the downstage wooden door; the Harvard 1870 promptbook says "R. 2. E.," which would be from the out-of-doors. In either case he does not at once come into the acting area, but wanders upstage through the outer room to the arch at upstage right; there he turns in and leans against a pillar, reading intently. When Polonius calls out to him, he looks up casually: "*Well* (low voice; he drops his eyes again to the book), God-a-mercy." His voice fades as if the interest in his book interferes with the vocal strength of his reply. At Polonius' "Do you know me, my lord?" he looks up again, comes forward to the chair below the right side arch, and lays his right hand upon it, having lowered his left hand with the opened book to his side: "*Excel*lent well (distinct articulation, slight upward accent of *well*, low tone and quiet demeanor; he draws the chair downstage). You are a *fish*monger (*fish* is prolonged)." Polonius protests that he is not. Hamlet sets the chair in position at about right center: "Then I would you *were* so *honest* a man (he sits)." [9]

[6] *43.* In later stagings, from the beginning of the Polonius passage the King and Queen were seated at the right and left of the center-stage table.

[7] *162-167.* Booth expresses in his Notebook considerable impatience with those "learned noodles" who have found something "indelicate and coarse" in Polonius' offer to loose his daughter for an encounter with Hamlet: "He simply means that he will remove the restriction placed upon Ophelia and let her converse with Hamlet. *Encounter* is merely their meeting."

[8] *167-170.* The precise instant of Hamlet's entrance varied in different stagings according to the scenic arrangements. When there was no outer room for him to wander in, he entered at the word "board." In his Notebook Booth remarks that Hamlet sees the King and Queen before they leave, suspects a trap, and "prepares at once to *bamboozle* the old man."

[9] *176.* In later stagings, when the table and chairs were set fairly well forward, he did not have to move a chair as he did in 1870, but simply sat

Polonius questions the word "honest." Hamlet, facing toward him, puts the book upright on his knee, with both hands on top of it. He looks at Polonius quietly with an air of courteous tolerance: "*Ay*, sir! To be *honest* as this world goes, is to be one man picked out of ten thousand (slow delivery, grave demeanor)." Polonius agrees with that. "For if the sun breed maggots in a dead dog (short sound of *dog;* he raises his left hand a little) being a *God* (pointing upward) *kissing carrion*—(upward accent)." [10] He drops his hand to the book again and pauses, looking at Polonius as if puzzled and drawing in his lower lip. He raises his left hand and reaches it out a little toward Polonius: "*Have you* a daughter? (change of tone to the more confidential)." Polonius says that he has one. "*Let her not walk* i' the *sun* (deep, warning tone). *Conception* is a blessing; but not as *your daughter* may *conceive* (he shakes his left hand lightly toward Polonius): —friend, *look to't, look to't* (upward accent; he raises the book with both hands and holds it open as if to read, shaking his head meaningfully at Polonius and gazing at him earnestly), *look to't*." He reads.

In an aside Polonius speculates on the meaning of this; then he turns to Hamlet and asks him what he reads. Hamlet looks up from the book, lifts his eyebrows, and turns the printed page toward Polonius: "*Words* (he holds the book a little tipped down in his right hand and strikes carelessly across it with the fingers of his left hand; he speaks as if to enlighten Polonius, but a little petulantly), *words* (he raises the book as if to read again and speaks as if in scorn both of the book and of Polonius' ignorance), *words* (scornfully, as if to be sure that Polonius does not misunderstand him)." [11] Polonius wants to know "what is the matter." Hamlet looks up in surprise, lifts his eyebrows, and drops the book down a little so that the print is showing: "Between who? (upward accent)."

Polonius corrects him: what is the matter that he reads? Hamlet raises the book and holds it in his left hand, laying his right forefinger on the page. He nods his head and speaks slowly: "*Slanders*, sir, for the *satirical rogue* says *here* that old men have *gray beards;*

on a stool in front of the table; he also delayed the sitting until line 187, "look to't."

[10] *181.* Booth could not or would not see any dark meaning in the image of the sun breeding maggots in a dead dog: "He is but 'guying' him after the fashion of the players"; it is only a "bit of greenroom 'chaffing.' "

[11] *194.* Booth wonders what motivation John Philip Kemble could have found for angrily tearing a leaf from his book at "Words, words, words."

that their *faces* are *wrinkled;* their *eyes* purging thick *amber* and *plum-tree gum;* and that they have a plentiful *lack* of wit, together with most weak *hams* (short sound). All of which, sir (the voice rising in a cheerful, assenting tone), though I most *powerfully* and *potently* believe, yet I hold it not *honesty* to have it thus *set down;* for you yourself, sir, shall be as *old* (prolonged) as *I* am (his voice drops as he continues) if, like a *crab* (he lifts his right hand with the fingers spread out), you could go *backward* (slow, sober pronunciation)." [12] He works his fingers up and down in imitation of a crab's movements.

Polonius retires to the center to give his aside. Hamlet looks after him with cautious, shrewd eyes, and then resumes reading. Polonius returns and invites him to "walk out of the air." "*In*to my *grave?* (heavy sound of *in*, which is interrogatory; *grave* has a falling inflection)." [13] The "grave" image appears to rouse some emotion in him, and as Polonius crosses to center for his long aside, Hamlet puts both hands on his book and stares out front for a moment, as if thinking about death; then, slowly, he raises the book and reads again. Presently Polonius calls out to him. Hamlet starts slightly, as if suddenly jogged from reverie. Polonius begs to take his leave.

Hamlet rises, and, for one of the few occasions in the play, his face grows bright and smiling; he turns toward Polonius as if a most agreeable piece of news had just been told him: "You *cannot*, sir (upward accent), take from me *anything* that I will more willingly *part* withal (upward accent; he bows a little); *except* my *life* (upward accent, but low voice and a sad, weary tone; he turns front at the chair), *except* my *life* (upward accent; he sits and rests one end of the book on his knees with both hands on it), *except* my life (upward accent, but the voice is fading)." His head drops a little,

[12] *207.* Booth found the meaning of the crab going backward, as he was fond of repeating (his Notebook, the Taylor 1890 promptbook, letter to Professor Corson in 1874), while he was fishing one day in the Shark River in New Jersey: "The natural *gait* of the crab is sidewise; it goes backward only when shedding its old shell—when it becomes, as it were—callow, and young —a fledging. This is the *method* which Polonius sees in Hamlet's madness."

[13] *210.* Clarke hears "Into my grave?" as a question. Mason says that Booth read it as an exclamation and *not* as a question. In the Taylor 1890 promptbook Booth confirms Clarke's hearing when he observes that *earlier* Hamlets gave this line "dolefully, not interrogatively." Booth means to convey, "Where else could I be *out* of the air?" The line is not to be spoken with a sigh. At line 220, likewise, "except my life" is to be spoken "with weary indifference, not despair."

and he looks front for an instant in gloomy thought. Then he starts, as if recalled to the present, lifts the book again, and reads. Polonius bids him farewell and goes out the left side arch. Hamlet turns at the word and bows slightly as Polonius goes. Then he scowls a trifle, and blurts out in unguarded relief, "These *tedious* old *fools!* (upward accent)."

228-333. "My excellent good friends!"

Polonius meets Rosencrantz and Guildenstern offstage, and we hear his voice from a farther room directing them to Hamlet. They enter through the left arch and come down left, calling out their effusive greetings. Hamlet looks up from his book, sees them with tempered joyousness, rises, crosses swiftly left, and takes their hands: "*My excellent good friends! How dost* thou, *Guildenstern?* Ah, Rosencrantz! [14] Good *lads*, how do ye *both? What news?*" Rosencrantz answers that there is no news but that the world is grown honest. Hamlet gives their hands a slight shake: "*Then* is *doomsday* near. *In* the beaten-*way* of friendship (releasing their hands and folding his arms), what *make* you at *Elsinore?* (his voice falls a little on *Elsinore*)." They have come only to visit him, says Rosencrantz. Hamlet, with arms folded, turns a little front: "*Beggar* that *I am*, I am even *poor* in *thanks!* but I *thank* you (upward accent)."

He stands back a little, arms still folded, and then raises his right hand to his chin: "WERE-you not *sent for?* (the voice falls in *for*).[15] *Is it* your-own *inclining?* (the voice falls in *inclining*). Is it a *free* visitation? (upward accent; pause). Come, come, *deal justly* with me. Come, *nay* (upward accent), speak (falling accent; holding his hands out before him)." Guildenstern asks what they should say. Hamlet drops his right hand to his breast: "*Anything* (he holds out his right hand again with fingers extended) —but to the *purpose*. You *were* sent for; and there is a kind of confession in your *looks* which your modesties have not *craft*-enough to color." He drops his right hand to his side and his left hand to the hilt of his dagger: "*I*

[14] *228.* In later productions, according to Pitman, Mason, and others, on greeting the friends Hamlet crosses behind the table (which is well forward) and throws his book down upon it. No further use is made of the book.

[15] *283.* At "Were you not sent for?" Booth remarks in his Notebook that Hamlet "here suspects the object of their coming." This perhaps accounts for the heavy emphasis which Clarke records for "*Were.*" Apparently Booth found the motivation entirely within Hamlet's mind, and required no especial stage action from Rosencrantz or Guildenstern to promote his suspicion.

know the good *King* and *Queen* have sent for you (slight upward accent)." "To what end?" says Rosencrantz. Hamlet raises his right hand: "*That* you must teach *me*. But let me *conjure*-you by the rights of our *fellowship* (he drops his right hand to his side), by the consonancy of our *youth*, by the obligation of our ever-*preserved-love* (upward accent; he raises his right hand again), and by what *more* dear a *better*-proposer could *charge* you *withal* (upward accent), be—*even—and direct* with me *whether you* were *sent for* or not."

He nods his head at them, turns away, and goes upstage toward the center table. Rosencrantz asks Guildenstern in a quick aside what they are to answer. Hamlet says in a low voice, aside, as he is going toward the table, "*Nay then*, I have an *eye* of *you*." He puts his right hand on the back of a chair near the table, and partly turning toward them, says over his shoulder, "If you *love*-me, hold-*not*-off." Guildenstern admits that they were indeed sent for. Hamlet nods. He turns to face them and brings his hand down heavily on the back of the chair: "*I* will tell-you *why;* so shall my *anticipation* prevent your *discovery*, and your secrecy to the *King* and *Queen* moult no feather."

He looks at them, and facing front leans against the table with both hands touching it: "*I have*, of *late*—but *wherefore* I *know not*—*lost* all my (short sound of *my*) *mirth* (the voice drops a little), *forgone* all custom of *exercises* (slight upward accent);[16] and *indeed*, it goes so-*heavily* with my disposition that this goodly *frame* the *earth* (his right hand giving a downward motion) *seems* to me a *ster*ile promontory; this most *excellent*-canopy, the *air* (leaving the table he steps slowly toward the right and points through the side arch as if out into the daylight), *look*-you, this *brave o'erhanging*-firmament, this *majestical roof* fretted with golden-*fire* (his voice drops a little; he looks back toward them, his hand still raised)—*why*-it appears *no other* thing to me (looking out toward the day again) than a *foul* and *pestilent* congregation of vapors (upward accent and slightly exclamatory tone)." He drops his hand and turns toward them, standing near the center table: "What a *piece* of *work* is a man! (short sound).[17] How *noble* in *reason!* (upward accent; he

[16] *308.* At "forgone all custom of exercises," Booth points out that elsewhere (V, 2, 221) Hamlet tells Horatio that he has been in continual practice of fencing ever since Laertes went to France. Apparently, however, he regarded this only as Shakespeare's slip of the pen rather than as a clue that Hamlet is launching a Homeric lie: he read this speech about melancholy with headlong earnestness and absolute sincerity.

[17] *316.* Booth indicates in his Notebook that this praise of "a man" is

lifts his hand for an instant toward his head) how *infinite* in *faculty!* (upward accent) in *form*-and-*moving*-how *express*-and-*admirable!* (level voice; holding his hand before him oratorically) in *action* how-like-an *angel!* (upward accent; looking upward) in *apprehension* how like a *god!* (upward accent; he raises his hand high, then drops it) the *beauty* of-the-world! (falling accent) the *paragon* (upward accent) of *animals!* (falling accent). And yet, to *me*, what-is-this *quintessence* of *dust?* (upward accent; he lifts his eyebrows and his upper lip in scorn, and gives his right hand a trivial swing outward). *Man* delights not me (clasping his hands at his girdle and leaning against the table); *no, nor* (upward accent; prolonged) *woman either* (long, high, indrawing sound of *e*, and upward accent; he starts forward and raises his right hand toward Rosencrantz, the index finger pointed admonishingly), though by your *smiling* (upward accent) you seem to *say* so (upward accent on the last two words)."

Rosencrantz denies that there was any such stuff in his thoughts. Hamlet has come down toward them at left and stands before them. His left arm lies across his breast, the left fingers resting on his right arm above the elbow. His right arm is bent up, the hand closed and held just below his chin: "*Why* (the *y* sound is prolonged, running on into the sound of *ee*) did you *laugh* then when I said *man*-delights-not me?" He looks at them with an air of half-thoughtful, half-bantering inquiry. Rosencrantz, changing the subject, tells of the coming of the Players.

334-407. "He that plays the King shall be welcome."

Hamlet steps back. His left hand falls to his girdle and he holds his right hand off at his side with the arm drawn back. He says quickly, almost eagerly, "He that *plays*-the-*King* shall be *welcome* (the voice falls)." He pauses an instant and then says, less eagerly but with more attention to his listeners, "His majesty shall have *tribute* of me (short sound of *me*); the-*adventurous knight* shall use his *foil* (upward accent) and *target* (downward accent; he reaches out both arms in a kindly fashion); the *lover* shall not sigh *gratis* (upward accent; he drops his left hand to his dagger and draws his right hand up before him a little); the humorous man shall end *his* part in peace;

intended to exclude women: "Woman holds a very low place in his estimation; since the very *root* of his veneration for her has been blasted by his mother's conduct."

and the *lady* (upward accent on the first syllable; prolonged; he nods and makes a gesture with his right hand before his breast, the index finger crooked a little) shall say her mind *freely*, or the blank verse shall *halt* for't.—*What players are* they?"

He takes a step toward them, his left hand on his dagger and his right hand before his breast. Rosencrantz tells him that they are Hamlet's favorite tragedians from the city. "How *chances*-it they *travel?* Their *residence* both in *reputation* and *profit* was *better*, both ways. Do they hold the same estimation they did when I was in the city? Are they so followed?" He folds his arms and looks at them inquiringly, his head a little to one side. Rosencrantz says that they are not.

Hamlet advances to them quickly. He puts his right hand on Guildenstern's shoulder and the fingers of his left hand on Rosencrantz' breast. He bends forward a little and says in a low tone and confidential manner, "It is not very *strange*, for *my* (prolonged) *uncle* (heavy sound) is *King* of Denmark; and those that would make *mouths* of him (looking from one to the other enigmatically) while my *father* lived, give *twenty*, *forty*, *fifty*, *an hundred* ducats, apiece, for his picture in little." He lifts from Rosencrantz' breast a miniature which is suspended on a string, and throws it back upon him lightly, with a short, dry, sarcastic laugh.[18] "There is something in this more than *natural* (leaving them with a casual swing of the arms, he comes down front center; and they cross up center to the table, looking at him wonderingly), if *philosophy* (upward accent on *philoso-*, downward accent on *-phy*) could-find-it-out (dry, ironical voice).

From off left is heard a flourish of trumpets, which Guildenstern identifies as announcing the Players. Hamlet turns toward them: "Gentlemen, you are welcome to Elsinore (he goes up center to them). Your *hands* (he takes a hand of each). You *are* (prolonged) welcome (upward accent of *wel-*, downward accent of *-come*). But

[18] *384.* In the properties list of the 1870 promptbook is the item, "*Two* Pictures on chains for Guildenstern and Rosencrantz." Mason, recording a later staging, shows Hamlet making more elaborate use of these miniatures, which are presumably of Claudius. He is standing just above Rosencrantz and Guildenstern, one at either side. When he asks if the tragedians still hold the same "estimation" as they did, he first notices Rosencrantz' miniature and touches it. At "my uncle is King of Denmark," he strikes it. At "his picture in little," he lifts *both* the miniatures, drops them, and walks away. At "my uncle-father" (line 395), he strikes Rosencrantz' miniature again.

(lifting their hands toward his face, and stooping a trifle forward with a faint, stealthy smile) my *uncle-father* (heavy sound of *uncle;* prolonged *ah* sound in *father*) and *aunt-mother* (prolonged *au* sound in *aunt*; he clasps both their hands between his own and lifts them to his eyes) *are* (long, upward, triumphant sound; smiling exultingly) *deceived* (prolonged; his voice falls)."

He casts their hands from him and comes down right. At Guildenstern's eager query of "In what, my dear lord?" Hamlet, facing front, throws back his head and lifts his eyebrows, and, motioning over his left shoulder with the fingers of his right hand, beckons them to come down to him. His left hand is on his dagger. Guildenstern comes down. Hamlet catches his right hand with his own left hand. Guildenstern bends back a little and Hamlet stoops toward him so that their faces are near together. Hamlet raises his right hand in front of Guildenstern's shoulder, the index finger pointing and crooked. Rosencrantz has followed down too, and stands a little upstage of them, listening attentively. "I am but mad *north-north-west;* when the *wind* (slight plause) is *southerly* (his voice falls a little; he nods and shakes his finger) *I know* a *hawk* from a *handsaw* (his voice falls)." He takes Guildenstern's left hand in both his own and looks at him with sober keenness. Then he leaves him and crosses to front center.

The voice of Polonius is heard calling from offstage left. Hamlet quickly returns to Guildenstern down right, takes his hand, bends toward him, and points back toward the left arches: "Hark you, Guildenstern and Rosencrantz—that *great baby* you see there (slowly) is not yet out of his swaddling-clouts (more quickly; upward accent and humorous tone)." Leaving them, he goes up near the center table, sits in a chair, and looks off left. Rosencrantz makes his little joke about an old man being twice a child.

Impulsively Hamlet rises and hurries down right again. He puts his right hand on the arm of Guildenstern and reaches toward Rosencrantz with his left: "I will prophesy he comes to tell me of the *players. Mark it.*" He steps backward a little, facing them, so that his back will obviously be turned to Polonius when he enters. He holds up his right hand as if in conversation, and his voice changes from a low, friendly tone to a louder, more formal one: "You say *right, sir:* o' Monday *morning* (upward accent); *'twas* so, indeed (his voice drops; he gestures with his right hand)." Polonius comes hurriedly through the left arch and down center, calling out, "My lord, I have news to tell you."

408-439. "My lord, I have news to tell you."

Hamlet repeats quickly, imitating Polonius' manner. "My lord, my lord, I have news to tell you," and leaving Rosencrantz and Guildenstern he crosses rapidly to meet Polonius at front center. He takes Polonius' wrist under his left hand, and standing very close to him says confidingly, "When *Roscius* was an *actor* in Rome— (full, even sound)." Polonius announces that the actors have come. "*Buzz, buzz!* (humming sound of the *z*'s; he faces front, waves his right hand to and fro before his face, and turns his face away impatiently)." He casts a quick glance toward Rosencrantz and Guildenstern as much as to say, "You see, my surmise was right." Polonius begins to protest, upon his "honor." Hamlet lays his left hand on Polonius' arm, takes a step forward, raises his right hand with fingers closed but the index finger extended and crooked, reaches up, looks forward and upward intensely, and says in a meditative yet expressive way, as if he were repeating something which he thought it necessary for Polonius to hear, "*Then came each actor* on his ass— (upward accent, as if the sentence were to continue)."

At the beginning of Polonius' gabbling speech about "the best actors in the world," Hamlet turns and looks at him as if in surprise and doubt. Gradually his face becomes grave, then sorrowful. He draws down his brows, parts his lips, and puffs out his cheeks a little, sadly. Near the end of the speech, he clasps his hands, and as Polonius concludes, he looks upward: "Oh (prolonged), Jepthah, Judge of *Israel* (heavy *s* sound rather than *z*), what a *treasure* (a little tremulously) hadst *thou!* (his voice drops; he raises his clasped hands before him and shakes his head mournfully)." Polonius asks in puzzlement, "What a treasure had he, my lord?"

Hamlet looks at him in sad surprise and lowers his hands: "Why (short sound; upward accent; he drops his left hand to his side, but holds his right hand in front of him; he smiles, as if at a memory of something which gave him pleasure mixed with pain), one *fair daughter* (gently, the voice rising on *fair* and falling on *daughter*, the stronger emphasis on *daughter*) and *no more* (he looks front and raises his right hand), the *which* he *lovèd* passing well (his voice rises softly but firmly in *lovèd*, declines in *passing*, and falls in *well*)." He drops his hands, and during Polonius' little aside, his upraised face alters from smiling to sorrowful. He turns and looks steadily at Polonius, and says in a tone of ordinary conversation, "Am I not i' the *right*, old Jepthah? (upward accent)."

Polonius acknowledges that he does have a daughter whom he loves passing well. Hamlet steps back a little and turns front with a disappointed and displeased look. He puts up his left hand: "Nay (prolonged; a contemptuous tone, as if correcting Polonius), that (the voice falls sadly) follows not." He turns toward the right, meditatively and almost grieving. Polonius asks what then does follow. Hamlet turns toward him slowly, a little surprised: "Why, as by *lot*, God *wot* (low, earnest tone; reciting with troubled face as if he could not remember what he wished to say)." He takes a step forward, facing front; he raises his right hand before him with fingers closed and looks up toward it as a devotee might look up toward a cross. He turns again toward Polonius: "And then, you know (he puts his left hand on Polonius' arm, and raising his right hand again, he looks toward the front), it came to *pass*, as *most like* it *was*." He hesitates, draws his right hand down to his forehead, and looks perplexed.

From offstage left the trumpets sound again. Looking relieved, Hamlet pats Polonius' arm and speaks in ordinary tones, as if glad to give over a subject he could not quite remember: "The first row of the pious *chanson* (pronounced *shaunson*) will show you more (the voice drops in *more*)." He turns and goes upstage a little as the Actors enter: "For *look*, my *abridgement* comes." Polonius clears the front of the stage by crossing to join Rosencrantz and Guildenstern at the right.

440-573. "You are welcome, masters; welcome all."

The Actors have entered from within the castle and they are coming forward through the outer room at the left. There are five of them: First Actor, Second Actor, Actress (a boy), and two others. "You are *welcome*, masters; *welcome all* (friendly tones)." He greets the First Actor as he comes through the left arch: "*Oh* (upward accent; prolonged), old *friend!*" He extends his hand. The First Actor steps in and kisses it, and then retires down left. Hamlet stands with his left hand on his dagger, his right hand at his breast: "Why, thy face is *valanced* since I saw thee *last*. Com'st thou to *beard* me (short sound of *me;* reaching out his right hand with a playful shake) in *Den*mark? (upward sound of *mark*)."

He looks at the "Actress," who comes next: "*What* (bright, upward sound), my *young lady* and *mistress!*" [19] He holds out his right hand, and the boy kneels and kisses it. "*By'r Lady,* your ladyship is nearer-to-heaven-than-when-I-saw-you *last,* by the altitude of a *chopine.* Pray heaven your voice, like a piece of *uncurrent gold,* be not *cracked* within the *ring* (upward accent)." He pats the boy's cheek, and the boy retires to the left. "You are *all welcome.* We'll e'en to't like *French falconers,* fly at *anything-we-see.*"

He goes toward front center: "We'll have a *speech,* straight; *come,* give us a taste of your quality (upward accent); come, a *passionate* speech." He folds his arms. The First Actor, from down left, asks what speech he wishes to hear. Hamlet unfolds his arms, drops his left hand to his dagger, and puts his right hand to his lips: "*I heard* thee speak me a *speech once*—but it was (dropping his right hand to his breast) *never acted;* or, if it *was,* not above *once* (he nods his head); for the *play,* I remember, *pleased not* the *million;* 'twas *caviare* (pronounced *ca-ve-a-ry*) to the *general.*" He takes a short step forward, looks at the Actor, and raises his right hand to his neck: "But it was an *excellent play,* well *digested* in the *scenes* (making a slight outward wave of the right hand), set down with as much *modesty* as *cunning.*"

He lowers his hand to his breast, droops his head, and looks down thoughtfully: "*One speech* in it I *chiefly loved* (he raises his head). 'Twas *Aeneas' tale* to *Dido* (nodding his head toward the Actor, he reaches out his right hand toward him and draws it back again in a confirmatory gesture), and *thereabout* of it *especially* where he speaks of *Priam's* slaughter (making a slight outward wave of the right hand and nodding his head). If it *live in your memory,* begin at this *line.*"

He faces front, lifts his left hand to his breast, and reaches up before him with his right hand, the fingers closed: "The *rugged Pyrrhus,* like the *Hyrcanian* beast (earnest voice) —'*Tis not so* (his voice falls)." He turns a little, drops his left hand to his side, lowers his head, and taps his forehead with the fingers of his right hand: "It *begins* with Pyrrhus." He looks up quickly and exultantly, faces

[19] *444.* The lines addressed to the Actress were not printed in Booth's 1878 edition (although as we find in the Taylor 1890 promptbook, Booth at times restored them). Mason, in noticing the 1878 omission, records that sometimes (as in 1870) the Actress was played by a boy, "who entered here in male attire, giving point to Hamlet's words: 'My young lady, etc' which Mr. Booth used to speak smilingly."

front, puts a foot forward; he lifts his right hand high before him, holds his left hand back and outward at his side, and declaims in a deep, eager voice: "*He*, whose *sable arms*, *black* as his *purpose*, did the *night* (sudden rise of tone) resemble (upward accent, but lower voice than in *night*), *old Grandsire* (low, tragic tone) *Priam seeks* (he takes a step forward, reaching out with his right arm)." Then he resumes his ordinary manner, and gestures courteously to the Actor to begin. Polonius, at right center, applauds and compliments Hamlet's good accent and good discretion. Hamlet acknowledges the applause with a short, polite bow, but with a sarcastic look. "So," he says; then, motioning to the Actor to begin, "*proceed you*."

The two minor Actors advance from left center and move a chair from upstage to downstage a little left of center. Hamlet bows his thanks to them and sits in it, facing left, his left elbow on the arm of the chair and his face resting against his left hand. The First Actor stands down left. During the speech Hamlet watches him closely.[20] When Polonius objects that the speech is too long, Hamlet rouses himself with a look of mild vexation, glances over his right shoulder, and motions Polonius to approach. He sits up and leans to the right, and as Polonius bends down to him, he puts his hand to his mouth and says in a low, confidential tone, "It shall to the *barber's*, with *your beard*." He looks keenly at Polonius, then turns again, rests his left elbow on the chair arm as before, and points his right hand toward the Actor: "Say on; come to Hecuba (authoritative but kindly tone)."

The Actor's next line refers to "the mobled queen." At the word "mobled" Hamlet starts a little, as if in curiosity. Leaning over the side of his chair and reaching out his right hand, he repeats in a voice of surprise, doubt, and admiration, "The *mobled* queen!"[21]

[20] *490-541.* Booth notes that the Pyrrhus-Hecuba speech "affords the *best* actor good opportunity to display some of his best powers."

[21] *526.* Eventually Booth rejected "mobled" and in revised issues of the Prompt-Book edition (after 1878) he printed the Folio word "inobled," which he took to mean "rendered ignoble." And whereas in 1870 he repeats "mobled" in tones of surprise, he would repeat "inobled" sadly, being preoccupied with thoughts of his "ignoble" mother. He spilled much ink to justify "inobled," claiming among other things that "mobled" was too common a word in Shakespeare's time to elicit comment from Hamlet and Polonius. "Why should Hamlet have caught at the Queen's *mob-cap*," he once exclaimed to William Winter (Folger, Y.c. 215 (342)); "it always strikes me as silly, and a useless interruption; he might with a shrewder meaning have caught at the blanket about her loins." Eventually (about 1887) one of his supporting actors, John Malone, who was something of a

Polonius exclaims that the word is "good." Hamlet turns and bows courteously to Polonius, but with a look which tells him to be silent. He faces the Actor again and motions him to go on. A few lines later the Actor, coming to his period, weeps, and Polonius bids him speak no more.[22] Hamlet looks at Polonius with an unusually sober face; then rises and faces the Actor: " *'Tis well* (low and quiet tone, signifying both commendation and dismissal). *I'll have thee speak out* the *rest* of *this soon*."

The Actor bows and goes up through the left arch. Hamlet goes to Polonius at center: "Good my lord, will you see the players *well bestowed*? Do you hear, let them be *well* (prolonged) *used* (prolonged), for they are the *abstract* and *brief chronicles* of the *time*. After your *death* you were better have a bad *epitaph* (upward accent) than their *ill report* while you *live* (slight upward accent)." Polonius agrees to "use them according to their desert." Hamlet steps nearer and raises his right hand to Polonius' breast: "*Much better* (upward accent on both words), sir. Use every man after his *desert* (marked emphasis and upward accent) and *who* (resting one finger on Polonius' breast) shall scape *whipping?* (upward accent; gentle, musical, but slightly sarcastic tone). Use them (the voice becomes a little admonitory) after your own *honor* and *dignity;* the less they *deserve* (upward accent) the *more merit* is in your *bounty*. Take them in." He steps aside courteously, with a passive wave of the hand. Polonius calls, "Come, sirs," to the Actors, who have gone up through the left arch, and they come forward a little. Hamlet says, "*Follow him*, friends (upward accent); we'll hear a play tomorrow." Polonius goes out the wooden door down left, followed one by one by the Actors.

The First Actor is the last to come down through the arch, and Hamlet, having sat again in the chair down front, motions him to stay. He begins to address him in a low tone: "Old friend—" but he breaks off suddenly, remembering that there are still others present.

classical scholar, traced the word to Aelius Lampridius' life of Heliogabalus, where it appears as *innobilitatus*, and wrote a little essay speculating on the likelihood that Shakespeare would have heard the word discussed by learned friends and would have adopted it. Malone's manuscript is in Booth's Notebook. See also Malone's recollections in "An Actor's Memory of Edwin Booth," *Forum*, July, 1893.

[22] *542.* Actors of Polonius had traditionally indicated that it is *Hamlet* who has "turned his color, and has tears in's eyes" (see the *Modern Standard Drama*). In his Notebook Booth corrects this queer error.

Rosencrantz and Guildenstern are lingering up center. Hamlet rises and faces upstage toward them: "My good friends, I'll *leave* you till *night*. You are *welcome* to *Elsinore* (his voice falls)." He bows to them and they go out at the rear. Hamlet sits and looks after them in silence long after they have gone. He shakes his finger after them, with a sagacious, watchful, "I'll-look-after-you" air, and with sharp, shrewd eyes.

At last he motions for the Actor to draw near again: "Can *you* (prolonged) *play* the *Murder* of *Gonzago?*" The Actor says he can. Hamlet leans over the side of the chair and nods his head: "We'll have it *tomorrow night*." He pauses for an instant and thoughtfully puts his hand to his face: "You *could* (looking up and extending his right hand with the index finger pointed) for a need (low tone and quiet, colloquial manner) study a *speech* of some *dozen* or *sixteen lines*, which I would set down and *insert* in't? *could-you not?* (downward accent)." The Actor agrees. Hamlet drops his hand and nods his head. "*Very well* (quietly; dignified but complaisant). Follow that lord (he motions courteously toward the door at the left)." The Actor bows, starts off, and halts. Hamlet calls after him, "And *look*-you (raising his right hand and pointing a finger warningly, yet smiling in a friendly way), *mock*-him *not* (upward accent)." [23] The Actor goes.

574-634. "Now I am alone."

Hamlet sinks back in one side of his chair, reaching out before him and grasping the opposite arm of it. His head hangs dejectedly and he is silent for a time. "*Now* I-am *alone* (slowly, in a deep, sad, reflective tone). Oh (he rises impulsively), what a *rogue* and peasant *slave am I!*" He strikes downward contemptuously with his right arm; then he raises it to his breast and stands looking toward the door at the left through which the Actors left the stage: "*Is* it *not monstrous* that this *player* here (he gives a short outward wave with his left hand, which then falls to his girdle), but in a *fiction*, in a *dream* of *passion*, could force his *soul so* to his own *conceit* that from her *working* all his visage wanned (short, flat sound and upward accent;

[23] *571.* In his Notebook, Booth says that his father read "And look you *mock* him not," but that his own reading (apparently invented later than 1870) is "And look *you* mock him not"—that is, "do not you mock him as you have just seen me do."

he turns front);[24] *tears* in his *eyes*, distraction in's *aspect*, a broken *voice*, and his *whole function* suiting with forms to his *conceit?* (downward accent; he raises his left hand to his breast). And all for *nothing!* For *Hecuba!* (the last syllable is pronounced *ah;* throwing his left hand a little outward). What's *Hecuba* to *him* or *he* to *Hecuba* that he should *weep* for her? (he strikes downward contemptuously with his left hand)."

He comes down to front center with hands partly clasped before him: "What would *he do*, had he the motive and the *cue* for passion, that I-have? He would *drown* the *stage*, with *tears*, and *cleave* the *general ear* with *horrid speech* (tremulous tones; the voice falls in *speech*), make *mad* the *guilty* and *appal* the free, confound *the ignorant, and amaze*, *indeed* (walking to the right front with clasped hands raised before him), the very *faculties* of *eyes* and *ears.* Yet I (he turns at the right and starts fitfully toward down center, raising his right hand), a *dull* and *muddy-mettled rascal* (tones of self-reproach and contempt; he stops down right center), *peak.* like (he turns and goes upstage a little, bringing his hands together for an instant but then casting them apart with a shake of the head) *John-a-dreams*, unpregnant of my *cause* (broad, long sound; he turns beside the chair at right center),[25] and can say *nothing* (he puts his right hand on the post of the chair): no, not for a *King*, upon whose *property*, and *most dear* life (he raises his right hand above his head and looks up bitterly) a *damned defeat was made* (his voice falters in those last five words)."

He throws himself sorrowingly, recklessly, into the chair at right center and bows his head in his arms so that his face is concealed. Then almost instantly he rises: "*Am* I a *coward?* (the *am* is intense, anxious, doubting; upward accent on *coward*)." He stands looking front, with anger, disdain, and pain in his looks: "Who *calls* me *villain?*" He reaches out his arms, spread wide, and looks into space as if calling for a reply: "Gives me the lie i' the *throat* as deep as to the *lungs? Who does* me *this?*" He omits the "Ha!" or only lets it slip out in a scornful sigh, a sound without emphasis. Suddenly he drops his arms, clasps his hands, and starts

[24] *580.* Booth rejects the Folio's "warm'd" and accepts "wanned" as suggested by the Quartos. He argues, citing Garrick as example, that all actors of feeling unconsciously have this power to turn pale, even as Polonius has just seen the First Actor do.

[25] *595.* This chair, which was brought forward at line 174, has not been used, nor has Clarke mentioned it, since Hamlet left it at line 228.

forward toward the left front. His voice drops to a humble, self-reproachful tone: "Why, I should *take* it (he bows his head and gives his hands a contemptuous outward throw); for it *can*not *be*, but I am *pigeon-livered*, and lack *gall* (his voice rises in volume; he turns at left front and starts upstage toward the center) to make oppression *bitter;* or ere this I should have *fatted* all the region *kites*, with this *slave's offal* (intense scorn)." He stops at left center and looks out through the left arches. He shakes his arm angrily in that direction: "*Bloody*, *bawdy*-villain! *Remorseless*, *treacherous*, *lecherous*, *kindless* (his voice rising) VILLAIN!"

He turns down to the chair at left front center, falls into it, and hides his face in his arms. For an instant he is motionless; then he looks up angrily, restlessly: "Why, what an *ass* am I! This is most *brave*, that *I*, the son of a dear *father murdered*, prompted to my *revenge* by heaven and hell, must like (his voice rises in a gentle upper tone of sorrow and reproach) a *bawd* (his voice falls) unpack (his voice rises again to the gentle upper tone) my *heart* with *words* (his voice falls) and fall a-cursing like a very *drab*, a *scullion!*" He strikes out with his right hand: "*Fie* up*on't!* foh!" He folds his arms. His face becomes stern, and he looks downward intensely: "*About*, my *brain!* (slowly)."

He strikes his forehead with his closed hand: "I have *heard* (looking up) [26] that *guilty creatures*, sitting at a *play*, have by the very *cunning* of the scene, been struck so to the *soul* (sitting up a little and thoughtfully holding his right hand out before him) that presently they have proclaimed their *malefactions;* for *murder*, though it have *no tongue*, *will speak* (he rises, holds his left hand up, and draws his lips a little together as if in sober self-communion) with *most miraculous organ!*" He brings down his left hand and stands by the chair, facing front, with his right hand on the chair post: "*I'll have* these *players* (slowly, in a calculating tone) play something like the murder of my (short sound) *father before* mine *uncle*. I'll observe his *looks*, I'll *tent* him (he throws his arm out and downward before him, and then draws it back to his breast) to the *quick*. If-he-*do-blench*, *I know my course* (deep, earnest tone)."

He steps down to the front: "The *spirit* (his voice sinks almost

[26] *618.* In the Taylor 1890 promptbook it is recorded that Booth sometimes omitted the bulk of this soliloquy and spoke only the last 17 lines, which lay out the plan to catch the King's conscience with a play. Kemble and other earlier actors cut it in this manner.

to a whisper) that I have seen *may be* a *devil* (upward accent, tone of alarm; he starts back a little, drawing up his shoulders, and casts a swift glance toward the rear; then he takes a step forward), and the devil hath *power* (low voice, excitedly) to assume a *pleasing shape;* yea, and perhaps, out of my (short sound) *weakness* and my *melancholy*—as he is very *pot*ent with such spirits—abuses (his voice rises a little) me to *damn* me." He draws his shoulders up quickly and bends back; his mouth falls open and he breathes hard. He puts his left hand to his forehead as if confused: "I'll have grounds (looking about resolutely) *more relative* (upward accent) than *this*. The *play's* the thing (he starts toward the left front, raising his right hand) wherein I'll *catch* (making a quick forward movement of the hand) the *conscience* of the *King*." Quickly he goes out the left door, holding his closed hand up before his face. The curtain falls on the second act.[27]

In this act, Clarke observes, Booth makes no conspicuous display of Hamlet's assumed madness. He conveys it more through insinuation than through any intense outbreak. He is only "passively a wanderer in mind." Thus, in his opening scene with Polonius he seems quiet, thoughtful, and now and then sarcastic. He never introduces his vagaries of speech with a bodily start. There might be a stoppage in the voice or a puzzled look, and then would come the surprising turn of thought; so that although his intellect seems to veer and tack, his passion is always under control. And every one of the barbed ironies which he shoots at Polonius is delivered with a courtesy of action which conceals its real rudeness.

When alone with Rosencrantz and Guildenstern he becomes more active and excitable. He moves about the room more. He treats them with more freedom, less deference, and more authority than he showed toward Polonius. His shifts of sentiment and strayings of thought are more obvious. At the same time we are aware that he is on guard—careful, distrustful, observing.

In the second passage with Polonius he displays the assumed madness openly. In greeting the old man he is abandoned and impulsive; in his first replies, spontaneously erratic; at Polonius' reception of the allusions to Jepthah's daughter, vaguely grieved; and at

[27] *634.* In Booth's latest stagings, according to the Taylor 1890 and the Harvard 1890 promptbooks, the curtain did not fall here: the action of Act III simply continued.

the end of their passage suddenly cheerful and serene. Throughout the scene with the Players, he of course comports himself with courtly dignity and friendliness, and with no sign of the assumed madness.

In the soliloquy, when he can put aside position and authority and abandon pretenses, Booth's essential Hamlet begins to emerge. He is bitterly self-accusative, passionate. He revels in empty self-analysis and the flow of words. Although he catches eagerly at the plan of testing the King's conscience with a play, he never really arrives at any deep decisiveness.

Clarke now enumerates several qualities which throughout the play seem to him peculiar to Booth's Hamlet. In the first place, this Hamlet is a thorough-bred gentleman, cultivated in court and school, and at all times he preserves a polite "outward habit of encounter." In the second place, being "controllingly phlegmatic," he is more excitable in words than in deeds. His "hot, sharp thought" does project itself into gestures, but never with extravagant energy; although always above languor, he never becomes "radically tempestuous." Although in his soliloquies "his soul appears to be running a wild zigzag course of self-reproach, philosophy, introspection, strong grief, and overwrought imagination, he never falls into vulgar ways of exhibition in making these things known." Further, he is always conscious of his position as a *prince*—not egotistically but as if through life-long habit. There is always "a gentle dignity and a quiet air of authority in his bearing." Toward Rosencrantz and Guildenstern, though gracious, he maintains a faint air of distance which marks their relative grade in the social scale. Toward Horatio he shows this distance much less; toward his mother not at all; and he can lay it by conspicuously when talking to the First Actor. Those around him, of course, treat him with uniform deference.

Here too Clarke calls attention to a technicality of Booth's speaking which is "one item in the many things which make up his mastery of this part"—that is, "the judicious use which he makes of *upward accents*." Unfortunately Clarke does not explain exactly what he means by this term; but the following sentence is suggestive: "Often in a passage there will be a special word or a phrase which he will deliver with an upward accent, giving its significance a peculiar turn or a new development." Clarke seems to suggest that this effect of vocal ambiguity was peculiar to Booth, or among Booth's roles perhaps peculiar to his Hamlet.

The text of Act II (line-numbering of the Globe edition).

The two scenes of this act are run together into one, only the last third of the first scene being spoken. The extensive cuts (258 lines) are traditional. In the first scene these are: 1-74a (Polonius and Reynaldo); 79b-80 (Hamlet's fouled stockings); 101, 103-106a, 111-117a (Polonius' analysis of Hamlet's madness). In the second scene these are: 5b-7a, 11-12 (in the King's opening speech); 34; 38-39; 40-45, 51-85 (Voltemand and Cornelius); 188; 231-240a, 243b-277a (some lines of bawdry and all the lines about prison and ambition); 281b-282; 337-338a; 346-347; 352-379 (the problems of the Players in the city); 384b ("'Sblood"); 389b-394a; 399b-400a; 438b ("where"); 449a ("Masters"); 458-459; 462-467a; 471b; 474a; 476-485, 496b-504 (in the Actor's speech); 522-523a; 535-541 (end of the Actor's speech); 554a; 561b; 575a; 599b-601a (pate, beard, and nose lines); 603a; 610 ("O, vengeance!").

In the first scene these wordings are altered: 76, "God" > "heaven"; 85-86a are moved down and inserted after 100. In the second scene are the following alterations: 176, "some of you" > "you"; 186, "as your daughter may conceive" > "not as your daughter may conceive"; 187, "look to't" is said three times; 202, "all which" > "all of which"; 204, "should" > "shall"; 218, "you cannot take" > "you cannot, sir, take"; 285, "come, come" > "come"; 287, "Why, anything" > "anything"; 297, "can" > "could" (Folio reading); 299, "sent for or no" > "sent for or not"; 323, "nor woman neither" > "no, nor woman either"; 399, "and you too" > "and Rosencrantz"; 409, "my lord" is said twice; 447, "God" > "heaven"; 469, "when" > "where"; 488, "God" > "heaven"; after 561 there is a rearrangement whereby 572-574 are spoken here—thus Rosencrantz and Guildenstern are dismissed early and do not hear the plans for *The Murder of Gonzago;* 614, "whore" > "bawd"; 626, "but blench" > "do blench" (Quarto reading).

The restorations total 21 lines. In the first scene these are: 82-84a; 120. In the second scene: 16; 22; 24; 137; 147b-148a; 163 ("Be you and I behind an arras then"); 190b-192a; 441; 446-447; 515-519, 529a, 531 (in the Actor's speech).

Act III

Act III, 1. *A Room in the Palace, called the Grand Hall of Audience.*
(Globe edition: Act III, 1. 196 lines cut to 185.)

The curtain rises on a Grand Hall of Audience even more spacious and splendid than the Hall of Arches of the second act (see Plates IX-XI).[1] The ceiling is again triple-vaulted. It is, in fact, the same ceiling that was used in the second act; and now, there being no stone screen under it to impede our view, we can enjoy to the full the interplay of its lofty springing curves. Architecturally, to be sure, it is an improbable construction, for the pendants with their heavy stone bosses serve no structural purpose, and they defy gravity with a bravado which in a real building might rather terrify than please. Nonetheless, as purely theatrical decoration the ceiling gives lift and majesty to the room.

Across the back, some ten to twelve feet above the stage floor, is a practical gallery. It is fronted by a carved stone railing and a lofty facing wall opened up by symmetrically disposed arches of pleasantly varying sizes. From the arches at either end of the gallery, great stone staircases with stone balustrades descend toward us. Beneath the gallery at center is the principal entrance—a very broad opening with a flattened arch—through which we see a paneled and windowed corridor crossing the stage behind. Lesser entrances are provided by low doorways under the stair heads.

In each side wall of the room, downstage from the stairs, are two large archways. These are curtained, but the curtains are drawn back, and the wall section and arch nearest us at each side is angled off somewhat so that we can look into anterooms or alcoves prettily lighted by stained-glass windows.

Consistent with the decor of the other interiors, the walls are of stone block, the arches everywhere are decorated with chevron and roll moldings with outside dentils, a chevron frieze runs along the top of the side walls, and there are displays of shields, spears, and banners. The floor is tesselated. Clarke was impressed by the "gilding, chasing, tracery" and by the general air of amplitude and richness.

[1] Booth's 1878 edition does not call for change of setting here: "The same as in Act Second." The Taylor 1890 and Harvard 1890 promptbooks do not call even for lowering of the curtain after Hamlet's last soliloquy of Act II, but continue the action with the entrance of the King and other characters into the same room.

A groundplan in the Harvard 1870 promptbook shows a profusion of furniture, most of it apparently decorative in Victorian parlor style, rather than useful to the action. Two small tables loaded with "Books, Urns, Fruit, and so forth" flank the central entrance, and several chairs and stools are scattered about. One chair far down right center will be used by Hamlet for "To be or not to be"; for its later uses, as we shall see, this chair must be set "*below first Grooves.*" Curiously, the groundplan does not show the one piece of furniture which is most necessary to the business of the first scene of the act. A fairly large table, with chairs about it, is called for at center, about midway between the second pair of side archways: the chair in front of this table will be used mainly by Ophelia.[2] A chair or window bench (but not the traditional *prie-dieu*) is needed for Ophelia in the stage left alcove.

Again as for the second act the set was erected during the entr'acte and will not be dismantled within sight of the audience, so that we need not be particularly concerned with its manipulation; but Bensen Sherwood's "Stage Plans" provides the stage manager's notes and groundplan, from which we can extract a few meaningful details including dimensions. The archway flats at either side of the stage, finished off at their downstage ends by "Column Tormentors," run from the first to the third grooves. Just upstage of them, about 21 feet beyond the curtain line, the stairways begin; the tops of the stairs (and consequently the central entrance in the wall below) are about 35 feet beyond the curtain line. The high "Table" (the floor of the gallery) to which the stairs connect runs straight across the stage, and at its stage left end it has an offstage access stair. The stone facing wall with arched openings which rises above the front edge of the Table is a painted drop flown in from overhead. The lower facade containing the central entrance is a painted drop hung from the front edge of the Table. Backing drops are hung on the back wall of the stage. The ceiling, as in Act II, is "Triple Arch Stone Borders to 5—Tabs in each E."

From the several extant pictures of this set we can observe the evolution and mutations of its form:

1. In the Booth-Hinton edition of 1866 is a drawing of the set (with the Play scene in progress) as it was first developed by Charles Witham in 1864 for the Hundred Nights *Hamlet* (see Plate

[2] The arrangement of furniture as Clarke describes it, dominated by the table at center, is common to later stagings, as indicated in the Pitman 1884 promptbook.

XVIIa). The ceiling is low, flat, supported by transverse beams, and trimmed across the front by an architecturally meaningless border cloth of stone block with blind arches and floral frieze. Altogether the set appears cramped and crowded. Yet in this version we can perceive the functional reason for its existence: the stair-and-gallery system was invented to frame up a "theatre"—an inner stage to house the play-within-a-play (see III, 3).

2. At the Museum of the City of New York is a small pencil sketch of the scene, apparently made by Witham, upon which the above drawing was based.

3, 4. At the same museum are two watercolors by Witham which are preliminary versions of the set as developed in 1870. Witham's new aim, on the vast stage of Booth's Theatre, was to create impressions of loftiness, airiness, and splendor: he replaced the flat ceiling by the triple-vaulted one created by five border cloths; added the facing wall above the gallery; doubled the number of side wall archways; and provided for more lavish hangings of banners, shields, and weapons.

5. When the production was completed, Witham painted the watercolor for the 1870 promptbook (see Plate IX). Here he made certain reductions of the details shown in the preliminary versions: five arches in the facing wall above the gallery instead of seven, fewer wall hangings, fewer border cloths, no tesselated flooring. Possibly this version is more faithful to what actually appeared on the stage in 1870 than are the preliminary versions; possibly, on the other hand, Witham has simplified it with a view to future reconstructions on smaller stages. The omission of the floor tesselation is certainly *not* true to the 1870 staging, for Clarke and other witnesses mention that the floor was tesselated.

6. In the Harvard Theatre Collection is a large (c. 33 x 23 inches) watercolor of Booth speaking "To be or not to be," painted in 1870 by William Wallace Scott (see Plate XI). Besides a careful rendering of Booth's costume, Scott gives us an exact representation of one of the "Hamlet" chairs, and in the background shows the stage left staircase, part of the wall hung with banners and a shield blazoned with a raven, a view of Ophelia seated in the side alcove, and the King and Polonius spying from a curtained arch in the gallery.[3]

[3] For many years the Harvard Theatre Collection has owned a photograph of this watercolor, endorsed and identified by Edwina Booth Gross-

7. In the Harvard Theatre Collection is a photograph of the Play scene in progress at McVicker's Theatre in Chicago in March, 1873 (see Plate X).[4] The Chicago reconstruction is obviously smaller than the original at Booth's Theatre had been. Twenty-three actors pretty well fill up the stage: at Booth's, as William Winter once reported (*Tribune*, December 5, 1871), there were sixty actors in the scene.

This set, along with the first act view of the Castle by moonlight and the fifth act Graveyard scene, stirred up extraordinary enthusiasm among the reviewers. The *Atlas* (January 8) singles it out as the most admirable of the interiors: it is "made superbly effective by its roofing of groined arches, its tapestried recesses, far reaching corridors, and its lofty gallery, to which access is gained by spacious and massive stairways." The *Albion* (January 8) calls attention to the ceiling "fretted with intricate traceries." The *World* (January 6) declares that the stairways "would bear the tread of a regiment." The *Sun* (January 6) calls it "one of the most superb scenes ever put upon the stage, brilliant in color, with stairs and corridors and arched recesses, and oratories with stained glass windows." The *Dispatch* (January 9), with perhaps more assertiveness than judgment, declares without reservation that it "surpasses, in sublimity, and scope, and detail, all previous attempts in scenic art," and "presents a set which has never before been available to English-speaking playgoers."

mann. In 1968 the collection acquired the painting itself, the gift of Mr. Warren Adelson. The catalogue of the Gilsey Collection (no. 238), a copy of which is preserved in the Bamburgh volume of Boothiana in the Harvard Theatre Collection, prints Scott's account of this painting. About a week after the opening of *Hamlet*, Scott visited Booth in his private rooms at the theatre and did a chalk-and-charcoal portrait of Booth's head and shoulders. "Mr. and Mrs. Booth pronounced it very admirable and the best likeness he had ever had taken!" (A month or so later, according to a notice in the *Tribune* of February 23, photographs of this drawing, prepared by Rockwood, were on sale at Booth's Theatre and in picture shops.) "Mr. Booth gave me an order," Scott continues, "to paint his wife as Desdemona in oil, and a full length of himself in Hamlet in watercolor." The watercolor, signed and dated on the crossbar under the chair, was finished in July, 1870.

[4] James Taylor, who played Horatio in this Chicago production (the figure standing down left), tells us that the photograph was a composite. The photographer took the actors in small groups and afterward assembled the groups upon a photograph of the set. The figure of Hamlet, lying at center, was actually posed by Taylor, and Booth's head was substituted for Taylor's during the recomposition (Philadelphia *Public Ledger*, September 15, 1893).

1-55. "And can you by no drift of conference. . . ."

The curtain rises not on an entrance of characters but a discovery. The King is standing or seated just to the left of the center table, with the Queen downstage of him and to his left. He is facing across to Rosencrantz and Guildenstern, who are near the bottom of the stairs at the right. Ophelia and Polonius are standing above the table at center. The King and Queen address inquiries to the spies, and the King sends them off to pry further into the matter of the play that is to be given this night. At line 28, "We shall, my lord," they go out "R. 2. E."—that is, out the archway nearest the foot of the stairs. The King dismisses the Queen and goes upstage center to confer with Polonius.

The Queen, after her gentle speech to Ophelia, goes out through the left archway, and Ophelia follows to the left. Polonius comes down to her at line 43, "Ophelia, walk you here," and handing her a breviary which he has fetched from the table, directs her to seem to be reading it. He walks her across the stage to the right as he explains how with "pious action we do sugar o'er the devil himself," and Ophelia retires through the right alcove.[5] The King comes down left for his soliloquy. At line 55 Polonius hears Hamlet coming, and he and the King withdraw, apparently by going up the left staircase and out the door at the left end of the gallery.[6] Ophelia then re-enters through the right alcove and slowly crosses the stage, reading; she passes through the downstage left archway and seats herself in the alcove.

55-90. "To be, or not to be, that is the question."

Hamlet enters from upstage left, through the small door under the staircase, and comes down right to the chair which is set below the first grooves.[7] He is without cloak or hat, and otherwise is clad in

[5] *46.* In later stagings Ophelia did not go out at this point, but at the King's exit at line 55, when she went all the way off *left.* She did not, then, re-enter and cross the stage, silently reading, as in 1870. In the Pitman 1884 and Taylor 1890 promptbooks, the prompter is warned to give Ophelia the "remembrances" while she is off left, these being in later stagings a jewel casket and a bundle of letters.

[6] *55.* Curiously the 1870 promptbook does not send them up the stairs, but simply out at upstage center. It is clear, however, from Clarke's account and from Scott's painting of the scene that they do their spying from the gallery. The direction to go "up Staircase" appears only in the Pitman 1884 promptbook.

[7] *56.* In later stagings, according to all the promptbooks, the chair used

the same dark costume as before. His dagger hangs at his girdle, the steel chain with his father's miniature is around his neck, and he wears the golden insignia of some order upon his breast. He enters with head bent down, his right arm crossing his breast and his left hand resting lightly on the left side of his chin.

His *walk*, Clarke says, is a study, bespeaking his intense abstraction. He comes very slowly, each step dragging a little: he draws his foot up by degrees to make a step, then swings it slowly forward. The movement is so hesitant and doubtful that one thinks he might stop at any moment. He reaches the chair and drops into it. He looks over the side of the chair into the audience, but even if his eyes fall directly upon one he appears not to see any external thing. One hand is at his temple, and two or three locks of hair fall over it. His face is taut with the concentrated working of his mind.

For ten or fifteen seconds he does not speak, but his eyes proclaim his thought almost as well as his voice could. "I forgot all about the man then," Clarke exclaims; "for the time I see right through his flesh and overlook his mind. He speaks—oh wonderful! It is not declamation. It is not recitation. It is the deep thought running right out at the lips, finding a vocal liberty. The power of it is not in the voice—though the voice is as apt as it could be—but in the spirit of the man Hamlet that shows itself behind. Every word gives me a shake, and then goes through me like a lance." With similar urgency the critic of the *Evening Mail* (January 6) reports the "suicide soliloquy," offering it as a perfect rebuttal to the anti-histrionic prejudices of Charles Lamb: "There was something deeply touching in the reckless, despondent attitude and the staring eyes, fixed on vacancy, betokening the complete misery of the man, while the intensity with

for the soliloquy stood beside the center table, usually to the left of it. Booth was the first actor in America to *sit* during this or any of the soliloquies. This touch of "realism" he had introduced in the early 1860's at the suggestion of Henry Tuckerman, the art historian; and on the same occasion, to the gratification of Mr. Tuckerman, he discovered the motivating line at which he could "rise from that chair with propriety and ease" (Asia Booth Clarke, *The Elder and Younger Booths* (New York, 1882), p. 154). A. C. Sprague points out that an English actor had sat for the soliloquy as early as 1854 (*Shakespeare and the Actors*, p. 385). By 1870 no one was astonished at the effect, although the critic of the *Times* (January 7) notices that "the free use of seats from which to deliver the soliloquys and long speeches gives variety to the scene, and is therefore commendable." Nym Crinkle in the *World* (January 9) thinks this "impulsive and unpremeditated negligence of attitude is infinitely superior to the delivery of the passage at the footlights in oratorical style."

which the words were spoken revealed his inmost thoughts with all the dark, gloomy forebodings. . . . The audience seems to feel that the man was alone with his thoughts, and that they were far removed from his consideration."

"*To be*, or (broad sound) *not* (slight pause) to be (subdued, searching voice; looking down and forward, with a sad, puzzled look), *that* is the question (free, almost colloquial delivery, yet very sober tones; his voice falls). Whether 'tis nobler in the mind, to *suffer* (slowly, the voice rising a little) the *slings* and *arrows* of outrageous *fortune;* or to take *arms* against a SEA *of troubles*, and, by opposing, *end* them? (he nods his head a little, and his hand slips up his temple to rest on the top of his forehead). To *die?* (the voice rises) —to *sleep* (the voice falls perplexedly) —*no more* (the voice very low and doubtfully conclusive; he shakes his head a trifle). *And* (upward accent) *by* a *sleep* (upward accents) to *say* we END the *heart-ache* (slowly and thoroughly pronounced; tone of speculation) and the *thousand* (slight upward accent in *thous-*, falling in *-and*) *natural shocks* that flesh is *heir* to (the voice drops in *to*)— 'tis a (he lifts himself to a more upright posture and his right hand gradually sinks from his temple to his breast) *consummation devoutly* to be *wished* (his voice falls; he looks upward for an instant, gives a slight outward toss of his right hand, and then brings it back to his breast). To *die* (tone of reflection and perplexity) —to sleep (slight upward accent and interrogatory tone; prolonged; he draws his head back a little, his brows contract, and his eyes start quickly with a new idea). To *sleep*! (slowly, but in an exclamatory tone; he draws back his right hand at his breast) per*chance* to *dream*— (upward accent). *Ay* (he sits back in the chair), there's the *rub*." [8]

He rises and stands beside the chair with his right hand on the post of it, his left hand drawn up to his breast. (Scott's watercolor seems to catch this precise moment.) He looks forward fixedly. Now he speaks a little more rapidly, as if he had slipped into a current of thought that relieved somewhat the earnestness of his reflections: "For in that *sleep-of-death*, what *dreams* may come, when we have *shuffled off* (the voice rises a little) this *mortal coil* (the voice declines into a deep, solemn tone; at the word *coil* he strikes his breast three or four times with the fingertips of his left hand) *must give us pause* (broad sound; his voice drops); *there's* the *respect*-that makes

[8] *65.* Booth's rising at exactly this point is marked in all the promptbooks.

calamity of *so long life* (he is facing front, his head bent down a little, his hands held loosely at his breast); for *who* (long, thin sound) *would bear* (upward accent) the *whips* and *scorns* of *time* (slight pause, but no fall of the voice), the *oppressor's wrong*, the *proud man's contumely* (the word is pronounced in four distinct syllables), the pangs of *despised* love, the *law's delay* (to this point in the list his voice does not vary much, but is like that of one counting up items in his imagination), the *insolence* (upward accent) of *office* (short sound, and his voice falls to its former level), and the *spurns-* (his voice rises) that- (his voice falls) patient-merit (his voice rises) *of the unworthy takes* (his voice falls smoothly and roundly) *when he himself* (lower tone) *might his quietus make* with a *bare bodkin?* (the words *bare bodkin* are spoken slowly and with slight contempt; his hand falls to his dagger, lifts it a little, and lets it go again). *Who* (upward accent; prolonged) would *fardels bear* to *grunt and sweat* under a *weary* (prolonged) life, but that (the voice drops and becomes a little solemn) the dread of something *after* death—the *undiscovered* (his voice rises softly) *country* from whose *bourne* (pronounced *boorne;* he looks upward and raises his right hand a little) *no traveller* returns (his voice falls) *puzzles* (his voice rises) the *will* (upward accent) and *makes*-us-rather *bear* those *ills* we *have* (his voice declines; he walks slowly to the right front, his right hand clasping his left hand before him) than *fly-to-others* (low voice; he stops) that-we-*know-not-of*. Thus *conscience*[9] (standing down right and facing toward the left) does make *cowards* of us all (his voice falls); and thus the native *hue* (prolonged) of *resolution* (downward accent) is *sicklied-o'er-by-the-pale-cast-of-thought* (low voice), and *enterprises* of great *pith* and *moment,* with *this regard* (upward accent) their *currents* turn *awry* (prolonged; slightly rising inflection) and *lose* (the voice falls to a low, bass, thoughtful tone) the *name* of *action*." He walks slowly toward front center.

90-133. "Soft you now! The fair Ophelia."

Ophelia emerges from the left alcove and moves toward the center, her eyes bent down on her book. Hamlet sees her and starts a little: "*Soft you now!* The fair *Ophelia* (slight upward accent; the tone of

[9] *83.* Booth mentions in his Notebook an emendation of "Thus conscience" to "This conscience," proposed by Friederich Bodenstedt. I do not know that he ever used it. He meant to convey "this consciousness of something after death."

one pleasantly wakened from meditation)." He walks quickly and quietly toward her, meeting her at left center: "*Nymph*, in *thy orisons* [10] be *all my sins remembered?* (upward accent; tone of general and courteous entreaty)." He bows to her with gentle deference. The coldness of her response—"How does your honor for this many a day?"—puts him off. He shrinks out of his attitude of graceful friendliness, looks at her a little rigidly, then drops his head a little, clasps his hands before him, and bows somewhat formally: "I humbly *thank you* (low, constrained voice). *Well* (upward accent and a tinge of sadness; he turns upstage), *well* (a little lower voice, and on a descending tone), *well* (the voice drops still lower; a faint expression of dignity and reserve)." He takes a step upstage with his hands clasped before his breast, and as he moves he throws his head back a little and puts his hands on his forehead.

At this instant, the King and Polonius enter the overhead gallery from the left and pass behind the hangings. Hamlet sees them.[11] He stops abruptly. He clutches his forehead. Then he makes a movement as if to go on, but he pauses and casts over his right shoulder a quick look of reproach at Ophelia. Her head being bowed as she disengages the "remembrances" from her dress, she does not observe his look or his action. He takes two or three steps upstage, with head bowed and an air of dejection which intimates his realization that she is betraying him. And from this moment, Booth says in his Notebook, he "*acts* the rest of this scene with Ophelia principally for the King."

She calls to him. He stops and remains motionless with his back toward her, his left arm across his breast and his right hand raised to his face. She speaks of the "remembrances of yours," and holding out

[10] *88.* Booth, and Lawrence Barrett too, always stressed the second syllable of "orisons," although, as Booth noted in the Taylor 1890 promptbook, "I have been severely censured for it." He cites Walker's *Pronouncing Dictionary* for authority and he collected notes demonstrating that Milton, Crashaw, and sometimes Shakespeare stressed the first syllable, and Shakespeare and others sometimes the second.

[11] *92.* Booth sees the King and Polonius either after "Well, well, well" or, according to the 1878 edition, three lines later as Ophelia is saying, "I pray you now receive them." Actors of the preceding generation mostly inserted this business some 40 lines later, just before "Where's your father?" The significance of Booth's early placement of the "seeing" is that it motivates Hamlet to "act" the scene for the King's benefit from the very beginning. The tradition of this "non-Shakespearean" bit of business—stoutly debated by purists even then—is not so old as might be assumed. A. C. Sprague traces it to a suggestion made by John Howard Payne in 1826 (*Shakespeare and the Actors*, p. 153).

a small packet toward him, begs him to receive them. He turns and looks at her, comes down as if to approach her, but goes to the center instead. He looks at her sadly and gravely: "*No, not I* (low, sober tone of denial). *I* never *gave* you *aught* (his voice falls)." He waves his hand at her disclaimingly; he turns to the right and stands with head bowed, his right hand on the post of the chair which is just downstage of the table, his left hand at his breast. She insists that he did give her these things and again holds out the packet to him. He looks over his shoulder at her irresolutely; then turns and comes quickly to her, smiling bitterly.

He seizes her wrist: "*Ha, ha!* (no heartiness in the exclamation) *are* you *honest?* (long, full sound in both stressed words, and neither rise nor fall of accent in *honest*)." [12] She cries out, but he will not be stopped: "*Are* (long, full sound) you *fair?* (descending accent)." She asks what he means. Now he holds her right wrist in his left hand and clasps her hand with his right. With her left hand she has taken the packet and replaced it in the pocket of her dress. "That if you be *honest and* (upward accent) *fair* (upward accent), you (his voice falls admonishingly) should admit no *discourse* to your *beauty*." She asks her riddling question whether beauty could have better commerce than with honesty. He lifts his brows and gazes at her informingly: "Ay (upward accent; prolonged), truly (falling sound), for (he nods and gazes earnestly into her face) the power of *beauty* will sooner transform *honesty* from what it is to a *bawd*, than the force of honesty can translate beauty into *his* likeness."

He clasps her wrist and hand so tightly that she has to move to keep her arm at ease: in this maneuver she passes in front of him, her back to the audience, until she is in front of the chair at his right. "This was *sometime* a *paradox*, but *now* (his voice falls) the time gives it *proof*. *I did* (he lets go her hand and wrist) *love-you* (he takes a step backward and upstage, holds up his hands before his breast, pauses, and looks at her with troubled face) *once* (slowly, in a low, sad voice; holding out both hands with the palms toward her)."

He turns then and walks a few steps upstage with head bowed

[12] *103*. According to Mason's notes, at "are you honest?" Hamlet *took* the "remembrances"; at "the time gives it proof" he stood gazing at them with his back turned to Ophelia; and at line 118, before "You should not have believed me," he thrust them into his bosom. No other witness records this arrangement.

and hands at the sides of his face. As he is moving away, she protests that he had once made her believe he loved her; but when he turns toward her abruptly and launches into vigorous denials, she sinks into the chair.[13] "You should *not* have *believed* me; for virtue (his voice falls, but he speaks rapidly and energetically; he starts toward her) *cannot so inoculate* our *old* (prolonged) *stock* (standing beside her) but we shall *relish* of it." He begins to turn upstage, but then looks at her resolutely and mournfully: "I (strong and prolonged, full of emotion) loved you *not*." These last four words seem forced out of him by his will, against the feelings of his heart.

He turns away suddenly and walks a few steps upstage. Ophelia says, "I was the more deceived," bowing her head upon the arm of the chair. Hamlet turns toward her, his face full of pity, love, and resolution: "*Get* thee to a nunnery (upward accent; tremulous tone; he comes forward and stands just above her chair with his right hand on a post of it). "*Why* (upward accent) wouldst thou be a breeder of *sinners* (the upward accent continues through *be*, then falls, then rises again in *sinners*). I am, *myself* (slight upward accent), indifferent *honest;* but yet I could *accuse me* of such things (he stands looking partly down at her, partly out from her, scowling a little as if in self-condemnation; he seems to be reaching ahead in his thought and only partially conscious of the words he is actually speaking; once he gestures outward with a wave of his left hand) that it were better my mother had not *borne* me; I am very *proud*, *revengeful*, *ambitious* (he pauses after each of these words, and utters them very distinctly, not so much attending Ophelia but covertly making sure that the King and Polonius hear him); with more *offenses* at my *beck* (he looks down at her with troubled face) than I have *thoughts* to put them in (upward accents), imagination to give them *shape*, or time to *act* them in. What should such fellows as *I* do, *crawling-* (prolonged; he stands back a little, his right hand on the chair post still, his left hand held out at his side) between *earth* and (full sound) *heaven?* (upward accent). We are *arrant knaves*, *all* (broad, deep sound); believe *none*-of-us." [14] He turns partly upstage, but then looks toward her again: "*Go* (upward accent) *thy ways* to a *nunnery* (slight upward

[13] *116.* According to later promptbooks, Ophelia did not sit until line 121, at "I was the more deceived."

[14] *132.* In the Taylor 1890 and Harvard 1890 promptbooks, after "believe none of us" he kissed her, or kissed her hand.

accent)." Still turned partly away, he reaches his arms toward her as if in pity. Then he turns toward her again and bends over her chair.

133-157. "Where's your father?"

His left hand rests on a post of the chair; his right hand is at his chin, the crooked forefinger touching his lip: "*Where's your father?*" He asks the question in a low tone, slowly, pronouncing each word deliberately and separately. The question is a test of her character. He looks down upon her anxiously, with mingled doubt, fear, sagacity, and just a trace of hopefulness. She replies, "At home, my lord"; then she raises her face, and her hand opens upward impulsively as if in entreaty to heaven to forgive her this deception. Hamlet starts slightly, and draws slowly back from her with a pained and saddened face. Then he bends over her again and raises his right hand.

His expression grows severe: "Let the doors be *shut* on him (emphatically, with a slight toss of the right hand) that he may play-the-*fool* (prolonged; upward accent that gives it a kind of delicacy which it would not have with a downward accent) *nowhere* but in's *own* (upward accent) *house* (downward accent)." [15] These words are uttered with a softness of tone, proceeding from the habitual courtesy of Booth's Hamlet, which smooths their real harshness. He speaks them more tenderly than he could have spoken them to a male character. Yet the words do not lack force and vitality. "Farewell." That word expresses much. It is gentle, earnest, harmonious; yet it conveys censure, regret at her conduct, and resolve to carry out a suddenly decided course of his own. He reaches a hand toward her, palm outward, and lets it fall.

He turns, walks quickly to the foot of the stage left staircase, and for an instant leans against the rail. Ophelia appeals for help to the sweet heavens.[16] "If thou dost *marry* (he runs back to her, kneels beside her chair, and takes her left hand), I'll give thee this *plague*

[15] *136.* Booth sees in the words "play the fool nowhere but in's *own* house" clear implication that Polonius is now playing the fool—that is, spying—in *this* house: "and this," he writes in his Notebook, "is proof enough that he has seen the 'espials.'" Thus the tiny word "own" becomes textual justification for the debated stage business.

[16] *138.* Mason says that Ophelia stood and crossed left on her first appeal to heaven, and crossed right again on her second at line 147. Thus in later stagings she was not seated but standing throughout Hamlet's last two tirades. The notations in the Taylor 1890 and Harvard 1890 promptbooks are similar to Mason's.

for thy *dowry* (he looks at her ironically, almost harshly). Be thou as *chaste* as *ice* (thin, warning voice; upward accents; drawing her hand toward him in both of his), as *pure* (prolonged) as *snow* (upward accents in these last four words), thou *shalt not* (his voice becomes deeper and more earnest, yet still ironical and taunting; he draws her left hand almost to his body and raises his right hand toward her, the forefinger partly pointed) *'scape calumny* (deep, full sound). He looks at her with bitter prophecy. Then his face falls a little, his lips close, his eyes lose something of their flash, and his cheeks raise a little with a look of tenderness. His right hand falls and closes over her left hand.

He draws back a little and gazes at her steadfastly and sadly: "*Get thee* to a *nunnery* (upward accent, but low voice full of pathos and entreaty)." She looks at him doubtingly. Once more his face hardens with ironic severity. He raises one knee and sets his foot on the floor, bending toward her again and still holding her left hand close to his breast. "Or-if-thou wilt *needs marry*, marry a *fool* (upward accent; prolonged; he looks at her with observant cunning), for *wise men* (he rises, still keeping his eyes on her face, and his voice falls into more natural, common tones) know *well enough* (upward accent; he lets go her hand and stands ready to turn away; the austerity clears from his face but remains in his attitude and in his eyes) what *monsters* [17] *you* make of them. To a *nunnery, go* (upward accent; authoritative tone)."

Raising his left hand to his head, he walks back to the stairs again and leans against the rail, his right arm reaching up along it. His left hand falls dejectedly to his side, and his head hangs down. Again Ophelia appeals softly to heaven for help. Hamlet comes a little forward: "I have heard (his voice is not loud, but warm and intense, with a sort of pathetic sarcasm) of your *paintings* (upward accent) too, *well enough* (upward accent). Heaven hath given you *one face* (he holds out his right hand toward her) and you make yourselves *another* (he swings his arm to the side, and bends a little forward accusingly). You *jig*, you *amble*, and you *lisp* (he is holding his right hand before him palm upward, and on each of these stressed words he gives it a little outward jerk such as card-players

[17] *144.* Booth observes in his Notebook that the gesture of the cuckold's horns is appropriate at the word "monsters," and in later stagings he adopted it. Mason records that he held up two fingers of each hand to the sides of his head.

do when dealing; he moves toward center), and nickname-heaven's-creatures (he stops at center upstage of the table, looking frontward toward her, reprovingly; her head is bowed upon the arm of her chair), and make your *wantonness* your *ignorance* (he pauses a little and looks at her steadily). Go *to*."

He crosses toward the right, casting a covert glance around toward the gallery. He stops at right center and looks at her: "I'll *no more of't*." He turns his face slowly from her and gazes offstage to the right. He tips his head a little back and to one side, showing that he is conscious of the spies in the gallery. Then he clasps his forehead with both hands, turns partly upstage, and says slowly, with deep emphasis and almost purposeless expression: "*It hath made me mad*." The delivery of these five words, Clarke says, is one of the greatest points in Booth's entire performance. The words seem not to rise out of the subject or the situation, and they sound singularly artificial, yet they express many meanings. To some extent they hint at regret for his feigned madness and for his blind censure of women. In the main they are a formula which Hamlet forces himself to utter in order to delude the listeners in the gallery, and as such they reach to the very limits of Hamlet's power to deceive. An incidental effect of the words is that they somewhat palliate the harshness of his raillery at Ophelia.

Now he looks at her again earnestly, and his voice drops to a grating tone near to hoarseness: "*I say*, we'll have *no more marriages* (full pronunciation and contemptuous tone). Those that are married *already—all but one* (low, solemn, meaningful tone) —shall *live*. The *rest* (pause; he looks at her severely) shall keep as they *are* (low voice, and decisive, dismissive tone)." He waves his right hand downward, turns right, and walks to the archway at the foot of the right stairs, his face still turned toward her. He pauses at the exit. His face is stern for a moment; then it becomes warm and pitiful, though still distrustful. He comes quickly down to her, and bending over he takes her right hand as it rests over the arm of the chair. At once she rises and stands close to him. His lips compress firmly.

Slowly he raises her hand, but when it is as high as her breast he lets go of it.[18] She holds it there motionless. Then very gently and tenderly he takes her cheeks in his hands, and holding her thus, looks earnestly down into her eyes. His face exhibits several emotions in

[18] *156*. In later stagings he *kissed* her hand after "The rest shall keep as they are."

turn: doubt, then tenderness and pity, then love. His lower lip draws in a little, his nostrils expand, his eyebrows gather, his eyes partly close. She puts her hand on his arm. He looks at her longingly, then with misgiving and regret. He quickly covers his eyes with his left hand, drops his right hand to her hand, throws his head back a little, and takes a step backward. He lets go her hand, turns away, and moves with irregular steps to the right archway, his hand at his face. Then looking again toward her he extends his left hand far from his shoulder with the palm open outward, and says in a broken voice, musical with pathos, his face miserable but resolute, "To a *nunnery, go* (upward accent and tremulous tone; prolonged)." He goes out hastily, his right hand held to his face.[19]

158-196. "Oh, what a noble mind is here o'erthrown!"

At Hamlet's exit, Ophelia sinks into the chair. Then she rises, speaks her soliloquy,[20] and goes out through the archway at the foot of the left stairs.[21] The King and Polonius come down the stage right staircase and advance to the center for their final colloquy. As they are going out to the left, three or four servants enter and begin to arrange the furniture for the Play scene. The set for the next scene, rising at the first grooves, conceals the servants as they work.

Clarke observes that the scene with Ophelia is one of the most difficult for the actor of Hamlet. It would be easy enough simply to upbraid Ophelia bluntly, play the madman, and run off wildly; but the actor must maintain the character of a cultivated gentleman and also reveal clearly the complicated motives for his actions. He must

[19] At the Winter Garden in the 1860's, according to Mason, the business of Hamlet's exit was arranged differently. Ophelia remained seated with head bowed, facing to the left. Hamlet returned to her slowly and irresolutely, looked around carefully to be sure he was not being observed, tremblingly laid his hand upon her head, and turned her about so that she was looking up at him. He gazed at her sorrowfully for a few seconds and then walked backward to the exit, saying, "To a nunnery, go," and adding "go" twice more. He made his exit backward, so that his face was visible throughout the exit.

[20] *167.* Booth caught at Ophelia's words "unmatched form" as another argument that Hamlet was not "fat."

[21] *169.* In later stagings, in which this scene was played as a continuation of Act II, Ophelia's soliloquy was the curtain speech. The following exchange between Polonius and the King (lines 170-196) were then spoken when the curtain rose on Act III, in the setting prepared for the Play scene. Mason and the Taylor 1890 and Harvard 1890 promptbooks record this divisioning.

show Hamlet's underlying sadness and keep us in mind of the weight of the Ghost's charge upon him. He must show at once that he loves Ophelia and is suspicious of her. He remembers that she has previously refused to see him or receive his letters, and now she lies to him in saying that her father is "at home." His mental struggle is intense: he longs to speak frankly to her; he is put off and angered by her present behavior; and he must play the madman in order to foil the spies who are listening in the gallery.

Booth passes through many phases of feeling in the scene, Clarke says. During the soliloquy and at the conclusion of it as he wanders in a desultory manner toward center, he is wholly rapt in thought. When he first sees Ophelia, a frank and genial pleasure possesses him; but at her cool response to his greeting, he recollects himself and instantly becomes ceremonious and distant. His discovery of the King and Polonius in the gallery at once turns him bitter. This discovery, which Booth sets early in the scene, has no warrant in the text, as Clarke notes; but it is of course extremely useful to Booth in motivating his subsequent harshness. From that moment on his flashes of, or relapses into, tenderness seem to be compelled by a deep emotional urge that runs counter to his intentions and his will.

When he has to say "I did love you—*once*" or "I loved you *not*," one senses that his feelings oppose the cruel words which must be spoken. He quickly overpowers these feelings, yet to the last his rejection of her is weakened by reluctance; his sternness is never steadfast. When she offers him the "remembrances," he holds her hand as if it gives him pleasure. His keen sarcasms, which cut and bruise, are almost always followed by some courtesy or kindness which smooths and excuses them. Yet every kindness only prepares the occasion for another form of attack.

Booth's intelligence in playing the madman is conspicuous. He is always convincingly distraught in counterfeit insanity, yet is never genuinely mad. The audience is always dextrously made aware that his madness is assumed.

The text of Act III, 1 (line-numbering of the Globe edition).

The few cuts (11 lines) are traditional. These are: 3-4; 10b-14a; 174-177a; 186b-188a (Polonius' dismissal of Ophelia). None of these are Hamlet-Ophelia lines.

A few slight alterations appear in Clarke's recording: 107, "your honesty" > "you" (Quarto reading); 135, "upon" > "on"; 149 and

151, "God" > "heaven"; 153, "on't" > "of't"; 154, "we will" > "we'll."

The restorations (12 lines) are as follows: 43a-44a; 46b-54 (including the King's soliloquy); 154, 162-163a (in Ophelia's soliloquy).

Act III, 2. *A Hallway in the Castle.*

(Globe edition: Act III, 2, 1-96. 96 lines cut to 88.)

Now, while the furniture in the Grand Hall of Audience is being arranged for the Play scene, Hamlet's Advice to the Player[s] and his conference with Horatio are performed down front as a "carpenters' scene." [22] The set, which rises at the first grooves, is a shallow front set consisting of a back wall with narrow doorway flats at either end. It contains a single chair down right center, which was placed "below 1st Grooves" for the preceding scene and so is in position for this one. The Harvard 1870 promptbook contains no watercolor of this set. Matthison mentions it as "an Arcade." According to Clarke, it is "a sort of anteroom or hallway with panelled walls."

1-50. "Speak the speech, I pray you, as I pronounced it to you."

Hamlet and the First Actor come on from the first enrance right, the Actor preceding and bowing Hamlet on.[23] They advance to front center, the Actor keeping to Hamlet's left. Hamlet holds out his right hand in an easy, familiar fashion: "*Speak* the *speech* I *pray you*, as I *pronounced* it to you, *trippingly* on the tongue; but if you *mouth* it, as many of our players *do* (slight upward accent), I had as lief the *towncrier* spoke my lines. Nor do not *saw the air* too much with your *hand* (short, flat sound) *thus* (prolonged; he gestures with his right arm, swaggeringly, once up and down and once down diagonally), but use *all* (broad sound) gently (these last four words slowly); for in the very *torrent*, *tempest*, and—as I *may say*—whirlwind of

[22] In Booth's 1878 edition, this set is prescribed as "A Hall in the Castle [First Grooves]." When in later stagings the Hamlet-Ophelia scene was made to conclude the second act (see above, footnote 21), and the third act set was made ready for the Play scene during the entr'acte, this present scene was not given a separate setting, but was played in front of the temporary stage set up for the *Mousetrap*.

[23] *1.* The Taylor 1890 promptbook marks this entrance as "from either L or R according to Mr. Booth's dressing room." According to Mason, in the 1860's at the Winter Garden Hamlet entered reading a paper—presumably the speech he had written to insert into the play. He rolled this up as he began his "advice," and used it to gesticulate with; then handed it to the Actor when he dismissed him.

your passion, you (the voice drops a little into a tone of friendly expostulation) must *acquire* and *beget*-a *temperance* that may give it smoothness (his voice drops roundly but gently). *Oh* (lightly; upward accent; pleasant but censuring tone), it offends me to the soul to hear a *robustious periwig-pated* fellow tear a passion to *tatters*, to very *rags* (contemptuously), to split the ears of the *groundlings*, who for-the-*most-part*-are-*capable*-of-nothing-but inexplicable *dumb shows* and *noise:* I would have such a fellow *whipped* for o'erdoing Termagant; it *out-herods* (upward accent) Herod (upward accent of *Her-*, falling accent of *-od*). *Pray* you (upward accent), *avoid* (upward accent) it." The Actor promises to do so.

"Be not too *tame* neither (upward accent), but let your own *discretion* be your tutor. Suit the *action* to the *word* (upward accent), the word to the *action;* with *this special* observance, that (slowly) you *o'erstep not* the *modesty* (upward accent) of *nature;* for *anything* so *overdone* (upward accent of *-done*) is from the PUR*pose* of *playing*, whose *end*, both *at the first and now* (broad sound of *and* and *now*, spoken slowly and warningly), *was*, and *is*, to *hold* as-'twere the *mirror up* (upward accent) to *nature;* to show (he speaks more freely and a little faster now, abandoning the admonitory tone) *virtue*-her-own-*feature* (upward accent), *scorn*-her-own-*image* (pronounced *im-aj*), and the very *age*, and *body* of the time, his *form* and *pressure*. *Now this* (upward accent) *overdone* (upward accent), or come *tardy of* (the word is *off*, but Booth says *of*), though (prolonged; frank, explanatory tone) it make the *unskillful laugh* (slight upward accent), *cannot* but make the *judicious grieve* (slight upward accent; prolonged), the *censure* of which *one* (upward accent) *must,* in your-allowance, o'erweigh a whole *theatre* (upward accent) of-*others*. Oh (upward accent; lightly scornful tone), there *be players* that I have seen *play*—and heard *others praise*, and that *highly*—not to speak it *profanely*, that neither having the *accent* of *Christians*, nor the gait of Christian (slowly and disdainfully), *Pagan*, *or* (prolonged broad sound) *man* (upward accent), have *so* (prolonged) *strutted*, *and* (prolonged broad sound) *bellowed* (prolonged; deep, contemptuous tone), that (his voice changes to an easy, colloquial tone) I have thought some of nature's *journeymen* (upward inflection) had made men, and not made them *well*, they imitated (low, sarcastic tone, but pleasant) *humanity* so *abominably*."

The Actor hopes that his company have reformed that "indifferently." Hamlet corrects him: "Oh, *reform* it *altogether*." He reaches out his right hand lightly toward the Actor. "And let those that play your *clowns* speak *no more* than is *set down* for them; for there *be*-of-them that will themselves *laugh* to set on some quantity of barren *spectators* to *laugh too; though* (upward accent; prolonged) in the meantime some necessary question of the *play* be then to-be-*considered; that's villainous* (upward accent); and shows a most *pitiful* ambition in the *fool* that *uses* it. *Go* make you *ready* (upward accent)." The Actor goes out backward to the left, bowing as he goes.

57-96. "Horatio!"

When Hamlet is alone, his tranquil and easy manner leaves him, and he seems again oppressed by responsibility. Weary and dejected, he crosses to the chair at down right center, sits, and gazes to the right through the open doorway. He sees someone there, lifts his head and arm quickly, and calls, "*Horatio!*"[24] In some performances he draws out the name slowly; in some he makes it a short, quick call as one does to catch the attention of someone passing by. Horatio enters and presents himself. Hamlet takes his hand and looks up at him confidingly: "*Horatio,* thou art e'en as *just* a man as *e'er* my conversation *coped* withal (slight upward accent; looking into Horatio's face in a thoughtful and friendly fashion)." Horatio begins to protest, but Hamlet's "Nay" cuts him off.

Hamlet rises as he speaks and they stand together with their sides toward the audience. Hamlet has taken Horatio's right hand in his own, and laid his left hand on Horatio's breast, the forefinger uppermost: "*Nay,* do not think I *flatter* (earnest and kindly tone): for what advancement may I hope from *thee,* that no *revenue* (pronounced re-*ven*-yoo) hast, but *thy*-good spirits to feed and clothe thee? *Why* (upward accent) should the *poor* be *flattered? No* (prolonged; giving his left hand an outward swing and stepping a little back), let the candied tongue lick *absurd pomp* and *crook* the *pregnant-hinges*-of the-knee where *thrift* may *follow fawning.* Dost thou hear?"

He puts his left hand to Horatio's right so that he encloses it in both his own: "Since my dear soul was mistress of her *choice* and could of *men distinguish* her election, she hath *sealed thee for herself;* for *thou hast been* as one in suffering *all* (upward accent; standing a little back, still holding his hand; looking at him with candid,

[24] 57. According to the Tayor 1890 promptbook, Horatio entered as the Actor withdrew, without waiting to be called.

sad admiration), that suffers *nothing;* a man that fortune's *buffets* and *rewards* (upward accent) has-ta'en with *equal-* (pronounced *e*-kwăl) thanks." He gives his left hand a short swing outward: "And *blessed* are *those* (upward accent) whose blood-and-judgment are so well *commingled* (slight upward accent) that they are not a *pipe* (upward accent) for *fortune's* finger to sound *what stop she please.* Give-me that man (putting his left hand again on Horatio's breast) that is not passion's-slave, and I will *wear* him in my heart's-*core, ay* (upward accent; prolonged) in my *heart* of *heart* (the first *heart* is sounded a little more heavily than the second; he drums two or three times on Horatio's breast) *as I do thee* (in these four words his voice falls into earnest, warm tones)." He shakes Horatio's hand.

Then, throwing his head back a little in an offhand and ingenuous way, he says frankly, as if to change the subject, "Something *too-much*-of-this." [25] Standing close to Horatio, he lifts his left hand, the forefinger pointed: "There is a *play* (sober, intense tone) tonight *before* the *King.* One *scene* of it comes near the *circumstance* which I have *told* thee of my father's *death.* I *prithee* when thou seest that *act afoot,* even with the very comment of thy *soul* (upward accent), *observe* my *uncle:* if his occulted *guilt* do not itself unkennel in one speech, it is a *damned*-ghost that we have seen: and my imaginations-are-as-*foul*-as *Vulcan's stithy:* give him *heedful* note (upward accent); for I mine eyes will *rivet* to his face; and after we will both our *judgments*-join in *censure* of his *seeming.*" A flourish of trumpets is heard from behind. Hamlet steps back and faces left. Horatio says, "Well, my lord." Hamlet, still holding Horatio's hand, says, "They are coming to the *play.*" He starts across to the left door, Horatio following. "I must be *idle* (caution and sarcasm in his voice)." He looks knowingly at Horatio, and taps his own forehead with the forefinger of his left hand: "Get you a place (friendly tone)." They go out the left door. Trumpets are sounding again, and almost at once the scene changes.

Booth delivers the advice to the Actor, Clarke says, in a very pleasant, friendly manner, at once maintaining his princely dignity and admitting a kind of equality which give his remarks a becoming

[25] 79. Here Mason comments: "More than any other Hamlet that I have seen, Mr. Booth emphasized Hamlet's affectionate intimacy with Horatio. He was constantly close beside him, and showed his affection uninterruptedly, by voice, action, and facial expression."

geniality. He expresses his opinions in a quick, authoritative, yet colloquial way, and seems to rely on the high intelligence of the Actor to fulfill his prescriptions. He gestures very little. His manner is that of one giving competent advice in a kindly manner upon a matter of mutual interest.

His talk with Horatio is serious and from the heart. In dwelling upon Horatio's qualities, he speaks with warm appreciation rather than enthusiasm. His way of saying "Something too much of this" is very manly. His charge to Horatio is by no means an appeal for help, but simply a giving of instructions to a friend of whose help he is thoroughly certain. In his apt pantomime of tapping his forehead at "I must be idle" he clearly indicates that he is about to assume his antic disposition.

The text of Act III, 2 (line-numbering of the Globe edition).

The cuts in this scene (8 lines) are traditional. These are: 51-57a (the entrance of Polonius, Rosencrantz, and Guildenstern, and Hamlet's dismissal of them); 93-94.

Slight alterations, as recorded by Clarke, are: 7, "of passion" > "of your passion"; 28, "off" > "of"; 30, "the which" > "which"; 36, "nor" > "or."

Act III, 3. *A Room in the Palace, called the Grand Hall of Audience.*

(Globe edition: Act III, 2, 97-417. 321 lines cut to 243.)

The trumpets sound, the set of the preceding scene sinks under the stage, and the Court is discovered assembled in the Grand Hall of Audience, waiting for the play to begin.[26] At stage right, forward of the staircase, the King and Queen are seated on chairs mounted on a rectangular dais two or three steps high. Polonius stands near them at the upstage end of the dais; later, when the play begins, he will take the chair "below 1st Grooves" at the right. Across the stage from them, backed against the curtained arch at the left, is a platform stage two feet tall and ten feet long, covered with a red cloth [27] and with a couch upon it. All around the rear, Clarke tells us, upon the stairs and across the gallery are groups and rows of attendants:

[26] In later stagings, when there was no change of scene here, after the words "I must be idle" Hamlet simply went upstage a little and to the platform stage, where he waited. Horatio went offstage either to the left or up center in order to bring on Ophelia. Then, while march music played, the King and Court entered to their places.

[27] Clarke reports a red cloth; the 1870 promptbook says it is green.

Guards, Chamberlains with torches, Courtiers, and Officers. A crowd of guests, many of whom are Ladies, are gathered up right center, where they will be seated when the action gets under way. According to William Winter (*Tribune*, December 5, 1871) there were sixty actors on the stage.

We have two pictures of the Play scene in progress (see Plates XVIIa and X), one from earlier years and one subsequent to the 1870 production, showing between them Booth's abandonment of the traditional in favor of "modern" staging of the play-within-a-play. The drawing in the Booth-Hinton edition of 1866 shows the *Mousetrap* going on in the alcove at the back—an arrangement such as we find in Daniel Maclise's famous painting of the scene in 1842; in the scenic directive in Bell's *Shakespeare* (1773) of "A Hall in the Palace. Theatre in the Background"; in the frontispiece to Hanmer's edition of Shakespeare (1744); and ultimately, we assume, in Shakespeare's own staging of the scene at the Globe.[28] The Winter Garden 1866 promptbook contains not only a groundplan which proves the alcove arrangement, but the curious stage direction, "Small bell rings & curtain front of set stage draws off R & L." That is to say, when Hamlet's play-within-a-play began, the traditional prompter's bell was heard just as in a "real" theatre. The photograph made at McVicker's Theatre in 1873 (following the new arrangement of 1870) shows how Booth, sensing at last the impracticality of the upstage center focus, abandoned his stage design, so to speak, and played the action crosswise of the stage. "This cannot but be deemed an improvement," said the *Sunday Times* (January 9), "for the counter-workings of the features of both Claudius and Hamlet are not only brought into more direct antithesis, but also more plainly put in sight of the audience."

The author of "How to Set a Great Play on the Stage" (Philadelphia *Evening Bulletin*, December 11, 1871) singles out this stage picture as "one of the most imposing known to the stage anywhere," and in describing it he dwells particularly upon its color values:

> The gray of the rich stone architecture is a delicious relief; the upper gallery, with its curiously hinged doors; the arrangement of the vaulted ceiling, with many vistas of solid pendentives; and finally the crowding over this almost cathedral-like background of living groups in the most

[28] Maclise's painting and the Hanmer frontispiece are reproduced in W. M. Merchant's *Shakespeare and the Artist* (London, 1959), Plates 8c and 46b.

softly-vivid dresses, the gallery thronged with soldiers, and the two long descents of stairs set with pages and flambeaux, all this combination proves that Mr. Peake and Mr. Deuel [29] comprehend the lofty truth that there is no chance for a true artist so fine as a great theatre stage with its easy relief of flats under different degrees of illumination, its ability to condone individual crudities of color by melting them into the larger harmonies, its unequalled resources of glooms and highlights, and its realities of drapery and moving color.

97-145. "How fares our cousin Hamlet?"

As the scene is discovered, Hamlet is coming through the central entrance at the back, and after him Horatio leading Ophelia by the hand. Hamlet, with arms folded and head bent, advances to the center, turns, and walks over to the platform stage, where he leans against it with his arm thrown up to rest on the end of the couch. Horatio moves a chair to the center, seats Ophelia there, and stands beside the chair with his hand on the post of it. As the music ceases, the King calls out, "How fares our cousin Hamlet?" Hamlet responds pleasantly: "EX*cellent* i' faith, of the *camelion's* dish (upward accent on the *me-* syllable; prolonged; then his voice falls): I eat the *air, promise-crammed* (upward accent on *promise*, and strong emphasis; his voice falls on *crammed*); you cannot (upward accent; pleasant tone) feed *capons* so (the tone of the last clause is that of an instructor speaking pleasantly to a young pupil)." He bows his head slightly, gives his right arm a graceful lateral wave, and then rests it again on the end of the sofa. The King rejects his answer, for these words "are not mine." Hamlet answers lightly, "*No* (slight upward accent), nor *mine* (upward accent) *now* (falling voice; full sound of *now*)."

He looks toward Polonius, and starting up with his right hand poised before his breast, he moves out toward the center: "My lord, *you* (prolonged) *played-once* in the *university* (marked sound of *ver-*, upward sound of *si-*, falling sound of *-ty*), you *say?* (his voice falls)." Polonius steps down in front of the throne and acknowledges that he did play then and was accounted a good actor. "And what did you *enact?*" It was Julius Caesar, says Polonius, killed in the capitol by Brutus. Hamlet lifts his brows a little and holds out his right hand in an easy gesture: "It was a *brute part* (upward accent) of *him* (he turns from Polonius with a partial bow, and walks down,

[29] J. L. Peake was the machinist of Booth's Theatre and J. P. Deuel was the manager of properties. The writer should also have mentioned Mr. Joyce, who was the costumer, and of course Charles Witham, the chief scene painter.

rounding in his course to front center) to kill so capital a *calf* there (dry quiet voice)."

He turns and looks upstage: "Be the *players ready?* (downward accent)." Rosencrantz, who is upstage left, says that they are, and Hamlet saunters toward the platform stage. The Queen calls to him to come and sit by her, but Hamlet moves toward Ophelia: "*No* (full though not prolonged sound), good *mother* (giving the Queen a short bow), here's metal (he reaches his left arm leisurely toward Ophelia) *more* (prolonged) attractive (upward accent)." He draws near to Ophelia, and Polonius in an aside bids the King to "mark that." [30] Hamlet stops at the left of Ophelia's chair, inclining his body a little toward her: "Lady, shall I *lie in your lap?* (slight upward accent)." Looking at her with a grave, sad, polite air, he drops his left knee on a footstool near her feet. She says that he is merry.

He throws his head back a trifle and drops his right hand out before him, palm upward: "Oh! your only *jigmaker!* (emphasis on *jig;* upward accent on *maker*). What (putting his right hand on the arm of her chair) should a man *do* (upward accent; prolonged) but be *merry?* (downward accent; he glances quietly at the Queen). For look you (his voice drops lower, to a sad and somewhat bitter tone) how cheerfully my *mother* looks, and my *father died* (he lowers his face sadly and reflectively and drops his left hand to his side) *within these two hours* (slowly, in low tones, as if in painful musing)." Ophelia insists that it is "quite two months." Hamlet glances up quickly, lifts his brows, and opens his lips with surprise: "so *long* (prolonged, wondering sound of *so;* upward accent of *long*). *Nay* (prolonged) then, let the *devil* (upward accent of *dev-*) wear *black*, for *I'll* (upward accent) have a suit of *sables* (long upward sound of *a;* slightly sarcastic tone). Die *two months ago* (slowly and reflectively; looking at Ophelia) and *not forgotten* (upward accent) *yet* (falling accent; the tone is sarcastic but sad; he drops his head and looks down thoughtfully). Then there's hope a GREAT *man's* memory may outlive his LIFE *half-a-year* (upward accent; he looks up with ironical cheerfulness); but by'r *lady* (he drops his head again, and speaks in a low voice almost at random) he must build *churches* then."

[30] *116.* In later stagings, according to Mason and the Taylor 1890 and Harvard 1890 promptbooks, as Hamlet approached Ophelia, Horatio crossed down left to the foot of the platform stage, so that he could conspicuously watch the King. The McVicker's Theatre photograph of 1873 (Plate X) shows Horatio in that position.

146-281. "What means the play, my lord?"

Since the pantomime is omitted, Ophelia cannot say "What means *this?*" but rather "What means the play?" Her motivation appears to be only to change the subject. Hamlet looks up at her alertly: "*Miching mallecho;* it *means* (he pauses for an instant and reaches out his left hand a little) *—mischief* (falling accent; he gives his hand a slight turn and lets it drop to his side)." She begs to know the argument of the play.

At this moment the Second Actor comes onto the platform stage from the curtained archway behind it to speak the Prologue. Hamlet's back is toward the platform, but he seems to hear him come. He starts up and crosses to Ophelia's right, exclaiming, "We shall *know* by *this fellow.*" He lies at Ophelia's feet, his head toward the platform, his feet toward the King, his body resting on a cushion. The Second Actor delivers his three-line jingle and retires. Hamlet turns his head to look at Ophelia: "Is *this* the *prologue* (pronounced *prol-og*) or the *posy* of a *ring?* (the words seem rather a general comment than a question)." Ophelia says it is "brief." Hamlet gives her a quick, quiet look, and then a long look round at the Queen, and says in a low, grave, sad, and sarcastic voice, "*As woman's love.*" Then he turns again toward the platform, where the First Actor and the Actress have entered.

During the first two speeches by the Actors, he watches them intently.[31] When the First Actor speaks again—"Faith, I must leave thee, love"—Hamlet turns and looks steadily at the Queen. As the Actress protests that second love in her would be treason, Hamlet rises a little on the cushion, holding his right arm down to his waist with the hand lifted a little toward the Queen. At the words "None wed the second but who killed the first," the King and Queen stir uneasily. Hamlet sinks back upon his cushion: "*Wormwood, wormwood* (low tone; prolonged; slightly grating voice)." He looks at the Queen with a smile of bitter gratification on his tightly closed lips.

Then he watches the Actors again. At "If once a widow, ever I be wife," he looks at the Queen, then at Ophelia. At " 'Tis deeply sworn," he puts his right hand upon Ophelia's hands, which rest in

[31] *183.* Here and at line 191, the Taylor 1890 promptbook records that Hamlet signaled Horatio to observe the King.

her lap, and says, "If she should *break* it *now* (light, exclamatory accents and sarcastic tones)." At the Player Queen's exit, he lifts up a little, resting his left elbow on the cushion, and looks toward the Queen: "*Madam* (upward accent), how *like* (downward accent; marked emphasis) you this *play?*" The Queen thinks that the lady protests too much. "*Oh*, but she'll *keep her word* (gentle emphasis of *word*, but peculiar sarcastic tone)." He turns his face toward Ophelia and lifts his right hand to her lap as if to touch her hands again.

The King demands to know if there will be any "offense" in the play. Hamlet turns his head toward the King, still keeping his right hand in Ophelia's lap: "No, no (light tone; lifting his eyebrows a little), they do but *jest*, *poison* (deep, full, strong sound) in *jest. No offense* i' *the world* (smooth, quieting pronunciation of *world*)." He looks sharply at the King, and then turns his head slowly toward Ophelia again. He also exchanges covert glances with Horatio, who stands behind Ophelia's chair. The King asks the name of the play. Hamlet turns his head toward the King suddenly: "The *Mousetrap* (briefly). Mary, *how?* (upward accent)." He takes his right hand from Ophelia's lap and partially sits up on the cushion, resting his left hand upon it: "Tropically. This *play* (motioning over his left shoulder) is the image of a *murder* done in Vienna. *Gonzago's* the *duke's* name; his *wife*, *Baptista*. You shall *see* anon. 'Tis a *knavish* (long, rounding sound of *a*) piece-of-*work* (upward accent), but *what of that?* Your majesty and we that have *free* (upward accent; prolonged) *souls* (upward accent), it touches *us not*. Let the GALLED-*jade* wince (leaning back on the cushions and eyeing the King keenly), *our* (prolonged; he taps his shoulder near the base of the neck) withers are unwrung (slowly; in a tranquil but ironic tone)."

The Third Actor enters as Lucianus. Hamlet sees him, casts a quick glance over his shoulder at Ophelia, and says to her, "This is one *Lucianus*, *nephew* to the *duke*." He looks at Lucianus. Ophelia says that Hamlet is as good as a chorus. He looks over his shoulder at her: "I could interpret *between you* and *your love* (he looks toward the platform again, and finishes the sentence in a lower tone), if I could see the *puppets dallying*." He looks at the King, then again toward the platform, and rises a little on his arm: "*Begin*, *murderer* (low, guttural tones). *Leave* thy *damnable faces* and *begin*. Come:

the croaking *raven* doth *bellow* (upward accent) for *revenge* (downward accent; these last four words are spoken slowly)." [32]

He turns his face toward the King with eyes unusually bright, lips parted, and brows gathered. During Lucianus' six-line speech, Hamlet's excitement grows; as the speech nears its climax, expectation, anxiety, and confirmed suspicion show in his face. He rises on the cushion to a sitting position, his right hand clenched before him, his head drawing back and lips parting. As Lucianus pours the poison into the Player King's ear, the certainty of the King's guilt seems to overwhelm Hamlet, and he sits upright, stares at the King, and cries in a hot, accusatory way, but too rapidly to be very deep or loud, "He *poisons him* i' the *garden* for his *estate.* His name's *Gonzago:* the story is *extant* and written in *very choice Italian:* you *shall see anon* (pointing swiftly over his left shoulder; all the guests start and stare at him, and the King listens terror-stricken) *how the murderer gets the love of Gonzago's wife* (his voice rises steadily to climax in *wife*)."

The King leaps up, calling for lights, and Polonius triples the cry. All but Hamlet and Horatio rush out distractedly, while trumpets flourish—the King, Queen, Polonius, and Ophelia up center, the others to right and left.[33] The Player King rises, and he and Lucianus bow and retire behind the curtain in the left archway.

282-346. "Why, let the strucken deer go weep."

As the crowd flees, Hamlet leaps up with glistening eyes and open mouth, smiling exultantly, and raising his arms and face runs toward the front crying, "Why let the *strucken deer* (turning at the front center and looking upstage with his arms upraised) go weep, the heart *ungallèd play* (he takes a few steps upstage), for some *must watch* while some (starting toward the front again, where Horatio has preceded him) must *sleep;* thus *runs the world* (upward accent and special emphasis) *away* (falling accent)." He drops into Horatio's arms, and with his right arm around Horatio's neck, leans on his breast. The last attendant just now vanishes from the hall. "Oh,

[32] *265.* In his Notebook Booth mentions at this line that the raven was an emblem of the House of Denmark. Thus "the croaking raven" bellowing for revenge is Hamlet himself.

[33] *281.* According to later promptbooks, such as the Pitman 1884, the stage lights were turned down somewhat as the attendants carried off their torches. The Harvard 1890 promptbook calls for moonlight through the stage right arches somewhat earlier in the scene.

good *Horatio* (he starts a little from Horatio's arms, puts his right hand on his shoulder and his left hand on his breast, and looks into his face), I'll take the ghost's word for a *thousand pound* (rapidly, with excited looks and hard breathing). *Didst perceive?* (heavy upward accent of *-ceive;* looking eagerly into Horatio's face)." Horatio says that he has seen it very well.

Hamlet draws back as if to get a clearer view of Horatio's face; he clutches Horatio's shoulder and breast, and his own face trembles with agitation: "*Upon* the talk of the *poisoning?* (upward accent; deep voice; hurriedly spoken)." Horatio repeats that he noted the King well. "Ah, ha! (the *ah* is an indrawn sound like a moan, the *ha* an expulsion of breath like a low, sorrowful, but triumphant laugh)."

He puts his left hand on his forehead and leans upon Horatio's breast, his face lifted and partly covered by his hand, his eyes closed, his right arm reaching around Horatio's shoulders. He remains so an instant, and then with a long breath drops his left hand to Horatio's face and looks into it as if emotionally confused. The two turn in toward each other slowly, and Hamlet puts his left arm around Horatio's shoulders. "*Come*, some *music* (low voice, scarcely above a whisper; he pats Horatio's shoulders restlessly two or three times as they move upstage). Come, the *recorders* (low voice, still almost a whisper; he motions with his right hand as he says *recorders*)." He takes his left arm from Horatio's shoulders and steps slowly toward the chair which Ophelia occupied at center. Horatio goes out the center entrance and to the right.

Almost immediately Rosencrantz and Guildenstern enter at upstage center, coming from the left, and advance toward downstage left, unperceived by Hamlet. Meanwhile Hamlet has drawn the chair down to front center, and he now sits in it, facing front, his right elbow on the arm of it, his forehead resting on his right hand, his left hand lying loosely upon his left leg. He looks down with brows gathered, lips open, and a look of intense and rapid thought upon his face. Guildenstern and Rosencrantz approach at his left, but not close to him, and Guildenstern begs a word with him. Hamlet starts, lifting his head from his hand, and looks aside at them in displeasure. Then with a look of enforced patience he lifts his brows, bows slightly, and gives his left hand a little outward turn, palm upward: "*Sir*, a *whole history* (low, courteous, but slightly fretful tone; sharp accent on *history;* he gazes at them steadfastly)."

Guildenstern says, "The King, sir—" and hesitates. "Ay, sir (Hamlet folds his arms and sits back nearly upright), *what of him?* (impatiently, and in a tone implying less regard for the King than he usually shows)." The King, says Guildenstern, is distempered. Hamlet shows faint signs of irritability. He scowls a little and looks at them with increased dignity: "*With drink*, sir? (he gives a slight jerk of the head)." Not that, says Guildenstern, but choler. "Your wisdom (sitting upright and looking at them with quiet reproval) should show itself *more richer* to signify *this* to his *doctor* (slight upward accent), for, for *me* to put him to *his purgation* would perhaps plunge him into *more* (full, broad sound; a short pause) *choler* (abruptly and disdainfully)." He sits back in his chair. Guildenstern urges him to "start not so wildly" from the matter. Hamlet rises: "I am *tame* (slight upward accent), sir (he bows a little and gives his arms a slow outsweep, palms upward); *pronounce* (slight upward accent)." He stands upright expectantly, his left hand at his side and his right hand before his breast with the fingers drawn together.

Guildenstern says that it is the Queen, in her affliction, who has sent them here. Hamlet lifts his brows a little, crosses left with measured steps, and takes Guildenstern's hand: "*You are welcome* (easy, polite tone and sober face; he looks steadily at him)." Guildenstern objects that this courtesy is not "of the right breed." Hamlet lets go his hand and steps back, looking at him gravely. Guildenstern insists on a wholesome answer. Hamlet folds his arms and turns as if to go to front center, but checks himself and looks at Guildenstern impatiently: "*Sir, I cannot* (quiet voice as if dismissing the claim; advancing his right foot as if to go)." "What, my lord?" says Guildenstern. Hamlet stops and drops his arms. "Make you a *wholesome answer;* my wit's *diseased*." He touches his forehead lightly with his forefinger: "But, *sir*, such answer as I *can* make, you (standing with his head held a little back and his right hand out at his side, palm upward) shall *command;* or *rather* (dropping his hand), as you say, *my mother;* therefore NO *more*, but to the *matter*. My *mother* (thrusting his head a little forward, and holding his right hand out before him, palm upward), you say—"

At this point Rosencrantz takes over the inquiry, and presently Guildenstern drifts upstage. Rosencrantz explains that the Queen has been struck into amazement and admiration by Hamlet's behavior. Hamlet stands erect, with head thrown back, brows raised, and hand held up to his breast, the palm outward: "Oh, *wonderful* (the first syllable prolonged) son, that can so *astonish* (dropping his hand and lowering his head) a *mother*. But is there no sequel at the heels of this mother's *admiration?* (he makes a slight outward gesture with his right hand). *Impart* (he nods lightly)." Rosencrantz says that she wishes to speak with him in her closet.

Hamlet takes a step backward and looks at them with polite dignity: "We shall *obey* (upward accent; holding his right hand out before him), were she TEN *times* (he raises his right hand above his head and makes a quick confirmatory gesture) *our mother* (his voice falls)." He takes a step toward front center, turns, and faces them: "Have you (reaching his left hand toward them, palm upward) any *further* TRADE (hard, sarcastic tone, implying in the word a reproach for their conspiracy against him) *with us?* (strong sibilant sound in *us*, and a dry, unfriendly tone hinting dislike of their presence)." [34] He turns from them coldly and walks toward the center.

347-389. "My lord, you once did love me."

Rosencrantz reminds him of their former love. Hamlet, in front of the chair at center, turns hastily, and bending his shoulders forward reaches out his hands toward Rosencrantz, the palms turned toward his own face and the fingers spread wide: "*And do* STILL, by these *pickers* (upward accent) *and stealers* (intense rising tone in both words; prolonged; he shakes his hands two or three times)." As Rosencrantz begins to reply, Hamlet drops his hands so that the right one rests on a post of the chair, and he looks at them wearily as if he longed to be alone. At the end of Rosencrantz' plea for his confidence, he sits carelessly, as if fatigued: "Sir, I lack *advancement*."

He crosses his legs, puts his left elbow on the arm of the chair, rests his chin on his hand, and looks at Rosencrantz with brows raised and lips closed, as if to say that merely out of courtesy he had spoken the first thing that came into his head, and as if he were weary of this conversation. But Rosencrantz pursues the subject: how can he lack advancement when the King has named him for succession to the throne? "Ay, sir (he drops his hand from his chin and gives his head a short toss, at the same time making a gesture of uneasiness with his right hand), but while the *grass grows* (he tosses his head, puts the

[34] *346.* Booth remarks in his Notebook and in the Taylor 1890 promptbook that here for the first time Hamlet uses the royal plural, and this sudden assertion of authority signifies that "he is determined to kill the King and assume his rights."

forefinger of his right hand to his forehead, and then impatiently dismisses the quotation) —the *proverb* is *something musty*." [35]

Meanwhile, Horatio has just entered upstage, followed by two musicians in long scarlet gowns, whom he leads forward toward the right of Hamlet's chair. Guildenstern, who has wandered up left, crosses over quickly and comes down behind them, as if to overhear whatever passes between them. Horatio touches Hamlet's arm. Hamlet looks up and nods, recalling the errand he had sent Horatio on: "Oh! The *recorders*. Let me *see* one (colloquial tone, pleasant voice)." Horatio takes a rosewood pipe from one of the musicians and hands it to Hamlet, who examines it cursorily and then says to Horatio in a tone of quiet authority, "To *withdraw* with you." This remark, which in the text is apparently something spoken to Rosencrantz and Guildenstern, is used by Booth, together with a sweep of the head, as a directive to Horatio to take away the musicians. Horatio does so.

Hamlet, still seated, then looks again toward Rosencrantz, bending forward, holding the pipe in his left hand: "*Why*-do-you go about to recover the *wind* (to rhyme with *find*) of me (short sound of *me*) as if you would drive me into a toil?" He asks this in a candid, direct manner, almost bluntly, quite differently from the suave manner he had used with them before. Guildenstern, at his right, puts in his quibble about duty being too bold and love too unmannerly. Hamlet looks at him doubtfully: "I do not well *understand*-that." He takes the pipe in his right hand and holds it out toward Guildenstern: "Will you play upon this-*pipe?*" Guildenstern protests he cannot. "I *pray* you." Hamlet sits motionless, looking steadily at him and holding out the pipe as if asking him to do a favor. But Guildenstern *cannot*. Hamlet looks at him an instant, his head raised a little as in surprise. He turns to Rosencrantz, leans on the left arm of the chair, and transferring the pipe to his left hand, holds it out toward him: "I do-beseech *you*." Rosencrantz claims to know no touch of it.

Hamlet looks from one to the other in mild surprise, then draws the instrument up before him, sitting upright: " '*Tis* (upward accent) as *easy* (prolonged; upward accent) as *lying* (upward accent

[35] *359.* Booth interprets the proverb as signifying in Hamlet's thought, "While the King lives there is no room for my advancement." In the Taylor 1890 promptbook Lawrence Barrett supplies the ending of the proverb: "the steed starves."

on the *y* sound; prolonged)." He holds the pipe out in his left hand and puts his right hand along it, covering the holes with his fingers. "*Govern* these *ventages* with your *fingers*-and-*thumb*, give it breath with your *mouth*, and it will *discourse* most *eloquent-music. Look*-you (upward accent of *you;* looking at them both), *these* are the *stops* (slight upward accent)." He points to the parts of the pipe, and holds it out toward Guildenstern. But Guildenstern protests he has not the skill. Hamlet looks at them with sternness and indignation. He holds the pipe before him: "*Why look*-you now, how *un*WOR*thy* a *thing* you make of *me!* You would play upon *me;* you would seem to know *my* stops (he drops the pipe to his left knee and touches his breast with his right hand); you would pluck out the *heart* of my (short sound of *my*) *mystery* (falling accent and quick pronunciation); you would sound *me* from my *lowest note* to the top of my *compass*."

He rises. He speaks in tones of accusation and displeasure: "And there is *much music* (upward accent), excellent voice, in this *little organ*." He holds out the pipe before him in his left hand and points at it with his right. Rosencrantz and Guildenstern draw a little nearer: "Yet *cannot* you make *it* speak. 'Sdeath (he drops his left hand, with the pipe, to his side), do you think *I* am *easier* to be *played on* than a *pipe?* (upward accent; making a frontward gesture with his right hand). *No* (upward accent and nasal tone). Call me *what instrument* you *will*, though you may *fret* me, you *cannot* PLAY upon me." He throws the pipe down into the chair, looks at them indignantly a moment, and moves toward the front. They retire a little, discomfited. Polonius enters at the back, calling "My lord! my lord!" and hastens forward.

390-417. "God bless you, sir!"

Hearing Polonius' call, Hamlet turns toward him, raises his right hand above his head with the palm toward Polonius, and says in a solemn, almost priestly way, "*God* BLESS *you, sir*." Polonius bows from right center and comes on. Hamlet crosses wearily, passing in front of Guildenstern, toward down right. The message Polonius brings is that the Queen would speak with Hamlet presently.

Hamlet seats himself in the chair down right center, facing toward the arched entrance. He looks offstage and motions over his shoulder for Polonius to draw near. He bends his head down gravely and peers through the arch: "Do you see *yonder cloud*, that's *almost* (slowly, in a tone of wonderment) in shape of a CAMEL? (downward accent, tone of affirmation)." Polonius bends down behind Hamlet, looks, and agrees "by the mass" that it is like a camel. "Methinks (turning his face to the front, and casting over his shoulder a cold, sharp glance at the point on the floor where Polonius is standing) it is like a *weasel.*" Polonius, still looking out the archway, agrees it is backed like a weasel. Hamlet turns still farther front, folds his arms, and looks angrily at the floor where Polonius is standing: "Or like a *whale?* (slowly, coldly, in a low voice as if drawing Polonius on)." Polonius agrees to the whale, and then straightens from his bent position.

Hamlet looks up at him sharply and irefully, his arms still folded: "Then I will come to *my* MOTHER by and (upward accent) *by.*" Polonius bows and goes up toward the center entrance. Hamlet unfolds his arms and turns restlessly in his chair: "They *fool* me to the *top* of my *bent* (quickly, in querulous tones, as if irritated even by Polonius' gullibility)." He turns in his chair and calls out, without looking back, "I will come *by* (upward accent) *and* (upward accent) *by* (downward accent; making a slight outward gesture with his left hand)." Polonius answers from the back and bows. Hamlet turns and looks at him: "*By and by* (he repeats the same accents; he inclines his body and gestures outward with his left hand) is *easily* (upward accent; prolonged) said."

He turns front and rises thoughtfully. As he starts toward the center, he sees Rosencrantz and Guildenstern, who are lingering upstage: "*Leave* me (short sound of *me;* pause), *friends* (downward accent)." [36] He bows slowly, with hands out at the sides. Rosencrantz and Guildenstern bow and go out.

With moderate steps, reflectively, Hamlet crosses to the right, leans against the pillar between the two archways, and looks out into the evening: " 'Tis *now* the very *witching time* (turning and facing front) of *night,* when (facing center) *churchyards yawn* (broad sound and slight upward accent; moving slowly toward right center) and *hell* itself breathes-out *contagion* to this *world.* Now could I drink hot *blood* (stopping at right center, facing left rear) and do such *bitter* business (looking down sternly) as the day would *quake* to *look*-on!" He brings down his clenched fist before his breast in a threatening stroke. He pauses briefly and drops his hand as if ponder-

[36] *405.* Mason records that at "Leave me, friends," Booth threw the flute down upon the platform stage. In the 1870 production he has left it in the chair.

ing his feeling, but then he keeps on: "Soft—now to my mother." He takes a step upstage: "Oh, heart (upward accent; semi-distinct, palatal sound of the *t*), lose-*not* thy *nature* (upward accent and appealing tone; looking up and placing his right hand on his breast); let not ever the soul of *Nero* enter this *firm* (long, grating sound) *bosom* (upward accent; tremulous sound)." He strikes his breast once or twice with his right hand: "Let me be *cruel* (upward accent), not *unnatural!* (strong voice and full articulation; giving a slight outward sweep with the right hand). I will *speak* DAGGERS *to*-her (lifting his right hand above his head conclusively) but *use* (prolonged) *none* (tremulous tone)." He brings his hand down before him energetically and starts toward the rear. As the set for the next scene rises up and shuts him from sight, he is walking upstage, his hands on his forehead, thinking intently.

This scene, in Clarke's judgment, is one of the greatest in Booth's *Hamlet.* Here Booth shows with remarkable clarity the central essence of his interpretation: Hamlet's resoluteness in minor matters and irresoluteness in major ones.

His attitudes toward his surroundings and toward the other characters are nicely distinguished. At his entrance he is sunk deep in meditation, seemingly unaware of the presence of the Court; but as he turns upstage from the front he adroitly effects a change from abstraction to perception. He wears his "madness" lightly: without ever quite departing from gracefulness or propriety, he carries himself with a freedom of movement and attitude just enough removed from courtly behavior to suggest mental aberration. In his little exchange with Polonius at the beginning of the scene he shows a fitting and natural delicacy. He does not throw into Polonius' face the words "to kill so capital a *calf* there," as Charles Fechter does, but utters them as a kind of aside while walking toward the front. Thus he avoids committing a crude insult. The audience hears the line, but Polonius and the Court do not.

His behavior toward Ophelia makes it clear that she is no longer important to him. He is formally gallant toward her, but severe at times and even ready with sharp retorts upon her. It is the play and the King's reception of it, not Ophelia, that occupies his attention, and although he stays close to her, he appears to forget her as the scene progresses.

He regards the Queen mournfully and with latent bitterness.

Several times during the passages of the Player Queen he attempts to rebuke his mother with stern looks, but she avoids his glances. He speaks the line "Oh, but she'll *keep her word*" with a fine mixture of deference and irony, referring it both to his mother's failure to keep her vows and to the parallel falsity of the Player Queen.

Toward the King he shows a suppressed defiance. He always answers the King's questions quickly, freely, and fearlessly. To this extent he is brave and decisive, without ever resorting to crude ferocity. His bravery is worked up toward a climax at the passage wherein Lucianus pours poison in the sleeper's ear; yet presently it becomes obvious that this bravery can never culminate in a grand tragic action. Hamlet's will gives way to his intelligence, and his directly vengeful, executive course gives way to the merely accusatory; he wants only to cut into the King's conscience and find proofs for his suspicions.

At this important turning point Booth shows Hamlet's weakness with surpassing skill: Hamlet ceases to be competent in action and becomes only skillful in observation. When the King rushes away and Hamlet comes forward, he shows in his face not the least determination to act, but only a wild certainty of the King's guilt. His feelings are a medley: gratification for the success of his scheme; regret and disappointment since now the duty imposed upon him by the Ghost bears more pressingly; a sense of weakness; a desire for vengeance but a pitiful giving way of the will to effect it. All these feelings flow in and out of his incoherent laughter. But there is no fury of intention, no sudden plan to kill the King, no suggestion of immediate revenge or of design for revenge in the future. He falls into Horatio's arms in a spasm of emotional bewilderment. Then he dispatches Horatio to fetch music, as if he wants to be soothed, and settles into a chair to ponder the events that have just occurred.

In the scene with Rosencrantz and Guildenstern he is once more in control of himself and once more the thorough gentleman. He does not bother to resume his counterfeit madness—except, of course, in the little side episode with Polonius; with the "friends" he is simply restrained, polite, cool, and ironic. His rebuke to them shows how efficient and stable he can be in minor matters. It is not a menacing or roughly delivered rebuke. He speaks it simply, firmly, with easy brevity. It contains no insolence and no threat, but it carries a warning, and its thorough earnestness quite disables the wits of the two courtiers. His dismissal of them, at "*Leave* me—*friends*," which is delivered in a tone of courteous authority, makes clear that he will continue to consider them "friends" in a technical sense, and that he will regard their past behavior with clemency; but it cautions them to cease meddling in his affairs hereafter.

The conclusion of the scene with the Players, Clarke says, is a fine example of Booth's skill in stage management. The Grand Hall of Audience itself, in its great size and elaborate embellishment, makes an impressive setting for so important a passage of the play. When the King takes fright and runs out of the room, the confusion which ensues is admirably arranged and executed, every person on the stage acting with well-planned uncertainty. The Players on the platform stage, for instance, stare in amazement and retire in doubt and chagrin. Horatio comes forward hurriedly, as if to get a place outside the frantic crowd where he can watch everything that happens. Hamlet comes down to him, his arms upraised, his face dark and tense with feeling; and just as he falls into Horatio's arms with a sorry laugh, the last one of the frightened spectators leaves the hall. The end of the episode has been reached by such superb combinations and processes of movement that Hamlet's action seems to top the whole and complete the tableau. And this is but one of the most striking instances of Booth's direction throughout the play. Everywhere great emotions or significant situations resolve themselves in brief pictures which give force, dignity, meaning, and dramatic effect. Yet the play is never sacrificed to these effects. They seem always to arise out of the natural order of events, and they are never stayed for.

The text of Act III, 3 (line-numbering of the Globe edition).

The cuts in this scene (78 lines) are traditional. These are: 120-128 (bawdy remarks to Ophelia); 130-131; 139a ("Oh, heavens"); 143-145; the dumbshow; 147a ("Marry, this is"); 152-158 (reference to the dumbshow, and some bawdry); 192-195, 198-223, 228-231 (from speeches of the Player Queen and Player King); 259-263 (bawdry); 276-278; 286-296 (Hamlet's bid for a place in a cry of players and his second set of rhymes); 303-304 (Hamlet's jingle); 415-417 (the rhymed ending).

There are numerous slight alterations: 108, "What" > "And what" (Folio reading); 132, "Oh God" > "Oh"; 136, "twice" > "quite" (Booth thought "twice" was a misprint, else Hamlet should say "four months" in his next speech); 146, "this" > "the play" (the dumbshow being omitted); 191, "That's wormwood" > "Wormwood, wormwood" (Folio reading); 235, " 'Tis deeply sworn" is moved back to follow "if ever I be wife"; 255, "nephew to the King" > "nephew to the Duke"; 360, Horatio and the musicians leave the stage after "To withdraw with you"; 370, "I do beseech you" is addressed to Rosencrantz, who then takes Guildenstern's next line; 386, "'Sblood" > "'Sdeath"; 387, "No" is inserted before "Call me"; 389, Polonius' "My lord" is taken from line 391, doubled, and inserted as a calling entrance.

The restorations (6 lines) are these: 166-168, 177-178 (in speeches of the Player Queen and Player King); 390 ("God bless you, sir!").

Act III, 4. *The King's Closet.*

(Globe edition: Act III, 3. 98 lines cut to 77.)

The setting for the King's Prayer scene, according to Clarke, "was simply a partition across the stage near the footlights, with panelings containing pictures of men in ancient armor engaged in warlike feats and struggles. At the center of this was a double door." When these doors were opened, they "disclosed a cell or cloister in which there stood an altar containing a cross and book of devotions."

To put it in other terms, it is a shallow front set which rises from under the stage at the first grooves. The main wall, which has an archway closed with double doors at center, is flanked at right and left by narrow door flats, and is met at the top by ceiling borders which come down from the flies.[37] The backing unit representing the inner cell and altar is put in place behind the closed double doors. The scene serves as a "carpenters' scene" to cover the preparation of the Queen's Private Apartment, which will appear next.

The scene design in the Harvard 1870 promptbook (see Plate XII) is not quite authentic for the 1870 production. What Clarke describes is pictured more accurately in the watercolor preserved in the Witham Collection at the Museum of the City of New York, in which we find the double doors of the center arch swung partly open, military tapestries hung in the two flanking blind arches, and such other expectable features as chevron and dentils on the arches and a chevron frieze around the top of the room. In preparing the design to be inserted into the promptbook, Witham "improved" it with happy afterthoughts. In lieu of the military tapestries, a motif which he had already used in earlier scenes, he converted the blind arches into windows and filled them prettily with religious subjects done in stained glass. He also simplified the stone work, eliminating the various orders of the arches and the chevron frieze around the top of the

[37] In later stagings, this set did not rise, of course, but was flown down or thrust on at the first grooves. The scene was never omitted, even when Booth gave up his own portion of it, being necessary as a "carpenters' scene."

walls. He abandoned the closed double doors. The design in the promptbook is perhaps the more attractive of the two, but it was not seen in this form during the run of the play at Booth's Theatre.

There is one piece of furniture in the room—the single chair down right center, "below 1st Grooves," which was placed there at the beginning of the act.

1-72. "I like him not, nor stands it safe with us. . . ."

The King, followed by Rosencrantz and Guildenstern, enters through the wooden door at the stage left end of the room and advances to the center.[38] After seven lines of directions from the King, the two courtiers bow and retire. At once Polonius enters from the right, announces to the King his plan to hide behind the arras in the forthcoming scene in the Queen's closet, and goes out left. The King throws open the doors revealing the altar in the inner cell, comes forward for his long soliloquy, and goes in to pray.

73-98. "Now might I do it pat, now he is praying."

Hamlet enters from the door at stage right, dressed exactly as in the Play scene except that he has put on a sword. He comes in slowly, arms folded and eyes down, as if absorbed in thought.[39] When nearly at center he glances into the cell, sees the King, and starts back a little to the right. He stands with his back partly toward the audience. His hands drop to his sword-hilt, and he says in a low whisper: "Now might I *do* it (slight pause) *pat* (this word has a peculiar labial and palatal pronunciation and the *t* is cut short; it sounds like a heavy emission of breath rather than a word, yet it is accented and it stands out distinctly; on the word he draws out his sword), now he is *praying*." He turns and crosses down right: "And *now I'll do't* (earnest, heavy whisper)." He runs suddenly and determinedly to the doorway of the cell, his sword held down at his right side, the blade pointing forward rigidly: "And *so* he goes (he pauses abruptly at the doorway) *—to heaven* (slight upward accent); and so am I *revenged?*"

He turns and faces the audience: "That would be *scanned*." He

[38] In some later promptbooks the King's entrance is marked as from the right, and the following exits and entrances are correspondingly reversed. In the Pitman 1884 promptbook, which records a quite different staging in which the King knelt and prayed at stage right, the entrances are all marked as from center, and the exits mainly to the left.

[39] Mason records, on the contrary, that Hamlet "enters rapidly."

steps away from the doorway, crosses to the chair down right center, and rests the point of his sword on the seat of it, with both hands resting on the hilt. He looks forward: "A *villain* kills my (short sound of *my*) *father* (meditatively, contemplating the situation and debating what had best be done), *and* for that, I, his sole *son*, do this same villain *send* to HEAVEN (upward accent, and a suggestion in the tone that he is withdrawing from his first quick purpose). *Oh* (upward accent; pronounced so that it sounds like *Why*), this is *hire* (upward accent) and *salary* (downward accent; he stops after the word *hire* as if the sense were complete, but then adds *salary*, tossing his right hand sidewise two or three times like a card-player dealing; he holds the sword on the chair seat as before, with his left hand on the hilt), *not* REVENGE (tone of self-censure)."

He looks toward the cell for an instant: "He took my *father* GROSSLY (he drops his right hand a little dejectedly), *full* of *bread* (looking forward with a peculiar sad expression), with all his *crimes broad-blown*, as fresh as *May* (clear, broad sound of *as* before and after *fresh;* slow, distinct utterance, and mournful but manly tone; looking upward and raising his right hand with palm upward); *and* (this word bends down, arc-like, to the middle and then rises at the end, implying a significant speculation to come) *how* (this word curves upward in the middle and down at the end) his *audit* (upward accent on the *au-* sound; prolonged) stands (flatly; downward accent), who-*knows* (tone of mournful inquiry; dropping his right hand to the sword-hilt and lowering his face a little) *save Heaven?*" He drops his head, then raises his eyes reverently for an instant. He pauses a little as if thinking of his father's condition: "But in *our circumstance* and *course* of *thought*, 'tis HEAVY with-him."

He gives a short, sorrowful shake of the head; then he closes his lips and looks down blankly for an instant. Then he rouses himself, as if getting back to consciousness of the present: "And am-I, then, *revenged*, to take *him* (looking toward the cell; with his right hand lifting the sword from the chair and swinging it lightly toward the cell, holding it out at last at the farthest point of the swing) in the *purging of his soul* (upward accent) when he (speaking faster now) is *fit* and *seasoned* (upward accent of *sea-*) for his *passage?* (slight upward accent)."

During these last few words he has left the chair and moved forward, facing the audience but in a position that gives him a full view of the doorway to the cell and a partial view of the kneeling

King: "*No* (emphatic and conclusive tone; giving his sword a decisive downward sweep). UP, sword (strong, rising accent on *up;* the voice falls on *sword;* he sheathes the sword quickly, keeping his left hand on the hilt), and know thou a more *horrid bent* (a gruff whisper, but clearly audible; he moves his right hand threateningly toward the sword, and turns to face the cell). When he is *drunk, asleep*, or in his rage; at *gaming, swearing*, or about some act (standing with his right foot a little back and his right hand down and a little to the rear, turned outward and with fingers closed tight) that has no *relish* of *salvation* IN'T."

He steps back a little and turns frontward: "THEN *trip*-him (slight upward accent; he looks toward the cell savagely), that his *heels* may KICK (raising his right hand with fingers clenched) at *heaven* (he tosses his hand upward and shuts his teeth exultantly, with a look of gross triumph), and that his *soul may be* as DAMN'D, and BLACK (he inclines his body forward and turns a little to the left, but without moving his feet; he lifts his right hand above his head with fingers clenched), as HELL (he strikes down vigorously, and smiles in a way that shows his teeth shut tightly together, his face resolute and exultant) *whereto* it *goes* (grim, grating whisper)."

On the last words he crosses the stage with long, firm, but noiseless steps, looking toward the cell as he goes. His left hand is on the sword-hilt, his right arm down at his side. He stops at the stage left door and rests his left arm against it: "My mother stays." He turns and lifts a finger threateningly toward the King: "*This* physic but *prolongs thy* sickly days." He goes out.

The King rises from the altar, closes the doors to the cell,[40] advances, speaks his final couplet, and goes out to the right. The lights are lowered somewhat, and the scenery sinks through the floor to reveal the Queen's Apartment.

Clarke finds this scene to be another superb exhibition of Hamlet as Booth conceived him—a man of strong intellect but very weak will. His brooding entrance accords perfectly with the mood and manner of his exit from the last scene. He is now on his way to his mother, and is reflecting upon how he will address her and rebuke

[40] No promptbook contains a directive for the King to close the doors. Yet in 1870 they had to be closed at this point in order to mask the removal of the backing unit (the altar), and to permit the wall to sink when the scene is ended.

her. His head is not dropped forward quite so far as usual; his lips protrude a little, hinting determination. He is alert, and when he first comes upon the King he seems about to kill him. But the acme of his resolution quickly passes; doubt and logic overcome his will, and he reasons himself out of the deed with a promise to accomplish it in the future.

In this scene is a fine instance of Booth's power of facial expression. At the line "Then trip him that his heels may kick at heaven," his face gradually loses its sadness and thoughtfulness; he smiles savagely with shut teeth; a mocking, triumphant expression starts from a dozen places in his face, and his look is "terrible, almost ferocious, and *humanly* malignant." When he says "as hell," his brows gather intensely, and here Clarke writes, "I was scared one night when sitting very near him to see that his eyes, naturally jet black, were almost white with light. It was the most notable change in the appearance of his eyes that occurred throughout the entire play."

Booth's vocal qualities, too—especially his undertones—are heard to especial advantage in this scene. It is a very clear, flexible, melodious voice, of considerable power and sturdy masculinity. Though not remarkably deep, it is round and sonorous. His speaking is distinct, and he is the master of rhythmical patterns adapted both to the soldier and the lover. "It is English with the pure Saxon accents," Clarke says, probably having in mind the contrast between Booth and Fechter, "not tinged by any other language or modes of pronunciation." His tones in this scene are low, sometimes sadly musical, again regular and reflective, sometimes gruff or sharp, now receding mournfully and again rising with governed vigor.

Clarke took exception to one failure of verisimilitude in the scene: that Hamlet was not sufficiently wary of being discovered with his sword drawn in the presence of the King. A man so cautious as Hamlet, who weighs every possibility and is over-prudent rather than rash, would be extremely vigilant to avoid discovery. Yet Booth stands down right center with the point of his sword resting on the chair for a long while, "not looking toward the King's position once a minute—no, not more than three or four times during his stay there."

The text of Act III, 4 (line-numbering of the Globe edition).

The cuts (21 lines) are traditional. These are: 5-23 (including

Guildenstern's and Rosencrantz' code of loyalty to the throne); 26b; 90 ("or in th' incestuous pleasure of his bed").

The restorations (63 lines) are these: 36-72, 97-98 (the King's soliloquy); 73-96 (Hamlet's soliloquy).

A note in Booth's 1878 edition warns that Hamlet's soliloquy is "sometimes omitted," and in the Taylor 1890 and the Harvard 1890 promptbooks it is cut. In Bell's *Shakespeare*, Francis Gentleman commended the eighteenth-century actors for deleting the speech "as being unnecessary, and next, as tending to vitiate and degrade his character much." One hopes that Booth did not participate in Gentleman's opinion, but it is very strange that having discovered the good of the speech and restored it, he should afterward give it up. One can understand that in his later years he may have needed rest before attacking the difficult scene with the Queen.

Act III, 5. *The Queen's Private Apartment.*
(Globe edition: Act III, 4. 218 lines cut to 144.)

The setting for the scene between Hamlet and his mother is a spacious room—Clarke says "extending twenty feet or so back from the footlights"—equipped with furniture. It was prepared while the King's Prayer scene was being acted—a process which, incidentally, involved the removal of the staircase units of the Grand Hall of Audience; and it is discovered when the King's Closet set sinks into the stage floor.

The decoration of the back wall, which stands at the third grooves, is consonant with the other interior scenes (see Plate XIII).[41] It is divided into three blind arches, or niches. Each arch consists of a chevron molding and a molding with a freer, perhaps floral, surface carving. The niches are hung with red arrases (practical, not merely painted), gold-fringed where they touch the floor. The lunettes of the three arches contain scenes from the Nativity: at stage right the shepherds sitting about their fire; at center the angel who appeared to them; at left one of the shepherds kneeling at the manger. On the capitals of the columns flanking the center niche are busts of a king and a queen. The wall above the arches is the customary stone block.

The side walls and ceiling are apparently made up of units

[41] The following account of the set is based upon the watercolor in the Harvard 1870 promptbook. Another design, basically the same but less attractive in details, is in the Witham Collection at the Museum of the City of New York.

repeated from earlier scenes. The ceiling, with its end-buttressed crossbeams and the arcade of tiny blind arches at the back, seems identical with the ceiling of Act I, 2; and in Bensen Sherwood's "Stage Plans" the same phrase, "Trick Borders," appears again to describe it. As for the side walls, the "Stage Plans" says that these are simply the side arch flats from the Play scene—i.e. Act III, 1 and 3. This may be true for 1873. The designs for 1870 suggest, however, that the upstage sections, with their large curtained archways, were repeated from Act I, 2; and the downstage sections with their markedly smaller arches, closed with wooden doors, were repeated from the Act II Hall of Arches. In any case, what with the consistency of decor throughout the production and the dim lighting of the scene about to be played, such repetition of units at this point is not only feasible but to be expected.[42]

At right center—closer to center and farther forward than is suggested in the watercolor—stands a cloth-covered table bearing religious objects: a crucifix, two or three burning tapers, an open Bible or missal. Just toward center from the table, and turned toward the table, is a chair. Another chair is at left center. Downstage right—not shown in the design but marked on the 1870 groundplan—is the inevitable chair "below 1st Grooves."

1-127. "He will come straight. Look you lay home to him."

The scene is dimly lighted. The Queen is discovered seated at her table, and Polonius is behind it giving his instructions. As Hamlet is heard from off left, calling in a low, sad voice, "Mother, Mother, Mother," Polonius hides behind the red arras in the stage left niche of the back wall. Hamlet enters through the wooden door at the left,[43] turns and shuts it, advances a few steps toward the Queen, and stands with his hands hanging at his sides, looking at her in mournful expectancy.

[42] Promptbooks of later stagings generally agree upon a quite different arrangement of the room and its entrances. In the Pitman 1884, the Taylor 1890, and the Harvard 1890 promptbooks, the principal entrance is a curtained archway in the middle of the back wall; the place where Polonius hides and is slain is a curtained archway in the stage left wall; in the stage right wall is a window or archway through which a calcium lamp pours moonlight, and through which the Ghost enters. The table is at center, with a stool in front of it and a chair to the right of it; when the scene opens, the Queen is sitting at the right of the table rather than the left.

[43] 8. Mason's notes show Hamlet entering from the right. In most later stagings he entered through the archway up center and came down to the right, behind his mother.

"*Now, Mother*, what's the *matter?*" The tone of his question is rigid with latent combativeness, as if he is ready to hear her words but has come here rather to speak than to listen. He is steady in his words and bearing, and this line and those that follow are low, firm, and short, yet gentle, as if he is uncertain of his direction until he sounds out the Queen's purpose. The Queen sits up and looks at him with dignity as she says, "Hamlet, you have your father much offended."[44] He answers softly, lifting his head a little, in a grave, distantly reproachful tone: "Mother (slight pause), *you* have *my* father much-offended (slight upward accent)." She challenges him with "Come, come, you *answer* with an *idle tongue*."

Standing with shoulders a little stooped, he raises his right hand a little before his breast, the palm obliquely fronting the Queen, and lifts his head: "*Go, go*, you *question* (slight upward accent) with a *wicked* tongue (low, evenly reproachful tone)." She rises: "*Why*, HOW *now*, Hamlet?" He lifts one shoulder, shifts his head as if in surprise, and looks at her: "What's the *matter now?* (tone of slight wonder and cool inquiry)." He gives these retorts randomly, as if they were a preface of little value to the business upon which he had come. "Have you *forgot* me?" she asks. He drops his head a little back, looks at her, and speaks with more animation: "*No*, by the Rood, *not so* (prolonged and very full sound of *so;* sarcastic tone). You are the *Queen* (prolonged), your *husband's brother's wife* (slowly, with little pauses between the words; sarcastic tone), and (he bows his shoulders a little) —would it WERE *not* SO!—you are *my* (low, aggrieved tone; slight pause; he bows his head and drops his hands to his sides, palms outward, as he adds) *mother*." Then he swings his hands outward, bows low, and drops his hands to his sides again. In this movement he seems to say that he recognizes her authority and will for the moment continue his reverence toward her.

She comes down front, saying that she will set those to him that can speak. Hamlet lifts his head slowly as if he has been lost in meditation; he seems visibly to rouse himself to the duty at hand, and becomes quick and alert. He crosses up to the chair she has left and draws it a little forward, saying with an air of resolute com-

[44] *10.* Clarke records the Queen's "thou hast thy father" as "you have your father," thus eliminating the contrast between the Queen's "thou" and Hamlet's hard "you." This may, of course, be a slip of the pen.

mand, but not ungently, "*Come, come*, and *sit* you *down;*[45] you *shall not* BUDGE (they meet at front center and he clasps her left wrist in his right hand). You *go not* till *I set you up* a *glass* (he lifts his left hand admonishingly before her) where-you-may-see the *inmost part* of you." She struggles to get loose from him, crying in alarm, "What wilt thou *do?* Thou wilt not *murder* me?" Hamlet has now got her left wrist in his own left hand, and his right hand is lifted either to make a gesture or to silence her voice. At the words "murder me," he gives a look of pained surprise and scornful denial, turns his face away, and raises his right hand disclaimingly between them, the palm toward her face.

As she cries "Help, help, ho!"[46] they struggle along the stage a few steps. Polonius cries out from behind the arras, "What ho! help!" At this, Hamlet turns quickly and faces toward the arras, still gripping the Queen's wrist in his left hand. He looks from the arras to her face, and again toward the arras: "How *now* (he looks again to the Queen), a *rat*, a *rat?*" As he repeats the word *rat* he slaps the back of her hand twice with his right palm. He drops her hand, draws his sword swiftly, and cries as he starts upstage toward the arras, "DEAD, for a *ducat*, DEAD!" His voice in these words is high, feverish, and impulsive. His face as he turns from her glows with a wild, inflamed purpose. He has resolved to punish the Queen by slaying the King before her eyes. Running to the arras he plunges his sword through it without stopping to make a thrust. The Queen gives a cry, and Polonius, groaning, falls and dies. The Queen cries, "Oh me! what hast thou done?"

Hamlet staggers backward from the arras, with his sword hanging in his right hand and his left hand on his forehead. He turns partly toward the Queen and walks mechanically toward upstage center, his hair falling over his temples, his face full of horror: "Nay, I *know not.*" He speaks slowly, word by word, in a heavy whisper, with a short movement of the neck and chin at every word as if he could barely articulate. Then suddenly he turns and faces

[45] *19.* The words "come, come, and sit you down" are struck out in the 1870 promptbook, and they are not printed in the 1878 edition; for the Queen does not sit until "Peace, sit you down" at line 35. By Clarke's recording, however, the cut words are spoken.

[46] *23.* For histrionic effect, the Queen always doubled the word "Help," and Polonius cried "Help" again. In later stagings Polonius was offstage left, not, as here, behind the arras in the back wall. Polonius never said, "Oh, I am slain," but only groaned.

the Queen. His knees project sharply, his body draws back, and his face reaches forward with gleaming eyes and trembling jaws. He holds his left arm out to the side with the hand up and fingers drooping, and in his right hand holds the sword with the point upward and forward. His entire upper body vibrates convulsively as if he were trying to speak but could not. Then, at last, he exclaims, "IS it (brief pause) the KING? (impetuous demand)." The sword flies from his hand and falls upon the floor several feet away.[47] He stands with open mouth, trembling jaw, and anxious, eager eyes, waiting motionless for the Queen's answer.

28-53. "Oh,[48] *what a rash and bloody deed is this!"*

She does not answer his question but only condemns his act. Coming to the front, he grasps her wrist again and cries in a high, almost shrill voice, "A *bloody deed* (upward accent) —almost as *bad*, good mother, as KILL a KING, and MARRY (utmost emphasis on *marry;* he looks down on her angrily and raises his right hand upward and outward as if to intensify the sense of *marry*) with his *brother!*" He gestures again with his raised right hand, throws her hand lightly but severely from him, and goes behind the table.

The Queen repeats his words "as kill a king" as an intense and emphatic question. He takes one of the lighted tapers from the table and starts up left toward the arras. Partway there he pauses: "*Ay*, lady, 'TWAS (nodding his head) my word (more slowly; more natural voice)." He goes to the arras and lifts it. He sees Polonius. He starts back and draws away the taper, yet still holds up the arras: "Thou *wretched*, *rash* intruding *fool* (tremulous tone; prolonged), FAREWELL! (the *fare-* is prolonged and uneven; plaintive tone on *-well*). I TOOK *thee* for thy *better* (tone of intense regret)." He bows his head, drops the arras, and turns away with an excited, half-desperate air.

He crosses to the table and puts the taper down upon it heavily. He looks wearily but determinedly toward the Queen, who is at the front pressing her hands together in agitated fright: "*Leave* wringing of your *hands—peace—sit you down* (he puts his hand on the top of the chair, motioning her to sit, and she obeys), and let

[47] *27.* All later promptbooks record the dropping of the sword exactly at this point.

[48] *28.* Booth remarks in his Notebook that "the effect of Hamlet's words & action depends largely upon the utterance of this 'O,'" and complains that the stupidity of actresses of the Queen often destroys it.

me wring your heart (strong sound of *t*)."[49] He stands in an attitude which expresses tiredness and disappointment; and he speaks in a voice which is strong and musical, but not loud, with occasional cessations of breath as one speaks after hard exercise: "For *so* I *shall* . . ." The word *shall* has a very peculiar pronunciation—a descending curve of sound which rises again in the final *l*, leaving the impression of an upward accent. It is as if he were fatigued and is uttering the very last word for which he has breath. The effect is very plaintive. ". . . if it be *made* (pronunciation similar to that of *shall*, but not so much mouthed) of PENETRABLE *stuff* (slight upward accent), if damned custom have not *brazed* it so, that it be *proof* and *bulwark* against *sense* (tone of reproach)." The Queen demands to know what she has done to draw this "noise so rude."

Hamlet stands beside her chair, looking down upon her, his right hand resting on the chair back. He opens his accusation as if the mere contemplation of her actions fatigues and sickens him; and his tones throughout his 11-line speech are those of one who is recounting something odious but yet is restraining himself to kindness and courtesy because of the son-mother relationship. "Such an *act* that *blurs* the-*blush*-and-*grace of* MODESTY . . ." These words, which draw the outlines of the subject, are spoken in a sort of light, skeleton voice, as if he found it difficult to touch the matter with sufficient delicacy. ". . . calls *virtue* HYPOCRITE . . ." These words are in a deeper tone; but for the next figure his voice lightens again: ". . . takes off the rose (spoken as if the dainty significance of the word could be damaged by a heavy tone, as a rose itself might be damaged by rude handling) from the *fair* (prolonged) *forehead* of an innocent *love* (the voice descends musically, giving exquisite beauty to the figure) and sets a *blister* there (a coarser though still smooth sound in *blister*); makes *marriage-vows* as *false* as *dicers' oaths* (the *as* both times is pronounced distinctly)."

He steps forward a little so that she can see him better, and he becomes more indignant and accusatory: "Oh, *such* a deed as from the body of *contraction plucks* the very SOUL." Again he becomes plaintive: "And *sweet religion* makes a *rhapsody*—of *words*—" He puts out his left hand, palm upward, and tosses it to the side two or three times swiftly, like a card-player dealing from the pack. Then

[49] *35.* Later promptbooks show the Queen sitting at the right of the table, and Hamlet sitting presently at the left of it; he does not rise until the business of the pictures at line 54.

his whole air changes, and as if abandoning the details of the matter and turning to its wider relations, he strongly affirms what he feels to be true: "Heaven's *face* doth *glow; yea*, this *solidity* and *compound mass*, with *tristful visage*, as against the *doom*, is thoughtsick at the *act*."

Throughout these words there is a dainty loftiness in his voice, a manner of delivery which lifts his denunciation to a level far above a merely vulgar view of her crime. Here is disclosed a high point in Hamlet's sensibilities. At the end, as if overwhelmed by the consciousness of her degradation, he impulsively leaves the chair and strides across to the left front, his hands clasped before him at his waist, his head hanging sadly forward. "Ah me!" cries the Queen, "*what* act?"

54-103. "Look here, upon this picture, and on this."

Hamlet turns at down left, lifting his eyebrows quickly as if affronted by her pretension of ignorance, and starts back toward her, fumbling in his bosom as he approaches her.[50] He stops beside her chair and draws out a miniature: "Look *here*, upon *this picture* (he holds it before her face, then kisses it reverently) and (slight pause; he reaches down and draws another minature from her bosom; change of tone from pleasure to contempt) *on* THIS."

He holds the King's picture before the Queen's face and his father's before his own, and he kisses his father's again: "The counterfeit presentment of (kneels on his left knee) *two* (prolonged)

[50] *54.* The endlessly debated problem of how to present the pictures of the two brothers is canvassed by A. C. Sprague in *Shakespeare and the Actors* (pp. 166-169). In 1870 Booth followed the practice of Edmund Kean, Thomas Cooper, Charles Young, Charles Kean, and others by presenting them as two miniatures, one worn by the Queen on a chain around her neck, one on his own chain. In later years he sometimes altered this to the system of having the King's picture in miniature at the Queen's neck and his father's picture painted full length and hanging on the stage right wall: according to the Taylor 1890 promptbook he tore off the Queen's picture from her neck and at line 72 threw it down. As for the oldest known practice of having both pictures hung on the walls, as shown in Rowe's 1709 *Shakespeare*, Booth argues lengthily against it in a note he inserted in the Taylor 1890 promptbook. The "modern" idea of "the way the author undoubtedly intended it"—that is, to dispense with pictures altogether and simply draw them in the air with words—had been broached in 1868 by Sol Smith in *Theatrical Management* (New York, 1868), pp. 218-220, but Booth would have none of it. In his Notebook he observes that Henry Irving does it this way, and on grounds of text and stage realism he dismisses Irving's "weak excuse for this silly omission."

brothers (tender voice)." He drops the King's picture, and taking his father's in both hands regards it intently: "See what a GRACE was seated on *this* brow." He holds the picture in his left hand and points to it with his right, extending his elbow over her lap and glancing toward her repeatedly to enforce her attention: "HYPERION'S (upward accent; prolonged) *curls*, the *front* of *Jove* himself; an *eye* like *Mars*, to threaten and command (flat sound)." Holding the picture earnestly up before him, forgetful of the Queen, he gazes at it affectionately and reverently, speaking in tones of admiration and pathetic remembrance: "A station like the herald *Mercury*, *new-lighted* on a *heaven-kissing hill;* a combination and a form, *indeed* (deep sound yet upward accent; he looks at the Queen resentfully), where *every god* (short sound) did seem to set his *seal* (prolonged) to give the world *assurance of a man.*" He kisses the picture, looks at it lovingly an instant, and then turns his face toward the Queen: "*This* (short pause) WAS (short pause; deeper tone) your husband (low sorrowful voice). *Look* you, *now*, what *follows* (low voice)." His throat and lips work with emotion, and he bows his head.

Then suddenly he seizes the miniature at his mother's bosom and holds it before her face: "Here IS your *husband*, like a *mildewed ear* (both words prolonged; strong, harsh voice; contemptuous tone) BLASTING his wholesome *brother*. *Have*-you *eyes?* (low, pleading tone)." He holds the picture before her, his mouth gathered mournfully, his left hand hanging down at his side, his whole attitude one of sadness and reproach: "*Could* you on this *fair mountain* (holding out his father's picture before him and gazing on it tenderly) leave to feed, and *batten* on this *moor?* (looking at the King's picture in his right hand, and then glancing rebukingly at her.) *Ha!* (short sound) *have*-you *eyes?* You *cannot* call-it (short pause) *love* (tone of dismissal); for at your age the *heyday* in the blood is *tame*, it's *humble*, and waits upon the *judgment* (low, reproachful tone) —and *what judgment* (rising tone and energetic manner; he lifts himself to his feet) would step from *this* (he raises his father's picture before him; then turns and holds the King's contemptuously before her) to THIS?"

He throws the King's picture into her lap angrily. He steps away to the left a little: "Oh, *shame!* (strong, intense voice and denunciatory tone; prolonged; he is standing at left center with his arm raised toward her, looking at her or over her head) where is thy *blush?* Rebellious *hell* (dropping his arm in a vigorous downward gesture), if thou canst *mutine* in a MATRON'S bones, to *flaming youth* let *virtue* be as *wax*, and MELT *in her own fire*." He gives an outward toss of the hand, indicating the hopelessness of virtue in such condition. He puts his left hand to his forehead and walks dejectedly toward the left. The Queen begs him to speak no more, and confesses to the black and grained spots in her own soul. Hamlet returns to her swiftly, grasps her wrist in his left hand, and stands over her with the forefinger of his right hand arraigning her: "*Nay*, but to *live* in the *rank* SWEAT of an *enseamèd* BED— (low voice, fast speech, tone of disgust; frowning, and his lips curling in contempt)." She begs, "No more."

He steps away a little, although still holding her hand, so that he can see her better:[51] "A *murderer* and a *villain* (loud, stern voice, expressing both contempt for the King and wonder and condemnation for the Queen's conduct), a SLAVE, that is not *twentieth part* the *tithe* of your *precedent lord* (tone of extreme disapproval) —a *vice* of kings; a *cutpurse* of the *empire* and the *rule*, that from a shelf the precious diadem STOLE (high voice; prolonged) and put it in his *pocket!* A king of *shreds* and *patches*— (high, angry voice)." He takes her hand in both his and looks down at her excitedly.[52]

104-137. Enter Ghost.

The Ghost has entered through the curtained archway at the right,[53] and comes downstage near them and a little below them. Hamlet sees the Ghost just as he completes the word *patches*, and he draws in his breath with a gasp of surprise and fear. He starts back, still clinging to the Queen's wrist with both hands.[54] The Queen rises, puts

[51] *97.* At "a murderer and a villain," according to Mason and the Taylor 1890 and Harvard 1890 promptbooks, Hamlet sat on the stool in front of the table, facing his mother, who was in the chair to the right of the table.

[52] *102.* All later promptbooks show that the lights have been dimming in preparation for the Ghost's entrance. Now they darken suddenly.

[53] *103.* On January 24 the *Herald* entered a jocular complaint: "We are taught to believe that such things as ghosts can come and go through solid walls of masonry, keyholes, etc., whenever necessary; yet the ghost at Booth's draws aside a heavy curtain before he can get into the room, and he never thinks of such a thing as replacing it as he found it. This, to say the least, is the height of ghostly ill manners."

[54] *103.* At the Ghost's entrance, according to the 1870 promptbook, "Hamlet starts & throws his mother round to L of him." Thus, in the action that follows, Hamlet would be *between* the Ghost and his mother. This would be an advantageous position for the actor, who could then turn from one to the other; but it violates the tradition (see Sprague, p. 166) that the Queen

her arms on his shoulders, and looks at him with alarm and wonder as he speaks: "*Save me* and hover *o'er* me with your *wings*, you *heavenly guards!* (faint whisper; appealing yet doubting tone)."

He stands back as if afraid of the Ghost and afraid that it might address his mother. Looking anxiously at it, he raises his left hand and puts it on his mother's right hand where it rests on his shoulder: "What WOULD your *gracious figure?* (slight upward accent; low, soft, supplicating voice; leaning forward a little and gazing intently at the Ghost)." The Queen cries out that he is mad,[55] and drops her head upon his breast. He holds her head: "*Do you not come* your *tardy son* to *chide* (low, plaintive voice) that, *lapsed*-in-*time*-and-*passion*, lets-go-*by* the important acting of your dread *command?* (flat sound; low, imploring, remorseful voice). Oh, *say!*"

One hears in this not only the tone of inquiry, but hopefulness that the Ghost has come only to visit him rather than to harm his mother, dread that the Ghost will rebuke him for his inactivity, and self-reproach. He raises his left hand, and tilts his head back inquiringly. As the Ghost adjures him not to forget his almost blunted purpose, he holds his arm out, listening. When the Ghost speaks of the Queen's "amazement," Hamlet puts both arms about her. The Ghost bids him speak to her. Hamlet glances down at her, but keeping his eyes mainly on the Ghost, says, "*How is it* with *you*, lady? (low voice; slowly and almost mechanically, as if not quite thinking what he is saying, yet tenderly and dutifully)." As the Queen responds he seems to listen, yet always with his eyes on the Ghost.

He turns a little, as if to direct the Queen's eyes into range with the Ghost's face, but she focuses only upon his own face, and demands at last what it is he is looking upon. "On *him!* on *him!* (impetuously, but not loudly)." He moves his left foot out toward the Ghost and reaches his left arm toward it: "*Look* you, how *pale* (low, tender, pitying tone; prolonged) he glares! His *form* and *cause conjoined*, preaching to *stones* (upward accent; prolonged) would make them *capable* (slight upward accent; sorrowful tone). *Do* not *look* upon me (slowly; moving a little forward, the Queen

must never turn her face toward the Ghost. Therefore, as Clarke records, Booth does not throw her to the left, but keeps her in the middle with her back to the Ghost. Persistently through the later promptbooks he addresses the Ghost "over Queen's shoulder," or "over Queen's head."

[55] *106.* At "Alas, he's mad," Mason shows the Queen kneeling to Hamlet, and he raising her at "How is it with you, lady." The later promptbooks do not concur.

moving with him, and reaching out his left hand beseechingly, but bringing it back at once to rest on the Queen's hand at his shoulder) *lest* with this *piteous action* you *convert* my stern *effects*. Then what I have to *do* will WANT *true* COLOR; *tears* (faint, sad tones; prolonged), perchance, for *blood*."

The Queen asks again to whom he is speaking. He looks down at her quickly. He puts his hand on his forehead for an instant as if perplexed. Then he drops it, takes her right hand in his and draws it out a little toward the Ghost: "Do you SEE (low, hushed tone) *nothing* (pause) THERE? (whispered)." The Queen looks all around slowly, and the Ghost drops his face. She can see nothing. Hamlet puts his hand on his forehead, bewildered, and asks quickly, "*Nor did you* nothing HEAR? (upward accent; prolonged)." As the Queen protests that she heard nothing but themselves, the Ghost crosses and stands to the left of them, looking at Hamlet's back.[56] "*Why,* LOOK you THERE!"

Hamlet points to where the Ghost has been, speaking in a tone of wonder and impatience. Then, when he looks at the spot and sees nothing, he draws in his breath with a gasp and starts backward, his hand flying to his forehead, his eyes full of terror. He turns about, drawing the Queen with him, until he sees the Ghost at his left, and again gasps in fear. The Queen clings to him in great alarm. The Ghost starts toward the left door. "*Look* how it STEALS AWAY! (energetic voice; pointing with his left arm). *My* FATHER . . ."

She cries out in fright at these words. He leaves her and starts toward the Ghost. ". . . in his *habit* as he LIVED![57] *Look* where he *goes* (following some eight or ten feet behind the Ghost) *even now* (noticeably nasal sound of *n*, round and full sound of *ow*) OUT (desperately, because the Queen cannot see it) at (falls to his knees at the left as the Ghost goes out the door, and reaching his arms after it) the PORTAL! (longing, sorrowful tone)." He holds his arms forward, his head thrown a little back, his lips apart, a yearning look upon his face. The Queen, with a cry of dread, sinks into her chair. Hamlet falls forward on the floor hopelessly, his face hidden by

[56] *134.* All later promptbooks specify that the Ghost's cross to the left is upstage and around the table, behind the speakers.

[57] *136.* Booth asserts in his Notebook that "habit" does not mean "clothes" but "general appearance, deportment." This signifies that the Ghost does not wear a "nightgown," but "complete steel" as in the earlier entrances. The call for the Ghost in the Pitman 1884 promptbook lists his "truncheon."

his hands, and lies motionless.[58] In a moment the Queen rises and goes slowly to him.

138-181. "This is the very coinage of your brain."

As the Queen speaks of Hamlet's "ecstasy" she stoops and touches him. Hamlet rises slowly, with an air of returning to the world of practical action: "*Ecstasy!* (slight upward accent, and tones of mingled exclamation, inquiry, and gentle sad denial; he shakes his head slowly) *my* pulse as *yours*, doth *temperately keep time . . .*" She has gone back to the center, and he follows her slowly, putting the fingers of his right hand on his left wrist and holding it out toward her. His slow, troubled voice expresses his belief in what he has just seen and wonderment that she could not have seen it: ". . . and makes as *healthful music*."

His tone becomes at once more matter-of-fact, as if he were not to be driven from his intention of arraigning the Queen; still emotional, as if he were newly conscious of the responsibilities which the Ghost laid upon him; and delicate, as if he were again aware of the painfulness of his errand to the Queen. "It *is not madness* that I have uttered (low, musical voice and pathetic tone); *bring* me to the *test* and I the matter will *re-word* (slight upward accent; tone of assurance) which *madness* would *gambol* (slowly) from.[59] *Mother*, for *love* of GRACE, *lay* (slight upward accent; tender and appealing tone) *not* THAT FLATTERING UNCTION *to your soul* (sharp sound of *s*, the vowel prolonged and plaintive) . . . " She is standing at center with her head bowed and her hands at her face, looking up at him piteously at times. He looks down at her with head bent for-

[58] *137.* Booth's business of following the Ghost to the left and falling prostrate there, which Clarke objected to as a breach of propriety, was later eliminated. What happened then, according to Mason and others, was that the Queen, while looking for the Ghost, got round to Hamlet's left; Hamlet remained at center, looking toward the left; at "my father, in his habit," the Queen shrieked and fell upon the stool before the table; after the Ghost's exit, Hamlet knelt to her (Taylor says with his head on her lap). The lights came up slowly after the Ghost's exit: Pitman mentions the footlights and the Harvard 1890 promptbook "unmasks" the calcium moonlight.

[59] *145.* According to Mason, Hamlet rose from his kneeling position at "Mother, for love of grace"; the Queen rose at "Oh, Hamlet, thou has cleft . . ."; Hamlet knelt again at "Oh, throw away the worser . . ."; and he rose at "go not to my uncle's bed." The later promptbooks vary these actions somewhat. In any case, in later stagings the positions were reversed from those of 1870, the Queen being to the left of Hamlet until the end of the scene.

ward and his arm held out adjuringly: ". . . that *not your* TRES*pass*, but my *madness*, speaks. It will but *skin* and *film* (upward accent in both the stressed words; flat, distinct sound of *and*) the *ulcerous place;* whiles *rank corruption*, mining ALL, *within*, *infects unseen* (tone of warning, yet gentle and respectful). *Confess yourself* (she starts to put her clasped hands imploringly upon his breast) to heaven (slight upward accent)."

He draws away from her, and she drops her hands quickly to her face: "*Repent* what's *past*." He walks slowly toward the left: "*Avoid* (holding his right hand toward her, but then clasping both hands before him and going farther left) *what is to* COME (slowly and sadly, as if his thoughts stifled further utterance)." The Queen takes a step toward him, reaching out her arms, cries that he has cleft her heart in twain, and buries her face in her hands.

Hamlet returns to her quickly, drops on one knee, and takes her left hand in both of his. He looks up at her as if rejoiced at having waked her conscience, but sorrowfully doubtful of the constancy of her good impulses. "Oh! *throw*-AWAY the *worser* PART of it, and live the *purer* with the *other half* (tone of earnest entreaty). *Good* night (his voice drops in *night*)." He lets go her hand, and she steps back a little. "But GO *not* (looking up again accusingly) to my UNCLE'S (heavy stress and tone of disgust) bed (pause; his head is bowed and his lips are contracted as with the thought of something vile). ASSUME (slowly and in a low voice, looking down and away from her, as if the sarcasm gave him pain) a *virtue*, if you HAVE IT *not*. *Once* more, GOOD *night* (low, tender voice; he bows his head)."

She looks at him and starts away with her hands at her face, but then turns impulsively and steps toward him, raising both hands over him as if to give him her benediction. Lifting his head sadly, he sees her hands, starts, draws in a breath audibly, reaches up and pushes her hands away as if preventing a sacrilege. She throws her head back a little with a look of misery as she understands his action. He rises slowly, with dignity, and says: "When YOU (prolonged) [60] are desirous to be *blessed*, I'll *blessing beg* of you (upward accent)."

[60] *172.* Clarke makes note of the fact that Booth omits the prefatory "And" in the line "And when you are desirous to be blessed." To have spoken it would have softened the line and pulled the emphasis away from the word "you," which Booth actually underscores in his Notebook. This little tampering was part of the old stage trick (see Sprague, p. 169) of rejecting the Queen's benediction.

He bows slowly, with a grave, sad face, turns toward the table behind them, and thence toward the arras which hides the dead Polonius. "For this *same* LORD I do *repent*." He points toward the arras and then comes down and takes her hand in a confidential way. He speaks in a kind and manly tone, thinking now, apparently, neither of the Queen's guilt nor of the Ghost, but only of the dead Polonius: "I will *bestow* him, and will answer *well* the *death* I *gave* him. So, *again* (taking her in his arms lovingly but sadly) good night!" She rests her head upon his breast, and he looks down upon her: "I *must* be *cruel* (regretful yet calculating voice) *only* to be *kind*. Thus *bad* BEGINS, and *worse* (slight pause; he looks up sorrowfully) *remains behind*."[61] He looks down upon her, drops his cheek against her head. "*Mother*, GOOD *night*." The curtain falls upon this tableau.[62]

This scene, in Clarke's estimation, is the most powerful of any in Booth's *Hamlet*. The scene with Ophelia is perhaps more delicate, but this one is more lofty and vigorous. The Play scene is great in its way, but it deals with but one idea. The Graveyard scene will be superb in its union of humor and pathos, and the closing scene full of energy and passion. But in none of these scenes does Hamlet labor under such a variety of strong feelings, with so many different memories, conditions, and prospects affecting him as in this scene with his mother. Every fine situation and sentiment of the play, including the awesomeness of the early Ghost scenes, is remembered and reviewed, or introduced, or foreshadowed here.

Throughout the scene Booth shows Hamlet driving to one main purpose, although he is interrupted by many emotional disturbances and shifts of feeling. Clarke despairs of giving a worthy account of its truth and beauty: "My comprehension is yet too cramped, my understanding too vague, and my observation too dull and inaccurate."

[61] *180.* In his Notebook, Booth records with amusement that Fechter thought that "worse remains behind" meant the "remains" of Polonius.

[62] *180.* From 1870 on, the promptbooks call for the curtain bell to ring on this picture of Hamlet and his mother in an embrace. In earlier times at the Winter Garden, according to Mason, the Queen left the stage two lines earlier, at "So again, good night," and Booth delivered the last couplet as a soliloquy. Prior to the Hundred Nights *Hamlet* he had added a little pantomime: he would take a candle from the table, go upstage, lift the arras, look at Polonius for a moment, and then glance around suspiciously as if dreading that he might be observed. He abandoned this business in 1865 and simply advanced to the chair down center and sank into it in deep meditation.

The three striking features of Booth's Hamlet at the beginning of the scene are: *quietude*, born out of powerful resolution; *intentness*, born of a purpose wrought up to the point of action; and *severity* toward his mother. He maintains the quietude only down to the moment when he seizes his mother and forces her to sit. His intentness he never loses, although it frequently shifts its direction. His severity toward the Queen is sustained throughout, although it is frequently broken into by touches of reverence: first, at the line "You are my mother," again when she fears he means to murder her, and at various points thereafter.

The stroke by which he slays Polonius, which he intends for the King, is by no means the opportune fulfillment of a design, but the stroke of an impulse, muscular but blind and breathless—sudden, violent, and frenzied. Upon discovering that it is not the King who is dead, he is sorely disappointed; but he at once recovers his purpose and renews his attack upon his mother.

His eulogy of his dead father rises to an ecstasy in which he almost forgets himself; but thoughts of the living King restore his indignation, and he upbraids his mother with stern, swift vigor, fiery and denunciatory. The appearance of the Ghost shatters this fierce mood in an instant. He falls into remorse, fearful of the Ghost's reprimand.

Two points in Booth's stage management impress Clarke as remarkably fine. The one is that moment when the Ghost moves from one side of the stage to the other while Hamlet is staring into his mother's face, so that when Hamlet turns to it again it seems to him to have vanished. Clarke can find no clue in the lines to justify this "trick," yet he accepts it as "quite efficient and very natural," and thinks it "increases the solemnity of the scene." The other "addition" is Hamlet's rejection of his mother's blessing: this is "full of terrible rebuke to the Queen and one of the most pathetic points in the scene." Clarke approves also of the flood of natural affection which crowns the ending. As Hamlet takes his mother in his arms with utmost tenderness and says, "I *must* be *cruel only* to be *kind*," he makes clear that his harsh words in the scene have "cut his heart and feelings no less than hers."

Three other points Clarke has doubts about. Booth ought not, after the departure of the Ghost, to fall prostrate. This seems an excessive collapse into weakness during a passage of great energy and excitement. Though willing "to yield to Booth's practice and superior insight into emotion," Clarke feels that this action is a "slight breach of propriety, and a superfluity." Certain of the critics shared Clarke's reservations about this fall. The *Sunday News* (February 6), for instance, having praised the fall in Act I, 5, after the first interview with the Ghost, suggests that here Booth is merely repeating a *coup de théâtre* because it worked so nicely the first time. The text, however, disallows it: the words "my pulse as yours doth temperately keep time," which he is about to utter, "forbids any performance calculated at least to disturb the circulation."

Clarke is further troubled that after Hamlet rises again and turns toward his mother, he does not once look around to be certain whether the Ghost "has really and entirely gone or not." And finally he wishes that out of the last long deleted passage Booth had managed to salvage the words, "That I essentially am not in madness, but mad in craft"—a statement which "with its adjuncts is of great importance to the play."

Clarke's assessment of the scene as the most powerful in the play is supported by widespread critical opinion. It was "probably the best scene," said the regular reviewer for the *World* (January 6),

> and certainly the one which received the most hearty and spontaneous applause. . . . The supernatural awe which invested this scene, the terror of the mother and son, and the admirable conduct of the Ghost, relieved it of the improbable, and oftentimes grotesque, character which inheres in the scene itself, and is peculiarly objective [*sic*] to the materialistic sense of today. To make the action of this episode as effective now as it was in the superstitious age for which it was written is . . . a triumph of histrionic art . . . impulsively recognized by the audience.

Three days later, to be sure, Nym Crinkle, who wrote the *World*'s Sunday pieces, rather blew up his colleague's unreserved approval of the scene. The "admirable conduct of the Ghost" became for Nym Crinkle only a "stage strut." The Ghost, he goes on to say, should not even be palpably present in the scene, but only heard; it is kept there only because of "English stage tradition." The power in the scene is provided not so much by Booth as by Miss Fanny Morant in the role of Gertrude. Booth is to be blamed here for abandoning the appeal to filial tenderness, which had so beautifully informed his first interview with the Ghost, and reverting unworthily to "the paralyzing terror of the supernatural business." Yet even so, Nym Crinkle was moved by the ensemble, and must confess it:

When, looking over his mother's shoulder, Hamlet addresses the shade, his face is convulsed, the ghastly and eager countenance seems to express a new and agonizing fear that he will now be forced to some act at which his soul revolts. Doubt, anxiety, apprehension, awe, have taken the place of sorrow and filial tenderness. When his mother has asked him, "Whereon do you look?" and he has answered, "On him, on him, look you how pale he glares," she turns so slowly and with such anxious hesitancy, and seeing nothing is so startled and overcome that a sympathetic thrill of terror runs through the audience.

The text of Act III, 5 (line-numbering of the Globe edition).

The extensive cuts (74 lines) are traditional. These are: 33b-34; 53; 72b-82, 86b-89a, 94-95a (from Hamlet's attack upon the Queen); 121-123a; 152-156, 162-171a, 174b-176 (from Hamlet's denunciation of sex); 181-217 (the entire last movement, including the counterplot against Rosencrantz and Guildenstern).

The alterations are these: 10, "thou" > "you"; 23, "Help" is doubled by the Queen, and Polonius triples it; 26a, "Oh, I am slain" > a prolonged groan; 172, "And when" > "when."

The few restorations (8 lines) are as follows: 6; 49b-52a; 95b-96; 115; 120; 218 (word order altered).

Act IV

Act IV. *A Room in the Palace, called the Hall of Arches.*
(Globe edition: Act IV, (1), (2), 3, (4), 5, (6), 7. 662 lines cut to 330.)

During the entr'acte, Arthur Matthison tells us in *Booth's Theatre: Hamlet,* the orchestra plays an arrangement of the "To be or not to be" solo from Ambroise Thomas' recent *Hamlet* opera.

The fourth act—or the half of it left after relentless cutting—is played continuously in a single setting (see Plate VIII).[1] According to the 1870 promptbook this is "Same Set, & scene as Act 2nd," and Arthur Matthison likewise identifies it as the same Hall of Arches in which the second act was played.[2] The furniture consists of a table with one or more chairs upstage in the central U-shaped room, a chair down right center, and a chair down left center. The lights are at full.

Shakespeare's first and second scenes, in which the Queen reports the slaying of Polonius and Hamlet eludes his pursuers, are both omitted. The act begins with scene 3.

2-70 (of Globe edition Act IV, 3). "*How dangerous is it that this man goes loose!*" [3]

When the curtain rises, the King is discovered alone in the vast hall, seated at the center table examining a scroll. He soliloquizes briefly. At the words "But never the offense" (line 7), Rosencrantz enters from the right, as from out-of-doors, passes through the side arch to the central room, and reports that Hamlet is under

[1] In Booth's latest stagings, as indicated in the Harvard 1890 promptbook, the play being then divided into six acts, this act was number five.

[2] By 1873, as we have seen (Act II, footnote 1), the Hall of Arches was discarded. Bensen Sherwood's "Stage Plans" patches together a set for the fourth act which consists of the back wall with center entrance from Act I, 2, standing at the third grooves; side arch walls from the Play scene; and three triple-arch stone borders for the ceiling. Later promptbooks call for *two* sets for the act. The first of these, used only for the scene of Hamlet's banishment, is indicated in the Pitman 1884 promptbook as follows: a back wall without center entrance at the third grooves; entrances in side walls at right and left; and downstage, near to the first grooves, a table and chairs at right center and a chair at left center. For the second set as given by Pitman, see below, footnote 7.

[3] In the Taylor 1890 promptbook this entire scene is cut, so that Booth did not appear at all in Act IV.

guard. As Rosencrantz calls off right to Guildenstern to bring Hamlet in, the King takes a position at the chair down left center, with his hand on the arm of it.

Hamlet enters boldly, with his arms folded, and strides with long steps and a self-confident, defiant air directly across the stage to the King.[4] He halts before him and looks him in the eyes, his features stern and ready. Guildenstern has stopped with Rosencrantz at about right center, and four Guards range themselves across the entrance. The King demands to know where Polonius is. Hamlet looks upward and lifts his brows a little arrogantly, as if ignoring the King's assumption of authority; he answers promptly, in a low, fixed voice, "At *supper*." The King, puzzled at this, says "At supper? Where?" Hamlet shifts his position a little, and his tone is ironical, yet coldly decorous: "Not where he *eats* (prolonged), but where he is *eaten*. A *certain convocation* (slowly; unfolding his arms and pointing downward with his right forefinger) of politic WORMS are e'en *at him*." Again, and harshly, the King demands an answer.

Hamlet looks at him, perfectly unaffected by his rough tone. Then, with animation, he takes a step forward and points upward with his right forefinger: "*In* HEAVEN (slight upward accent; solemn and earnest but bizarre tone)." He drops his finger and points it loosely at the King: "*Send* thither to *seek*. If your messenger *find him not* THERE (slowly, plainly, in a grave but sarcastic tone), *seek him* in the OTHER *place* (slight pause) YOURSELF." He takes a step to the King's side and points downward with his right forefinger. The King starts away to the left a little, clasping his hands as if grieved and irritated by Hamlet's mood. Hamlet watches him with a subtly malicious look. The King returns as if about to speak, but Hamlet continues: "But indeed (more commonplace tone) if you *find him not* within the *month* you shall NOSE (contemptuous tone; prolonged) him as (his voice drops a little; he points quietly toward the door at down right) you go *upstairs* into the *lobby!* (slight upward accent)."

[4] *15.* In later stagings, according to the Pitman 1884 and Harvard 1890 promptbooks, the entrances were made from the left rather than the right, and the stage pictures were generally reversed. Thus, Hamlet confronted the King down right rather than down left; Guildenstern went off left to seek the dead Polonius; etc. In later stagings two Guards, rather than four, seem to have sufficed. At Hamlet's entrance these two crossed their spears and Hamlet came through them.

The King orders Guildenstern to go seek him, and Guildenstern starts for the down right door. Hamlet watches him go, and then stops him with a quick and authoritative "*Sir* (this word is an addition to the text)." Guildenstern stops at the door. "*He will* STAY (upward accent) till you *come* (upward accent; calm, assuring tone)." He adds a short, affirmative nod or movement of the hand, and looks after the departing Guildenstern with wary eyes. Then he turns to the King again and folds his arms. The King tells him that because of this deed and for his safety he must be sent to England. Hamlet listens to this with head bowed but with eyes fixed steadily on the King: "FOR *England?* (slowly, as if considering the subject carefully; tone of curiosity and exclamation rather than of interrogation)." The King reaffirms it. "GOOD (ready, conclusive, and approving tone; very grave and earnest)."

The King says, "*So* is it, if thou knew'st our purposes." Hamlet looks up instantly, with an open, sagacious expression. He closes his lids a little and gazes knowingly at the King. He raises his hand: "*I* SEE (upward accent) a *cherub* (slight upward accent; gazing at the King he points upward to the left, and then looks sharply upward where he is pointing) *that sees* THEM (low, earnest, cunning tone)."[5] He drops his eyes to the King's face with a crafty look, and then turns slowly away, keeping his eyes on the King until he has veered so far that the King is out of his vision. The King is uneasy. Then suddenly Hamlet starts and strides upstage toward the right side arch, crying, "But COME, *for* ENGLAND! (clear voice; triumphant tone)."

He stops at the side arch, his body thrown back a little and his hand raised aloft like a standard-bearer. He pauses a moment, and then turns quickly. An affectionate and sorrowing look crosses his face, and he comes swiftly down to the King, falls on one knee before him, and takes both his hands in his own: "*Farewell* (sorrowful tone; prolonged and tremulous), DEAR (tender; prolonged)

[5] *48.* Apparently, from Clarke's account, Booth sees the "cherub" in the air over the King's head. But sometime later he contrived a remarkable piece of business here, which puzzled and annoyed many observers. He peered into the King's eyes so closely that he could see his own reflection there: that is to say, the "cherub" that saw the King's purposes was himself. By way of justification of this he records in his Notebook passages from *Love's Labor's Lost, The Merchant of Venice*, and *King John*, in which Shakespeare plays with the notion of seeing oneself in another's eyes.

Mother (upward accent)."[6] He draws the King's hands near to his lips and respectfully and lovingly bows his head over them. The King bends down a little as he says, "Thy loving father, Hamlet." Hamlet leaps up and backs away quickly as one might from a reptile, not with detestation but as from something repugnant. He stops at center: "*My* MOTHER (upward accent), sir (this word is an addition to the text; tone of denial as if protesting a point with a stranger)."

Then he steps nearer to the King, and as if he were recognizing him as a representative of his mother, he speaks more affably. "*Father* and *Mother* (upward accent in both words) is *man* and *wife;* man and wife is *one flesh* (upward accent); and *so* (pause) *my* MOTHER (low, reverent tone)." He looks at the King softly for a moment; then severely, as if he had asserted a fact which the King must believe; then angrily, as if throwing a farewell defiance into the King's teeth. He drops his right hand out before him as if to give point to what he has just said. Then he turns quietly toward the right side arch, jauntily straightens his shoulders, lifts his chest, raises his arm enthusiastically, and cries, "COME (tone of command), for ENGLAND (tone of exultation)." He strikes upward with his right hand and walks off right with a martial tread. The King orders the others to follow him, and Rosencrantz and the four Guards go out. The King delivers his brief apostrophe to England, and goes out through the arches to the left.

In this scene, Clarke observes, Hamlet is self-possessed, coolwitted, and quite fearless—and, of course, fantastic. He shows no thought of wanting to kill the King. He takes the announcement of his exile to England philosophically, and acquiesces without a hint of remonstrance. Indeed, Clarke thinks, he seems actively jubilant about the expedition, as if it raises some latent hope in him; as if, perhaps, he expects from it some recuperation of moral force to make him better able to execute his purpose when he returns.

The fourth scene, containing the passage of Fortinbras' army and Hamlet's soliloquy of "How all occasions do inform against me," is omitted.

[6] *49.* Booth says in his Notebook, "I think I was the first to kneel and address the King as *mother.* The traditional method was to speak as to the absent parent without reference to the King."

1-74 (of Globe edition Act IV, 5). "*I will not speak to her.*" [7] As the King goes out to the left, the Queen and Horatio [8] enter from up right and come forward to the chair at right center, where the Queen sits. (About now, offstage right, the prompter is readying Laertes, Marcellus, and "all the gentlemen" of the company to "shout and fight.") The Queen refuses to see Ophelia; but Horatio persuades her in a couple of lines that she should do so, and going upstage he beckons off right. Ophelia at once enters, as from out-of-doors, passes through the right side arch, and comes down center.

Once more, as in Act I, 3—since Clarke fails us and the 1870 promptbook notations are minimal—it is profitable to incorporate Mason's record of Helena Modjeska's stage business when she played Ophelia to Booth's Hamlet in 1889—remembering always that these are the especial inventions of a starring actress, and doubtless go far beyond the routine acting of Blanche de Bar in 1870.

Ophelia enters rapidly, looking from side to side as if searching: "Where is the beauteous majesty of Denmark?" [9] The Queen calls out to her. She sings two stanzas of "How should I your true love know," repeats the last line of it ("At his heels a stone"), clasps her hands over her eyes, and cries, "Oh!" The King has entered through the left arches; he starts as he sees Ophelia, and comes down near the chair at left center. Ophelia does not notice him, but comes to front center and sings the third stanza, during which the Queen rises and crosses slowly to join the King. At the end of the song, the King calls out to Ophelia, and on the words "the owl was a baker's daughter" she crosses to him quickly. But at "Lord, we know what we are," she wanders up to the right side arch again, stops, and returns. She stands quite near the King to sing the first stanza of the Saint Valentine song; then she breaks into a song without words, dancing up the stage and down again, swaying her body and waving her arms like a Bacchante.

[7] In later stagings there was a scene change here, and in Booth's 1878 edition what follows is called "Scene Second." Mason describes the new scene as "A room in the Castle. Full stage. Large open entrance, centre." The Pitman 1884 promptbook says "Change not disturbing the furniture." Apparently then all that happened was that the back wall of the preceding scene slid or flew away revealing a farther back wall with center entrance.

[8] *2.* The "Gentleman" in charge of Ophelia in 1870 is Horatio. In Booth's 1878 edition and in all later stagings he became Marcellus.

[9] *20.* In the Taylor 1890 promptbook, which is perhaps recording Modjeska, Ophelia carries two white roses.

As she begins (but does not complete) the second stanza with the words "Then up he rose and donned his clothes," her voice at first chokes with smothered laughter and then breaks out in loud, full laughter. She plucks a flower from her bosom and throws it on the floor. Her laughter changes to hysterical weeping. She sinks down and covers her face with her hands, sobbing. The King asks how long she has been thus. She rises to her knees, and at "My brother shall know of it" she starts to her feet, speaking vehemently. As she says goodnight to the "ladies," she goes upstage, bowing to right and left. When she is at the right side arch she sees something outside (perhaps she imagines Hamlet out there); she throws up her hands, screams, and runs off swiftly, laughing loudly and wildly.

75-157. "Follow her close; give her good watch, I pray you."

The King dispatches Horatio to watch Ophelia. As he then laments to the Queen that sorrows come "not single spies, but in battalions," we hear from off right an increasing noise of shouts, clashing swords, and cries of "Laertes! Laertes!" [10] The King calls out, "What is the matter?" and Marcellus runs in from the right to warn him of the insurrection to make Laertes king. The King calls for his Switzers. Marcellus beckons off left, whence enter six Guards who rush across the stage and out toward the noise. The cries and sound of fighting die down. In a moment Laertes is heard shouting, "Where is this king?" and he rushes in through the right side arch with sword drawn, turning back to order his followers to wait outside. He demands his father. The Queen, crying, "Calmly, good Laertes," runs across and throws herself upon him.

The King addresses Laertes calmly and bids the Queen to let him go. When he says "Let him go, Gertrude" the second time (line 126), he crosses to her, detaches her from Laertes, and passes her behind him to the left. He then stands about center, facing Laertes, to receive his demands. At about line 152 we hear voices from outside again, and among them Horatio's voice crying, "Oh, poor Ophelia!" [11] The Queen sits at left center; the King says "Let her come in," and goes to stand beside her. Ophelia enters slowly to the

[10] *97.* In Taylor and the Harvard 1890 promptbooks the crowd noise offstage is augmented with trumpet flourishes and tramping feet. Pitman calls for drums.

[11] *152.* Pitman and Taylor direct the prompter, rather than Horatio, to cry, "Oh, poor Ophelia!" and offstage voices, rather than the King, to say (repeatedly), "Let her come in."

center, looking at no one. Laertes starts as he sees her, and crosses behind her to the right.

157-200. "Oh rose of May, dear maid, kind sister, sweet Ophelia."

As Laertes addresses Ophelia, he moves toward her, but she repels him by raising her right elbow toward him and comes farther forward. Laertes withdraws toward the right. Ophelia sings a snatch of "A-down, a-down," and Laertes drops to his knees at "This nothing's more than matter."[12] She turns toward him and cries "Ah!" as if she recognizes him, runs to him, and lays her hands on his shoulders; but after a moment her face goes blank. Slowly she gives him the rosemary and the pansies. She is wandering slowly across toward the King and Queen as she says, "That's for thoughts." Laertes sadly rises. She gives the King fennel, and the Queen rue. At "here's some for me," she sinks to her knees. At "There's a daisy," she rises joyously and wanders to the center, looking at the flower; but in a moment she forgets it and lets it fall to the floor. "I would give you some violets" is spoken plaintively, but after "my father died" she breaks into a light laugh and says "he made a good end" in a sprightly manner. She sings "For bonny sweet Robin is all my joy" very gaily.

Laertes, after his speech at line 189, goes upstage to the nearest column and leans against it weeping;[13] the King goes up left a little and stands with his back toward Ophelia; the Queen remains seated at left center. Meanwhile Ophelia has sat upon the floor at center, strewing flowers before her over an imaginary bier. She sings the lamentation, rising to her knees at "He is gone, he is gone." After the song, at "I pray God," she rises and stands for a moment with clasped hands, facing front. Then she goes left to the Queen, to whom she says, "God be wi' *you*." She kisses the Queen's forehead, turns, and goes slowly to the right side arch, singing again, "And will he not come again?" She goes out, still singing. Her voice can be heard, ever more faintly, during the King's speech which follows, and it fades so gradually in the distance that we scarcely know when it ceases.

[12] *170.* But this scrap of song and Laertes' following line appear to be cut in 1870.

[13] *189.* This direction to lean against a column appears in the 1870 promptbook only. In later stagings Laertes sat in a chair (Mason), or threw himself on the ground (Taylor).

200-219. Ophelia's exit.

Before the King speaks, and while Ophelia is still heard singing offstage, he comes down to the Queen, raises her from her chair, and walks her across to the door down right. She leaves the stage. Laertes meanwhile crosses up left and thence forward. The King returns to him, and after his promise of giving satisfaction, and Laertes' entering his complaints about the circumstances of Polonius' death, the dialogue proceeds into that of the seventh scene. (The sixth scene, between Horatio and the sailors, is omitted.)

1-196 (of Globe edition Act IV, 7). "*So must your conscience my acquittance seal.*"

The text here is problematic. In the 1870 promptbook the first 35 lines of the scene are deleted, but notations in Booth's hand declare the passage "In," because "This dialogue is necessary to the plot." To effect this restoration he has cut the final couplet of the fifth scene and soldered the transition by slightly rewording the opening lines of the seventh. Whether he made this restoration before, during, or after the 1870 production, one cannot tell. The passage explains why the King has not heretofore dared to act against Hamlet and why he is now ready to assist in Laertes' revenge. No stage directions exist, and apparently, if the passage is in fact spoken, the two men simply face each other near the center, without remarkable changes of position.

At line 36 Bernardo enters from the right, as from out-of-doors, bringing two letters from Hamlet, one of which he gives to the King;[14] a moment later he bows and goes out the arches to the left. The King reads out Hamlet's announcement of his return to Demark, conceives the "exploit now rife in my device" to bring about Hamlet's death, and flatters Laertes' skill with the rapier. No stage directions occur until line 127:[15] when Laertes says "To

[14] *36.* In the Pitman 1884 promptbook the call for Bernardo directs that one of his letters be "*Blank,*" the other "*Wn.*" That is to say, according to traditional stage practice, the letter Bernardo gave to the King had to be fully written out so that the actor could actually read it and need not memorize it.

[15] *42 ff.* Later promptbooks give various movements for the two men which perhaps occur in the 1870 production as well. During the letter-reading Laertes walks up and down, and at "Know you the hand?" he goes to the King (Taylor); at line 53, "Can you advise me?" the King sits (Pitman); etc.

60-106. The Harvard 1890 promptbook cuts *all* these lines having to do

cut his throat i' the church" he crosses to the right. The King proposes the use of an unbated foil. Laertes offers to envenom the point, and the King promises to poison Hamlet's drink.

At line 162, the Queen is heard crying offstage, and she enters from the down right door to tell that Ophelia is drowned. The King goes upstage left. On the words "Fell in the weeping brook," the Queen crosses to left center and sits, and the King turns down and stands beside her.[16] Laertes crosses to the King as he says, "Adieu, my lord," and lays his sword before him; at the end of his speech he turns and goes out the door down right. The curtain falls on the picture of the Queen seated and the King holding Laertes' sword.

The text of Act IV (line-numbering of the Globe edition).

The extensive cuts in this act (332 lines) exceed tradition. Of IV, 1, the *Modern Standard Drama* cuts 23 lines, but Booth cuts all 45; of IV, 2, *MSD* cuts 5 lines, but Booth cuts all 33; of IV, 4, both *MSD* and Booth cut the entire 66 lines; of IV, 6, *MSD* cuts none, but Booth cuts all 34.

In IV, 3, the cuts (21 lines) are somewhat fewer than traditional. These are: 1; 7b-11a; 22b-34 (of kings, worms, and beggars); 61-64a. In IV, 5, the cuts (77 lines) are somewhat fewer than traditional. These are: 3-13 (description of mad Ophelia); 17-20 (the Queen's soliloquy); 36; 52-55, 59-67 (the bawdy stanzas of Ophelia's song); 79b-96a (the King's listing of the battalions of sorrows); 99-100; 103-105; 109-111; 113-114a; 140-148; 153-157a, 161-163 (parts of Laertes' lament); 170-173; 199; 215b-217. In IV, 7, the cuts (56 lines) are somewhat fewer than traditional. These are (without reckoning the opening 35 lines, which are cut in the promptbook but marked by Booth for retention): 40-41a; 74b-77a; 84-96 (description of the Norman Lamord); 101b-103a; 111-124 (the King's temporizing on "love"); 149-154; 157; 171-172 (dead men's fingers); 176-187a (part of the death of Ophelia); 192b-195 (the King's final speech to the Queen).

There are a few slight alterations. In IV, 3, at 31, "Sir" is inserted;

with Hamlet's mastery of sword play—a deletion of 27 more lines than in 1870.

[16] *176.* In the latest stagings, according to the Taylor 1890 and the Harvard 1890 promptbooks, at the end of the Queen's narrative four Guards brought on a bier with Ophelia's body, placed it diagonally at the center of the stage, and departed. Laertes uncovered her face, delivered his final speech, and threw himself across her body. The curtain fell on this tableau. The Birmingham (England) *Daily Post* of December 13, 1882, credits Booth with this innovation. Whether it was Booth's idea or that of his English producer, Wynne Miller, is moot, but Booth and others used it thereafter. As A. C. Sprague notes in *Shakespeare and the Actors*, p. 173, an American critic objected to it in the Booth-Barrett production in 1887, and an English critic to F. R. Benson's use of it in 1890.

53, "sir" is inserted. In IV, 5, at 151 the unassigned line "Let her come in" is spoken by the King; 199, "God" > "heaven"; 200, "And of all Christian souls, I pray God" > "And peace be with all Christian souls, I pray heaven." In IV, 7, at 1, "Now" > "So"; 3, 4 are altered and reduced to "When you have heard that he which hath your noble father slain."

The restorations in IV, 3 (11 lines) are: 43-44a; 45b; 47a; 57; 59; 64b-70 (the apostrophe to England). In IV, 5 (6 lines), they are: 77-79b (battalions of sorrows); 125-126a; 131b-133a. In IV, 7 (31 lines), they are: 2, 5b-24 (the King's excuses for not having moved against Hamlet); 27b; 34-35; 59; 79b-82a; 129-130; 189b-190a. The total of restorations in the act is 48 lines.

Act V

Act V, 1. *A Churchyard.*

(Globe edition: Act V, 1. 322 lines cut to 286.)[1]

"This," says Clarke, "was the wonderful graveyard scene. It was produced at Booth's with a richness and perfection of mechanical arrangements that invariably caused great applause the moment that the curtain rose" (see Plate XIV).

It is a night scene, draped in shade, with moonlight flooding the church and falling in streaks through the branches of the trees. A faint mist, a damp, dewy look, seems to hang about it. All the standard scenic elements—wings, borders, cut pieces, built pieces, and backdrop—combine to provide the most ideally romantic and yet convincingly real illusion of a country churchyard.

The scene is framed at the sides by "Moonlight Wood Wings" showing gaunt trees through the leafage. These, according to Bensen Sherwood's "Stage Plans," fill five grooves at stage right and four grooves at stage left. Overhead the scene is framed by heavily leafed branches ("Cut Wood Borders") which cross the entire stage above the downstage entrances. The moonlight falls from stage right, so that the trees at the left are strongly lighted. Well upstage and just to the right of center a large bushy tree rises on two trunks; toward the left, just below the third grooves, is a blackish pyramidal yew, also double-trunked.

Beyond this yew, set well on stage at the fifth entrance, is a church building in Gothic style, washed with moonlight. Its facade, topped by a low cross, gives toward center stage. The church is "practical": its portal, with two steps leading up to it, is the entrance through which the funeral procession is to come. At one side of the steps is a gravestone which has split, and Clarke notes that the moonlight glancing across it "where the piece has flickered off" gives a particularly lifelike touch to the scene.

Upstage of the church, in the sixth entrance, a narrow platform crosses the stage, forming a raised path along which Hamlet and Horatio will enter. This platform is two feet high, but toward the left it rakes up to a four-foot platform concealed behind the church. Thus Hamlet and Horatio, entering from the left, will appear to be coming down from higher ground, will cross the stage

[1] In the Harvard 1890 promptbook this is called "Act VI."

along the path, and will descend to stage level by a small raking platform at stage right.

The backdrop, hung at the sixth grooves, shows "foliage retiring vaguely into the perspective, with a far-off spire announcing itself against the hazy night-lights in the background." Over all is the lightly clouded sky.

In the right foreground, under a thicket of trees, are several stone slabs and obelisks, one tall cross, and three low tombs, one of them bearing a recumbent stone effigy. The tomb near the center, its end toward us, is three or four feet tall; it has a pitched marble roof and it rests on a stone base two steps high. The stage floor beyond the first grooves is completely concealed. "All was grass and sand, very naturally interspersed," says Clarke, "the grass and vegetation growing everywhere save in spots where earth seemed to have been taken for purposes of burial, or had been thrown when dug from adjacent graves."

The focus of the scene, where the illumination is strongest, is down left center (but above the first grooves) at the newly opened grave. To the left of the grave and behind it is a mound of fresh-dug earth; beside the mound is an ancient Celtic cross. A spade is stuck in the mound. A stone jug and two lengths of rope lie near the foot of the grave.[2]

The reviewers, like Clarke, were enraptured by this scene, and many of them sought to re-create the feel of it for their readers. Thus the *Atlas* (January 8): "The graveyard scene presents a grassy and uneven surface which appears to undulate over long-forgotten graves and wind picturesquely amid monuments, while trees of venerable seeming rustle their foliage against the walls of an antique church, and cast suggestive shadows over the consecrated ground. This scene, with its solemn funeral cortege, is without doubt the best arranged and most effective exterior tableau ever placed upon a stage." The *Sunday Times* (January 9) congratulates the artists for stopping short of introducing "real" foliage, which bits of "arborescent reality among a canvas whole are fatal to the harmony

[2] In several promptbooks the property list for the grave includes "boxes of damp earth" for the Gravedigger to shovel from. When the play toured, a properly positioned gravetrap could not be counted on because of lack of traps. Sometimes, as in the Pitman 1884 promptbook, the grave seems to have been at center. Sometimes, as in the Taylor 1890 promptbook, it was set toward the left but built above the level of the stage floor and surrounded by an "incline."

of many a stage scene"; and then: "In all the adjuncts of the scene —the pure, pellucid sky, the faint church towers, the worn tombstones, the dim chime of bells—the ideas of depth and distance, of solitude and sanctity, were perfectly preserved." Nym Crinkle in the *World* (January 9) was the only reporter shrewd enough to recognize that "the subject matter has been bent to make a point": that is to say, for no other reason than the scenic one the funeral has been made to take place *at night.* But the artistic success of it justifies the liberty: "By some new process this factitious moonlight is made to shed itself in mellow effulgence equally over the view, falling only in a mass upon the round limbs of a gaunt tree (which, thus silvered, stands out in clear relief against a mysterious background) and in a broad shaft across the end of the little chapel. The effect of this studied arrangement of light is charming." Some weeks later in the *Spirit of the Times* (February 5), Nym Crinkle builds up another paragraph about "the *chiaro oscuro;* the infinity and reality of details; the atmospheric effect of distance; the dainty disposition of light"; and he declares that it gives him a sense of "looking through the proscenium out upon an actual English landscape." The *Evening Post* (February 28) prints a response to the play from a pious country cousin, a lady who signs herself "M." She has told us that, although she has never been in a theatre before, next after the Bible Shakespeare is her favorite reading, and she loves *Hamlet* best of all. She has not been altogether pleased with the production—put off not a little by the staginess of the actors—and hereafter she shall content herself with "the companionship of the well-worn volume." But the scenery she has found of unimagined beauty: "The graveyard scene is beautiful and picturesque beyond description; surely no 'God's acre' was ever more lovely than this! the moonlight streams calmly on the little church, the green hillocks, the marble tombs, the graceful figure of Hamlet, and the sturdy and loquacious grave-digger who sings at his work, keeping time with his shovel as he throws up the earth and now and then a skull."

1-72. "Is she to be buried in Christian burial. . . ."

As the curtain rises, the Gravediggers are discovered—the First Gravedigger waist deep in the grave working with one of his two spades, the Second holding a pickaxe and sitting on the marble tomb at center. The First Gravedigger carries on his clownish-logical argument opposing Christian burial for suicides. At "Give me leave" (line 17), he climbs out of the grave, comes downstage, and lays his spade on the ground: "Here lies the water." The Second Gravedigger has come downstage also.

The First takes from him the pickaxe, stands it to the left of the spade, and pops his cap onto the top of the handle: "Here stands the man." The chain of argument is concluded at line 23, and the Second sits on the tomb again: "But is this the law?" The First, at "crowner's quest law," puts on his cap again, and, taking the pickaxe, stands near the grave. At "Come, my spade" (line 33), the Second fetches him his spade and takes back the pickaxe. Then follows the riddle game about who builds the strongest houses. At "Go, get thee to Yaughan, fetch me a stoup of liquor" (line 68), the Second takes the stone jug, wanders upstage and off through the trees at the left. The First Gravedigger jumps into the grave again, digs, and sings.

73-154. "Has this fellow no feeling of his business?"

Hamlet and Horatio have already (at about line 63) entered down the path behind the church, crossed at the back, and advanced slowly through the tombs at the right.[3] Hamlet is dressed in black, with a fur cloak and fur bonnet, and he wears his sword. Horatio is soberly dressed, though in lighter hues than Hamlet. As they listen to the Gravedigger singing, they come to rest down right. Hamlet is leaning on Horatio lightly, his left arm over Horatio's right shoulder. Hamlet points with his right hand. "*Has this fellow no feeling* of his *business*, that he *sings at gravemaking?* (slowly, pronouncing all the syllables distinctly; tone of sympathy as well as inquiry; seemingly recalled to the present from a more remote train of thought)." Horatio replies that custom has made the Gravedigger easy at his work. " 'Tis *even so* (Hamlet nods assent, and continues reflectively). The-*hand* of LITTLE *employment* hath the daintier-sense."

They move slowly toward the center tomb, watching the Gravedigger with sober curiosity. As the Gravedigger sings again, he throws up a skull. Hamlet has come to the center tomb, and he rests his left hand on the corner of it; Horatio stands a little behind

[3] *63.* In later stagings, in which there was no deep woods to wander through, Hamlet and Horatio delayed their entrance nearly to the end of the Gravedigger's song. The Taylor 1890 promptbook says they entered "arm in arm through opening in flat (foliage) R. C."

him. "That *skull* (slowly, in a meditative tone) had a *tongue in it* (upward accent), *and could* SING (upward accent, affirmative tone), once (downward accent). *How* (upward accent) the *knave* jowls it to the ground, as if it were *Cain's* (upward accent; prolonged) *jaw-bone* (downward accent), that did the first *murder!* This might-be the pate of a *politician* (upward accent), which *this* ASS now *o'er-reaches;* one that would circumvent *heaven* (upward accent, slight pause), *might it* NOT?" Horatio agrees that it might. The Gravedigger gets hold of a bone projecting from the wall of the grave. He twists it, jerks it from side to side, and pulls it out. He throws it to the left, hitting the spade stuck in the mound of earth. He tugs out another bone and hits the spade again. Hamlet sounds perplexed: "Did these *bones* (perplexed and mournful tone; prolonged) cost-no-*more* (downward accent) the *breeding* (slight upward accent; slowly) but to play *at loggats* with them?" [4] His shoulders shrink and he turns a little toward Horatio: "*Mine* ACHE to *think* on't."

The Gravedigger sings again, and throws up a second skull. He stops as he throws it, as if trying to remember something about it. This skull is partly covered with a leather cap or band, very old, much worn, and discolored.[5] Hamlet continues: "*There's* ANOTHER." He points with his right hand and nods: "*Why* may not *that* be the skull of a LAWYER? Where be his quiddits *now*, his *quillits*, his *cases*, his tenures and his *tricks?* (contemplative tone). Why does he suffer this rude knave now to knock him about the *sconce* with a *dirty* (upward accent) *shovel* (downward accent) and *will not tell him* of his *action* of *battery?*" He looks at Horatio gravely, and points toward the Gravedigger: "I will *speak* to *this fellow* (sober tone)."

He nods toward Horatio, steps away from the tomb and stands at the foot of the grave: "*Whose* (prolonged) GRAVE's (prolonged) this, sirrah? (slowly, in a courteous yet authoritative tone)." The

[4] *100.* Booth would not have his Gravedigger shovel out the bones "as is usually done," but made him throw them by hand and hit the shovel, so that the game of "loggats" be suggested. Clarke, who got the point, likened loggats to the modern game of penny-pitching.

[5] *105.* Booth says in his Notebook that the idea of dressing Yorick's skull in a remnant of a leather fool's cap came from an illustration in Knight's *Shakespeare.* The illustration was in fact in the Kenny Meadows *Shakespeare* from which the text sheets of the Harvard 1870 promptbook were taken.

Gravedigger says, "*Mine*, sir," and sings again. Hamlet turns to Horatio and lifts his brows, partly as if in surprise, partly as if annoyed at having his train of thought broken by such a reply. He looks down at the Gravedigger until he stops singing: "I think it be THINE, *indeed*, for thou LIEST (prolonged) in it (slowly and earnestly; in the manner of one accustomed to repartee and confident of getting the information by this process)." He looks curiously at the Gravedigger.

The Gravedigger returns the quibble. Hamlet looks up and shifts his position carelessly. He replies as one who is willing to beguile the time between important matters with trivial conversation. He speaks in a grave voice, declaratively, yet as if he desired and expected a reply: "Thou DOST LIE in't (prolonged), to *be* in't, and say it is *thine*. 'Tis for the *dead*, not for the *quick; therefore* thou LIEST (prolonged; the whole speech slowly spoken and fully pronounced; yet gentle and not harsh in tone)." The Gravedigger calls it a quick lie.

Hamlet speaks at once, as if driving for an answer, but not impatiently: "*What* MAN (flat sound) *dost thou* DIG it for? (slowly, in an authoritative tone)." The Gravedigger says it is for no man. "What *woman* then? (persistently)." For none. Hamlet stands with arms folded and an air of resignation as if he finds this inquiry onerous but intends to persevere: "*Who* is to be *buried* in it?" The Gravedigger says that it is one that *was* a woman but she now is dead. Hamlet looks at the Gravedigger with casual interest, and turns to Horatio, smiling a little: [6] "How *absolute* the *knave is!* We must speak by the CARD, or *equivocation* (upward accent) will *undo* (upward accent) us."

He sits on the steps at the near end of the tomb at center, his left foot on the earth, his right foot on the bottom step. His right arm rests on his right knee with the hand fallen just below the knee, and his left hand rests on the step beside him: "*How long* (inquiring tone; prolonged) hast thou been a *gravemaker?* (prolonged; slowly, and uttering every consonant distinctly)." The Gravedigger lays down his spade and becomes earnest and interested.

[6] *148.* Clarke insists that this is the only time that Booth smiles in the entire scene. In later years he seems to have played in a more relaxed manner: the Taylor 1890 promptbook notes at line 120 that Hamlet "looks occasionally at Horatio with a smile at the Gravedigger's wit."

155-239. "Of all the days of the year, I came to't. . . ."

He replies that he began his profession on the day the late King Hamlet overcame Fortinbras. Hamlet asks quietly, softly, less formally than before: "*How long* is *that since?*" It was the day that young Hamlet was born, he that is mad and sent into England. Hamlet, seated, raises his head and glances up to his left at Horatio, who has come round behind the tomb and stands beside him: "AY (long upward sound as if drawn up in the throat by suction rather than pushed up by force of breath; a tone of recollection), *marry* (slowly, and sounding both *r*'s; his voice returns from the height of *ay* to its proper level), WHY (long, upward sound of *y* that turns into *ee*) *was* HE *sent* INTO ENGLAND? (upward accents)." Because he is mad and will recover his wits there, or it will not matter there. "Why? (simple inquiry)."

It will not be seen in him there, says the Gravedigger, for there all are as mad as he. "How *came he mad?* (air of one inquiring into a matter of which he knows little)." Very strangely. "HOW (downward accent; pause) STRANGELY? (upward accent; prolonged)." With losing his wits, says the Gravedigger. Hamlet draws his head back a little. His lip curls and he gives an upward toss of his left hand as if annoyed by the frivolous answer. He appears to be weary of the dialogue, but bending forward he asks one more question: "Upon *what* GROUND? (slowly and earnestly)." The Gravedigger says, "Why *here*," slapping the earth, "in *Denmark*"; and he adds that he has been sexton thirty years.

Hamlet sits back against the tomb quietly, as if he were not ready to go on. Then he starts up a new subject, as if he wished to talk further: "How *long* will a man lie i' the *earth* ere he ROT? (short sound)." A tanner, says the Gravedigger, will last nine years. "*Why* HE MORE (prolonged) than *another?*" The Gravedigger explains about tanned hides keeping out water; and he takes up the second skull, which he says has been buried three and twenty years. "WHOSE (prolonged) *was it?*" The Gravedigger would have him guess. Hamlet tosses his left hand, shakes his head lightly, and lifts his brows a little: "*Nay* (prolonged), ***I*** *know* not (tone of disclaimer and indifference)." It was Yorick's skull, the King's jester.

Hamlet rises and moves to the grave: "*This?* (upward accent)." He reaches down quickly to take the skull, and the Gravedigger gives it. Hamlet turns frontward with it and holding it before his waist gazes down upon it with great interest. Then he raises it slowly nearer his face: "*Alas!* (low, sad tone; he shakes his head gently from side to side) POOR (tenderly; prolonged and tremulous; he raises his head a little on the word) *Yorick!* (he nods his head once or twice mournfully)." This sentence is spoken, Clarke says, in a wonderfully thoughtful, pathetic, musical way—not in awe as one would remember a great man, not in reverence as one would remember a saint, but in a kindly and regretful manner as if speaking of one loved for genial, pleasant qualities. He adds that if he had never *heard* of Yorick Booth's pronunciation of these words would have erected a monument to Yorick in his memory.

"I KNEW HIM, Horatio (upward accent)." He drops the skull to his waist and looks at Horatio: "A fellow of *infinite* jest, of most *excellent* fancy (slight upward accent). He hath borne *me* on *his back* a *thousand* (slight upward accent) times (slight upward accent). And *now* how *abhorred* in my *imagination* it *is!*" He draws back his head and gives a gesture of disgust: "Here hung those *lips* (lifting the skull and looking down on it) that I have *kissed* I know not *how oft*. Where be your *gibes* NOW? Your *gambols?* Your *songs?* Your flashes of *merriment* that were wont to set the table *in a roar? Not one now*, to mock your *own grinning?* QUITE *chap-fallen?*" These questions, Clarke says, are put slowly, gravely, pityingly; the last two of them are musing comments rather than interrogations. "*Now get you* (soberly, in a warning tone; raising the skull with his left hand and putting his right hand upon it) to my lady's *chamber*, and tell her, let her paint an INCH *thick* (his voice drops to a solemn undertone; slow and meditative), to *this* favor MUST *she come*. Make her LAUGH *at that*."[7] He looks at the skull

[7] *215.* An absurd little critical storm raged around the line "Make her laugh at that"—significant only because it demonstrates the microscopic attention which expert playgoers of the last century paid to every detail of an actor's performance. On January 22 a "warm admirer of Booth" who signed himself R. S. T. reported to the *Leader* that at an earlier time (in Boston in 1867, he says) Booth had misinterpreted "make her laugh at that": on the word "that" he had pointed his finger at the skull, as if telling Horatio to make "my lady" laugh at the skull, instead of telling the skull to make my lady laugh at death. In the next Monday's *Tribune* (January 24) William Winter accused R. S. T. of faulty observation and defended Booth from the "grave injustice" of this "loose and silly" charge. In the *Leader* on January 29, R. S. T. struck back at Winter and rejected the imputation that he was "a liar and a villain." But in the same issue of the *Leader* he was attacked by one J. K. K., who denounced his naive and "almost incredible credulity" in mis-reporting Booth's business and meaning; and on February 5 J. K. K.

closely; then suddenly he puts it at arm's length from his face as if offended by it, and looks up as if awakened from a train of thought: "*Prithee*, Horatio (lighter, speculative tone) *tell me* ONE thing." Horatio, who has moved forward to the right, asks what thing. Hamlet steps forward and stands beside him: "Dost thou think that *Alexander* looked o' *this* fashion i' the earth?" Horatio thinks so. "And *smelt* so?" He turns from Horatio and lowers the skull with an air of aversion. "*Pah!*" His lips part with repugnance. He hands the skull to the Gravedigger.[8]

He takes Horatio's arm, with his head dropped down in thought, and walks him forward from the grave a little. By this time the Second Gravedigger has returned with the jug of liquor, and stands under a tree at the left. As the First Gravedigger turns to reach for the pickaxe, the Second raises the jug significantly; but the First, with a glance toward Hamlet and Horatio, makes a warning gesture, and the Second hides the jug near the tree. The First climbs out of the grave, and the two of them fasten the ropes across it in readiness for the burial.

From down left center Hamlet and Horatio turn and walk toward the right: "To what BASE *uses* may we *return*, Horatio! (tone of pity). WHY *may not imagination* trace the noble-dust of *Alexander* (stopping thoughtfully at front center) till he find it stopping a *bunghole?*" He puts his hand on Horatio's breast. Horatio thinks that that were to consider too curiously. Hamlet responds with animation: "*No*, faith, *not a jot*, but to *follow him thither* with *modesty* ENOUGH, and *likelihood*-to-*lead*-it. As *thus:* Alexander *died* (upward accent), Alexander was *buried*, Alexander-*returnèd* to *dust;* the *dust* is *earth;* of earth we make *loam* (slight upward accent); and *why*—of *that earth* whereto he was converted (slowly, methodically, separating the words, as if pointing a piece of logic) —might *they not stop* a beer barrel?"

He puts his left hand on Horatio's breast and speaks the quat-

savaged R. S. T. further with laborious sarcasm. Later in February J. K. K. scolded Charles Fechter for mispronouncing "contumely," after which R. S. T. (by now no longer a "warm admirer of Booth") responded by enumerating half a dozen errors in Booth's performing which, he claimed, Fechter did *not* commit.

[8] *221.* In later stagings, as Mason records, when Hamlet gave the skull back to the Gravedigger he wiped his hand with a handkerchief. Booth in his Notebook records Fechter's "offensive" business of smelling his fingers and making a grimace—"o'erstepping the modesty of art if not of nature."

rain. "*Imperious* CAESAR, DEAD and *turned* to *clay*, Might *stop-a-hole* to keep the WIND (rhymes with *find*) *away*. Oh, *that* THAT *earth* which kept the WORLD (pause) in AWE (full sound; downward accent), Should PATCH a *wall* t'*expel* the *winter's-flaw!*" The words of these couplets are all clearly pronounced. The first two lines are spoken assertively; the last two more slowly, and in a deliberate, meditative manner.

240-269. "But soft! but soft! aside! Here comes the King."

At the end of the couplets, a bell begins to toll, and solemn organ music is heard from the church. The church door opens. Hamlet pauses for a moment, and then goes up center toward the church door: "*But soft! but soft! aside!* (his voice is barely audible above the strains of the organ)." He stops before the church door and looks in: "HERE *comes* the KING, the *Queen*, the *courtiers. Who is this that they* FOLLOW, and with such *maimèd rites! This* doth betoken *the corse they* FOLLOW *did*, with desperate hand, *foredo* its own life (slight upward accent)." He stands several feet from the church looking in, his left hand raised in curiosity. Then he starts toward the front again: " 'Twas of *some estate*. COUCH WE *awhile*, and *mark*." He takes Horatio's arm and they retire into the shadows at the right. Horatio stands behind the tall cross and Hamlet stands above him with his right hand on his shoulder. When the coffin appears, a moment later, they reverently remove their caps.

The procession emerges from the church and comes slowly forward. First is the Priest, who takes his place downstage of the grave with his back to the audience. Four Ladies in white, with bunches of flowers, are the coffin-bearers; they bring the corpse of Ophelia around to the front of the grave, lay it across the ropes, and then retire upstage.[9] Laertes takes his place at the foot of the grave. The King and Queen, she with a basket of flowers, stand above the grave. Ladies and Gentlemen of the Court stand about in groups, the Gentlemen carrying torches. Soldiers form lines across the rear.

When all have come to a halt, the Gravediggers lower the

[9] *245.* Booth claims in his Notebook to have been the first American producer of the play to use women as corpse-bearers: the Winter Garden 1866 promptbook calls for "6 Girls with coffin." He claims also to be the first in America to present the corpse swathed and strapped to a board, rather than on a bier or in a coffin; but this innovation was apparently made later than his edition of 1878 and probably did not occur until the 1880's.

corpse by means of the ropes and retire to the left. The music ceases.[10] Laertes asks what ceremony else. Hamlet says aside to Horatio, "*That* is LAERTES, a very *noble* youth (low, sympathizing tone)." Laertes repeats his question, and the Priest explains that the ceremonies are ended, that further rites would be a profanation. In rage Laertes speaks the words which make Hamlet understand what the scene is about: "I tell thee, churlish priest, *a ministering angel shall my sister be*, when thou liest howling."

Hamlet starts wildly. His left arm flies outward toward Horatio, then upward in a despairing gesture. He throws his right arm over Horatio's shoulder, and rests his left arm on Horatio's breast: "What (low, exclamatory tone), the *fair* OPHELIA! (prolonged and tremulous; he clings to the word as if unwilling to let it pass his lips)." This cry moved Charles Clarke deeply. It is, he said, the heart using the tongue. Its intense grief and musical pathos are inexpressibly touching. There is no bewilderment in it. Hamlet instantly recognizes the significance of the fact, and his sad nature seems, in Booth's voice, to have taken full account of one more bitter truth to bear it down. It is neither a combative cry nor a resigned one, but a cry of pain and of simple, heartfelt understanding. "When I heard Booth's Hamlet say that," Clarke writes, "I felt that some part of his spirit had broken suddenly."

Hamlet seems about to fall, but Horatio supports him and walks him to the tomb at center. Hamlet sits on the steps of the tomb, his back toward the funeral. Horatio kneels before him, and Hamlet throws his arms about his shoulders and bows his head in Horatio's arms. So they remain while the Queen strews flowers into the grave. At her words, "I hoped thou shouldst have been my Hamlet's wife," Hamlet grasps Horatio's body convulsively.

269-322. "Oh treble woe fall ten times treble on that cursed head."

As Hamlet hears Laertes blame him for this disaster, he rises with a shocked expression on his face and looks across the tomb at Laertes. He steps to the end of the tomb, Horatio striving to deter him by holding his arms. When Laertes leaps into the grave,[11] Hamlet re-

[10] *245.* The Harvard 1870 promptbook says that the bell continues to toll throughout the scene. Clarke does not say so, however, and the Winter Garden 1866 and the Pitman 1884 promptbooks specify that both bell and music stop when the corpse is in the grave.

[11] *272.* The direction for Laertes to leap into the grave is scratched from the 1870 promptbook, yet plainly from Clarke's account Laertes does so. He

coils and rests in Horatio's arms, throwing his left arm around his neck. Horatio draws him upstage right, under the trees, moving quickly as if anxious to get him away from the place. Hamlet goes vaguely, his left arm still about Horatio's neck, his right hand on his own forehead. They stop near one of the lines of soldiery.

Twice Hamlet attempts to turn back but Horatio stays him. When Hamlet speaks, Horatio lets him go: "*What is* HE whose *grief*[12] (he is standing where a shaft of moonlight, penetrating the treetops, falls across his face) bears such an *emphasis!* (low, even voice, but interrupted with the efforts to get free from Horatio, who still holds his hand). Whose *phrase of sorrow* (breaking from Horatio, he stands free, looking forward; he draws his shoulders back and gathers strength as he continues in a stronger voice) *conjures* the *wandering* STARS and *makes them* STAND like *wonder-wounded hearers?* (downward accent; bold but pathetic tone). This is ***I*** (defiant tone; prolonged), HAMLET (deep sound; he starts forward) *the* DANE."

Laertes leaps from the grave, uttering his curse, meets Hamlet at front center, and grasps his throat savagely. Hamlet, not expecting the attack, is almost thrown down. Laertes forces his head back. Hamlet seizes Laertes' hands and speaks in a hoarse, half-articulate voice: "Thou prayest not *well.* I prithee, *take* thy FINGERS *from my* THROAT (low, expostulatory tone, as if he did not wish to quarrel with Ophelia's brother); for *though* I *am* not *splenetive* and *rash,* yet *have I* IN *me* something DANGEROUS, which *let* thy *wisdom fear* (tones of admonition and warning). HOLD *off* THY HAND! (sudden fierceness)." He throws off Laertes instantly, and without looking at him starts toward the grave.

The King orders someone to pluck them asunder, and several Courtiers step forward, but they stop when they see that Hamlet is free. Hamlet, at the foot of the grave, is almost face to face with the King. He looks back at Laertes, and says excitedly: "Why, I will *fight* with him *upon this* THEME, until my EYELIDS will *no longer*

does so in the 1878 edition. In later stagings, according to Mason, the business was eliminated: "Laertes does not leap into the grave, but prepares to do so."

[12] *277.* In later stagings, according to Mason and the Pitman 1884 and Taylor 1890 promptbooks, Horatio led Hamlet offstage sometime after line 265, "What, the fair Ophelia?" Then Hamlet's speech beginning "What is he whose grief" was shouted from the wings, and Hamlet exploded upon the stage at "This is I, Hamlet the Dane."

wag (vehement, desperate)." Disregarding everybody, he drops on one knee at the foot of the grave. Laertes crosses to the front of the grave and regards him angrily. The Queen, behind the grave, cries, "*What* theme?" Hamlet looks into the grave, clasps his hands, and holds his arms downward toward Ophelia: "I LOVED OPHELIA! (sad, earnest, piteous tones; prolonged). FORTY THOUSAND BROTHERS (downward accent, slightly contemptuous tone) COULD *not*, with ALL THEIR (more slowly, each word pronounced separately) *quantity* of *love* (tender tone) make up MY (upward accent, plaintive tone) sum." He sees Laertes and starts up impetuously: "*What* WILT-*thou* DO for her? (tones of challenge, but grief-shadowed)."

The Queen cries out that he is mad, but almost without waiting for his cue, Hamlet plunges on in fiery defiance: "*Come*, SHOW *me* what thou'lt DO." He throws out his right arm toward Laertes as if daring him to competition: "Wou'lt WEEP? (gives his head a side toss). Wou'lt FIGHT? (another side toss). Wou'lt *fast?* Wou'lt TEAR thyself? (he holds out his left arm and seizes it with his right hand). I'LL do it." He steps back a little and throws his hands out at his sides. "*Dost* THOU *come here* but to WHINE? (prolonged). To outface ME (upward accent; prolonged; he stands with his body bent a little forward, his arms held out at his sides in mad inquiry) with leaping in her GRAVE? (upward accent). Be buried QUICK-*with-her* and so will-*I* (upward accent)."

He stands upright: "And if thou *prate of* MOUNTAINS (giving his left hand a fierce toss at Laertes), let them *throw* (holding out both hands with the fingers closed) MILLIONS (deep sound of *mill-*; heavy, defying tone; throwing his head back and stretching his arms apart, upward and outward) of ACRES ON US (high, powerful tones; furious irritation) till *our ground, singeing his pate* AGAINST the BURNING ZONE (prolonged; his left arm at his side, his right reaching upward) make OSSA (pointing upward, his hand quivering) *like* a WART! (his voice drops in *wart*, but gives a distinct emphasis; tone of contempt)." He casts his right arm down scornfully and looks at Laertes with disdainful indignation. His nostrils dilate and his lip is drawn upward at the left corner. He points at Laertes suddenly: "*Nay* (low voice; prolonged)." He speaks suddenly as if to interrupt something that Laertes was about to say—but in fact, says Clarke, to prevent the audience's applause, which is always about to break in at this point. He bends forward, his left arm down at his side: "An *thou'lt* MOUTH (prolonged;

slowly; low, hard tone expressing defiance and partly a sneer) *I'll* RANT *as well* as *thou* (slight upward accent; casting his right hand out toward Laertes)." He turns his back on them all, goes to the front, and puts his face on Horatio's shoulder.

During the Queen's speech Hamlet remains motionless. Then he lifts his head and reaches his left arm out toward Laertes: "*Hear you*, sir (tone of entreaty, friendly and remorseful). *What* is the *reason* (upward accent) that you USE *me* thus? I *loved you* EVER." He steps a little toward Laertes, reaching out, though still resting his right hand on Horatio's arm. Laertes raises his right hand angrily, palm toward him, motioning him away, and turns his back. Hamlet's face becomes hard. He steps back and lets go of Horatio: "But it is NO (slight upward accent; prolonged) *matter*." He looks about swiftly at the King and the Court; then he shakes his shoulders with a reckless air and stands aside where all can see his face.

He looks at Laertes: "Let *Hercules* HIMSELF (raising his left arm with the hand clenched, and looking upward, his lips drawn up) do *what* he *may* (flat sound, upward accent), the cat WILL (dropping his hand and giving his head a side nod) *mew*, and DOG (very short sound, and as if it were spelled *dawg*) will *have his day*." He shakes his clenched hand in the air in a random, distracted way, and runs off the stage to the right.

His manner of going has something of dignity and earnestness in it, yet it is also desperate, and it reminds one, Clarke says, of a moody child running from someone who has displeased it. The King dispatches Horatio after him. Laertes moves up to the foot of the grave while the King speaks the final lines.[13] Organ music is again heard from the church as the scene is "closed in" by the next set.

In reviewing the scene, Clarke notes how from the first Booth expresses Hamlet's mental preoccupation. Although Hamlet is not familiar with the place (he does not know the Gravedigger, who has worked here for thirty years), he pays no attention to his surroundings. He does not look at the church as he comes in. He notices no monument. He never looks up at the trees or takes direct notice of where he treads. He lays his hand on the tomb abstract-

[13] *320*. The tableau on which the scene ended, according to the Taylor 1890 promptbook, was composed by the King and Queen standing in front of the grave, and Laertes falling weeping beside it.

edly. It appears that he and Horatio have been discussing Hamlet's return and matters at the court, but that Hamlet has not yet fully confided to Horatio his feelings and intentions. There is in Horatio a quiet, waiting manner which tells that something between them has not yet been talked of, but that he expects that in the order of events it soon will be. They turn toward the Gravedigger as if toward something to fill the time until Hamlet's mood is ready to indulge in confidences.

The scene with the Gravedigger, Clarke says, is "not defaced with any levity on Hamlet's part." The Gravedigger's dialect and manner draw Hamlet's attention, but not strongly; nor does the Gravedigger's humor stir any merriment in him. His own repartee rises, as it were, from instinct, from habit, and Booth does not use it to lighten the scene. Hamlet is ruled by reflection and sorrowful memories, and these make sober every thought that passes through his mind. Indeed, only once does he smile—when he says to Horatio, "We must speak by the card or equivocation will undo us"—and then it is a sad or slightly sarcastic smile, but by no means a ripple of buoyancy.

Certain small points of stage management impress Clarke with the thoroughness of Booth's producing hand: the Gravediggers' business with the jug of liquor when the Second Gravedigger returns; Hamlet's and Horatio's reverently taking off their caps at the sight of the coffin. "Both of these pantomimic trifles were done in the shadows, and probably were not noticed at all by two-thirds of the audience. But how much they helped to fill in the naturalness and sentiment of the scene to those who did see them!" Clarke admires too the care with which Booth, after struggling free from Horatio in the shadows of the trees, finds the exact spot to stand where the moonlight illuminates his face.

The last part of the scene is turbulent enough. Hamlet is thoroughly enraged—bold, fiery, outspoken—yet wonderfully controlled. It is a *clear* rage, devoid of bluster and full of pathos. His consciousness of Ophelia in the grave runs through it all. He stands near the grave when he defies Laertes, he kneels beside it once, he turns to it; in all his vehemence he cannot forget it. As for the King and Court, he quite disregards them, noticing them only once when at the last he glances toward them as, overcome with grief and anger, he utters his last couplet and runs distracted from the stage.

The text of Act V, 1 (line-numbering of the Globe edition).

The few cuts (36 lines) are traditional. These are: 90-99a; 112b-128a; 150-153; 181-182; 207a; 287b-288; 296; 299; 321-322.

The alterations are these: 199, "loam" > "earth"; 297, "Swounds" > "Come."

The restorations (4 lines) are: 39-42.

Act V, 2. *A Portico of the Castle.*
(Globe edition: Act V, 2, 1-236. 236 lines cut to 167.)

The Churchyard set has disappeared in an instant behind a set which rises at the first grooves (see Plate XV). It is now the day after Ophelia's funeral. We are in a shaded porch or an outside gallery of the castle, looking through three spacious arches onto a brightly lighted landscape. In the middle distance we see a low plain covered by foliage and crisscrossed by a shining river; beyond the plain the horizon is bounded by low whitish mountains. The arches of the porch are supported by sturdy columns which rest upon tall, handsomely carved square pedestals. At the ends of the porch, at right and left, archways provide entrances. Sunlight streams in from stage right.[14]

The scene which takes place is all talk and little action. Clarke notes that the first 74 lines of it—Hamlet's narrative of his adventures at sea—are traditionally omitted on the stage, being "of little interest save to the literary people, or precisians," and "detracting from the activity of the play"; these lines, he says, are not even printed in the "Book of the Play" which is sold in the lobby.[15] He recognizes that Booth has restored the passage principally in order

[14] The author of "How to Set a Great Play on the Stage" (Philadelphia *Evening Bulletin*, December 11, 1871), in describing the rise-and-sink machinery, says: "The pleased surprise at this novel mode of setting a stage is felt progressively during the play up to the very last, when, to mask the operation of arranging the back for the fencing-act, a lovely screen rises, representing distant river scenery viewed from the arches of a loggia, and bathed in an Arctic intensity of light." To the reviewer of the *Evening Post* (March 16), by the way, the beauty of this scene was based in error. The light on the landscape appeared to him to be "tropical" rather than "Arctic," and the distant "snow-covered mountains of Alpine height" are "features of natural scenery that do not exist at all on Danish soil." The loggia set was, of course, not essential to the scene, and in later productions it disappeared. According to The Players 1876 promptbook, the set was "Wood in 1."

[15] The "Book of the Play" would be the Booth-Hinton acting edition, first published in 1866 but kept in print by Hinton and still hawked in the theatres when Booth performed.

to give the carpenters more time to get rid of the elaborate Churchyard set and replace it with the Court set which is to follow. There is so little action in the passage, in fact, that once Clark has got it under way he merely transcribes the verses and marks them for stresses.

1-80. "So much for this, sir; now shall you hear the other."

Hamlet and Horatio enter through the stage right archway, both wearing their cloaks and caps as when we last saw them. Hamlet is speaking as he comes. "So much for *this*, sir; now shall you hear *the other*." He stops at right center, with his right arm on Horatio's left shoulder. He is very quiet and easy in deportment. "You *do remember all the* CIRCUMSTANCE?"

Horatio. Remember it, my lord!
Hamlet. *Sir*, in my *heart there was a kind* of *fighting*
That *would not* let me *sleep*. Methought I *lay*
Worse than the *mutines* in the *bilboes. Rashly*—
And praised be the RASHNESS *for it*—let us know,
Our INDISCRETION *sometimes serves us well*
When our *deep plots* do *pall;* and that should teach-us (low reverent voice)
There's a DIVINITY that SHAPES-our-*ends*
Rough-hew them *how we will.*
Horatio. That is most certain.
Hamlet. *Up from my* CABIN
My *sea-gown* SCARFED ABOUT ME, in the *dark*
Groped *I* to find them out; had *my* DESIRE;
Fingered their *packet, and, in fine*, WITHDREW
To mine *own* ROOM again; *making* so bold,
My fears forgetting-manners, to UNSEAL
Their *grand commission;* where I *found, Horatio,*
Oh, ROYAL *knavery!* an EXACT *command,*—
LARDED with *many several sorts of reasons,*
Importing *Denmark's health*, and ENGLAND'S *too,*
With, *ho!* such *bugs* and *goblins* in *my life,*—
That on the *supervise*, no LEISURE *bated,*
NO, not to stay the *grinding of the* AXE,
My HEAD *should be struck off.*
Horatio. *Is't* POSSIBLE?
Hamlet. *Here's the* COMMISSION (giving a packet); *read* it at *more* leisure.
But wilt thou *hear*-me how I did *proceed?*
Horatio. I BESEECH you.
Hamlet. BEING THUS *benetted-round* with VILLAINIES,
ERE *I could make* a *prologue* to my *brains,*

They had *begun the* PLAY—I *sat* me *down;*
Devised a *new commission;* wrote it *fair.*—
I *once* did *hold* it, as our STATISTS do,
A BASENESS to *write* FAIR, and *labored much,*
How to FORGET that learning; *but,* sir, *now*
It *did me yeo*MAN'S service. Wilt thou know
The *effect* of *what I wrote:*

Horatio. *Ay,* good my lord.

Hamlet. An earnest *conjuration from the* KING,
As ENGLAND was his *faithful tributary*
As LOVE between-them like the PALM *might flourish,*
As *peace* should *still* her *wheaten garland wear,*
And *stand a common 'tween their amities,*
And *many suchlike* AS'S of GREAT CHARGE,—
That, on the *view* and *know* of *these contents,*
Without *debatement farther,* more-or-less,
He *should* the BEARERS put to SUDDEN DEATH,
Not SHRIVING *time allowed.*

Horatio. How was this sealed?

Hamlet. *Why, even in* THAT was *heaven* ORDINANT.
I had my *father's* SIGNET in my *purse* (upward accent)
Which was the MODEL of that *Danish seal* (upward accent);
Folded the *writ* UP in form of the OTHER,
Subscribed it; gave't the *impression;* placed it *safely,*
The CHANGELING *never* KNOWN. Now the *next day*
Was our SEA-FIGHT; and what to *this* was *sequent*
Thou knowest *already.*

Horatio. So Rosencrantz and Guildenstern go to't.

Hamlet. *Why, man,* they did *make* LOVE to this employment;
THEY *are not* NEAR MY *conscience; their defeat*
Does by *their own insinuation grow.*
'Tis DANGEROUS when the *baser nature comes*
Between the *pass-and-fell-incensèd-points*
Of *mighty* OPPOSITES.

Horatio. Why, what a King is this!

Hamlet. *Does it* NOT, *think'st thee,* stand me now *upon*—
He that hath KILLED MY KING, *defil'd my* MOTHER;
Popped-in between the *election* and *my*-HOPES;
Thrown OUT *his* ANGLE for my *proper-life*
And with such COZENAGE—IS'T *not perfect conscience*
(upward accent)
To QUIT *him* with *this* ARM? and is't not to be DAMNED
(upward accent)
To let this canker of *our* NATURE *come*
In further evil?

Horatio. It must be shortly known to him from England
What is the issue of the business there.

Hamlet. It WILL *be* short; the INTERIM—is MINE;
And a MAN'S LIFE NO-MORE—than to *say*, ONE.
But I am *very* SORRY, good *Horatio*,[16]
That to *Laertes* I *forgot* MYSELF (upward accent);
For by the image of MY *cause*, I *see* (upward accent)
The portraiture of *his;* I'll *count* his *favors;*
But-sure, the *bravery* of his grief did put-me
Into a TOWERING *passion*.[17]
Horatio. *Peace!* who comes here?

The passage interests Clarke very much because it reveals Booth's power of elocution in reading a narrative, and it is the only such passage in the play. He acknowledges that his marking of the stresses is but a "coarse and inadequate denotement": only by hearing Booth can one appreciate the exquisite characteristics of his delivery of the passage.

Booth has nothing to do in the passage but to stand beside Horatio with a hand on his shoulder, or now and again to gesture gently. He is not impassioned, though very much in earnest. One senses in him, through his vocal tones, through an occasional light in the eyes, or a change of position, or a disposal of the hand, that Hamlet has now improved somewhat in steadfastness of purpose. Yet behind the bolder words he speaks, there lurks the old moodiness and weakness: his heart and will seem perplexed with unrest.

It troubles Clarke that sometimes in his commentary, as perhaps here, his "fancy puts wings upon Booth's tones," and that he catches from their echoes meanings which have not been expressed. "But I write as I think and feel": Booth's acting is such that each word and motion is, as it were, a "stereoscope through which some great glowing view of a grand emotion or a magnificent idea is for the instant placed before my eyes." When he considers all that Booth has done for him—to drill his mind, to put edge upon his sensibility, to instruct his emotions, to inform his imagination—his impulse is to reach up his arms and cry with longing and admiration and humility, "Oh Booth! Booth!" It is as if Booth's identity and

[16] *75.* In the traditional acting versions the scene begins at this reference to Laertes, so that there is an immediate linking to Hamlet's quarrel with Laertes at the grave. In his earlier and later stagings, in which less time was required for the change going on backstage, Booth began here too.

[17] *80.* Booth observes in his Notebook that Hamlet has not a word to say here of "poor Ophelia." This is another bit of evidence for Booth's case that Hamlet's love for Ophelia did not amount to much.

power were in the air overhead, and he were looking up to them as to a source of mental health and light.

80-189. "Your lordship is right welcome back to Denmark."

Osric enters from the left and addresses Hamlet with an elaborate bow. Hamlet returns the bow slightly: "I *humbly thank you*, sir." He turns to Horatio, and they start slowly off to the right: "Dost KNOW this *waterfly?*" He speaks in an undertone, with a contemptuous wave of the hand toward Osric, but not so that Osric can see it. Horatio denies the acquaintance. "*Thy state* is the *more gracious*, for 'tis a VICE to *know* him (low tone)."

Osric calls after him. They pause, and Hamlet partly turns back, looking annoyed but making an effort at politeness. Osric says he would impart something from his majesty. Hamlet faces Osric, and moves two or three steps toward him: "I will *receive* it, sir, with ALL (prolonged; speaking slowly and with dignity) *diligence* (folding his arms) of spirit. —Your *bonnet* to its *right use* (gentle but authoritative tone; he indicates Osric's cap with his right hand, and motions him to put it on). *'Tis* for the *head* (short sound)." Osric demurs: it is very hot. Hamlet stares at Osric with an ironic expression, his arms folded and his head dropped forward a little: "*No, believe*-me, 'tis very COLD (pause as for a period). The WIND is *northerly* (making an outward movement with his right thumb)." Osric agrees that it *is* indifferent cold, and bows. Hamlet swings his shoulders round toward Horatio with a glance which expresses ridicule of Osric. Then he swings back and looks at Osric steadily as before: "But *yet*, methinks (doubtingly), it is very *sultry* and *hot* (short sound), or *my complexion*—" Osric agrees, and speaks stammeringly, and finally collapses into a deferential bow as he exclaims, "***I*** cannot tell how." [18] Hamlet turns from him weariedly. Horatio comes to him and Hamlet puts his right arm on his shoulder.

Osric speaks of the King's wager and plunges on into his message, but Hamlet interrupts him: "*I beseech* you (tone of request; he points to Osric's cap with his left hand, and makes an upward gesture toward Osric's head) *remember* (upward accent; tone of authority and slight displeasure)." Osric begs to be excused, for his "ease," and he bows again. Hamlet withdraws his stare, and

[18] *104.* Booth seems to have instructed his Osrics to put an especially strong emphasis on "I." A note he added to the Taylor 1890 promptbook explains the significance: "as if to say it is as *you* say, my lord; whatever *you* say it *is—it is.* I must not gainsay you!"

turns toward Horatio with an air of compelled resignation. Osric speaks of the newly come Laertes and goes on with his elaborate description of Laertes' gentlemanliness.[19]

Hamlet faces Horatio the while, with only side glances at Osric, but at last he turns quietly: "*What imports* the *nomination* of this *gentleman?* (upward accent; tone of slight impatience)." [20] Osric says "Of Laertes?" as if surprised by the question. "OF HIM, sir (upward accent)." Osric reminds Hamlet that he is not "ignorant of" Laertes' excellence. Hamlet interrupts him as if irritated by his tediousness: "I DARE NOT *confess that*, lest I should *compare* with him in excellence; but to know a man *well* were to know *himself*." He looks at Osric as if he did not care whether he had made himself intelligible or not.

Osric speaks of Laertes' weapon. "What IS his weapon? (slowly, as in forced courtesy)." It is rapier and dagger. "That's TWO (gentle, ironic tone) of his weapons (changing his position and folding his arms again). *But* (nodding, and as if he were to make a comment), well (upward accent, and in an indifferent tone, as if deciding *not* to make a comment)." Osric speaks of the King's wager of Barbary horses against French rapiers,[21] and rattles on about the "carriages." Hamlet, the while, stands at arm's length from Horatio, his hand on his shoulder, and looks at Osric with staid politeness: "What CALL *you* the CARRIAGES? (upward accent; slowly)." The carriages, says Osric, are the hangers. "The phrase would be more german to the *matter*, if we could carry a CANNON by our sides (turning his look toward Horatio, so that the sarcasm seems rather an aside than a thrust at Osric)."

Again Osric explains the terms of the wager, and how it remains for Hamlet to agree to the match. Hamlet drops his hand from Horatio's shoulder and folds his arms: "*How* if I *answer, no?* (slight upward accent)." Osric rephrases the matter. Hamlet raises his right arm from his breast and rests his hand against his chin, with the forefinger pointing upward. He looks at Osric with more

[19] *110.* At the mention of Laertes, Booth says in his Notebook, Hamlet suspects that some danger is brewing. The Taylor 1890 promptbook records here that Horatio comes to Hamlet and they converse in dumbshow.

[20] *133.* Booth says in his Notebook, "Ask this slowly & impressively and with a searching gaze at Osric."

[21] *156.* When Osric used the word "impawned" he affectedly pronounced it "imponed." The Taylor 1890 promptbook records that Hamlet would then turn to Horatio and repeat the word in an undertone.

interest and favor: "Sir, it is the *breathing time* of *day* with-me. Let the foils *be brought:* the gentleman *willing*, and the King *hold his purpose, I will* WIN for him *if I* CAN; if *not*, I will gain *nothing*-but-my-*shame* and the *odd* HITS." Osric asks if he is to report this. "To this EFFECT, sir; after what *flourish* (waving his left hand gracefully) your nature will." Osric goes to the left archway and bows low. Hamlet bows his head a very little and looks at him intently. Osric goes out and Hamlet turns to Horatio with an air of relief.

219-236. "You will lose this wager, my lord."

Horatio warns Hamlet that he will lose the match. Hamlet rests his hand on Horatio's shoulder, and speaks confidently: "I do not *think* so. Since he went into France, I have been in continual *practice.*[22] I shall win at the *odds.*" Sauntering a little toward the right, they stop at center: "But thou (low, solemn tone; looking at Horatio sadly) *would'st not think* how *ill* ALL'S here *about my* HEART (his voice drops soberly; slow speech)." He taps his side with his left hand; then raises his left hand with a gesture of dismissal: "But it is *no matter.*" Horatio starts to protest, but Hamlet goes on: "It is but *foolery;* but it is such a kind of *gain-giving* as would, perhaps, trouble a *woman* (slowly, in a troubled tone)." His reference to *woman* is not contemptuous, but rather as if he himself were subject to some peculiarity of temperament that was womanish. Horatio begs him not to proceed with it, and offers to carry excuses to the King.

Hamlet drops his hand from Horatio's shoulder, and takes his left hand in both of his. They start toward the left. "Not a *whit* (pause, as for a period), we DEFY (slight pause) AUGURY (sound of every syllable). There is a *special providence* in the *fall of a* SPARROW." They stop near the left entrance: "If it BE *now*, 'tis *not to* COME (gravely, as if surveying a fatality); if it be *not to* COME, it WILL be NOW; if it *be* NOT NOW, yet it WILL COME; the *readiness* (starting to the left) is *all*. Since no man of *aught he leaves*, KNOWS, what is't to leave *betimes. Let be* (his voice drops, as if concluding the matter)." He pats Horatio's hand adjuringly as they go out: "*Let be*, LET *be.*" In the last "let be" he stops, raises his right hand to the side of his head, gives it one or two forward

[22] *221.* Booth calls attention in his Notebook to the curious inconsistency of this with "I have forgone all custom of exercises" (II, 2, 308).

jerks, and goes out. The repetition of "let be" is, as Clarke notes, an addition to the text, but it is in character, for Hamlet frequently utters final words, as "Well, well, well" or "Words, words, words," three times. As they go out, the Porch set sinks through the stage floor.

In this scene, Clarke says, Booth's showing of Hamlet's superiority to Osric is remarkably delicate. Hamlet is never arrogant, but simply treats the courtier as someone he dislikes. In doing so, and in making Osric look ridiculous, he manages not to offend Osric's feelings. His wit is exhibited to the audience or to Horatio, but is never directed to sting Osric's vanity. He is so courteous that Osric leaves him as friendly as when he came.

Booth's way at Osric's exit is a fine transition. He seems to fathom the value of Osric's obeisance with a single look. Then, with a slight shrug, he turns to Horatio, and without reference to Osric's absurdity, as if it has spoken for itself and needs no comment, they turn to sober discussion of the wager and the coming trial at arms.

His manner is compact with meaning as he speaks of his forebodings. He is depressed, his face full of doubt and perplexity, his voice troubled and prophetic. His presentiment is so distinctly sombre that one will think back to it when the final catastrophe takes place.

The text of Act V, 2 (line-numbering of the Globe edition).

The cuts (69 lines) are traditional. These are: 86b-90; 116-132 (euphuistic description of Laertes); 136-137; 139-142; 148-150; 162-163; 167-171; 180-181a; 190-218 (ridicule of Osric; the entrance of a Lord).

The following alterations are made: 1, "See" > "hear"; 9, "learn" > "teach"; 27, "now" > "me"; 29, "villains" > "villainies"; 30, "Or" > "Ere"; 42, "comma" > "common"; 44, "knowing" > "know"; 64, "whored" > "defil'd"; 78, "court his favor" > "count his favors" (Folio reading); 95, "put" is omitted; 102, "for" > "or"; 165, "germane" > "german"; 236, "Let be" is tripled.

The restorations (80 lines) are these: 1-74 (Hamlet's narrative); 78b-80a (cut in the promptbook but recorded by Clarke as spoken); 232-236 ("If it be now," etc.).

Act V, 3. *A Room in the Palace, called the Grand Hall of Audience.*
(Globe edition: Act V, 2, 237-414. 178 lines cut to 98.)

The evidence for the final set is contradictory. According to Arthur Matthison's pamphlet, *Booth's Theatre: Hamlet,* it was a new and special "Grand Banqueting Hall" designed by Russell Smith, and "here all the architectural, armorial, and decorative splendours of that chivalrous age are revived and united, being a gorgeous finale to this chain of ancient, yet novel, scenic pictures; and forming altogether a worthy framework to this grand inspiration of the master writer!" The Harvard 1870 promptbook, however, includes no watercolor of such a set as Matthison describes; and its groundplans indicate clearly that the set is the same Room of State in which the Court first convenes in Act I, 2. Moreover the watercolor of that Room of State set (see Plate V) shows a pair of throne chairs mounted on a dais: these throne chairs, as we have seen, are not used in Act I, 2, and they *are* required for the final scene.

But Charles Clarke's account agrees with neither Matthison nor the promptbook; and his scenic notes at this point, though perfunctory, are decisive. The set is a "hall of state in the castle," he writes, "the same one seen many times before during the play." That disposes of the Russell Smith "Grand Banqueting Hall," which certainly has not been seen at all during the play; and it puts in question the Act I, 2, Room of State, which has been seen not "many times" but only once. "The throne filled the end," Clarke goes on, "and the King and Queen sat upon it. At [stage left] was a table with drink; at the [right] another table with foils and weapons upon it. At the rear and sides were chairs and seats filled by the court, and upon the stairs and in the gallery were groups and rows of spectators." This reference to stairs and galleries can mean no other set than the Grand Hall of Audience—the great staircase set of the third act (Plate IX). That set has not been seen "many times," to be sure, but it has been seen twice (in Act III, 1 and 3), and it is the only interior that has been seen more than once.

I would account for the contradictions in the following manner. Matthison, whose pamphlet was printed before the opening night, based his account of the final set upon Russell Smith's *design* of it; and for reasons unknown (but in the theatrical situation never far to seek) that design was scrapped and the great staircase set was reintroduced in place of it. But the shift from the full-stage Graveyard set to the full-stage staircase set was a cumbersome and complicated operation, feasible only on a stage as well equipped and manned as Booth's stage was in 1870. Therefore, when the promptbook was made up with a view to future reproductions in other theatres, and the watercolor was painted for it, Booth and Witham settled for the simpler expedient of reintroducing the shallower single-level Room of State set of Act I, 2.[23]

It is, of course, slippery to speculate on these matters, but some such sequence of events must have occurred to produce three contradictory bodies of evidence. In any case, it is clear from Clarke's account that we are to imagine the final scene, as of 1870, being mounted in the great staircase set.

Flourishes of trumpets cover the scene change, which is effected almost instantaneously as the Porch set drops down through the floor of the stage. The Court is discovered all assembled, the King and Queen seated on throne chairs mounted on a dais upstage center between the staircases, Laertes standing to their right and Osric beside him. Courtiers, Ladies, and Guards fill up the spaces at either side and range up the staircases and across the gallery.

237-314. "Come, Hamlet, come, and take this hand from me."

Hamlet and Horatio enter from down left, wearing their capes as in the preceding scene with their caps hanging behind their shoulders. Hamlet, with a self-confident but deferential and courtly air, advances directly in front of the throne and bows low. Horatio bows from down left. At the King's invitation to take Laertes' hand, Hamlet does so readily and heartily: "Give me your *pardon*, sir; I've *done you wrong*. But *pardon* it, as you're a *gentleman*. Let my disclaiming from a *purposed* EVIL *free me so far* in your *most generous thoughts* that I have *shot my arrow* O'ER the *house* (upward accents; raising his left hand), and *hurt* (pause) *my brother* (tender, friendly tone)." Laertes allows that he is satisfied "in nature," and accepts Hamlet's offered love. Hamlet takes both Laertes'

[23] By 1873, according to Bensen Sherwood's "Stage Plans," Booth had reverted to something very like the Act I, 2, set even at his own theatre; only the ceiling was noticeably different, being composed not of "Trick Borders" but of "Juliet Chamber Borders." The Players 1876 promptbook actually specifies "2nd Sc of Act 1."

hands in his: "*I* EMBRACE it FREELY (joyous tone), and will this BROTHER's wager *frankly* play." [24]

He lets go Laertes' hands, inclines his head toward the throne, takes a step backward, and turns and comes down near the table at the left: "GIVE *us* the foils (eagerly)." [25] Horatio helps him remove his cloak, and he tightens his waistbelt: "I'll be YOUR foil, Laertes. In mine ignorance your *skill* shall, like a *star* in the *darkest night*, stick *fiery off indeed*." Laertes accuses him of mockery. "*No* (upward accent; throwing up his hand for an instant and then busying it again at his belt), by this *hand* (slight upward accent)." The King orders Osric to give them the foils, which are on the table at right, and asks Hamlet if he knows the wager.

Hamlet receives a foil from Osric and passes it at once to Horatio without examining it; he continues to adjust his belt: "*Very* WELL, my lord, *Your grace* hath laid the *odds* on the *weaker side*." He looks up now, having prepared himself, and takes the foil from Horatio. Across the stage Laertes is objecting to the foil given him, and is conspicuously exchanging it for another; Hamlet, not noticing this, begins to test his own. Holding it at tip and hilt, he bends it. He jams the point against the floor. Holding it horizontally he tosses it up and catches it: "THIS *likes* me *well*. These foils have *all* a LENGTH?"

The King speaks a dozen lines of instruction, and drinks; trumpets and cannon sound; he orders them to begin.[26] Hamlet and Laertes advance to front center and face each other: "COME ON, sir." [27] First come the introductory flourishes. Laertes then bends back and stands motionless, and Hamlet formally touches his breast

[24] *264.* In later stagings, according to Mason and to the Taylor 1890 promptbook, Hamlet and Laertes here stood before the King with their backs to the audience and Hamlet's left arm across Laertes' shoulders. They bowed together to the King.

[25] *265.* The Taylor 1890 promptbook records that Hamlet here removed his pouch from his girdle and gave it to Horatio; also that he wiped his hands with a handkerchief.

[26] *289.* The 1870 promptbook names the cup-bearer in this scene Francisco. The edition of 1878 and the later promptbooks name him Bernardo. The later promptbooks record that when the King drank Hamlet's health, the fencers stood at salute and the whole Court bowed.

[27] *291.* The Pitman 1884 promptbook calls for "Fight music" to play behind the scenes from this point until the moment the Queen swoons (line 314); then the musicians are to return to the orchestra. The Taylor 1890 and Harvard 1890 promptbooks concur. A pianoforte reduction of the fight music is preserved in the Theatre Collection of the New York Public Library.

with the point of his foil. Then Hamlet stands motionless and Laertes formally touches him. The bout begins. They cross the stage once or twice. Suddenly at center there is a swift circling movement wherein Hamlet wards a thrust from Laertes, spins round so that his back is toward Laertes, passes his sword beneath his own arm so that its point is near to Laertes' breast, looks, pushes it, and touches Laertes.[28] He steps away with a look of triumph: "*One* (quietly)." Laertes objects. "*Judgment* (Hamlet turns toward Osric)." Osric grants the hit, the "palpable hit," and they are ready to play again.

The King stays them; he calls for the drink, which Francisco brings from the table at left. The King drops the promised pearl into it and pretends to drink, while drums and cannon are heard from without. Hamlet, while waiting, gives his sword a wave or two, brings the hilt to his forehead, and bows to the King in acknowledgment of the "health." The King orders Francisco to take the cup to Hamlet, but Hamlet declines it: "I'll play *this bout first. Set it by awhile* (authoritative but easy tone, as if he were eager to play). *Come*." Trumpets sound, and they fence as before, crossing the stage once or twice, until Hamlet hits Laertes a second time. "Another hit? What *say you?*"

Laertes admits the touch, and the Queen, who has beckoned Francisco to her, calls out that she is carousing to Hamlet's fortune. She drinks. Hamlet, who is moving toward the left table, stops and bows to her: "GOOD *madam* (courteously)." As the King tells the Queen, aside, not to drink, Hamlet is at the left table, handing his sword to Horatio and wiping his hands with his handkerchief. The King mutters to himself that it is the poisoned cup. Laertes, at the right table, is anointing the tip of his sword, and Hamlet is drinking at the left table. Presently Hamlet returns to the center, speaking with especial animation as if stirred by the heat of play and by the wine he has just swallowed: "*Come for the third*, Laertes. *You do* but *dally*. I *pray you*, *pass* with your *best violence*. I am *afeared* (upward accent) you make a *wanton* of me (short sound of *me*)."

They play with great ardor, passing swiftly back and forth

[28] *291.* The *Citizen's Round Table* (January 8) was outraged by this eccentric bit of gymnastics: "When did a duellist ever execute an entire revolution on his heel, and stab his adversary with the complicated backward thrust with which he kills Laertes?" (Observe that Booth did *not* use the tricky maneuver to kill Laertes, but only to make the first point in the game of skill.) Many critics in years to come would voice similar objection, but Booth could not be talked out of the business.

across the stage, ever more vehemently. Presently Laertes stabs Hamlet in the breast. Hamlet staggers backward to the center, though not as if hurt severely. Horatio starts toward him. The King rises and calls to the attendants to part the fighters; several step forward. At this moment the Queen swoons. But Hamlet straightens up resolutely, breathing hard: "*Nay* (upward accent and commanding tone, but huskily), *come again* (short sounds, as if he were in increasing pain, and impetuously)." He starts forward as he speaks, his left hand at the wound. They play across the stage but once. Hamlet is now infuriated. Laertes wards the thrusts, but Hamlet drives him down right and closes with him as if to pay back the wound he has received.

Their swords become caught between them. Hamlet seizes Laertes' foil, the point of it being near Laertes' breast, and wrenching it from him, with a sudden stroke drives it home.[29] Laertes starts back, and Hamlet, holding both Laertes' foil and his own together, staggers to the center. He rests on Horatio there, who falls on his knees before him, opening his coat at the breast to see the wound. Hamlet looks down at it.

314-404. "Look to the Queen there, ho!"

It is Osric who cries out that the Queen needs help, and several of the Ladies assist her down from the throne and toward the left. Hamlet turns and looks fixedly at the Queen, seeming not to listen to Horatio's cry of "How is't, my lord?" or Osric's "How is't, Laertes?" or Laertes' cry that he is killed by his own treachery. "*How* DOES the *Queen?*" As the Queen is led off to the left, supported and attended by all the court Ladies, she blames the drink and cries out that she is poisoned.[30]

At this Hamlet raises his right hand over his head, grasping the foils by the middle of the blades and holding them horizontally. He turns them two or three times: "Oh *villainy!* Ho!" He breaks from Horatio and starts up and to the left where the Queen has gone out.

[29] *313.* It is plain here that Hamlet seizes Laertes' foil and keeps them both. There is no *exchange* of weapons. In summary notes near the end of his manuscript, Clarke objects that the exchange is omitted. The printed directions in Booth's 1878 edition include the words from the Folio "In scuffling they change rapiers." But apparently Booth never used that business: the later promptbooks do not mention it, and in the Taylor 1890 promptbook it is clear that down to line 331 Hamlet has both the foils in his hand.

[30] *321.* In the printed directions of the 1878 edition and in Mason's recording, the King left the stage along with the Queen and then returned to the throne.

"LET THE DOOR be *locked*. TREACHERY! *Seek it out* (excited and resolute)." But the fallen Laertes calls him, and going quickly down right, he kneels before Laertes and hears the brief facts of the poisoning, his own imminent death, and the guilt of the King. As he listens, his head sinks forward, his brows project, his left hand falls out at his side with the fingers drawing in like a bird's talon. He breathes quickly, his nostrils dilate, his eyes stare. His left hand touches the foil, and as Laertes concludes, he runs his hand along the foil toward the tip. Then he turns on his knees, drops his own foil, raises Laertes' foil quickly, and facing the audience, catches the point in his fingers. "The point ENVENOMED *too!* Then, *venom, to thy* WORK!"

He rises desperately, fury in his face. Horatio, seeing his intention, catches at his arm to stay him. Hamlet races across the front of the stage toward down left. Horatio keeps pace with him, but suddenly Hamlet turns inward, throws off Horatio, and darts toward the throne. The King is on the throne, apparently giving directions to the Courtiers and Guards who surround him. As they see Hamlet coming they cry "Treason!" and draw swords against him. But he sweeps down their weapons, drives them aside, bounds up the throne, and seizes the King's throat in his left hand. With his right he plunges the foil through the King's neck twice, saying on the second thrust: "*Here*, thou *incestuous*, *murderous*, DAMNED DANE, *follow* my *mother* (tone and energy of mad exultation, but the utterance cramped as if coming from overworked lungs or closed lips)." He throws the King off, who falls backward into the arms of those below.[31]

He casts up his left hand with the fingers open, looks after the King with a stare of horror, and then reels uncertainly down the steps of the throne with his left hand on his forehead. He drops his foil as he comes down. Horatio receives him in his arms at the foot of the steps. Laertes is saying that the King is justly served. Hamlet, supported by Horatio, moves down to Laertes' side and falls on one

[31] *338.* According to Mason, when Hamlet killed the King, he then went up to the throne and sat on it; he rose and came down at line 349, "Horatio, I am dead." The Taylor 1890 promptbook, on the contrary, says that the King fell onto the throne as he died. The critics generally reported the killing of the King as "thrilling" or "truly horrible"; but the *Citizen's Round Table* (January 8) faulted Booth for rushing past the King to an upstage position and assuming a "theatrical and picturesque attitude," instead of striking the death blow at once.

knee. Laertes begs to exchange forgivenesses. They reach out and clasp right hands. Laertes' last wish is that "mine and my father's death come not upon thee; nor thine on me!" He falls back in death, Hamlet looks down on him with a sad and pitying face: "Heaven *make thee free*-of-it." He drops his head a little, despondingly: "I *follow thee* (upward accent; pathetic tone)."

He rises with Horatio's help, and walks toward the Guards and Courtiers who surround the throne: "You that look pale and *tremble* (upward accent; tremulously) at this chance, that are but *mutes* or AUDIENCE (upward accent, in a gentle voice full of pathos and desire; leaning on Horatio, his body stricken with lassitude) to this act, HAD *I but time* (these four words on one breath, gropingly, as if wishing to explain but lacking the power to do so) —as this fell sergeant, *Death* (deeper tone, and a pushing out of the voice; he turns before the throne and thrusting his breast out he grasps Horatio) is STRICT in his *arrest*—Oh, I *could tell you*—but *let it* BE. *Horatio*, I am *dead*." He slips down in Horatio's arms and sinks on one knee at right center: "*Report me* and my *cause* aright to the *unsatisfied* (soft and pathetic tone; he seems to have lost most of his vigor)."

Horatio, seeing the poisoned cup, which has been left on the table at the left, runs to it and snatches it; and coming halfway back toward Hamlet, offers to drink it. Hamlet looks up commandingly: "*As* thou art a *man* (starting up, he runs to Horatio and grasps the cup), *give me* the cup. *Let go*. By *heaven* (determined tone, hoarsely), I'll *have it!*" He wrenches the cup from Horatio and throws it offstage left. He falls to his knees, with Horatio supporting him. He smiles up at Horatio with friendly reproval and continues weakly: "Oh, *good Horatio*, what a *wounded name* (upward accent), things standing thus *unknown* (upward accent), shall *live* behind me! (short sound of *me*). If thou didst *ever* hold-me in thy heart, *absent* thee from *felicity*-awhile, and in this *harsh world* draw thy *breath in pain* (slight upward accent) to tell *my story*. *Oh!* I *die* (upward accent; prolonged; tone of regret), Horatio!"

He rises a little, and turning, falls backward into Horatio's arms, his head toward the audience.[32] One or two Courtiers come

[32] *363*. In later stagings, according to Mason and Taylor, the position Booth took for dying was with his head upstage, lying partway up the steps to the throne. Mason records at length how in the Hundred Nights *Hamlet* at the Winter Garden Booth worked up a more spectacular dying. At the words "to tell my story" a languor passed over him and he seemed nearly dead. But then: "he raises his head, and looks wildly round. His expression

forward to help Horatio support him. "The *potent poison* quite o'ercrows my spirit. The *rest* is *silence* (slowly, in a low, sad tone)." He drops his head and dies. Horatio speaks the two lines of benediction and lowers him to the ground. Drums and a march are heard.[33] All turn to the left and look offstage expectantly as the curtain slowly falls.

In recapitulating this scene, Clarke emphasizes first of all Booth's gracefulness. "Nothing could be more admirable than the ease and finish of the movement . . . through the fencing; and in the dying there was no distortion but at all times a harmony of action and posture."

It fascinates Clarke that to the very end Booth shows Hamlet's weakness when great responsibilities are thrust upon him. Under extreme provocation, incited to desperation by the multiple treacheries about him, he kills the King. But the instant that deed is done he shrinks from it. His conscience is outraged. His will is appalled, for it has overdone itself. And so he staggers from the deed, coming down from the throne in a bewildered way, as from a climax that is too high to be maintained. His vigor wanes, his resolution vanishes —and not from the effects of the poison only, for he can rally strength to snatch the cup from Horatio. The deed is done; his purpose is fulfilled. But he cannot vindicate himself, cannot assert the justice of his course. He cannot brace himself against the world's criticism.

His death is supremely pathetic. In the pained words "Oh, I die, Horatio" one senses in him a desperate return of feeling as if he wants to live still. He rises up and drops into Horatio's arms with a slow fall which foreshadows death, and therein is especially chilling. Yet it is death in the arms of a friend, and that eases the rude-

has changed, and his face now shows the sharpest agony; his eyes dilate, the muscles of his face become rigid, and, with a low shuddering cry, he rises, tremblingly, to his feet, with the words: 'O, I die, Horatio!' As he rises, Horatio and Osric support him, and he turns, convulsively, in their arms, as he speaks his last words. They lower him slowly to the stage—the head toward the footlights."

[33] *371.* This music was not heard at the beginning of the run. On January 27, the *Daily Star* reported that "Mr. Booth has added a feature purely 'Shakespearean,' yet quite novel and touching. As Hamlet dies, the distant strains of martial music are heard, which announces the approach of Fortinbras." The *Sunday News* (January 30) describes it as a "joyous and inspiring melody." It is apparently no. 13 in the *Hamlet* score preserved in the Theatre Collection of the New York Public Library.

ness of it. "*The rest is silence.*" The words are slow, sad, contemplative. And they are an intellectual recognition: they express at once weariness of the world, willingness to exchange it for the life hereafter, and no distinct hope that the life hereafter exists.

The text of Act V, 3 (line-numbering of the Globe edition).

The cuts (80 lines) are, except for a couple of lines, traditional. They are: 239-251 (part of Hamlet's apology); 255b; 257b-261; 278; 298b-299 ("He's fat," etc.); 304-306; 312-313; 315a; 335; 337; 339; 344b; 360b-363a; 365-369a; 372-414 (the Fortinbras ending).

✠

PART III

THE FINAL YEARS

CHAPTER VII

Hamlet in Repertory, 1870-91

Throughout Booth's tenure of his theatre he kept the *Hamlet* production in stock.[1] His grand intention was to build in Booth's Theatre a matchless production of every important play in the modern legitimate repertory, so that eventually not only he but other leading actors of the day would be able to exhibit their art in perfect settings. He mounted *Rip Van Winkle* for Joseph Jefferson, for instance, and *The Winter's Tale* for Lawrence Barrett. From his own repertory he produced *Romeo and Juliet* and *Othello* in the first season, *Hamlet* and *Macbeth* in the second. In 1870-71 he added *Richelieu* and *Much Ado About Nothing*, in 1871-72 *Julius Caesar* and *Richard III*, in 1872-73 Payne's *Brutus*.

That was the end, however. The more grandly Booth strove, the worse he fell behind financially. The cost of these productions (and there were many lesser ones), together with unpaid mortgages on the theatre, ran up debts beyond Booth's power to understand, much less cope with. By 1873 he was desperate. Turning over the management to his brother Junius Brutus, he took to the road to raise funds. It was too late. During the financial panic which occurred that autumn, his creditors closed in on him, and in the following January he filed petition of bankruptcy. Never again would he attempt to own a theatre or assume management or produce plays on his own account,

[1] In December of 1871, while preparing *Julius Caesar* at Booth's Theatre, Booth revived *Hamlet* for a three-week run. In November of 1873 he revived it again under his brother's management, the scenery by then being somewhat simplified.

but would only act his roles as best he could in whatever companies and whatever scenic investitures other managements would afford him.

With Augustin Daly at the Fifth Avenue, 1875

For two seasons, from the fall of 1873 through the spring of 1875, he roamed about the northern and eastern cities and was not seen in New York at all. On October 25, 1875, he took up an engagement with Augustin Daly at the Fifth Avenue Theatre. Daly, who was eager to extend himself in the Shakespearean line, gave him decent mountings of several of his regular plays, plus *Richard II*, which he had never acted before, and *King Lear*, which he had not performed in New York since 1857. The actors at the Fifth Avenue, all of them attuned to comedy, supported him with perhaps more enthusiasm than tragical aptitude.

He opened, of course, in *Hamlet*. The applause which greeted him, according to the *Herald*, was "instantaneous, electrical, universal." The audience was not only welcoming him home to the city, but expressing their gratitude that he was still alive. Two months earlier he had suffered a violent carriage accident near his summer home in Connecticut; for days he had lain unconscious, stupefied by drugs, while the newspapers cried alarm. His opening was postponed three weeks beyond its announced date while he recovered from the accident and the subsequent ministrations of the surgeons; his left arm, badly broken and badly set, rebroken and set again, would never recover its full use. When opening night came he acted with unexpected vigor, although his left arm dangled helplessly at his side and he could gesture only with his right one. Yet "Briareus himself could not have done better," exclaimed the *Herald;* "the wonderful wealth of gesture he revealed with one arm alone might be compared to the performance of Paganini on a single string of the violin." The critics were for the most part disposed to be generous.

A Modernist Attacks Booth's Hamlet: The Psychological View

His return in *Hamlet* was the occasion for one devastatingly negative study, however, which, though at odds with majority opinion of the day, is nevertheless of unusual interest. It is an essay of great length and particularity, divided between the November 20 and 27 issues of *Appleton's Journal*. The author, O. B. Bunce,[2] had reviewed Booth's Hamlet in *Appleton's* five years earlier (February 5, 1870), and taking exception then to Booth's interpretation, had promised a more extensive treatment in the future: the sword dropped in 1875.

Bunce admits fairly that Booth's Hamlet is at present "the best on the American if not on the whole English-speaking stage." He admits, too, that Booth's physical appearance is peculiarly appropriate to the role, and that much may be forgiven him for having "rid his style of the strut, pomp, and sounding declamation of the traditional stage." Yet Booth's Hamlet falls far short of what in Bunce's mind the ideal Hamlet should be.

He objects, in the first place, to the trickishness and to the ceaseless change in Booth's performances—not change in order to improve the ideal of Hamlet (for rather like Nym Crinkle, Bunce thinks Booth *has* no adequate ideal of it), but merely in a stagey way to gratify the eye or the ear by novel effects. As an example of this sort of thing Bunce points to Booth's first entrance. Whereas heretofore Hamlet has either entered with the court or been discovered seated among them, Booth now chooses to make a late entrance—and a brisk one, too—just before the cue for his first speech. Thus he absolutely destroys our first impression of the "wistful, brooding, melancholy" Hamlet.[3] As another example, Bunce instances the "fantastic nonsense in the fencing business" (the under-arm maneuver by which Booth delivered the first thrust to Laertes). This, Bunce says, is not only unprincely but childish, and Booth should give it up.

He objects to Booth's manner of reading. The delivery of the long speeches is superficial, hasty, deficient in use of pause, without

[2] Though Bunce was hostile to Booth's Hamlet, he had greatly admired Booth's Theatre. In the *Appleton's Journal* of May 28, 1870, he had published a long illustrated article called "Behind, Below, and Above the Scenes" describing the theatre in detail. This article was at once republished in pamphlet form under the title *Booth's Theatre. Behind the Scenes.* The pamphlet was issued again in 1873.

[3] Booth had invented this late entrance during his recent road tours. He caused it to be printed in the Prompt-Book edition of 1878. He was still using it in England in 1880. (See Percy Fitzgerald, *Shakespearean Representation* (London, 1908), p. 12.) He abandoned it before 1886, according to the actress Kitty Molony. Miss Molony explains the reason for it: the audiences were determined to greet the star with an ovation, and the only way Booth could secure a proper hearing for the King's opening speeches was to keep out of sight until they were finished. See Goodale, pp. 176-178.

thought or feeling. In the first soliloquy, for instance, Booth does not give us Hamlet's inward feelings "sometimes musingly, sometimes hesitatingly, sometimes as if he brooded over the thought, sometimes with a rush and explosion of feeling"; he rather "gallops" over the sentences like a "not very well-trained elocutionist." As for "To be or not to be," although he begins it in a profoundly meditative mood, it quickly degenerates into "rapid and characterless declamation . . . flung off at a heat, as if learned by rote." The speeches to his mother in her chamber "seem to us to lack light and shade, and commonly to be uttered in an off-hand dash that ignores all the shades of meaning." [4] In yet another attack upon Booth's reading Bunce accuses him of an "amazing fondness" for prepositions and pronouns. He offers as examples, "Seems to me all the uses *of* this world" and "With which she followed *my* poor father's body." In 1870 he had cited "And batten *on* this moor." [5]

Bunce's most acute, most persistent—and most convincing—charge is that Booth fails to convey Hamlet's "fever of the brain." The failure, he says, is not unique with Booth, for to judge by the records no actor before him ever properly conveyed "this hysteric wildness, this intense feeling that can only find expression by abnormal methods." In a word: "The psychological Hamlet is yet to arise." Booth is altogether too determined to convince us that Hamlet is sane, purposeful in everything he does, perfectly in control, only *assuming* an antic disposition. At every moment when Hamlet ought to behave hysterically, Booth finds an explanation for his behaving logically. "Explanation! This is the thing so many commentators are wrecked upon. . . . To force explanations upon us of Hamlet's conduct is to destroy its mystery, its illusive, fascinating undertouch . . . its profound agitations that ascend from depths of feeling and suffering, which, while they perplex, are still recognized as genuine."

[4] This charge of excessive speed of speaking is, of course, almost inexplicably at odds with Charles Clarke's account and others in 1870. Had Booth staled so much in five years? Or was Bunce, as an armchair Shakespearean, simply not willing to listen fast enough and respond fast enough to stage performance?

[5] In these three instances, Clarke in 1870 had marked *uses*, *poor*, *batten*, and *moor* as the stressed words. The point is a delicate one, and much depends upon the hearer. The critic and elocutionist Alfred Ayres, terror of all late-century American actors, attacked Booth mercilessly for stressing unimportant words. See Alfred Ayres, *Acting and Actors, Elocution and Elocutionists* (New York, 1894), pp. 234-236; and *Theatre Magazine*, March 8, 1902.

The principal examples Bunce develops are these. (1) Booth no longer uses the lines in which Hamlet calls the Ghost in the cellarage by irreverent names, but even in the days when he did so they and the other "wild and whirling words" did not spring from intense feeling rising into hysterical mirth: they were only a practical device to confound and confuse his listeners. (2) When Booth puts on his antic disposition in the second act, he does so with no hint of inner turmoil. "He is light-hearted, not wild-brained. He is jovial with Rosencrantz, Guildenstern, and Polonius, not fitful with a strange fever. . . . He is not Hamlet, but a very good comedy gentleman playing pranks upon his friends." (3) His delivery of the "Now I am alone" soliloquy is his most signal failure, for there is no frenzy in it. The tumult in this speech "should be limited only by those laws of art by which effect is not destroyed by extravagance." He does not "unpack his heart with words" to express an inner agony, for he feels none. (4) In the scene with Ophelia Hamlet ought to be shaken to his depths by the collision of warring elements: he loves Ophelia, and she is false to him. If the scene is played rightly, "he is deeply stirred, profoundly agitated; wild and hysterical sentences break from his lips; he gives rein to his feverish fancy; he riots . . . in a whirl of words and bitter objurgations." But Booth has *explained* the situation to us by the old device of discovering the King and Polonius eavesdropping: thus his outrageous remarks are simply a cunning counterattack upon the spies. Booth is resolved, too, that Hamlet must not be brutal to Ophelia. Thus his "Get thee to a nunnery!" which ought to be a frenzied command, becomes tender, tearful advice; his "Why wouldst thou be a breeder of sinners?" is softened to an urgent solicitation that she forgo hope of marriage; his "I am myself indifferent honest" is an apology that he is unworthy of a woman's love. He reduces the agonized Hamlet to a "tender lover taking a last farewell of his mistress."

When Bunce declared that Booth had no adequate ideal of Hamlet, he ought rather to have said that from his own point of view Booth had the *wrong* ideal of Hamlet. His recognition that Booth's Hamlet was a "sane" Hamlet was absolutely correct, and therein lay the "ideal" of Hamlet which Booth intended. Booth took his stand on a literal acceptance of Hamlet's own words, "I essentially am not in madness, but mad in craft." [6] He interpreted every bit of Hamlet's

[6] Booth's daughter says that he inscribed these lines on a picture of himself as Hamlet (Grossmann, pp. 19-20). See above, Introduction, pp. xxii-xxiv, and notes to key passages in Chapter VI.

erratic behavior as the assumption of a cunning disguise, a weapon of defense in the life-and-death struggle against his mighty opposite the King. In his Notebook he explains that his lunatic entrance to Ophelia in her closet is only "play-acting." He talks crazily to Polonius only to "bamboozle" the old man, who he knows is conspiring against him. In the scene he acts with Ophelia, he is hardly thinking about Ophelia but is concentrating on the King behind the curtains. For Booth, as for most of his audience, *Hamlet* was a straightforward morality play, a contest of good against evil. There was room in it for heavenly and hellish mystery, and for fearful response to mystery of that sort—or for the mystery of the defeat of man's will by the pressures of man's fate; but not for the mystery of abnormal behavior, for the boiling up of irrational drives from the subconscious, which Bunce, well in advance of his time, was asking for. Not until well into the twentieth century would the "psychological Hamlet" arise.

A Tour of the South, and the First Return to San Francisco, 1876

Booth's reputation was on the upswing throughout the country, and it was time to reap the advantages. In January and February of 1876, under the management of John Ford of Washington, he toured the southern states, which he had not visited since 1859, playing fifty-two performances in sixteen cities. The desire to see him drew people from many miles around the places he visited, as William Winter tells us: "The hotels were thronged. Legislatures regulated their hours of meeting, with a special view to attendance upon his performances. Social parties gave precedence to the theatre. . . . There was a multitude at every stopping-place, to welcome the actor; and often, at way-stations, the doors of the cars had to be locked, in order to keep out the rush of spectators." [7] Booth's profit was $30,000. Next he cut a swathe eastward from Chicago, even venturing across the Canadian border to Hamilton and Toronto.

In the autumn of 1876 his friend John McCullough, manager of the California Theatre in San Francisco, engaged him for an eight-week stand. San Francisco had not seen Booth for twenty years, and the rush to honor its "graduate" was tremendous. Wealth and ease were speedily transforming the place from an outpost to a metropolis, but its taste in theatricals, at least among the men of the

[7] Winter, *Life and Art of Edwin Booth*, pp. 159-160.

press, was somewhat rougher than Booth was used to serving. The reviewers were disappointed in his "etherialized" Hamlet, "with much of the grosser part of his humanity purged away." The *Chronicle*[8] finally put it down as "passable," inferior to his Richelieu and far beneath his "wonderful" Iago. It was a Hamlet for the "attentive student," but "not that which the human flesh and blood which has trod the stage in this part in times gone by has accustomed us to expect." The great Irish barnstormer Barry Sullivan had recently passed through, and after Sullivan's "human flesh and blood," his muscularity and brazen resonance, Booth's genteel Hamlet must indeed have seemed tame. Not to the ladies, however. The ladies there, as everywhere, worshiped Booth. One disgruntled male complained to the *Chronicle* that "the dear creatures being, of course, lamentably incapable of finding fit terms with which to express their adoration of him, have found their accustomed consolation in violent abuse of the unhappy wretch who dares to disagree with them." Prate as this fellow would of the superior powers of Fechter, Sullivan, and Barrett, cry down as he would Booth's truckling to the modern preference for the "quiet style," the taste of the ladies governed the box office. Booth's profit from San Francisco was nearly $50,000.

The Booth-Winter Prompt-Book Editions

During this year of touring Booth felt the need for an up-to-date acting edition of his mainstay plays. All that he had to work with as he moved about from company to company was the old Henry Hinton editions from the 1860's; and these flimsy booklets, closely printed in double columns with narrow margins, were hard to read and awkward for actors to use as part books. Nor were their texts accurate, for during the last decade Booth had altered the cuts, the exits and entrances, and other basic directions. He had come to loathe the Hinton books, especially the *Hamlet* with its cover-portrait which, as he wrote William Winter, "represents me as a drunken *Dumas*—(or some other nigger) & excites the indignation of my wife." There was little demand for them as souvenir copies: "Many ask for *my* version of the plays & will not accept Hinton's book."[9]

[8] San Francisco *Chronicle*, September 8, 10, October 29, 1876.

[9] Booth first proposed the Prompt-Book scheme in a letter to Winter on April 18, 1876; he acknowledged receipt of the *Hamlet* book on February 24, 1878. Dozens of Booth's letters to Winter concerning the Prompt-Book edition are in the Booth file at the Folger Shakespeare Library, Y.c. 215 (232 ff.)

He asked Winter to edit the new series. He would provide Winter with prompt copies "precisely as we do the plays." His versions of *Richard III* and *King Lear* were available at once for Winter to work from and he had at Cos Cob "a beautifully marked promptbook of *Hamlet*—three to begin with." Winter, for his pains, was to take all the income after the costs of printing. Between the end of 1877 and the end of 1878 fifteen titles of the Prompt-Book edition appeared. They are attractive little books, bound in blue-gray paper, printed in well-spaced ten-point type at 40 lines to the page; those intended for backstage use are printed on recto only, so that the left-hand page is free for actors' or stage managers' notations. For each play Winter wrote one or more explanatory essays and gathered interpretative statements from famous critics. His essay on the character of Hamlet includes the following typically empyreal flight: "He is a compound of spiritualized intellect, masculine strength, feminine softness, overimaginative reason, lassitude of thought, autumnal gloom, lovable temperament, piteous, tear-freighted humor, princely grace of condition, brooding melancholy, the philosophic mind, and the deep heart. His nature is everything noble. He is placed upon a pinnacle of earthly greatness." Booth was delighted with this sort of thing. "I like the *Hamlet* exceedingly," he wrote. "You certainly *hit* my idea of Hamlet, whether or not I succeed in illustrating it is questionable." The Prompt-Books served Booth throughout his career and, although soon dated, they were still being reprinted fifteen years and more after his death.

Second Trial of London, 1880-81

In 1880 Booth yielded once more to his old ambition, frustrated in 1861, to prove his art in England. On November 6 at London's new Princess's Theatre he made his debut as Hamlet. Again as in 1861, between miscalculation and circumstance, the venture ran into trouble. As the Haymarket had then been, the Princess's was now—the wrong theatre. Once famous for Charles Kean's fashionable Shakespeare productions, it had long since descended to blood-and-thunder melodrama and a vulgar clientele. Its owner, Walter Gooch, having decided to "go legitimate," had torn it down and rebuilt it, and had engaged Booth to inaugurate its new program. But the habits of playgoers are not mended overnight: fashionable Londoners were as uneager as ever to pay attention to a tragedian from America, and they certainly did not expect much in the way of "art" at the Princess's. Gooch, moreover, was a low-grade commercial manager, with neither the purse nor the imagination to provide supporting actors and scenery worthy of his star. The rehearsals were beset with accidents: one of the actors fell through a hole in the stage floor and was killed; another, involved in a dispute with a rival management, was legally enjoined from playing. Booth was distracted by his wife's illness. For several years Mrs. Booth had been subject to fits of hysteria; not only was her mental condition rapidly worsening but she had contracted a lung ailment which could (and indeed within a year did) prove fatal.

The choice of Hamlet as the role to open with was a dangerous lapse of tact. Although Booth had once upon a time played Hamlet for a hundred nights, and in America he *was* Hamlet, more recently in London Henry Irving had played it for *two* hundred nights, and in English eyes the role belonged to Irving alone. For Booth to open in it could be construed as a gesture of defiance toward Irving, or even a snap at the taste of the town. Winter had urged him to avoid *Hamlet* or at least to postpone it until later in the run. But Mrs. Booth had demanded that he open with it and he yielded to her manic insistence. The reviewers taught him that Winter had been right.[10]

An American who was in London at the time related afterward that within forty-eight hours of the opening he read seventeen criticisms written from seventeen standpoints expressing seventeen conflicting opinions of Booth's worth.[11] Their significance, he claimed, was that "Outside of our right-little, tight-little isle there is no dramatic art worth mentioning." The aging Charles Reade, outraged by the critics' insular condescension toward Booth, denounced them with a cantankerous shout: "The London press is an ass!"[12] The press was not, in fact, so unanimously chauvinistic or hostile as these overstatements suggest; but it was clear to Booth that at best he was being damned with faint praise.

[10] Booth ought to have remembered the hostility Charles Fechter aroused in 1870 when he played Hamlet in New York in competition with Booth. Irving was much more tactful when he visited America: he did not play Hamlet at all in his first season, and did not lead off with it in his second.

[11] Arthur Warren, "Reminiscences of a Scribe," Boston *Home Journal*, October 20, 1888.

[12] As reported by E. H. House, "Edwin Booth in London," *Century*, LV (December, 1897), 271.

Poor Clement Scott of the *Daily Telegraph*,[13] whom everybody read and whom everybody took to be Henry Irving's tied critic (Scott was to Irving more or less what Winter was to Booth), was reduced to near idiocy by the pressures of the situation. He disliked Booth's Hamlet intensely and wanted to strike it down; at the same time he knew it was his business to be polite to strangers. From sentence to sentence in his first notice he wobbled rudderlessly from reluctant half-compliments to outright condemnation. "We may have our opinions," he began darkly, and then, flaunting his sense of fair play—"but we are not so bigoted as to taint them with prejudice." On the positive side, he reported that the audience applauded generously and called Booth before the curtain many times with repeated cheers. Booth's "clear and measured delivery" of the long speeches "called down extravagant enthusiasm." Booth seized the attention of the audience and never let them go. There was not in his Hamlet "one grain or trace of unworthy trifling or vulgarity." The audience will look forward eagerly to his future impersonations. That was about all that Scott could squeeze out, drop by drop, in the way of praise. The rest of his message is unmistakably clear. Booth's performance is entirely wrong. What we want on the stage nowadays is something other than a mere reading of the part. Booth's Hamlet is only an "actor's Hamlet," built upon old-school methods, forcing our attention upon the performer rather than the role. "The days of the old classical school are dead and buried," as everyone knows, yet Booth in his tangled black hair and dingy costume looks as if he has just "stepped out of some old theatrical print in the days of elocution and before the era of real and natural acting." Booth is cold and classical to a fault, intellectual, rhetorical, neat. He lacks sympathy. The Play scene was "singularly cold"; the scene with his mother "failed in effect"; although the Graveyard scene "interested the audience at a late hour," the closing scene, "robbed of all poetic significance," was "commonplace." As the play proceeds, "the naturally ideal Hamlet seems omitted from the program."

In the long run, Booth worked his way out of the critical box. His Richelieu and Lear, when he got around to offering them, were praised warmly on every hand, and gradually the Londoners came to appreciate his remarkable lucidity of speech—an element of the art which Henry Irving was not much interested in and which,

[13] London *Daily Telegraph*, November 8, 1880.

indeed, avant-garde actors of many generations have bypassed as insignificant, but which always gratifies audiences when it reappears. In May of 1881, Irving paid Booth the high honor of taking him into the Lyceum, where for six weeks the two stars alternated in Iago and Othello. In June Booth took his dying wife home. With the Lyceum engagement he had won his laurels, and his English reputation as an acceptable tragedian, if not as a Hamlet, was set.

The English Provinces, 1882

When he returned to England two years later for a brief stand in London and a tour of fifteen provincial cities, his "old-school" affinities were simply taken for granted, and within that context he was accepted, especially in the provinces, as a master. "He is a cultured artist," said the Liverpool *Courier* (December 4, 1882); "a tragedian of whom America may well be proud." His stage portraits are "intellectual and not merely muscular"; he is faithful to the text, free from staginess, rant, and point-making, and strong in passion where passion is called for. The Dundee *Advertiser* (October 8, 1882) thought his Hamlet "infinitely" superior to his Richelieu, and although quiet, by no means tame: "for there was such an admirable judgment governing the utterances and such a true appreciation of the poetic meaning of the text that silent enjoyment was the universal feeling." The Birmingham *Daily Post* (December 13, 1882) observed that his Hamlet was attended in such rapt silence that "one might almost have supposed that the audience had seen the drama for the first time." Whereas in 1880 Booth had been condemned for shabby dress and scenery and for failure in his acting to live up to Irvingesque realism, in 1882 these very "faults" were transposed into virtues. "He condescends but little," said the Liverpool *Daily Post* (November 28, 1882) approvingly, "to the modern taste for being surrounded with realistic accessories, or for conspicuously living from moment to moment the life which the personage represented would have lived in real life." An "Occasional Critic" in a Glasgow paper (October 16, 1882), with a covert fling at Henry Irving, remarked that Booth and his kind are superior to the "most recent school" in that they "read very little *into* the characters they play. They act objectively, subjecting themselves to the author."

Booth won his English victories only by persistent and exhaustive application. Even after his stand at the Lyceum (which, by the way, was never repeated), he could never be quite certain that he had taken London. As he wrote Winter on his way home in May of 1883, "I don't care to waste my efforts on Londoners—*fashion* alone secures success there & nothing could make me fashionable; it would be labor lost—I've got all I can possibly get out of the English & am satisfied." [14]

The German Adventure, 1883

To fulfill another old ambition he went to Germany. For many years various German stars had been visiting America, playing sometimes to German-speaking, sometimes to general audiences, and had been lionized; but no American tragedian, with the exception of the expatriate Negro Ira Aldridge, had ever carried American acting to the Continent. Booth had been urged to do so by the German Bogumil Dawison when Dawison was his guest at the Winter Garden in the 1860's. Dawison was dead by now, but Friederich Haase and others continued to assure Booth that Germany would welcome him. Their predictions were, in the main, justified.

From Berlin to Vienna, between January and April of 1883, Booth played in eight cities. His roles were Hamlet, Lear, Othello, and Iago. The performances were bilingual, of course. Booth knew hardly a word of German, and the actors of the local stock companies for the most part had no English, but there was little need for communication. The Germans knew "*Unser Shakespeare*" well, and having been coached in advance by Emanuel Lederer, a bilingual actor who was schooled in Booth's stage business and interpretations, they managed to keep the curious *zweisprachigen Zusammenspiel* going.

Wherever Booth went the houses were sold from orchestra to rafters, and at the end of his tour in Vienna his engagement was extended for several days. The German actors loved him, called him "*Meister*"—greater than Talma, greater than Devrient—and embarrassed him with hand-kissings and continental embraces. At Leipzig one of the leading actors, Max Grube, arguing that macaronic Shakespeare would be inartistic, declined in advance to play Iago to Booth's Othello; but as he watched Booth's opening per-

[14] Booth to William Winter, Paris, May 1, 1883. The Folger Shakespeare Library, Y.c. 215 (441).

formance of Hamlet he was so astounded by its power and beauty that after a sleepless night he hurried round to his director to submit his *pater peccavi* and reclaim the "joy and honor" of supporting Booth.[15] It was the custom of the German companies to present distinguished guests with gold or silver crowns of laurel leaves, each leaf inscribed with the name of an actor, and Booth accumulated several of these.

The critical response was mixed. In the more internationally minded northern cities, Berlin and Hamburg, where the tour began, many of the reviews were little more than celebrations. Two of the most eminent German Shakespeare scholars, Professors Karl Friederich Werder and Friederich Leo, were known to have put their blessings on Booth's visit, and the crown prince and his English-born princess attended his performances, so that respect was the order of the day. As Booth moved into the provinces, however, and finally to Vienna, the reports sharpened. Some thought the English language itself positively ugly, objecting especially to the non-German lisping sounds (*lispeln*) and the guttural noises (*gurgeln*). A Bremen critic was offended by the "*Mischmasch*" of the two languages spoken together.[16] Hugo Wittmann of Vienna thought that the art of the theatre had never been brought so low as by this mixture of tongues in which the performers took cues from each other like mechanical dolls.[17] In the wake of *King Lear* in Vienna, a cartoon appeared which showed two fat ladies watching Booth tear his hair in anguish. One of them asks, "What is the old man crying about?" and the other answers, "No wonder he's crying; he can't understand a word his own flesh and blood says to him."[18] In various quarters the venture was dismissed as a sort of publicity stunt—such hard words were invoked as "*Barnum und Humbug.*" One Viennese writer who apparently knew no English was exasperated at those who pretended to know it. "*Ach ja, das Englisch, ach ja, das Englisch,*" he exclaimed, "that is the only way to interpret Shakespeare—but one needs to understand it first."[19]

Booth's own limitations came under fire. In German eyes he lacked the physical stature, in comparison with Tommaso Salvini,

[15] Max Grube, *Am Hofe der Kunst* (Leipzig, 1918), pp. 28-31.

[16] *Bremer Nachrichten*, February 26, 1883.

[17] Vienna *Neue Freie Presse*, April 4, 1883.

[18] Vienna letter to the London *Daily News*, reprinted in the New York *Times*, April 30, 1883.

[19] *Illustrirtes Wiener Extrablatt*, April 1, 1883.

Ernesto Rossi, and many German actors, to qualify as a tragedian. His voice was held to be inadequate—small, weak, and aging—and he indulged in queer vocal mannerisms: effeminate vibrato, extreme prolongation of vowel sounds (like a locomotive whistle, somebody said), shrieking, sobbing, speaking in the throat, growling like a wild beast. He lapsed into monotonous "*Singsang*," or into the tedious intonations of a preacher haranguing a "*nordamerikanischen Campmeeting*."[20] He was far too restless and busy for German taste, forever rising and sitting and roving about among the furniture; forever manipulating sword and dagger, rather in the manner of a juggler, some said, than a tragic actor. He made too many gestures and he depended too much upon literally illustrative fingerplay.

These are all technical and surface objections, some of them trivial, some ignorant, some obviously spiteful. The brilliant young Berlin critic, Otto Brahm, acutely defined Booth's more fundamental limitation.[21] Brahm genuinely loved to watch Booth, and declared at the end of the Berlin run that "the memory of this distinguished guest, to whom we are indebted for such stimulating and pleasurable evenings, will surely for all theatre lovers in this city be long-lasting." But he cut to the center of what seemed to him the softness of Booth's playing. Booth stirs us in many a moment of moving pathos, Brahm thought, but he never sweeps us off our feet with tragic passion. He is incapable, for instance, of expressing overpowering anger. Shakespeare's Lear is "a choleric man, he has too much blood—and Booth has too little." Booth is always gentlemanly, princely, even kingly, as the role demands (so much so that even his Iago becomes a prince in disguise); but pity (*Mitleid*), not tragic terror, is the strongest emotion he arouses: "Profound sympathy is what his Lear, his Othello inspire in me; poor, poor Othello, poor miserable Lear, I want to call out to him—how your fate touches me, what deep compassion it wakes in me." In Brahm's view, though he was too gracious to put it bluntly, Booth's appeal was mainly sentimental. As for Booth's Hamlet, Brahm found in it countless brilliant and affecting moments of actorship, but no compelling tragic effect. This Hamlet was, as Rosencrantz says, "*Ganz wie ein Weltmann*," every inch a prince—a man of exquisite manners, charm, wit, emotional vitality, piety; but to Brahm he

[20] Bremen *Courier*, February 27, 1883.
[21] Berlin *Vossische Zeitung*, February 8, 1883.

conveyed nothing that bespoke tragic burden, tragic destiny. "I read in the program that Mr. Booth is a 'tragedian,' but much as I admire his splendid art, it is precisely this that I am not convinced of."

Booth knew very little or nothing of what the German critics said, nor would he have cared anyway, for by this time of life he had little use for "crickets" in any language. As he had written to a friend before going abroad, "My sole ambition now (so far as Europe is concerned) is to obtain the German endorsement," and midway in the tour he referred to it as "the most important engagement of my life."[22] The full houses, the adulation of the actors, the "silver wreaths . . . flowers, laurels, and ribbons galore," and the excitement of adventure and accomplishment satisfied him completely. He always looked back upon his German expedition as the climax of his career.

The Irving Competition, 1883-84

When Booth returned to the American stage in the fall of 1883, he was just turning fifty. Prematurely and rather swiftly he was feeling and looking old. His hair was graying, his stomach rebelled against food, he was easily exhausted. The last year abroad had wearied him more than he knew. He was worried about money, for the English and German tours had cost him more than they brought in. Especially he was worried about his daughter Edwina, who was in a state of depression after her marriage plans had gone awry. Her suitor, young Downing Vaux, had suffered a mental collapse, and the engagement was perforce broken off. Booth, who had so lately been freed from the care of a lunatic wife, could be grateful that Edwina had been saved from a similar trial, but that did not mend her present grief.

It was a bad time professionally too. Henry Irving chose this season to bring to America half a dozen of his splendid Lyceum productions, and wherever Irving went the crowds and the reviewers followed. Booth was embarrassed. He would have liked to reciprocate Irving's Lyceum hospitality, but with no theatre of his own (even the theatre which bore his name had ceased to exist), he could not. He could not even act in the same cities where Irving was acting, for that would look as if he were competing. For decency's sake he dared not appear to rival Irving, but, worse still,

[22] Booth to Mary Booth, New York, May 25, 1882; and to David Anderson, Hamburg, February 18, 1883. See Grossmann, pp. 230, 244.

had he chosen to rival him he would have been out-rivaled at the box office.

Every newspaper reminded him of that sorry fact, for the more the critics praised the Irving ensemble, the stronger the insinuation grew that Booth was at fault for not having provided as much for America. The king of the American theatre was reduced to an itinerant beggar, skulking about the fringes of his kingdom. While Irving played in New York, Booth kept to Boston. When Irving moved to Boston, Booth slipped into New York. Defeated and doom-eager, he fell in with incompetent managements. In Boston, at the Globe, he acted with what the *Gazette* (December 2, 1883) called "one of the worst organizations for the playing of tragedy that we have had here in many years." At the Star in New York things were not much better, and the *Life* critic (January 3, 1884) was outraged that Booth let his plays be "merely pitchforked upon the stage." He even acted badly. His Hamlet, said the *Spirit of the Times* (December 22, 1883), "shambled about the stage ungracefully; it was indistinct in its elocution; it was absurd in most of its business. . . . Our unprejudiced judgment of the play, on Monday, was that the King had the best of it and was fully justified in trying to put such a Hamlet out of the way." This reviewer could make no sense of Booth's behavior, declaring that he "can act a hundred times better; we have seen him act a hundred times better." He need not "rally around the American flag" in the face of the Irving opposition, but he ought "not to disgrace the Danish flag"; and if he hears his work unfavorably compared with Irving's he ought not to sulk.

Altogether it was a wretched, discouraging season. Booth's temper at the end of it is reflected in a letter he wrote to a young friend to dissuade him from joining the profession. He said in part:

> Had nature fitted me for any other calling I should never have chosen the stage; were I able to employ my thoughts and labor in any other field I would gladly turn my back on the theatre forever. An art whose professors and followers should be of the very highest culture is the mere makeshift of every speculator and boor that can hire a theatre or get hold of some sensational rubbish to gull the public. I am not very much in love with my calling as it now is (and, I fear, will ever be); therefore you see how loath I am to encourage any to adopt it.[23]

[23] Booth to an unknown correspondent, July 27, 1884. Published in the New York *Herald*, June 7, 1893.

With the Boston Museum Company, 1884-86

By the autumn of 1884 he seems to have shaken off this black humor, accepted the inevitable, and readied himself for a fresh beginning. He would give up carpetbagging. He bought a pretty house on Chestnut Street in Boston, settled into it with Edwina, and engaged himself for the season with R. M. Field, the manager of the Boston Museum. This was a comfortable move, not an ambitious one; it might even be regarded as a voluntary retreat from status. For the Museum was a local theatre, a family theatre, and above all a comedy theatre, its actors unaccustomed to the buskin. Yet these actors were a *company*, not a scratch gathering of wandering nobodies and rising stars competing with falling stars—a company, moreover, with a forty-year tradition of responsibility and inner harmony. Field would mount Booth's plays with decent care; the actors would support him with devotion if not genius, and Booth would take the company with him when he went to New York and on the road. The arrangement lasted through two seasons.

In this congenial atmosphere, warmed by the praise of the Boston critics, who were gratified by the alliance of the great actor with the company which was Boston's own, Booth's acting flowered again. His Hamlet, with which he opened, was praised enthusiastically, and the *Globe* (November 18, 1884) hailed it as the beginning of "a renaissance of tragedy—a revival of Shakespeare in a way that bids fair to make him even more dear to every man who wants to see the drama take the place among us it deserves." When Irving brought his Lyceum company for a second American visit, Booth did not this time appear to be skulking. When he moved the ensemble to New York in mid-season, clearing the way for Irving's move to Boston, it looked less like flight and more like sensible strategy.

When Irving chose during this season to exhibit his long-awaited Hamlet, the critical response broke out exactly as Booth could have wished it. His friend William Winter diplomatically accorded Irving's Hamlet the golden compliments which were appropriate to the art of a distinguished visitor. That nicely squared the matter of protocol. The rascally Nym Crinkle expectedly *over*-praised Irving's Hamlet as a thing of "flesh and blood," and went out of his way to ridicule Booth's Hamlet as one whose sole idea is to "look as pretty and feel as bad as he can." [24] The average New York opinion, fairly represented by the critic of the *Herald* (November 28, 1884), found Irving to be "unnecessarily sombre," "melodramatic, grim and weird"; he was monotonous in soliloquies, vitriolic with Ophelia, moody and morose with the Players; his Hamlet would never be popular in America, and he would do well to drop it from his American repertory. Booth could rest comfortably in the knowledge that Winter had satisfied the amenities and that by majority opinion his own Hamlet was master of the field.

Booth's Older Hamlet: What It Meant to Hamlin Garland

Meanwhile in Boston an obscure and impoverished youth named Hamlin Garland had been rifling his food budget for what it cost him every night to attend Booth's performance. At the age of twenty-four, Garland had come east from the Dakota plains to pursue truth, literature, and culture at the intellectual center of America. Garland could never become a proper Bostonian. He was neither an esthete nor a reclusive scholar, but a doughty young frontiersman, progressive and utilitarian, interested in art for its practical usefulness, determined to get at its secrets and fix them according to modern scientific principles. He studied Darwin's *Expression in Man and Animals*, Helmholtz on the physics of sound, and the evolutionary philosophy of Herbert Spencer, and he read Shakespeare and the poets in the light of these modern doctrines.

His preferences led him from literature as the written word to literature as the spoken word, and by 1885 he was "teaching literature" and bore the title of "Professor" at Moses True Brown's Boston School of Oratory. The Boston Museum, whenever Booth played there, had been, so to speak, Garland's graduate school and laboratory. He worked up a series of lectures on "Edwin Booth as a Master of Expression" and on Booth's Hamlet, Macbeth, and Iago, which he delivered in 1885 at the Wentworth Club in Boston, at Tufts College, and perhaps elsewhere. He sent his lectures to Booth for comment and correction, and got back friendly if not deeply committed approval. As late as 1903 he would still be de-

[24] In the *World*, as quoted by Laurence Irving in *Henry Irving* (New York, 1952), p. 446.

livering them at the University of Chicago.[25] The promise he made from time to time that the lectures would appear in book form was never fulfilled, but to the end of his days he talked and wrote about Booth's acting as the most profound educative experience he had ever known.

Garland's response to Booth in the 1880's reminds us of Charles Clarke's response in 1870; and when Garland recalls the effect upon him of "that magic velvet voice" ("neither time nor space nor matter existed for me—I was in an ecstasy of attention"), it might almost be the young Clarke speaking. Like Clarke he studied Booth with feverish devotion:

> What an education that was! With reckless disregard of the expenditure I paid my thirty-five cents and stood night after night in the semi-dark of my position taking no account of aching limbs. I was only a brain. My mind was at once a photographic plate and a phonographic film. Nothing escaped me. The grace, the majesty of Booth's movements, the velvet smoothness of his voice, the beauty and precision of his speech were precious revelations to me. Each night I staggered down the stairs, my limbs benumbed, my mind in a tumult, and found my way back home across the Common to my den like a sleepwalker, so profoundly stirred that nothing physical mattered.[26]

That was Clarke's experience all over again; and like Clarke, too, Garland jotted notations of Booth's gestures, inflections, and emphases in a notebook—the depository of facts from which he developed his lectures.

Garland's image of Booth's Hamlet is significantly different from Clarke's.[27] The difference, we may assume, does not depend much upon the eye of the beholder, for the two witnesses closely resembled each other in taste and temperament—Clarke a young man with a literary flair whom chance carried off to a life of agriculture and business on the frontier; Garland a young frontiersman who turned to a career in practical literature; both of them out-

[25] The Chicago lectures were reported at length by James O'Donnell Bennett in the Chicago *Record-Herald*, August 16, 1903.

[26] Hamlin Garland, *Roadside Meetings* (New York, 1930), p. 12. Garland mentioned Booth often in his autobiographical writings. See *Roadside Meetings*, pp. 48-53, 88-89, and *A Son of the Middle Border* (New York, 1921), pp. 264-267, 329-331.

[27] Garland's opinions of Booth's Hamlet are cited and quoted, with the permission of the Garland heirs, from the typescript of his lecture-essay, now filed in the Garland Papers at the Library of the University of Southern California.

siders to the theatrical profession, and both experiencing Booth's Hamlet above all as a moral and spiritual awakening. What their reports reveal is the change between the Hamlet Booth projected in his middle thirties and the Hamlet of his fifties. Clarke saw a Hamlet still elastic with youth and promise, and what impressed him most was the pathos of Hamlet's weak will, the baffled and frustrated collapse of this beautiful young man caught in circumstances too terrible for his powers to resolve. Garland saw a gray-haired Hamlet—settled in wisdom, strong and purposeful, far less pathetic and far more a subject for tragic admiration.

He is "the passive suffering center," says Garland, "the good man enduring." The very qualities of the characters who surround him—the King's treachery, the Queen's fickleness, Ophelia's childlish innocence, Osric's butterfly existence, the sly jesting of the courtiers—set off in relief Hamlet's virtues and mature strength: "The senile jests of Polonius raise but a faint and hollow laugh, while the central figure of all, the Prince, with white, brooding, intent face hears death's monotone beneath the swirl of pipe and tap of drum." It is no boyish, capricious Hamlet, says Garland (perhaps silently contrasting him to the notorious twenty-year-old Hamlet of the English actor Wilson Barrett, who pranced about American stages in the 1880's), but "a sombre philosopher, a student of life and a man burdened with doubt."

From the opening Court scene Garland recalls the rigid restraint on Booth's face and his hardened voice—"his brows on level, his lips motionless, his eyes introspective." After receiving the frightful message of the Ghost, Hamlet fixes upon the single idea of vengeance as if caught in a monomania; he becomes self-contained, secretive, master of himself and all about him. His antic disposition is by no means madness, although it first emerges in a swirl of conflicting emotions: it is a weapon of control. "Henceforth no smile of joy will light his face. He will laugh only in the convulsions of hysterical excitement. His voice will be low, deep and musical, with but few inflections, its tones denoting that the same monstrous thought comes again and again. . . . He will brood more than plan, and plan more than execute." In the great soliloquy after the scene with the Players ("Now I am alone") he is "a man fully roused, a resolute, rapid and crafty man. His voice is firm and decisive. . . . His eye is bright, his face stern and commanding, and for the moment he seems a healthy, well-poised man of action."

The scene with Ophelia meant to Garland beyond an instant's doubt that Hamlet is passionately in love with Ophelia. The tragedy of it is that Hamlet must break from her; he cannot keep his promises to her, cannot drag her with him to death and ruin. He must save her. Therefore, half-crazed with self-torture but inexorable in purpose, he slanders her and reviles all womankind. His manifest intention is, at whatever cost to himself, to smother her love for him in disgust.

And so on to the end of the play, Garland finds Booth's Hamlet strong-minded and steadfast, driving relentlessly along his chosen path toward vengeance and certain doom. There are moments of relaxation, of course—his Advice to the Players; his affectionate eulogy of Horatio, the "man that is not passion's slave"; the almost merry interview with Osric; the "level" lines, "If it be now, 'tis not to come," which were Booth's favorites—yet all these in their passing serve only to accentuate the enveloping tragic blackness. Remembering the Graveyard scene, the Gravedigger's rude jests, Hamlet's question of how long will a man lie i' the earth ere he rot, and his address to the skull of Yorick, Garland unabashedly sets down a vision of eternity: "As I listened to him, the roar of the city's traffic died in silence, the brick walls were as mist, warring kingdoms seemed but the shadows cast by a passing cloud, and the whole mighty stream of hurrying humanity became like the passing of a shadowy whispering river rushing endlessly into night. I lost sight of Booth the player. The eternal thought which Hamlet voiced seemed the only reality before me."

How much of Garland's reporting as we have it reflects his immediate response to Booth's performance, and how much it owes to meditation feeding upon itself years after the event we cannot say. It is, however, the vividest, most meaningful account that comes to us of the Hamlet of Booth's later years, and I think we are not far misled if we accept it as evidence of the extraordinary authority with which Booth finally invested the part. It is confirmed here and there by certain later reviewers, when we can find those rare ones who were able to look upon the performance unjaded by too frequent exposure.

The Booth-Barrett Partnership: The National Tour of 1886-87

In the fall of 1886 Booth put himself under the management of Lawrence Barrett, and began that series of national tours, three of them transcontinental, which brought his career to its close. During the first of these, carrying a repertory of ten plays, he visited nearly sixty cities and played Hamlet nearly a hundred times. The schedule was almost more strenuous than Booth could endure. Indigestion troubled him constantly and he was subject to spells of dizziness. At Minneapolis in September he caught a severe cold, which lingered through the next month with "incessant headaches, bone-aches, & a cough"; in New York in November this developed into pneumonia and the theatre was dark for ten days. From Memphis in February he complained to Barrett of the horrors of night travel:

> The trip here was to me a fearful one! Not a wink of sleep, & all the d--nable "movement cures" . . . hell-conceived, were applied to me for ten or twelve hours; I thought I would go mad &, seriously, I believe such experience would soon—if oft repeated—put me in an asylum—or a box; then to act with nerves prostrated, a raging headache and "sick to me stummic"! Great *gord!* . . . For God's sake let us avoid night travel next season. Dost thou not suspect mine years—I'm a shaky fellow, go to! [28]

On March 7, 1887, he arrived for a long pleasant stay in San Francisco.

The triumph of Booth's San Francisco opening in *Hamlet* has been affectionately celebrated by Katherine Goodale (then the actress Kitty Molony) in *Behind the Scenes with Edwin Booth.* She timed the ovation when the audience first caught sight of Booth (it was five minutes); she counted the calls at act and scene endings (over forty-four when she stopped counting); she describes the bedlam which broke loose in the auditorium at the end of the play, with ladies climbing upon their seats and screaming for Booth! Booth! She tells of her own gratified exhaustion after the "Jove's lightning bolts" of Booth's performance ceased to fly.[29]

The spirit, if not the statistics, of Kitty Molony's reporting is faithful to the event. When it comes to the hard facts of what

[28] Booth to Lawrence Barrett, Memphis, February 11, 1887. The Harvard Theatre Collection.

[29] See Goodale, pp. 176-183. For her account of Booth and the wig, see pp. 154-175.

really happened, however, she is not quite to be trusted. Through several chapters, for instance, she builds up the exciting behind-the-scenes story of how she alone, at the instance of Mr. Barrett and Mr. Chase the manager, persuaded Mr. Booth at last (and on that night for the first time) to conceal his gray hair under a dark brown wig which faithfully re-created the hair style of his younger days. Now it is certainly true that for a month or longer Barrett had been urging Booth to make this concession to his audiences, and sometime later in the season Booth apparently submitted. But not on the opening night in San Francisco. The *Chronicle* of March 8 mentioned that Booth's aging was undisguised by makeup. The *Examiner* said that "silver streaks his hair, and shows his years are waning . . . and even the silver in his hair did not induce him to wear a wig." The *Argonaut* of March 12 spoke of the "glint of gray in his locks," and lamented that he had had his hair cut short.

The San Franciscans did not complain, however. "A feeling of veneration took hold of the audience," said the *Examiner*. Many there present had not been born when Booth first played Hamlet, but all their lives they had heard of him, and since he had last played there he had proved himself (to patriotic eyes) the greatest Hamlet in the world. "How long were they to enjoy his genius? When again? These were thoughts which added pathos to the evening."

It occurred to no one on this occasion to belittle Booth by measuring him against others. "When we saw him before," said the *Chronicle*, "we were still in the old school. . . . Like a breath of air from some intellectual dramatic world comes Edwin Booth in Hamlet, comes Edwin Booth in anything." He brings neither the boisterous elocution of the so-called "legitimate," nor the "namby-pamby crushed hat colloquial of the modern hero." He has long since outlived the enthusiasm of youth which leads to extravagances, and with the years he has "gradually polished and finished his conception of the part and reduced his delivery of it to absolutely as natural a point as Shakespeare can ever be brought."

You cannot see the slightest sign of claptrap in Booth; he speaks no lines to get the applause of the unthinking. . . . Those have always been his characteristics, of course, but now one appreciates the perfect command of delivery, the knowledge of the meaning and value of every line, the wonderfully graceful emphasis which never misses its syllable or its word. Booth does not now pay so much attention to the outward appearances. In Hamlet he shows his age, an age which contrasts rather sharply with the surrounding figures, but it is questionable if he could by make-up conceal his years, and they have only matured his intellectual vigor, given to him a more certain and notable control over his dramatic power, which now has become an instrument upon which he plays with an ease that is fascinating of itself. Still he seems to grow older as the piece progresses, his face seems to carry with it more and more with every scene the troubles he is enduring, and Hamlet at the close is a man to whom even the execution of revenge does not bring back the joy of life. It is now a play, the end of which is naturally a complete tragedy.

The ebullient reviewer for the *Argonaut*, "Betsy B.," observed that Booth had given body to a book-wraith that had been waiting for him for almost three hundred years: "And therefore it is that Hamlet was born with Edwin Booth, and that Hamlet will die with Edwin Booth."

The Last Seasons

There is little more to add. In 1887-88 and 1888-89 Barrett accompanied him on national tours. They played *Hamlet* occasionally, although *Julius Caesar* and *Othello* were better suited to show off the double stars. On May 21, 1888, there occurred at the Metropolitan Opera House one of the most remarkable events in the American stage history of *Hamlet*—a benefit performance for the lately retired manager Lester Wallack in which every role was taken by a well-known actor or a famous star. Booth played Hamlet, of course, and Barrett the Ghost. The King was Frank Mayo, the Queen Gertrude Kellogg, Polonius John Gilbert, the Gravediggers Joseph Jefferson and W. J. Florence. The Ophelia was Helena Modjeska, whose inspired acting is said to have roused Booth from an indifferent performance to an impassioned one. One hundred and thirty actors and actresses, dozens of them eminent in the profession, crowded the stage as extras. Walter Damrosch conducted the orchestra.

Presumably as a result of this encounter with Modjeska, Booth partnered with her for the 1889-90 season. Carrying a program in which Modjeska starred in her own vehicles and supported Booth in his, they toured the eastern half of the country. By now Booth's energies had run so low that, as Otis Skinner tells us, his Hamlet was at times merely mechanical: "It was as if he allowed the part to play itself."[30] Or, as the reviewer for the Boston *Traveller* (Jan-

[30] Otis Skinner, *Footlights and Spotlights* (Indianapolis, 1924), p. 99.

uary 28, 1890) explained in kindly terms: "The great actor lacks the old-time identification with the part, and seems to go through the piece lovingly and sympathetically and yet regretfully, as if he were simply allowing his imagination the pleasure of reliving old scenes and incidents." Yet Modjeska was incomparably the finest Ophelia he had ever had, and her beauty of person and emotional warmth brought to portions of the play illuminations which Booth's audiences had never known. Because of "her length and delicacy of limb, her clear-cut intellectuality, and her sinuous grace," Nym Crinkle adoringly compared her to Thorvaldsen's "Venus."[31] If to some critics her personality was too imposing for the faint Ophelia they were accustomed to, if to some she over-embroidered the mad scenes with histrionic virtuosity, yet the pathos of her responses in the Nunnery scene and her rising terror throughout the Play scene were sparks which could sometimes set even Booth's wearying Hamlet on fire.

The story dwindles out sadly at a matinee at the Brooklyn Academy of Music in the spring of 1891. In late March of that year Lawrence Barrett, who was not only Booth's manager but his dearest colleague and companion, suddenly died; and two weeks afterward, on April 4, Booth went over to Brooklyn to play his last Hamlet, his last appearance on any stage. There was no fanfare to announce the event, but rumor got about that this was the end, and over three thousand persons crowded the auditorium. It was a sorry occasion. The faithful William Winter was there to memorialize it in a last violet-colored notice. Others reported it less amiably but more truly —the shabby costumes and mismatched scenery, the butchered text, the listless, inept supporting company, the wretched stage management, and Booth's own inadequacy. "Mr. Booth spoke so faintly that much of his speech was inaudible even in the front of the house," said the reviewer for the Brooklyn *Eagle*, "and several times he heightened the difficulty by delivering long speeches in a low tone with his back to the audience." His farewell speech was murmured so softly that few knew what he had said.

[31] New York *Dramatic Mirror*, November 9, 1889.

INDEX

Adams, Edwin, 66
Adams, John Cranford, 112
Adelson, Warren, 25n, 185n
Agassiz, Louis, 12
Aldrich, Thomas Bailey, 93, 120n
Aldridge, Ira, 296
Anderson, David C. (Polonius), 84, 86-87, 138n, 299n
Anderson, Mary, 88
Andrews, W. S. (First Gravedigger), 84n, 88
Arendt, Carl, xx
Ayres, Alfred, 288n

Badeau, Adam: letters to Booth, vi, 21-22, 27-29; "Vagabond" essays, 5, 18-21, 27; personal relations with Booth, 5, 21, 28-30; career and personality, 18n; professional assistance to Booth, 18-29; on filial affection in Ghost scenes, 21, 141-142; relations with Mollie Devlin, 29, 31, 33, 34-35; on Booth and spiritualism, 49-50; mentioned, 52, 54, 55n
Baker, Ben, 9, 10
Barrett, Lawrence: as Booth's manager, xx-xxi, 111, 306-307, 308, 309; on Hamlet, xxiii; annotations in Taylor promptbook, 111-112, 130n, 131n, 212n; death, 309; mentioned, 138n, 190n, 285, 291
Barrett, Wilson, 304
Barron, Charles, xxi
Barry, Thomas, 10, 12
Barrymore, John, xv
Bateman, Kate, 66
"Bayard": praises Booth's Hamlet (1864), 53; on Booth's return to the stage (1866), 62
Bell's *Shakespeare*, 203, 223
Belleforest: *Histoires tragiques*, 153n
Bennet, James O'Donnell, 303n
Bennett, James Gordon, 62
Benson, F. R., 248n
"Betsy B.": praises Booth's Hamlet (1887), 308
Betterton, Thomas, 63, 71, 89
Bierstadt, Albert, xxv, 26, 54
Boaden, James, 22
Bodenstedt, Friederich, 189n
Booth, Edwin:
Career: in California (1852-56), 3-9; death of father, 4; first performs Hamlet (1853), 4-7; ap-

prenticeship in lesser roles, 4; returns to the East (1856), 9-10; in Boston (1857), 10-13; in New York (1857), 16-17; relations with Adam Badeau, 18-30, 34-35, 49-50; friendship with artists, 25-26, 52, 54; relations with Mollie Devlin, 30-36; in Boston and New York (1860-61), 37-43; in London (1861-62), 43-47; in Boston and New York (1862-63), 47-50; death of Mollie Devlin Booth, 48-50; in New York (1863-64), 51-53; manages Walnut Street Theatre, 53-54; manages Winter Garden Theatre (1864-65), 53-62; the Hundred Nights *Hamlet*, 54-62, 101, 112; the Booth-Hinton editions, 55-56; in Boston (1865), 61; assassination of President Lincoln, 62; return to the Winter Garden (1866), 62; Winter Garden fire (1867), 65; Booth's Theatre (1869), 65-66; second marriage, 66; the 1870 *Hamlet*, 67-98, 101-114, 115-281; loss of Booth's Theatre, 285; maimed in carriage accident, 286; Daly engagement (1875), 286; national tour (1876), 290-291; the Booth-Winter Prompt-Book editions, 291-292; in London (1880-81), 292-295; death of second wife, 293, 295; Lyceum engagement (1881), 295; in the English provinces (1882), 295-296; in Germany (1883), 296-299; doldrum season (1883-84), 299-300; Boston Museum engagement (1884-86), 301-302; national tour (1886-87), 306-308; last tours, 308-309; the Wallack benefit *Hamlet* (1888), 308; the Modjeska season (1889-90), 308-309; death of Barrett, 309; the last Hamlet, 309

Character and personality: response to personal disaster, xiv, 4, 48-50, 62, 65, 285-286, 301, 304; moral standards, xv, xviii-xix, 32, 72; gentlemanliness, xix-xx; generosity to fellow actors, xx-xxi, 42, 54, 67, 86; intellectual limitations, xxiv, 46-47, 90-93, 287-290; conservative attitude toward the arts, xxiv-xxv; beauty of person, xxv-xxvi; affection for father, 3-6; belief in the supernatural, 5, 49-50; moral lapses, 8, 9, 27-28, 48; ambition, 9-10, 28, 43-44, 52, 53-54, 285, 292-293, 296, 299

General acting style: appearance, xxvi, 13, 42, 59, 63, 90, 297-298, 303-304; voice, xxvi, 13, 16, 42, 90, 294-295, 298, 303-304; power, xxvii, 50, 59, 90, 93, 304-305, 307-308; influence of father, 3-6, 11, 16, 40, 48; apprenticeship in ephemeral roles, 4, 8; carelessness of early working methods, 8; decision to become a star, 9-10; coarseness of early style, 11-13, 19-20; repertory of roles, 11, 39-40, 52-53, 64; movement and gesture, 13, 16, 59, 63, 286, 298, 303; the Forrest method, 13-15, 24, 41, 51; imputed effeteness, 15, 41, 92-93, 291, 303; influence of Adam Badeau, 18-28; romanticism, 19; idealism vs. realism, 20-21, 31-32, 46, 94; study of actors of the past, 20-22; the lesson of Consuelo, 24; influence of art and artists, 25-26, 43, 52, 54; influence of Mollie Devlin, 30-36, 49-50, 54; the "conversational, colloquial" style, 32, 37-38, 43; esthetics of Victor Cousin, 33-34; addiction to flashy histrionics, 39-40, 42, 51-52, 63, 287-288, 298; rejection of the Fechter method, 44-47; avoidance of point-making, 48; feminine qualities, 63-64; failure in youthful romantic roles, 64; imputed false readings, 257n, 287-288; imputed lack of psychological understanding, 289-290; imputed lack of tragic stature, 298; decline of powers, 299-300, 306, 308, 309

Hamlet: idealized by audience and critics, xiii, xv-xvi, 6-7, 60-61, 69-70, 89, 93-95, 96, 292, 307-308; identification of actor and role, xiii-xv, 3, 5-6, 26, 38, 42-43, 60, 63, 69, 70, 90, 96; intelligence (intellectuality) and sanity, xiv, xxii-xxiii, xxvii, 11, 24, 73, 91-92, 96-97, 136, 162n, 179, 180, 187-188, 196-197, 202, 215-217, 221, 237, 243, 263-264, 272, 280, 289-290, 304-305; weakness of will, xiv, 24, 96-97, 159, 180, 215-217, 221, 268, 280, 304; steadfastness, xiv-xv, 303-305; acting version, xvi-xix, 37, 55-57, 291-292, *see also* notes on text at end of each scene in Chapter VI *passim;* gentlemanliness and dignity, xix-xx, 7, 12, 15, 42, 60-61, 63, 92, 94-95, 129, 159, 179-180, 193-195, 196-197, 201-202, 215-217, 229, 272, 292, 304-305; attitude toward Ophelia, xxi-xxii, 7, 196-197, 215, 305; emotional power, complexity, and control, xxii, xxvii, 6-7, 49-50, 59, 90-91, 127, 136, 147, 159, 179-180, 195, 196-197, 215-218, 236-238, 243, 264, 272, 297, 303-305; displays of madness, xxii, 179-180, 196-197, 202, 216, 288-289; clarity, xxiii-xxiv, 59, 90-91, 288-289, 294; movement and gesture, xxiv, 13, 42, 51-52, 59, 63, 90, 126, 136, 146, 159, 180, 187, 201-202, 208, 280, 286, 298; beauty of, xxv-xxvi, 12, 13, 15, 36, 42, 59, 60-61, 63, 90, 93-95, 292, 303-305; influence of his father (filial piety), 3-6, 21, 38, 92, 95, 124n, 141-142, 144, 146, 148; first performance, 4, 6-7; naturalness and quietude, 11, 37-38, 42-43, 47-48, 63, 129, 136, 237, 287, 307; comparative failure in early years, 11-13, 16-17, 37-43; acclaimed by Cambridge intellectuals, 12; voice, 12, 13, 16, 21, 37, 63, 92, 144, 180, 187, 222, 229, 268, 288n, 298, 303; facial expression and eyes, 13, 15, 36, 37, 69, 136, 144, 146, 222; imputed effeteness, 15, 80, 91-93, 291, 298-299, 301-302; imputed lack of controlling idea, 15, 80, 91-93, 287-289; ideas of Hazlitt, 22-23; ideas of Goethe, 23, 36; influence of artists, 25-26, 43-44, 52, 54; opinions of Mollie Devlin, 36; faults in performance, 42, 46-47, 51-52, 61, 81-82, 90, 91-93, 151-152, 222, 237-238, 257n, 276n, 278n, 286, 287-289, 294, 297-299, 300, 308-309; comparison to Fechter's Hamlet, 44-47, 97-98; the Hamlet bust, 52; the Hundred Nights *Hamlet* (1864-65), 53-61, 101-102, 279n; scenery, 54-58, 65, 69-70, 71-73, 75-83, 108-109, 115-117, 121-124, 137-138, 140, 147-148, 160-161, 182-185, 195, 202-204, 218-219, 223-224, 240, 244n, 250-252, 265-266, 273-274, 293, 295, 309; the Hamlet medal, 65; at Booth's Theatre (1870), 67-98, 101-281; costume, 73-75, 124-125, 134n, 141, 162n, 186-187, 204, 212, 223n, 253, 266, 294, 295, 307, 309; spirituality, 94, 136, 146, 159, 237, 281; poetic artifice, 97-98; stage management and business, 102-114, 147, 217, 237, 264; Booth's promptbooks and notebooks, 107-109, 109-110, 110-111, 112-113; citations from, *see* footnotes in Chapter VI *passim;* lighting, 115-117, 124, 138, 140, 147, 151, 160, 204, 208n, 221, 224, 231n, 234n, 250-252, 265; music, 115, 120, 124, 127, 141, 169, 172, 202, 204, 240, 259-260, 274, 275, 280; machinery, 116n, 122-124, 137-138, 140, 148, 198,

215, 218, 221, 265, 272; at Daly's Fifth Avenue Theatre (1875), 286; imputed lack of psychological understanding, 288-290; national tour (1876), 290-291; in London (1880-81), 293-295; in the English provinces (1882), 295-296; in Germany (1883), 296-299; declining powers, 299-309; national tours (1886-91), 306-309

Principal critiques: Advertiser (1860), 37-38, (1865), 61; *Atlas* (1870), 251; Badeau, Adam (1857), 18-21; "Bayard" (1863), 53; Brahm, Otto (1883), 298-299; Bunce, O. B. (1870), 142, (1875), 286-290; *Chronicle* (1876), 291, (1887), 307-308; Clarke, Charles (1870), 96-98, 104-107, 115-281; Curtis, George William (1865), 60-61; *Daily News* (1860), 40; Devlin, Mollie (1860), 36; *Dispatch* (1860-61), 40-41; *Evening Post* (1865), 58-59, (1870), xiii, 252; Ewer, F. C. (1853), 6-7; Garland, Hamlin (1880's), 302-305; *Globe* (1870), 82-83; Hurlburt, William (1860), 40, 41, 43; Matthison, Arthur (1870), 71-74, 273; Nym Crinkle (A. C. Wheeler) (1870-93), 14-15, 79-80, 83, 85-87, 91-93, 142, 238-239, 252; "Perdu" (1871), 122-123, 203-204, 265n; *Post* (1862), 47-48; Scott, Clement (1880), 294; "Shakespeare" (1870), 70-71; *Spirit of the Times* (1870), 70, 75-76, (1883), 300; Stedman, E. C. (1866), 63-64; *Sunday Times* (1870), 95-96, 251-252; *Times* (1870), 89-91; *Transcript* (1857), 11, 12; *Traveller* (1857), 12-13; *Tribune* (1860), 42; White, Richard Grant (1870), 80-83, 152; Wilkins, E. G. P. (1860), 43, (1863), 51, (1864), 59; Winter, William (1862), 48, (1863), 51-52, (1870), 85-86, 93-95, (1878), 292; *World* (1870), 72, 76, 238

Booth, John Wilkes, xiv, 9, 62

Booth, Junius Brutus: urges Booth to play Hamlet, 3; Booth's affection for, 4-6, 48; influence on Booth's acting, 5-6, 13, 16, 40; miniature portrait, 5-6, 124; mentioned, 89, 91, 162n

Booth, Junius Brutus, Junior: management in San Francisco, 3n, 4; management of Booth's Theatre, 285; mentioned, 30, 86

Booth, Mary ("Mollie") Devlin: letters to Booth, vi, 5n, 31-35; death, xiv, 48-50, 62; on Booth's father, 5; influence on Booth's morals, 9; portrait, 25; engagement to Booth and retirement from stage, 29, 30-31; on Booth's acting style, 32; on Matilda Heron, 32; on immoral plays, 32; on Victor Cousin, 33-34; on Badeau, 35; book of critiques, 35-36; birth of daughter, 44; influence after death, 50; on theatrical management, 54; mentioned, 23, 37, 64, 81

Booth, Mary Runnion McVicker: book of critiques, 35n; lunacy and death, 62, 293, 294; acting, retirement, and marriage, 66; portrait, 185n; mentioned, 57n, 74

Bosworth, Hallam, 113

Brahm, Otto: analysis of Booth's acting, 298-299

Brennan, T. F. (Second Actor), 84, 88

Brignoli, Pasquale, 28

Bronte, Charlotte, 19

Brooke, Gustavus V., 79, 87, 89

Brougham, John, 68

Brown, Moses True, 302

Bryant, Dan, 68

Buckstone, J. B., 44

Buggles, 120n

Bulwer-Lytton, Edward: popularity of his *Richelieu*, 39; "Talent and Genius," 107; mentioned, xxv. *See also* Plays and Dramatic Characters
Bunce, O. B.: on Booth's delayed first entrance, 124n; on the Ghost scenes, 142; article on Booth's Theatre, 286n; attack on Booth's Hamlet (1875), 286-290
Bundy, Murray, 102-103
Burbage, Richard, 129n
Burton, William, 16

Carlyle, Thomas, 19
Carroll, Pat, 107
Cary, Emma, 26, 59n
Cary, Richard, 43, 48
Castiglione, Baldassare, 34
Cazauran, August R., 93n
Chase, Arthur B., 307
Chilton, R. S., 16-17
Church, Frederick, 19, 26
Churchill, Charles, 20
Clarke, Asia Booth, 3n
Clarke, Charles W.: description of Booth's Hamlet, vi-vii, xxvii, 115-281; definition of Booth's Hamlet, xiv, 24, 96-98; method and style, 102-107; biography, 103-104; compared to Hamlin Garland, 303-304; mentioned, 77, 95, 108, 112, 288n
Clarke, Emma, 104
Clarke, John Sleeper, 53, 54
Coleman, Thomas L., xx
Colman, George, 10. *See also* Plays and Dramatic Characters
Cooper, Thomas Abthorpe, 229n
Cornwall, Barry (Bryan Waller Procter), 22
Couldock, Charles, 87
Cousin, Victor: his esthetics, 33-34, 58, 81
Crashaw, Richard, 190n
Curtis, George William: describes Booth's Hamlet, 60-61; mentioned, 38
Cushman, Charlotte, 20, 38, 79, 87

Daly, Augustin: Booth's engagement with, 286; mentioned, 57
Damrosch, Walter, 308
Darwin, Charles, 302
Davenport, E. L., 19, 79, 87
Davies, Thomas, 22
Davis, Andrew Jackson, 86
Davison, Bogumil, 296
de Bar, Blanche (Ophelia), 84, 86, 139, 244
Decker, Nelson (Guildenstern), 84, 88
Deuel, J. P., 204
Devlin, Mary ("Mollie"). *See* Booth
Devrient, Gustave Emil, 296
Dickens, Charles, 45, 67
Drummond, William (Priest), 84, 88
Dumas, Alexandre, 19, 57n, 291. *See also* Plays and Dramatic Characters
Dumfries, Mr., 4n
Dunphie, Charles, 113
Dyce, Alexander, 120n

Edmonds, Laura, 49
Everett, Edward, 93
Ewer, Ferdinand Cartwright: praises Booth's Richard III and Hamlet (1853), 6-7; mentioned, xxivn, 8, 22

"F.": praises Booth's Hamlet, 12
Falconer, Edmund, 64
Farnie, H. B., 72
Fechter, Charles: as Hamlet (1861), 44-45, 74; as Othello, 44-46; acting method, 44-47; Booth accused of imitating, 48, 92, 146n; production of *Hamlet* (1864), 55n; in New York (1870), 67-68, 293n; attends

Booth's *Hamlet*, 69; attacked by Winter, 95; his Hamlet contrasted to Booth's, 97-98, 222; Booth's objections to his readings, 119n, 134n, 236n, 258n; adopts Booth's business with sword, 146n; mentioned, 58n, 60, 90, 257n, 291
Fenno, A. W. (First Actor), 84, 87
Field, R. M.: Booth's engagement with (1884-86), 301
Fitzgerald, Percy, 287n
Flohr, Henry, 112
Florence, W. J., 308
Ford, John T., 290
Forrest, Edwin: acting style, 13-14, 24; attacked by Stuart, 14; praised by Nym Crinkle, 14; dispraised by Badeau, 20; competes with Booth (1860-61), 38, 39, 40-42; hostility to Booth, 42n; approved by "Shakespeare," 71; mentioned, 6, 10, 47, 52, 53, 79, 87, 89, 91
Fox, George, 68
Furness, Horace Howard, xxv, 143n

Garland, Hamlin: interpretation of Booth's Hamlet, xiv, 302-305
Garrick, David: Booth compared to, 20; terror in Ghost scenes, 21, 142; Davies' *Life*, 22; Booth cites authority of, 135n, 177n; mentioned, xix, 10, 22, 60, 89, 146n
Gentleman, Francis, 223
Gifford, Sanford: "The Coming Storm," 26; mentioned, 54
Gilbert, John, 308
Gluck, Christoph W., *Iphigenia*, 115
Goethe, Johann Wolfgang von: on Hamlet, 23-24, 36; mentioned, 45, 72, 74
Gooch, Walter: Booth's engagement with (1880-81), 292-293
Goodale, Katherine (Kitty Molony): affection for Booth, xx-xxi, 306; her incompetent acting, xxi; on Booth's power, xxvii; on the delayed first entrance, 124n, 287n; on the first night in San Francisco (1887), 306; on the Hamlet wig, 307
Gottschalk, Louis, 19
Grant, Ulysses S., 18n, 30
Grossmann, Edwina Booth: portrait, 25n; birth, 44; on the Hamlet burlesque, 68; on the 1870 promptbook, 107-108; on W. W. Scott's watercolor, 184n; on Hamlet's sanity, 289n; failure of marriage plans, 299; in Boston (1884-86), 301; mentioned, 49
Grube, Max, 296-297
Guizot, François, 71

Haase, Friederich, 296
Hackett, James H., 66
Hamilton, Theodore (Claudius), 84, 85
Hanford, Charles, xx
Hanmer, Thomas, 203
Harrigan, Edward, 79
Hazlitt, William: on Hamlet, 22-23; mentioned, 7, 20, 24
Heenan, John, 68
Heister, George, 65
Helmholtz, Hermann L. F. von, 302
Henderson, John, 155n
Heron, Matilda: realistic acting in sensational plays, xix, 19, 20, 32
Hicks, Thomas, 25, 26n
Hillyard, Henry, 75
Hind, Thomas J. (Rosencrantz), 84, 88
Hinton, Henry L. (Marcellus): editions of Booth's plays, 55-

56, 110, 183, 203, 265n, 291; as actor, 84, 87-88
Hogan, Henry (Francisco), 84, 88
Hollister, G. H., 27
Honaker, Gerald L., 66n
Horace, 40
House, E. H., 293n
Howard, Joe, 93n
Howe, Julia Ward, 12, 64
Hudson, William Henry, 72
Hugo, Victor, xxv, 33, 52, 68
Hurlburt, William: condemns supporting company (1860), 40; praises Booth (1860-61), 41, 43
Hystorie of Hamblet, 153n

Irving, Henry: his staging of the Kings' portraits, 229n; his 200-night Hamlet, 293; invites Booth to act at the Lyceum, 295; first American tour (1883-84), 299-300; second American tour (1884-85), 301-302; mentioned, 44, 50n, 58n, 294

"J. K. K.": reports details of Booth's Hamlet, 145n, 257n
Jackson, A. W., 40
Jameson, Anna B., 72, 151n
Jefferson, Joseph, 66, 285, 308
Johnson, Eastman, 25
Johnson, Samuel, 71
Joyce, Thomas, 204n

Kean, Charles: his production methods a model for Booth, 53, 54, 57, 76; his acting versions, 56, 72; asymmetric scene designs, 78; mentioned, 58n, 60, 89, 229n, 292
Kean, Edmund: Booth compared to, 20, 21; Barry Cornwall's *Life*, 22; and Hazlitt's ideal of Hamlet, 23; tenderness toward Ghost, 142; mentioned, xiii, 60, 229n
Keene, Laura, 8, 9
Kellogg, Gertrude, 308
Kemble, Charles, 76
Kemble, John Philip: Boaden's *Life*, 22; and Hazlitt's ideal of Hamlet, 23; Lawrence's painting, 60; mentioned, xiii, 71, 89, 155n, 164n, 178n
Knight's *Shakespeare*, 254n

Lamb, Charles, 21, 72, 187
Lander, Jean Davenport, 8
Lawrence, Sir Thomas, 60
Lay, Oliver, 124n
Leclercq, Carlotta, 69
Lederer, Emanuel, 296
Leo, Friederich, 297
Leutze, Emanuel, 25, 65
Lewes, George Henry, 46
Lewis, Minard, 75
Lincoln, Abraham, xiv, 39, 62
Lowell, James Russell, 12

"M.": on graveyard scenery, 252
McCloskey, J. J.: tales of Booth's early days, 4n
McCullough, John, 290
McEntee, Jervis, 25, 26n, 54
Maclise, Daniel, 203
Macready, William Charles: influence of, 15, 16, 19; creates Richelieu, 39; production methods, 53; "freaky" Hamlet, 71; asymmetric scene design, 78; mentioned, xviii, 89
McVicker, Mary Runnion. *See* Booth
Maginn, William, 71
Malone, John, xx, 174n
Marlowe, Julia, 88
Marshall, Thomas F., 79
Mason, Edward Tuckerman: record of Booth's stage business, 110, 113; citations of, *see* footnotes in Chapter VI *passim;* record of Modjeska's stage

business, 112, 139-140, 244-247
Massinger, Philip, 10. *See also* Plays and Dramatic Characters
Matthison, Arthur (Bernardo): pamphlet on the 1870 *Hamlet*, 72-74, 148n, 240, 273; as actor, 84, 88. *See also* Plays and Dramatic Characters
Mayo, Frank, 308
Meadows, Kenny, *Shakespeare*, 108, 254n
Meissner, Johannes, 125n
Melville, Herman, 26n
Miller, Dr. Erasmus, 48-49
Miller, Wynne, 248n
Milton, John, 190n
Modjeska, Helena (Ophelia): Mason's record of her stage business, 112, 138n, 139-140, 244-247; as Ophelia (1889-90), 308-309
Mollenhauer, Edward, 73
Molony, Kitty. *See* Goodale
Morant, Fanny (Gertrude), 84, 85, 238
Moray, John, 93n
Morse, Jem, 68
Mounet-Sully, Jean, 155n

Norris, Charles (Osric), 84, 88
Nym Crinkle. *See* Wheeler, A. C.

Odell, G. C. D., 52, 84n
Orcagna, 74, 124

Packard, Frederick, xxvin
Pastor, Tony, 68
Payne, John Howard, 153n, 190n, 285. *See also* Plays and Dramatic Characters
Peake, J. L., 204
Peirce, Benjamin, 12
"Perdu": on scenes and machines in the 1870 *Hamlet*, 122-124, 203-204, 265n
Peters, Charles (First Grave-digger), 84, 88
Pitman, James R.: promptbooks, 111; citations of, *see* footnotes in Chapter VI *passim*
Pitou, Augustus (Horatio), 84, 87
Plays and Dramatic Characters: *The Apostate*, Richard Lalor Sheil (Pescara), 10, 39; *As You Like It*, Shakespeare (Rosalind), 10, 63; *Bertram*, Charles Robert Maturin (Bertram), 10; *The Black Crook*, Charles M. Barras, xix, 72, 82; *Brutus; or, The Fall of Tarquin*, John Howard Payne (Brutus), xxi, 10, 14, 47, 153n, 285; *Camille*, Alexandre Dumas (Armand Duval, Camille, DeVarville), 8, 10, 19, 20, 32, 45; *Coriolanus*, Shakespeare (Coriolanus), 63; *Don Caesar de Bazan*, Dion Boucicault, xxi; *The Duke's Motto*, John Brougham, 68; *Enoch Arden*, Arthur Matthison, 66, 85, 88; *Fazio*, Henry Hart Milman (Bianca), 38, 86; *The Fool's Revenge*, Tom Taylor (Bertuccio), 32, 52, 64; *The Forty Thieves*, H. B. Farnie, 72; *Guy Mannering*, Daniel Terry (Henry Bertram, Meg Merrilies), 38, 66, 85, 86, 88; *The Heir at Law*, George Colman (Dick Duberly), 4; *Henry II*, G. H. Hollister, 27; *Henry IV*, Shakespeare (Falstaff, Prince Hal), 66, 85; *Hippolytus*, Julia Ward Howe, 12, 64; *Iphigenia in Aulis*, Sophocles (Iphigenia), 34; *The Iron Chest*, George Colman (Sir Edward Mortimer), 10; *Julius Caesar*, Shakespeare (Brutus, Soothsayer), 34, 64, 79, 87, 285, 308; *King John*, Shakespeare, 57, 242n; *King Lear*,

Shakespeare, xvi, 10, 38, 64, 73, 78, 286, 292, 294, 296, 297, 298; *The Lady of Lyons*, Edward Bulwer-Lytton (Beauséant, Claude Melnotte, Pauline), 4, 64, 66, 85, 86; *Leah the Forsaken*, Augustin Daly, 66, 85; *Lesbia*, Matilda Heron, 32; *Love's Labor's Lost*, Shakespeare, 242n; *Love's Ordeal*, Edmund Falconer (Eugene de Morny), 64; *Macbeth*, Shakespeare (Banquo, Duncan, Macbeth, Macduff, Lady Macbeth), xiii, 14, 38, 39, 41, 53, 63, 64, 73, 85, 87, 285, 302; *The Marble Heart*, Charles Selby (Raphael), 8, 53; *Mary Warner*, Tom Taylor, 66, 79, 85, 92; *Medea*, Mario Uchard, 19, 32; *The Merchant of Venice*, Shakespeare (Portia, Shylock), 44, 47, 53, 57, 60, 63, 64, 65, 242n; *The Merry Wives of Windsor*, Shakespeare (Falstaff, Ford, Page), 66, 85, 87; *Much Ado About Nothing*, Shakespeare (Claudio, Leonato), 87, 285; *Narcisse*, Tom Taylor, 116; *A New Way to Pay Old Debts*, Philip Massinger (Sir Giles Overreach), 10, 11, 16, 41, 44; Oberammergau Passion Play, xix; *Othello*, Shakespeare (Desdemona, Duke, Iago, Othello), xiii, xxi, xxvi, 14, 26, 27, 38, 40, 44, 45, 47, 53, 63, 64, 66, 87, 285, 295, 296, 298, 302, 308; *Ours*, Tom Robertson, 92; *Richard II*, Shakespeare, 64, 286; *Richard III*, Shakespeare, xvi, xxi, 4, 6, 8, 10, 11, 12, 13, 16, 20, 27, 38, 39, 44, 53, 57, 60, 64, 90, 285, 292; *Richelieu*, Edward Bulwer-Lytton (Louis XIII, Richelieu), 10, 11, 32, 39-40, 41, 42n, 44, 47, 52, 56, 57, 62, 64, 79, 87, 285, 294, 295; *Rip Van Winkle*, Dion Boucicault, 66, 285; *Romeo and Juliet*, Shakespeare (Capulet, Escalus, Juliet, Nurse, Romeo), 30, 58, 64, 66, 85, 87, 285; *Ruy Blas*, Victor Hugo, 52, 68; *The Taming of the Shrew*, Shakespeare (Petruchio), 10, 64; *The Tempest*, Shakespeare, xvi; *The Two Gentlemen of Verona*, Shakespeare, 57; *Venice Preserved*, Thomas Otway (Jaffeir, Pierre), 3; *Virginius*, Sheridan Knowles, 63; *The White Fawn*, James Mortimer, xix; *The Winter's Tale*, Shakespeare (Florizel, Polixenes), 87, 285

Powers, Hiram, 19

"R. S. T.": on Booth's faulty readings, 257n

Rachel, 60

Raphael, 33, 60, 81

Reade, Charles, 293

Robertson, Tom, 92

Rogers, John, 145n

Rosene, Charles (Second Gravedigger), 84, 88

Rossi, Ernesto, 298

Rowe's *Shakespeare*, 229n

Salvini, Tommaso, 297

Sand, George, *Consuelo*, 19, 24

Schlegel, August Wilhelm von, 72

Scott, Clement: reviews Booth's Hamlet (1881), 294

Scott, William Wallace: portrait of Booth, 124n, 184, 186n

Seymour, James, 88

Seymour, William (Actress), 84, 88

"Shakespeare": praises Booth's Hamlet (1870), 70-71

Sheil, Richard Lalor, 10, 39. *See also* Plays and Dramatic Characters
Sheridan, Mr., 109
Sheridan, William E. (Laertes), 84, 87
Sherwood, Bensen: "Stage Plans," 109; citations of, 117, 123, 161, 183, 224, 250, and footnotes in Chapter VI *passim*
Siddons, Sarah, xiii, 22, 146n
Sinclair, Catherine, 42n
Skinner, Otis, 308
Smith, Russell, 75, 273
Smith, Sol, 229n
Socrates, 33
Spencer, Herbert, 302
Sprague, Arthur Colby: on Hamlet's suspicion of Marcellus, 155n; on sitting during soliloquy, 187n; on seeing the espials, 190n; on the Kings' portraits, 229n; on rejecting the Queen's blessing, 235n; on the burial of Ophelia, 248n
Stark, James, 7, 30
Stedman, E. C.: essay on Booth's style (1866), 63-64
Stoddard, Elizabeth, 9
Stoepel, Robert, 54
Stuart, William (O'Flaherty): attacks Forrest, 14; management of the Winter Garden, 54, 56; and the Hundred Nights *Hamlet*, 60, 70n, 102; mentioned, 93n
Sullivan, Barry, 79, 291
Sullivan, John T., xx

Talma, François Joseph, 296
Taylor, James: on blonde wigs, 74-75; on the McVicker's Theatre photograph, 185n; his 1890 scrapbook and promptbook, 111-112; citations of, *see* footnotes in Chapter VI *passim*
Taylor, Tom, 52, 79, 92, 117. *See also* Plays and Dramatic Characters
Telbin, William, 55n
Tennyson, Alfred, Lord, 15, 19, 66, 88
Thomas, Ambroise, *Hamlet*, 240
Thompson, Launt: the Hamlet bust, 52; mentioned, 25, 54
Thompson, Lydia, 72
Thorne, John, 54, 75
Thorvaldsen, Albert Bertel, 309
"Touchstone": on the Hundred Nights *Hamlet*, 60
Tree, Herbert Beerbohm, 44, 57
Tuckerman, Henry, 187n
Turner, J. W. M., 19

Vaders, Emma, xx
Vaux, Downing, 299
Vining, Edward, *The Mystery of Hamlet*, 63-64
Voltaire, 33

Walker, John, *Pronouncing Dictionary*, 190n
Wallack, J. W., 19
Wallack, Lester, 308
Waller, D. Wilmarth (Ghost), 84, 85-86
Waller, Emma, 66, 86
Warren, Arthur, 293
Werder, Karl Friederich, 297
Wheeler, A. C. (Nym Crinkle): praises Forrest and attacks Booth, 14-15; critical principles, 79-80, 93; attacks Booth's staging, 79-80; praises ensemble acting, 83-84; on Fanny Morant, 85, 238-239; on D. W. Waller, 86; on D. C. Anderson, 87; on Augustus Pitou, 87; attacks Booth's interpretation of Hamlet, 91-93, 156n, 238, 301; on scenery, 117, 252; on Ghost scenes, 142, 156n; on Closet scene, 238; praises Irving's Hamlet,

301; on Modjeska, 309; mentioned, 18, 81, 89, 95, 96, 146n, 187n, 287
White, Richard Grant: attacks historical staging, 59n, 79-82; objects to Booth's stage fall, 83, 152; mentioned, 71
Whitman, Walt, 93, 94
Whytal, A. Russ, 111
Wilkins, E. G. P.: reviews Booth's Hamlet (1860), 42-43, 51
Wilson, James Harrison, 18n, 25n, 49
Winter, William: edits Booth's Prompt-Books, xvii-xviii, 56n, 140n, 291-292; on Forrest's hostility to Booth, 42n; praises Booth's acting (1862), 48; excuses Booth's overacting (1863), 51; defends historical staging, 82; on Theodore Hamilton, 85; on D. W. Waller, 86; on Blanche de Bar, 86; praises Booth's Hamlet (1870), 93-95; literary style, 93-95; his copy of the Prompt-Book *Hamlet*, 113; counts actors in Play scene, 185, 203; defends Booth from imputation of error, 257n; on Booth's tour of the South (1876), 290; advises against London opening in Hamlet, 293; praises Irving's Hamlet, 301-302; reviews Booth's last Hamlet, 309; mentioned, 50n, 58n, 64n, 68, 96, 156n, 174n, 296
Witham, Charles: watercolors in the Harvard 1870 promptbook, vi, xxvii, 73, 108-109; designs for the Hundred Nights *Hamlet* (1864), 54, 160n, 184; drawings in the Hinton edition, 56-57, 183-184; designs *The Merchant of Venice* (1867), 65; designs for *Hamlet* (1870), 75-79; later work, 79; versions of Act I, 2, setting, 122n; versions of Act II setting, 160n; versions of Act III setting, 183-185; "improvements" in King's Closet design, 218; versions of Act V, 3, setting, 273-274
Wittmann, Hugo, 297

Young, Charles Mayne, 229n